THE IRONY OF DESEGREGATION LAW

In loving memory of Dr. Stephen Winters

and of Sylvia Davis

The Irony of Desegregation Law

by

MARK WHITMAN

Markus Wiener Publishers
Princeton

For information write to:
  Markus Wiener Publishers, Inc.
  231 Nassau Street, Princeton, NJ 08542

Library of Congress Cataloging-in-Publication Data

The irony of desegregation law, 1955–1995: essays and documents/
  Mark Whitman, ed.
    Includes bibliographical references.
    ISBN 1-55876-119-5 hardcover
    ISBN 1-55876-120-9 paperback
    1. Segregation in education—Law and legislation—
United States—History.
  I. Whitman, Mark, 1937–
  KF4155.I76   1997
  344.73'0798—dc21   97-22314
                                             CIP

Printed in the United States of America on acid-free paper.

Contents

Preface

This volume sets itself a straightforward task, to trace the development of the case law which grew up in America around the momentous constitutional and social issue of school desegregation. I begin with *Brown II*, having treated *Brown I* extensively in an earlier book, and end with a discussion of the most recent Supreme Court decision dealing with desegregation as of this writing, *Missouri* v. *Jenkins* (the Kansas City school case). My focus, however, is not only on the Supreme Court. There is a great deal of analysis of litigation in the lower courts.

Accompanying the text are a series of documents which I think essential in telling the story. In choosing these documents, I have been guided by two, sometimes conflicting, criteria: I wanted to make available material which has never been published previously. But I also thought it helpful at times to select excerpts from decisions and briefs which reinforce the analysis I am attempting, even though their full text is already in print.

In the desire to follow what I see as the main line of development in desegregation law, I found it necessary to forswear as much comprehensiveness as I would have liked. Thus, regretfully deleted are extended discussions I had originally planned of the taxation issue as it relates to school desegregation, and of the constitutionality of state initiatives concerning pupil assignment.

I have not sought to derive from my study any overarching thesis about American desegregation law, nor to undertake a critique or a vindication of "busing" or "compulsory integration." Others are doing that brilliantly already. I am satisfied if I can illuminate some of the legal and institutional background of major doctrinal shifts in school law, as they arose in the district and circuit courts, and to recount the often tortuous process by which the Supreme Court justices arrived at some of their principal desegregation decisions.

But if there is one theme which runs through this account, it involves the ironic contrast between the behavior of our courts, especially the Supreme Court, during the two clearly demarcated phases of American desegregation law.

The justices of 1954–1955 felt keenly that the social and political dimensions of the endeavor they were undertaking would strain judicial authority to the limits, even if the goal to which desegregation was generally thought to aspire at the time—merely ending racial classifications in education—seems modest compared to later expectations. The Court was careful, therefore, to announce a unanimous decision in *Brown I*, and to frame that decision in simple and comprehensible language (though the language, in fact, hid some long-term ambiguities about its meaning). Chief Justice Earl Warren noted that he consciously wrote a short opinion, so that any interested layman could read it in its entirety.

A year later, a still unanimous Court spelled out its approach to compliance, based on "all deliberate speed." This turned out to be an excessively cautious approach, but it flowed from a reasonable, even a humble, appreciation of the tenuousness of the rule of law in the uncertain atmosphere the justices were necessarily creating. During the next decade, the lower courts, at their best, threaded their way carefully, but often with ingenuity and courage, through the thicket of compliance with *Brown*.

Yet beginning in 1968, when the Court sanctioned a far more radical revolution in American society, when it required integration and massive busing, first in the South, then, inevitably in the North, it did so disingenuously, not to say dishonestly, in opinions lacking any doctrinal consistency or coherence.

These decisions, through *Keyes* v. *Denver* in 1973, still clung to the much-cherished principle of unanimity in school cases, but it was a unanimity which concealed serious divisions in the Court. Consequently, the institution as a whole failed utterly to do what Earl Warren had thought so essential in *Brown I*. It consistently obfuscated, instead of clarifying, what seemed to be the real reasons for its actions.

Nor did the justices seem to be sobered by the gravity and the perilousness of the social experiment they were decreeing, until they were confronted with the prospect of ordering busing across city-suburb lines in 1974. Then, a Court which had slipped up the hill so furtively in the previous five years slipped back down again. By a 5–4 vote in *Milliken* v. *Bradley*, it slyly crept away from its commitment to "racial balance," keeping busing out of the suburbs and signaling that in the long run it would end everywhere. By our own day, both foes and advocates of the Court's confused integrationist offerings of the early seventies have come to feel that the justices instituted a circular and self-defeating requirement.

This is not to say that decisions forthrightly explaining the constitutional imperatives of busing would have nourished a willingness on the part of the American people to accept the need for its rigors. It is highly doubtful that a revolution as profound as the long-term integration of America's schools could have been accomplished by judicial fiat under any long-term circumstances.

Indeed, some have suggested that the unpopularity of what the justices were trying to do between 1968 and 1973 explains their disordered product, that they were consciously and cleverly hiding their purposes behind bland, convoluted, legal decrees. Examination of the justices' papers, however, tells a more complex and less deliberative tale. In any event, I must respectfully disagree with the view that the judiciary could, or should, have attempted to surreptitiously maneuver Americans into accepting its conception of the educational good during the 1970's, or any other period. That is scarcely the function of an institution which has a special responsibility under our constitutional system to deal in reasoned argument.

There existed plausible and dignified (though certainly debatable) rationale for justifying integration if one was going to impose it. Individual justices embraced them during consideration of the major desegregation cases, but the Court as a body never did.

In 1959, Professor Herbert Wechsler of Columbia Law School argued that a truly principled decision in constitutional law must rest on reasons which in their sweep and in their neutrality transcend the immediate result they might achieve. He asserted that *Brown* v. *Board of Education* was not buttressed on such "neutral principles." I believe Professor Wechsler was wrong. But his condemnation could apply all too easily to many of the judicial opinions considered in this study.

April 1998

THE TWO SIDES OF
BROWN II

I

"We conclude that in the field of public education the doctrine of 'separate but equal' has no place. Separate educational facilities are inherently unequal. Therefore, we hold that the plaintiffs and others similarly situated . . . are, by reason of the segregation complained of, deprived of the equal protection of the laws guaranteed by the Fourteenth Amendment."[1]

With these words of May 17, 1954, the Supreme Court of the United States redeemed itself from its own shameful past and pointed the way toward a revolution in American constitutional law and social development. The decision in *Brown* v. *Board of Education of Topeka* struck down, in education at least, the doctrine established 58 years earlier in *Plessy* v. *Ferguson*: that separate facilities for the races are constitutionally permissible, so long as the facilities were approximately equivalent. In defending such a proposition in 1896, Justice Henry Brown had argued that if African-Americans somehow got the notion segregation comprised deliberate discrimination against them, it was a figment of their imaginations. "We consider the underlying fallacy of the plaintiff's argument," said Justice Brown, for a majority of eight, "to consist in the assumption that the enforced separation of the two races stamps the colored race with a badge of inferiority. If this be so, it is . . . solely because the colored race chooses to put that construction upon it."[2] The Court's unanimous conclusion upon this matter in 1954 now vindicated the brave and noble dissent in *Plessy* of Justice John Marshall Harlan, who asserted that segregation "puts the brand of servitude and degradation upon a large class of our fellow-citi-

1

zens, our equals before the law."[3]

Brown could certainly lay claim to being "the most important American governmental act of any kind since the Emancipation Proclamation."[4] Yet the concluding paragraph of the decision made it plain that the constitutional rights affirmed by the Court would not immediately be available to Linda Brown and her fellow plaintiffs in Topeka; nor to those plaintiffs in Prince Edward County, Virginia, Clarendon County, South Carolina, and in Delaware and the District of Columbia, who had brought the suits argued alongside the Kansas case in 1952, then reargued in 1953. "[B]ecause of the wide applicability of this decision, and because of the great variety of local conditions, the formulation of decrees in these cases presents problems of considerable complexity,"[5] the justices admitted. Consequently, "[i]n order that we may have the full assistance of the parties in formulating the decrees," they set the *Brown* cases down for "further argument"[6] at the October 1954 term of the Court. There, the proceedings would focus exclusively on the issue of desegregation—on how, in short, to go about dismantling a dual school system. The attorneys general of all states requiring or permitting segregation in public schools were invited to appear as *amici curiae* (friends of the court).

This was unprecedented in American judicial history, the first time a court articulated the existence of a constitutional right, yet delayed execution of the means for bringing it about. By contrast, when the justices held segregation in graduate and law schools unconstitutional in 1950, they simply reversed the lower court decisions at issue and ordered immediate admission of the plaintiffs to the institutions they sought to enter. Any African-American student then became eligible to demand a similar right. But for elementary and secondary school students, in the controversies at bar, and in the thirteen other states affected by the Court's desegregation ruling, *Brown I* would have to be followed by *Brown II*.

This hiatus was decreed, to be sure, in order for school officials to examine the administrative and educational mechanisms for breaking up dual systems. But the justices' invocation of "local conditions" also signaled their awareness of the enormous magnitude of what they were up to in the school cases, especially in the deep South. *Brown* was probably the most far-reaching judgment the Supreme Court had ever rendered, the most drastic attack on people's settled mores and social institutions. The reach of the decision bred a natural inclination to approach compliance with caution. Indeed, the very idea of ordering a delay before meditating on the process of implementation gave warning that the process ultimately approved might be a deliberate one, especially if one looked at the specific questions on implementation which the justices ordered the parties to address on "further argument." These were questions four and five of the series propounded for the 1953 reargument, but "necessarily subordinated" at that time to the three questions actually dealing with "the constitutionality of segregation in public education."[7]

> 4. Assuming it is decided that segregation in public schools violates the Fourteenth Amendment,
>
> (a) would a decree necessarily follow providing that, within the limits set by

normal geographic school districting, Negro children should forthwith be admitted to schools of their choice, or

(b) may this Court, in the exercise of its equity powers, permit an effective gradual adjustment to be brought about from existing segregated systems to a system not based on color distinctions?

5. On the assumption on which questions 4(a) and (b) are based, and assuming further that this Court will exercise its equity powers to the end described in question 4(b),

(a) should this Court formulate detailed decrees in these cases;
(b) if so, what specific issues should the decrees reach;
(c) should this Court appoint a special master to hear evidence with a view to recommending specific terms for such decrees;
(d) should this Court remand to the courts of first instance with directions to frame decrees in these cases, and if so, what general directions should the decrees of this Court include and what procedures should the courts of first instance follow in arriving at the specific terms of more detailed decrees?[8]

By their very phrasing, these inquiries suggested that as early as 1953 the justices were settling on an incremental approach to compliance with any decision which proscribed school segregation. Thus question four presented the parties with a set of alternatives, "Assuming it is decided that segregation in public schools violates the Fourteenth Amendment." One alternative followed out the implications of the view that constitutional rights must be granted immediately, once affirmed; a decree would "necessarily follow" admitting youngsters "forthwith . . . to schools of their choice." The other alternative, however, was disturbingly novel, especially to Thurgood Marshall, and the brilliant group of attorneys he headed at the NAACP Legal Defense Fund. For it held out the possibility that the Court could, "in the exercise of its equity powers," allow "*an effective gradual adjustment*" to non-segregated school systems. Question five did nothing to assuage Marshall's concerns, based, as it was, on the proposition "that this Court *will exercise its equity powers to the end described in question 4(b).*"

In fact, by the time of the Court's initial (and ultimately inconclusive) conference on *Brown* in December, 1952, six of the justices who would join the eventual opinion were pretty well committed to gradualism, particularly when they thought of desegregation as it applied to the middle and lower South. Justices Harold Burton and William O. Douglas, who favored outlawing segregation from the outset, assumed that compliance would be slow. Burton noted, "We have Constitution and must be guided by [it] . . . .But we can use time."[9] His own notes on Douglas state, "Simple Const. question—will take a long time to work it out."[10]

Justice Hugo Black, another unquestioned advocate of striking down school segregation, said nothing about time frames in his 1952 conference remarks. But his doleful predictions about the problems such a decision would create in the South stamp him as a gradualist from the beginning. *"Segregation per se violation?* [But] to so hold would bring drastic things."[11] (Black made his cautious views on remedy quite explicit in early 1954. "Let it simmer . . . .It can't take too long."[12])

Justices Robert Jackson and Tom Clark, ambivalent on the merits in 1952, but willing to be won over to reversing *Plessy*, clearly premised such acquiescence on the assumption that southerners would get an interval to adjust to radical change. Desegregation *"must* be done in certain period,"[13] Jackson said. Clark indicated, according to Justice Douglas at least, that he could "go along" with a judgment against segregation, but only if it gave "lower courts the right to withhold relief in light of troubles."[14]

Justice Felix Frankfurter had been thinking about the shape of a compliance decree from the time the Court agreed to hear the school segregation cases. And from the outset, as Richard Kluger points out, "he was convinced that any desegregation process that the Court might order should not be a drastic one, instant and universal; it would probably have to allow the South time to make the adjustment."[15] In a penciled note, entitled "Segregation," the justice noted, "Is equity to be unmindful to the psychological truth that change, especially drastic change, takes time?"[16] It was Frankfurter who drew up the subtly loaded questions on relief, which the Court initially promulgated on June 8, 1953, in its order for the 1953 reargument.

In posing these questions, Frankfurter and his colleagues may have been influenced by a Justice Department brief filed for the argument of 1952. This contribution, amicus curiae, of the United States government was the first document in *Brown* to formally propose to the justices a gradual approach to desegregation. Its principal author, Special Assistant to the Attorney General Phillip Elman, had served as law clerk to Justice Frankfurter a decade before and remained a close confidant of the justice, though he denies discussing the brief with Frankfurter before filing it.

In any event, Earl Warren, assuming the reins as chief justice in October, 1953, quickly joined the incrementalist consensus emerging among his brethren. At the initial conference on *Brown* following the 1953 reargument, Warren argued eloquently for the demise of educational segregation, but felt the need for measured implementation. "It would be unfortunate," he said, "if we had to take precipitous action that would inflame more than necessary."[17] The varying conditions in the states with segregated schools must be taken carefully into account. "How we do it is important . . . .[M]y instincts and feelings lead me to say that . . . we should abolish the practice of segregation in the public schools—but in a tolerant way."[18] Justice Sherman Minton, a firm proponent since 1952 of doing away with separate schools, agreed with this basic approach, telling his colleagues at a January, 1954 conference that, on implementation, he was "not given to throwing the Court's weight around."[19] Similarly, Justice Stanley Reed, the lone potential dissenter on *Brown*, was won over by Warren and Burton in the spring of 1954, partly through the promise of a tactful approach to remedy.

By the day of the great decision, therefore, the justices harbored preferences concerning the desegregation issue more definite even than their questions four and five portended. Just how far into the future the process of dismantling separate schools could permissibly extend remained unclear. But "effective gradual adjustment" comprised an accurate reading of the Court's pulse as it resolved the substance of the *Brown* cases, then put them back on the docket.

Thurgood Marshall and his colleagues had already made plain their distaste for such a course. In a first pass at questions four and five, part of their 1953 brief, they vigorously rejected the notion of any delay in the granting of constitutional rights. "[We] are unable, in good faith, to suggest terms for a decree which will secure effective gradual adjustment because no such decree will protect [plaintiffs'] rights."[20] Their "infant" clients, they pointed out,

> are asserting the most important secular claims that can be put forward by children, the claim to their full measure of the chance to learn and grow, and the inseparably connected but even more important claim to be treated as entire citizens of the society into which they have been born. We have discovered no case in which such rights, once established, have been postponed by a cautious calculation of conveniences . . . .
>
> The Fourteenth Amendment can hardly have been intended for enforcement at a pace geared down to the mores of the very states whose action it was designed to limit. The balance between the customs of the states and the personal rights of these appellants has been struck by that Amendment.[21]

"It follow[ed]," therefore, that the only proper course in equity was to send the school cases back to the federal district courts (which everyone agreed should be done), and direct lower court judges to issue the decree specified in question 4(a), a decree requiring that the injured parties "be admitted forthwith"[22] to non-segregated schools.

II

The 1955 reargument on *Brown* resolved itself down to a road check of the Court's preference for the approach to implementation "that the Justice Department had recommended from the very beginning."[23] Oral arguments in the case were originally planned for just after the 1954 congressional elections, but had to be moved to April of the next year because of the death of Justice Robert Jackson and the delay in confirming his successor, Judge John Marshall Harlan (grandson of the great dissenter of *Plessy*). In the meantime, the District of Columbia and Topeka, Kansas went forward promptly with desegregation efforts. Delaware too made progress, especially in the Wilmington area. The conundrum of the deep South remained.

By 1955, the NAACP had modified its position on relief somewhat. Marshall and his colleagues still called for a "forthwith" decree, and, as in *Brown I*, they introduced considerable sociological and psychological evidence to demonstrate the efficacy of their approach. Relying again upon the work of Professor Kenneth Clark of C.C.N.Y., among others, they held up to the Court studies "which support the position that gradualism, far from facilitating the process [of desegregation], may actually make it more difficult."[24] Receding deadlines and grade-by-grade plans, they argued presciently, created more problems than solutions.

Cognizant of the judicial mood, however, the NAACP brief reluctantly conceded the possibility of putting off full desegregation until the beginning of the 1956 school year. "Certainly, to indulge school authorities until September 1, 1956, to achieve desegregation would be generous in the extreme. Therefore, we submit that if the Court decides to grant further time, then the Court should direct that all decrees specify September, 1956, as the outside date by which desegregation must be accomplished."[25]

The Justice Department, represented by Solicitor General Simon Sobeloff, reiterated its commitment to "gradual adjustment," though Sobeloff cautioned against any tolerance for stalling or evasion of duty. While the government did not believe the Court should impose a definite time limit for completing desegregation, it did recommend that when the justices referred the various cases back to the district courts they provide that school authorities be required to submit within ninety days plans for ending racial separation "as soon as feasible."[26] District judges should then set deadlines for the completion of these desegregation plans, though such limits could be flexible where authorities displayed good faith.

Customs and institutions "that have persisted for generations," Sobeloff told the Court, could not "be erased with a single stroke of the pen. No practical person will overlook that situation."[27] On the other hand, lower court judges must understand the purpose of the leeway granted them. They must "not . . . permit delay to be had for the mere sake of delay . . . . The district courts ought to have it made plain that in the view of this Court a time shall be allowed, but not for the purpose of paralyzing action or of emasculating the Court's decision of last May."[28] Virginia and South Carolina, of course, offered nothing sensible or realistic to the debate over implementation.

Predictably, this range of arguments did little to change the Court's basic cast of mind, however useful they may have proved in clarifying mechanisms and procedures. Indeed, John Fassett, Justice Reed's law clerk at the time of *Brown I*, believes that Earl Warren had settled on the main outlines of a compliance decree by the time he left Washington for California in the summer of 1954. "I take it," says Fassett, "that he agreed that reasonable efforts to start the integration process is all the Court [could] expect in view of the scope of the problem, and that an order to immediately admit all negroes in white schools would be an absurdity because impossible to obey in many areas."[29]

When the Court met in conference on April 16, 1955, two days after the close of arguments on remedy, Warren laid out the path he wished to follow. He had yet to sketch out a detailed decision, he told his colleagues, but he was certain of a few things: The Court should not specify any deadline for completing desegregation, nor require lower courts to set such deadlines; it should not even require district judges to demand a precise plan of desegregation, though they obviously possessed the authority to do so. Rather, *Brown II* should focus on the "circumstances to be taken into account"[30] in implementing the initial decision. Among those the chief justice included problems relating to finance, redistricting, and plant conversion, but he rejected any consideration of psychological or sociological factors.

Warren's approach resembled the one which Justice Frankfurter articulated in a memorandum to his colleagues, circulated on the last day of oral arguments. Frankfurter favored "a decree which would take due," but "not detailed, account of [the] considerations relevant to the fashioning of a decree in equity," though he included as a consideration "what are loosely called 'attitudes' as well as physical, financial and administrative conditions."[31] He opposed setting a time limit, because it would "seem to be an imposition of our will," and would "tend to alienate instead of enlist favorable or educable local sentiment."[32]

No one at the April 16 conference quarreled with the chief justice's comments, except Hugo Black. He remained wary of the intense opposition to desegregation sure to explode in the South; one of his law clerks, he remarked, came from Alabama and was firmly convinced that children of different races would not attend school together "in this generation."[33] Justice Black inclined, therefore, toward an approach to compliance which Frankfurter had mentioned in his memorandum, but rejected—a "bare bones"[34] decree simply enjoining segregation and returning the cases to the lower courts. "How to say and do as little as possible" represented Black's "present desire."[35] But he willingly ceded initiative in drafting an opinion to the chief justice, for like the rest of his colleagues he wanted a unanimous decision.

The second *Brown* v. *Board of Education of Topeka*, dated May 31, 1955, reflected the Supreme Court's desire to eschew peremptory commands, yet at the same time not to appear weak-kneed about the massive changes it was ordering. The school cases were remanded to the district courts "[b]ecause of their proximity to local conditions," and because of the undoubted fact that local school officials "have the primary responsibility for elucidating, assessing, and solving" the various logistical problems which impeded "the transition to a system of public education freed of racial discrimination."[36] In overseeing this transition, lower court judges could "properly take into account the public interest in the elimination of . . . obstacles [to desegregation] in a systematic and effective manner," a way of intimating, perhaps, that they could pay some attention to the mood of their communities. But "it should go without saying that the vitality of . . . constitutional principles cannot be allowed to yield simply because of disagreement with them."[37]

The justices mentioned no time limits of any sort. The district courts, however, must "require that the defendants make a prompt . . . start toward full compliance with our May 17, 1954 ruling." Once local officials did something positive, "the courts may find that additional time is necessary to carry out the ruling in an effective manner." Still, the "burden rests upon the defendants to establish that such time is necessary . . . and is consistent with good faith compliance at the earliest practicable date."[38]

The Court's carefully modulated approach to remedy in *Brown II* is capsulized in the phrase which quickly became synonymous with the decision. "[T]he cases are remanded to the District Courts to take such proceedings and enter such orders . . . as are necessary and proper to admit to public schools on a racially nondiscriminatory basis *with all deliberate speed* the parties to these cases."[39] These celebrated words were originally used in connection with *Brown* by Justice Frankfurter, in a memo he sent to his colleagues just after the 1953 argument.[40] Frankfurter was actually quoting from a 1918 opinion of Oliver Wendell Holmes.[41]

By definition, *Brown II* was directed only at the five localities involved in the litigation. Furthermore, after much discussion, the justices ordered their relief limited to the actual plaintiffs who had filed suit in the various controversies. At the remedy level, in other words, the Court refused to treat the school cases the way it treated them in *Brown I*, as class action suits: suits implicating not only the named plaintiffs, but all others who were "similarly situated"—meaning large numbers of additional African-American children in the five jurisdictions who were subjected to segregated education. This expansive concept was not invoked in *Brown II*, though Justice Frankfurter never believed its use or non-use made any practical difference. By definition, he felt, the justices were dealing with questions which involved not only the rest of the school children in Topeka or Wilmington or Washington, D.C., but hundreds of thousands of others as well. "[We] are asked in effect to transform state-wide school systems in nearly a score of states."[42]

The NAACP's instant reaction to the second *Brown* decision was by no means unfriendly. Writing in the summer of 1955, Thurgood Marshall and his chief assistant, Robert Carter, pronounced the decision "a good one."[43] While the Court's approach to remedy differed from their own, "chiefly in regard to the fixing of a deadline for compliance," they concluded that "the formula devised is about as effective as one could have expected."[44]

Marshall and Carter even allowed themselves to speculate on whether failure to set a deadline might not be a wise thing. Any date decreed by jurists in Washington, they noted, "would have been open to attack as . . . arbitrary, unrealistic and unfair to the South, and this would have given the demagogues a great opportunity to secure support for an attitude of open defiance."[45] But since the justices had perpetrated nothing of this sort, and with local judges in charge of desegregation, "what more could the South realistically ask for except repudiation of the May 17th decision?"[46] The district courts would wind up setting the deadlines, breeding in much of the South an "attitude . . . of resignation to living within the law."[47]

Of course, Prince Edward County, Virginia and Clarendon County, South Carolina, to say nothing of communities in Mississippi and Alabama, would find ways to delay action for a while. But Marshall and Carter did not believe such recalcitrants would get away with indefinite postponement. Eventually, they "have to come to grips with the facts of life—the law must be obeyed."[48] The defendants in Virginia and South Carolina might even "spring a big surprise on the country and bring forth a good faith desegregation program."[49]

If this essay engendered the suspicion that its authors were putting a cheery "spin" upon a disappointing result, such suspicions are belied by a private phone conversation which Marshall had in June of 1955 with the editor of the *Baltimore Afro-American*, Carl Murphy.

> MURPHY: . . . . [M]y thought is that we can go with this.

> MARSHALL: I'm sure of it. I was telling the guys up here—the guys kept on woofin' and I told them—I said, you know, some people want most of the hog, other people insist on having the whole hog, and then there are some people who want the hog, the hair, and the rice on the hair. What the hell! The more I think about it, I think it's a damned good decision! . . .

> MURPHY: What are you going to do, Thurgood?

> MARSHALL: . . . [W]e're going to do [it] state by state, that's what I hope . . . .Virginia, we're going to bust wide open!

> MURPHY: I don't see any reason why, if we beat Virginia and Carolina, the rest of them aren't going to wake up.

> MARSHALL: You're darned right they are. You can say all you want but those white crackers are going to get tired of having Negro lawyers beating 'em every day in court. They're going to get tired of it . . . .[50]

The ensuing decade, as is well-known, would not be kind to such sanguine predictions about the efficacy of "all deliberate speech."

III

Brown II, and the arguments preceding it, also cast light, though far more dimly, on other issues raised by its predecessor, issues less publicly prominent during the first years of school desegregation than the speed of compliance, yet with even deeper implications for the fate of desegregation law. These concered what *Brown I* really meant to proscribe, and the exact nature and scope of the remedial obligations it imposed.

Chief Justice Warren's opinion, of course, condemned state-imposed segregation as "inherently unequal," even if physical facilities were equivalent. His reasoning followed earlier Supreme Court decisions proscribing such segregation in law and graduate schools on the ground that, regardless of "'tangible' factors,"[51] there were intangible elements making for the inequality of all-black institutions. Thus in *Sweatt* v. *Painter*, the chief justice noted, the Court found a separate law school inadequate, relying for the most part on "those qualities which are incapable of objective measurement but which make for greatness in a law school":[52] prestige of the faculty, respect in the community, and clout of the alumni. In *McLaurin* v. *Oklahoma State Regents*, the justices demanded that an African-American student admitted to a white graduate school not be separated from the other students within the school. Again, they placed heavy reliance on "intangible considerations," the student's "ability to study, to engage in discussions and exchange views with other students, and, in general, to learn his profession."[53]

Then came the celebrated passage applying this type of analysis most directly to the case at hand.

> Such considerations apply with added force to children in grade and high schools. To separate them from others of similar age and qualifications solely because of their race generates a feeling of inferiority as to their status in the community that may affect their hearts and minds in a way unlikely ever to be undone.[54]

To reinforce the point, Warren quoted with favor a passage from the lower court decision in the Topeka case

> Segregation of white and colored children in public schools has a detrimental effect upon the colored children. The impact is greater when it has the sanction of the law; for the policy of separating the races is usually interpreted as denoting the inferiority of the negro group. A sense of inferiority affects the motivation of the child to learn. Segregation with the sanction of law, therefore, has a tendency to [retard] the educational and mental development of negro children and to deprive them of some of the benefits they would receive in a racial[ly] integrated school system.[55]

Whatever the state of psychological knowledge in 1896, "this finding," the Court announced, was "amply supported by modern authority."[56] Documentation for the "modern authority" appeared in footnote eleven of the opinion, which cited a number of sociological and psychological works on segregation and race relations. A study by Kenneth Clark led the list. Gunnar Myrdal's great classic, *An American Dilemma*, concluded it (though none of this evidence, it should be noted, documented academic performance among African-American children). Clark and a number of other social scientists had testified at the trial level of the various cases.

In a literal sense, *Brown* merely abrogated the laws in seventeen states requiring or permitting segregated education. But one might read the language used by Earl Warren and his colleagues as widening critically the range of those who could be held in violation of the decision, for the researches of Kenneth Clark, and of other social scientists, purported to show that the allegedly benign segregation in the schools of New York and Boston produced among African-American students social pathologies of the same sort detected in South Carolina—feelings of inferiority, doubts about identity, and stunted motivation.[57] (Certainly such separation also cut them off from the mainstream of society.) The issues adjudicated in *Brown*, of course, were not officially relevant to this so-called "de facto" segregation of the North and West: racial separation in schools caused, supposedly, by residential choice rather than by discriminatory state action. And Earl Warren's opinion, therefore, contained no statements going to the matter of whether all segregation was constitutionally suspect. Yet he did cite the passage from the Kansas opinion inferring something very much along these lines. "Segregation of white and colored children in public schools has a detrimental effect upon the colored children. The impact *is greater when it has the sanction of the law*." This raised the question of whether the rationale of *Brown* might reach segregation not formally mandated by statute. In Professor Frank Goodman's words, "Though *Brown* left the legal issue of de facto segregation undecided, it may have gone far toward foreclosing a critical factual issue. In finding that '[s]eparate educational facilities are inherently unequal' and separation of the races in school 'has a detrimental effect upon the colored children,' the Court may have supplied the central empirical premise for the argument that de facto segregation amounts to a constitutional denial of equal educational opportunity."[58] Within a month of *Brown I*, Professor Clark was claiming that the decision applied to the North, and, by the late 1950's, plaintiffs in northern communities were on the attack against de facto racial separation, maintaining that *Brown* actually stood for the view that all such separation caused psychological harm and crippling social isolation, and was thus "inherently unequal." (Some complainants, though, began to supplement their arguments with empirical data showing lower academic achievement among African-American students isolated in all-black schools).[59]

But this expansive interpretation of the *Brown* decision rested on what many regarded as a fragile foundation, most particularly in its demonstration of "feelings of inferiority." The Court's reference to "modern authority" was made rather casually, and a number of the lawyers who advised the NAACP in the school cases belittled the psychological evidence used by the plaintiffs as vigorously as did the lawyers for Prince Edward and Clarendon counties. As early as 1952, the editors of the *Yale Law Journal* pointed out that Professor Clark's data on attitudes among African-American youngsters did not control for the factor of school segregation, as opposed to home environment (something which the social scientists frankly admitted), and that it showed more pronounced feelings of inferiority in children attending northern schools than in those attending southern schools. Such flaws not only cast doubt on the general applicability of the evidence to education, but seemed to render it inapplicable to the *Brown* cases themselves.[60]

One of the first and most sensitive analyses of *Brown I*, published less than a year after the decision, voiced similar concerns about its factual underpinnings. Professor Edmond Cahn of N.Y.U. Law School praised the result, but found the social science data unconvincing. Cahn thought there were many flaws in the celebrated tests with paper dolls which Professor Clark had used to demonstrate feelings of inadequacy among African-American younsters, and he too noted that the tests were not equipped to distinguish the effects of home and school settings. " . . . I would not have the constitutional rights of Negroes—or of other Americans—rest on . . . such flimsy foundation as some of the scientific demonstrations in these records."[61]

Such criticisms pointed toward the possibility that the actual intent of *Brown* was both more narrow and more broad than some of the wording in the opinion intimated. In this view, the justices were simply asserting that state-sponsored separation of human beings from the social mainstream because of race, whether in education, or, by implication, in any other area, was manifestly harmful to minorities, served no sensible governmental purpose, and hence was unconstitutional per se. The chief justice's references to "hearts and minds" and "feeling[s] of inferiority" were seen as merely underlining the palpable discrimination inherent in racial categories. As Professor John Kaplan articulated the point,

> A reference to the facts of . . . *McLaurin* v. *Oklahoma State Regents* makes [the reasoning of *Brown*] somewhat more clear. In *McLaurin*, all facilities were equal, indeed identical, except for the fact that school authorities on the basis of race prevented the plaintiff from normal contact with his schoolmates. Certainly, the mere fact that one person is denied the right to associate in school with other persons cannot be said to be a constitutional violation. Unless a school authority operates only one school it must always divide the school population in some way or other and thus prevent some students from having contact with some others. In some ways a student in one school might even be harmed by his inability to associate with students in another. But even such harm would not mean that the separation was constitutionally prohibited. The *McLaurin* case merely stood for the principle that, at least in higher education, *race* might not be made the criterion for separation of one group of students from another. The practical positions of the two races in the United States made it clear that this very separation made the two groups unequal, and thus outside of the rule of *Plessy* v. *Ferguson*. In the *Brown* case, the Court merely took the view that the *McLaurin* principle was equally applicable to segregated education in the grade and high schools, and that, as in *McLaurin*, it was the racial separation, rather than any inequality of facilities or other educational benefits, that was the essence of the plaintiffs' claim. This view explains the Court's

language that "such considerations apply with added force" to children in grade and high schools because of the psychological harm these children suffer. The Court was asserting that *Brown* was in a sense an easier case than *McLaurin* and *Sweatt* v. *Painter*, where this type of harm to young children was not to be expected, rather than to show that harm to Negro children or inequality of schools was the essence of the constitutional violation . . . .

This view of *Brown* is reinforced by examining the type of evidence that was available to the Court on the question of the actual harm visited upon Negro children by school segregation. Several commentators have pointed out that though a large quantity of expert testimony was introduced as evidence in the cases and in briefs, it was by no means sufficiently definite, unambiguous, uncontradicted, or sweeping to allow the Court to find as a fact, irrefutable in all future cases, that regardless of the area of social climate, even deliberate state-imposed segregation in schools would work such harm on Negro children as to require a finding of unconstitutionality . . . . Thus, *Plessy* held that racial classifications did not offend the Constitution so long as they did not cause some type of harm. *McLaurin* and *Brown* found the necessary harm inherent in the separation by racial classification in education . . . .[62]

Even if the harm discussed by the Court in *Brown* went beyond the mere *fact* of separation, this harm was scarcely difficult to locate, argued Professor Charles Black of Yale Law School, in an unforgettably eloquent essay. But Professor Black, who assisted the Legal Defense Fund at all stages of the school litigation, felt that the justices, perhaps consciously, had looked in the wrong place for the deleterious effects of state-imposed apartheid, had not followed fully in the footsteps of the first Justice Harlan. In their solicitude for southern feelings, Black suggested, they had failed to focus on the most wrenching evil of segregation, the fact that its central purpose, whatever feelings it did or didn't arouse in its victims, was to degrade and humiliate an entire race of people. The racial classifications wrought by segregation were unconstitutional above all because they were an organized racial insult.

Segregation in the South comes down in apostolic succession from slavery and the *Dred Scott* case. The South fought to keep slavery, and lost. Then it tried the Black Codes, and lost. Then it looked around for something else and found segregation. The movement for segregation was an integral part of the movement to maintain and further "white supremacy." . . . It is now defended . . . on the ground that the Negro . . . is not fit to associate with the white . . . .

Northern people may be misled by the entirely sincere protestations of many southerners that segregation is "better" for the Negroes, is not intended to hurt them. But I think a little probing would demonstrate that what is meant is that it is better for the Negroes to accept a position of inferiority, at least for the indefinite future.[63]

Any "feelings of inferiority" generated in African-American youngsters by school segregation were merely symptoms of a larger disease. The Court's acknowledgement of them, Black felt, was just "corroboratory of [the] common sense" notion that "such treatment is generally not good for children," and was undoubtedly intended as a rebuttal to *Plessy's* smug assertion that any demeaning implications of segregation existed "*solely because the colored race chooses to put that construction upon it.*"[64]

Black's analysis, like Kaplan's, was aimed only at the de jure segregtion of the South, but focused on the transparent, systemic racism which lay behind it. If southern plaintiffs in future years took advantage of the constitutional tool the Court offered them, and adverted to the psychic damage caused by school segregation, they did not need to think they were referring to an abtruse concept. To say that segregation harms, felt Professor Cahn, was like asserting "that fire burns," or "that a cold causes sniffles . . . . Segregation does involve stigma; the community knows it does . . . . The moral factors involved in racial segregation are not new—like the science of social psychology—but exceedingly ancient."[65]

Judge Harvie Wilkinson cites an incident which, though occurring in the 1960's, conveys aptly what a Jim Crow social order habitually meant to southern blacks. "Mary Hamilton, a Negro, appeared in Alabama court as her own witness in a [court] hearing. Though the state's attorney had addressed white witnesses as 'Mr.' or 'Mrs.,' the following colloquy took place:

Q:What is your name, please?

A: Miss Mary Hamilton

Q: Mary, I believe you were arrested—who were you arrested by?

A:My name is Miss Hamilton. Please address me correctly.

Q:Who were you arrested by, Mary?

"She refused to answer; the trial judge held her in contempt; the Supreme Court of Alabama affirmed . . . ."[66] (In 1964, the Supreme Court summarily reversed.)

IV

If *Brown* v. *Board of Education* was directed at racial classifications, it seemed to apply to facets of public life other than education, spelling the demise of *Plessy v. Ferguson*. Indeed, within a year, the Court, merely citing *Brown*, struck down official segregation of public beaches and golf courses; within two years, it destroyed *Plessy* directly by outlawing racial segregation in transportation.[67]

Yet in the sphere of education itself, the racial classification theory of *Brown* looked, at first glance, in a restrictive direction, especially as it concerned the critical issue of remedy in desegregation law, of what authorities found in violation of the decision must do to bring themselves into compliance. Seemingly, its command of desegregation imposed upon officials in dual systems only the requirement of doing away with racial categories, and the harmful legacy they represented, and replacing them with some neutral and impartial method of assigning children to schools, whether integration developed or not. The most logical way to accomplish this, presumably, was to create a setup where neighborhood or some method of free choice replaced race as the basis of assignment.

Some degree of biracial association would normally result from such neutral educational arrangements, and to this extent "desegregation" and "integration" could be spoken of synonymously. Still, integration, in such a view, was not the necessary result of desegregation. In Professor Paul Kauper's words, *"Brown v. Board of Education* . . . . does not mean that the states are required to establish school districts in such a way as to insure racial integration . . . . Nothing in the Court's opinion can be interpreted to interfere with the normal districting of school areas on the basis of geographical lines."[68]

Professor Kauper's approach assumed, however, that there was such a thing as "normal districting" for formerly de jure school systems, that there existed a genuine principle of neutrality in student assignment which could efface racial classifications and the harms they wrought, short of actual integration. Whether such a principle actually existed, and whether, even if it did, it could offset the ingrained evils of segregation, as observers like Professor Black described them, would be vigorously debated in future litigation

Furthermore, though an analysis like Black's applied only to the South, it possessed the capacity to transcend regional boundaries, since it corresponded, almost certainly, to the deeper convictions of plaintiffs and lawyers who argued that psychological as well as social harm inhered in all forms of segregated schooling. For did not many of them see such schooling as tied to a historically rooted and legally sanctioned system of racism which was almost as pervasive in New York or Detroit as it was in Richmond, even if laws officially segregating schools no longer operated in northern cities? And could this not lead to the proposition that equal protection of the laws was attainable only through integrated school systems, as the pathway to an integrated society?

Brown I, after all, cited Gunnar Myrdal as well as Professor Clark. And while Myrdal's monumental work of 1944 perceived genuine differences in northern and southern attitudes toward race, he had documented unsparingly the state-abetted segregation, discrimination, and pathological hostility toward African-Americans which characterized northern society. When rampant "segregation and discrimination" needed to be justified in the North, Myrdal noted, "[t]he rationalizations run in terms of the alleged racial inferiority of the Negro, his animal-like nature, his unreliability, his low morals, dirtiness and unpleasant manners . . . . [T]he development of prejudice against Negroes is usually one of [an immigrant's] first lessons in Americanization."[69]

Whether assessments like Black's and Myrdal's, and the integrationist ideal put forward because of them, provided a sound constitutional basis for the condemnation of all forms of school segregation, and the foundation for a judicially attainable requirement of nationwide integration—whether, in fact, the Supreme Court was covertly embracing such views by the early 1970's. These would turn out to be the most important questions in the history of American desegregation law.

V

The Court's terse opinion in *Brown II* was scarcely intended as a definitive gloss on the intricacies of Earl Warren's words of the year before, especially as they might concern violation. But there are definite indications that in 1955 the justices, and the plaintiffs as well, assumed, without as yet elaborating on their assumptions to any great degree, a distinctly conservative posture toward remedy in desegregation law, one which taxed school officials only with the task of replacing racial classifications with what was thought to be neutrality in student assignment. The briefs and oral arguments in *Brown II* never focus in detail on what the participants expected a unitary school system to look like, consumed, as they were, with questions of pacing. Signs abound, however, of a restrained view of compliance, certainly as we would define compliance today.

Evidence of this tendency surfaces in the first question held over for the 1955 reargument, the very question which posed a radical alternative on timetables. "Assuming it is decided that segregation in public schools violates the Fourteenth Amendment, . . . would a decree necessarily follow providing that, *within the limits set by normal geographic school districting*, Negro children should forthwith be admitted to schools of their choice . . . ?" An exchange between Thurgood Marshall and Justice Frankfurter in 1952 presages the wording of this question, and illuminates the mindset behind it.

> JUSTICE FRANKFURTER: You mean, if we reverse, it will not entitle every mother to have her child go to a nonsegregated school in Clarendon County?
>
> MR. MARSHALL: No, sir.
>
> JUSTICE FRANKFURTER: What will it do? Would you mind spelling this out? What would happen?

MR. MARSHALL: Yes, sir. The school board, I assume, would find some other method of distributing the children, a recognizable method, by drawing district lines.[70]

Similar exchanges occurred in 1955.

JUSTICE FRANKFURTER: I do not imagine this Court is going to work out the details [of desegregation] in all the states of the Union.

MR. MARSHALL: I certainly would not want to be a party to thinking about it. But that is why, it seemed to me, that the real basic issue as I said in the beginning, is that what we want from this Court is the striking down of race.

Now, whatever other plan they want to work out . . . . That has been an administrative detail since we have had public schools . . . .

Put the dumb colored children in with the dumb white children, and put the smart colored children with the smart white children—that is no problem.[71]

✳ ✳ ✳ ✳ ✳ ✳ ✳ ✳ ✳ ✳ ✳ ✳

JUSTICE FRANKFURTER: I should like to have you spell out with particularity just what would happen in [a] school district.

MR. MARSHALL: Well, I would say, sir, that the school board would sit down and take this position with its staff, administrative staff, superintendents, supervisors, et cetera. They would say, "The present policy of admission based on race, that is now gone. Now we have to find some other one." The first thing would be to use the maps that they already have, show the population, the school population, then I would assume they would draw district lines without the idea of race but district lines circled around the schools like they did in the District of Columbia.[72]

Accordingly, the NAACP brief on compliance hewed to the goal of simply eliminating race as the basis for admission to public schools. The psychological damage flowing from segregation argued imperatively for speed in the implementation of constitutional rights, but at this point for nothing else. "Each day relief is postponed is . . . a day of serious and irreparable injury; for this Court has announced that segregation of Negroes in the public schools 'generates a feeling of inferiority as to their status in the community that may affect their hearts and minds in a way unlikely ever to be undone . . . .'"[73] Objections raised in the brief to the desegregation plans proposed for Kansas and for the District of Columbia concentrated on a lack of neutrality in aspects of those plans; there was no exploration of the sufficiency of the notion itself. If officials in the District established a *genuine* neighborhood school system, said the students' attorney, James Nabrit, that was all his clients could ask. Jack Greenberg, counsel in the Delaware desegregation case, went a step further in a book published in 1959. "If . . . there were complete freedom of choice, or geographical zoning, or any other nonracial standard, and all Negroes still ended up in certain schools, there would seem to be no constitutional objection."[74]

Chief Justice Warren's 800 word opinion in *Brown II* blended in with the tone of the briefs and court proceedings. The task of desegregation, said Warren, was "to effectuate a transition to a racially nondiscriminatory school system," where authorities would admit students "to public schools on a racially nondiscriminatory basis."[75] A memorandum by Justice Frankfurter entitled "Districting," undated, but almost certainly written at the time of *Brown II*, expressed the prevailing view of remedy very directly. "Non-segregation does not mean compulsory mixing . . . ."[76]

Lower court judges to whom the school cases went, relied, quite understandably, on the most accessible reading of the Court's language. The three judge panel in Kansas, authors of the passage which most stamped *Brown I* as an "integrationist" decision, now stated: "Desegregation does not mean that there must be intermingling of the races in all school districts. It means only that they may not be prevented from . . . going to school together because of race or color."[77] If a school district was "inhabited entirely by colored students, no violation of any constitutional right results because they are compelled to attend the school in the district in which they live."[78]

The remand in South Carolina produced an especially influential commentary on *Brown*, the work of the highly respected John J. Parker, Chief Judge of the Fourth Circuit Court of Appeals and presiding judge in the Clarendon County case. "The Constitution," he stated flatly," . . . does not require integration. It merely forbids discrimination."[79] Parker's words echoed endlessly through southern courtrooms during the next decade, a barrier against any attempt to extend the reach of compliance.

Judges in northern jurisdictions could invoke such sentiments as well, to prove that *Brown* had nothing to do with their communities unless officials gerrymandered school districts or otherwise manipulated attendance patterns with a racial bias. In one of the first challenges to de facto segregation to reach the federal judiciary, a district court in Michigan noted,

> If [a school board] builds schools in areas where need exists, without arbitrarily fixing attendance areas to exclude any given segment of the school population, it is carrying out [its] duty . . . . The fact that in a given area a school is populated almost exclusively by the children of a given race is not of itself evidence of discrimination . . . . The plaintiff has no constitutionally guaranteed right to attend a public school outside of the attendance area in which she resides.[80]

These views would undergo radical transformation in the years ahead.

I. *BROWN II*: INTIMATIONS OF DEFIANCE

In *Brown I*, as in *Brown II*, the briefs submitted by Prince Edward County, Virginia, breathed an unremitting air of hostility. And this time, South Carolina, no longer speaking with the gentlemanly voice of John W. Davis, also hinted grimly of non-compliance with the desegregation decisions.

These sentiments, forerunners of massive resistance and of Little Rock, highlight the context in which the justices felt they must move with such caution.

1. BRIEF OF PRINCE EDWARD COUNTY

I

INTRODUCTION

The decision of this Court of May 17, 1954, has raised over most of the Virginia scene the spectre of impending educational chaos. If this Court is now to order immediate amalgamation of the races in the public schools of Prince Edward County, the spectre becomes a reality; if this Court now permits a reasonable time for the problems raised by its decision to be weighed and for alternatives to be considered without the heat of emotion created by unreasonable haste, the children in Prince Edward may still go to school. It is for that reason that the school authorities of Prince Edward County, supported by the Commonwealth of Virginia, now appear before this Court.

We make clear at the beginning that Virginia has no plan or panacea that will result in complete solution of this problem. We do not foresee a complete solution at any future time. Government still derives its foundation from the consent of the governed. The people of many sections of Virginia have stated forthrightly that they will not consent to compulsory integration of the races in the public schools. Neither court decree nor executive order can force in those sections a result so basically opposed by a united majority . . . .

III

ARGUMENT

1.

The Power to Permit Gradual Adjustment . . . .

If the Court had no power to permit gradual adjustment, it would simply have entered an order on May 17 reversing the decree of the court below with instructions to grant the relief sought. That the Court did not enter such an order is of itself evidence that it possesses the power to permit gradual adjustment.

Of course, the entry of such an order then as now would destroy the public schools of Prince Edward County . . . .

This Court has now made clear, in broad outline at least, the nature of the rights of the Appellants by its decision of May 17, 1954. We do not discuss here the nature of those rights; what is at issue here is the remedy to enforce those rights. Whether a present right leads to an immediate remedy, even if the right has a constitutional basis, remains a matter for the discretion of this Court in the light of all the circumstances.

This Court has without question the power to permit time for adjustment to new conditions which produce patent complexities.

2.

The Necessity for Gradual Adjustment . . . .

As this Court has recognized by its refusal simply to reverse and remand the decision of the court below, there are weighty considerations impelling the conclusion that action in this field must not be too hasty . . . .

The community attitude of Prince Edward County, Virginia, has already been made clear. There is attached to this brief as Appendix A a resolution adopted on July 12, 1954, by the Board of Supervisors of the County. The Supervisors are not trained perhaps to legal niceties but they reflect in quite an accurate manner the community attitude of Prince Edward County.

This case concerns, of course, only Prince Edward County and any action taken by the Court will bind only Prince Edward County for its school officials are the only ones before the Court. But Virginia is naturally interested on a broader basis and any action taken here would have its impact on other Virginia communities. For that reason, we point out that the attitude expressed by the community of Prince Edward is identical with that of many other Virginia localities. More than thirty counties and cities, through their legislative or school bodies, have expressed this attitude by resolutions filed with the Governor of Virginia. A list of these is placed at the foot of Appendix A. All that this means is that, if this Court's opinion of May 17, 1954, is ever to be accepted by the people of many sections of Virginia, and it may never be, a substantial period for adjustment must be permitted by this Court. Without community acceptance, public education as we know it now will not survive in those localities.

This brings us to the second major problem in Virginia as a whole. Ratio of population is of great significance in the solution of segregation . . . .

The question of ratio of population has particular significance in Virginia. The percentage of Negro school children ranges from zero in Buchanan, Craig and Highland Counties to 77.3% in Charles City County . . . .

In general, education in Virginia has operated in the past pursuant to a single plan centrally controlled with regard to segregation of the races. It would be most unfortunate if the decision of this Court on May 17, 1954, affected adversely the schools in Craig County where there are no Negro pupils as well as those in Charles City County. So some plan for local variation must be devised . . . . But if no time is permitted for the establishment of such a plan, the majority in Virginia are so determined that it is possible that all of Virginia's public schools will be closed for the period required to establish a new system, a period perhaps of years.

In the preparation of any plan, there are many other factors for consideration. The Court implies in its questions that the geographic location of residence is alone significant. But this seems perhaps an oversimplification. Is it not relevant to consider the general level of educational capacity and attainment between the two races? Should not general standards of health and morals be considered? What of the teacher force? If white parents and children are opposed to Negro teachers, should not some plan be worked out to minimize dissension and yet be fair to the Negro teachers? These are only a few of the many problems for consideration in the development of a new educational system . . . .

The problem facing Virginia is a difficult one. It is the problem of coping with the decision of May 17, 1954. How best can Virginia coordinate that ruling with the feeling of a majority of her people and the requirement that her children be educated? That is the basic problem under consideration. To reach the proper answer requires time. Even a generation may not be long enough for solution, but to find the beginning of the path to solution requires a substantial period of adjustment.

These in broad outline are the reasons why, in our view, this Court should permit a gradual adjustment. Otherwise, it may well drive Virginia's children from her schools.

3.

The Final Decree . . . .

We do not believe that this Court should attempt to establish any specific limit of time. This Court cannot know (nor, in fact, do we) how long will be required, if the public school system is to be preserved, for the full operation of its new rule as to segregation by race or color. Conditions over which we have no control make it clear that a very substantial period of time will be required . . . .

Are the Appellants so determined that segregated education be destroyed that they are willing to destroy all of education? That would indeed be a Pyrrhic victory . . . .

IV

CONCLUSION

In conclusion, we reiterate that we know of no short path to solution of the problems raised by this Court's decision of May 17, 1954. No money judgment may be entered and paid and the case then put aside to gather dust in the files. We anticipate continuing problems and, perhaps, prolonged social disorder; the generation of litigation foreseen with trepidation by some members of this Court will not be forestalled by any action now taken.

Our desire is to minimize any conflict that may now result and to preserve the public education of Virginia's children. We have outlined in this brief the best way in our opinion that the chances of achieving this aim may now be enhanced. We know that some of the alternatives that others will suggest will frustrate the achievement. The future is still cloudy and shows few signs of clearing; the path that we suggest seems to us the safest to follow in the difficult days that now lie ahead for our public education.

1.

Resolution Adopted by the Board of Supervisors of

Prince Edward County

At a meeting of the Board of Supervisors of Prince Edward County, held on July 12, 1954, the following resolution was adopted:

WHEREAS, the Supreme Court of the United States has in a recent decision purportedly held that the provision of the Constitution of Virginia requiring segregation in public schools to be unconstitutional, and the said Court having indicated its intention to enter a decree implementing the decision some time in the future; and,

WHEREAS, it is the opinion of this board that such decision is to the detriment of public education in Virginia and an invasion on the rights of the citizens of the Commonwealth.

NOW, THEREFORE, BE IT RESOLVED BY THE BOARD OF SUPERVISORS OF PRINCE EDWARD COUNTY, VIRGINIA:

1st.

That the said Board is unalterably opposed to the operation of nonsegregated public schools in the Commonwealth of Virginia.

2nd.

That this Board is of the opinion that it is not only impracticable, but that it will be impossible to operate a nonsegregated school system in the Commonwealth of Virginia.

3rd.

That the said Board intends to use its power, authority and efforts to insure a continuation of a segregated school system in the Commonwealth of Virginia.

4th.

That it urges all the officials of the Commonwealth to take such action as may be necessary to insure the continuation of a segregated school system in the Commonwealth of Virginia.

5th.

That the Clerk of this Board be instructed to send a copy of this resolution to the Governor, Attorney General, State Senator and Representative in the House of Delegates.

2.

List of Virginia Localities Where Boards of Supervisors and

School Boards Have Adopted Resolutions
Opposing Amalgamation.

BOARDS OF SUPERVISORS

Albemarle	Hanover
Amelia	Lunenburg
Amherst	Mecklenburg
Appomattox	Middlesex
Brunswick	Nansemond
Buckingham	New Kent
Charlotte	Northumberland
Culpeper	Nottoway
Cumberland	Pittsylvania
Dinwiddie	Powhatan
Essex	Prince Edward
Fauquier	Southampton
Greene	Stafford
Greensville	Surry
Halifax	Sussex

SCHOOL BOARDS

Brunswick	Powhatan
Greensville	Southampton
Mecklenburg	South Norfolk
Nansemond	Surry
New Kent	

2. REBUTTAL BRIEF OF PRINCE EDWARD COUNTY

III

IMPEDIMENTS TO INTEGRATION

The Appellants would have the Court believe that there are no reasons why integration may not be directed overnight. They speak of "documented experience with desegregation" that indicates that "gradualism . . . may make it more difficult." . . .

But none of the "experience" that they cite has any relevance to the present issue. The primary and secondary schools to which they refer are in localities remote from the Southern States; in the Southern States the practice of segregation has existed with legal sanction ever since the beginning, and there the greatest concentration of the Negro population still exists . . . .

Virginia is confronted with many problems. They are problems arising primarily from the determined unwillingness of its people to support, financially and otherwise, a system of integrated public schools. This position is not taken out of racial dislike. There are many practical reasons.

1. *Level of Educational Attainment:* More than 31,000 Virginia school children in the eighth grade annually are given a standard silent reading test. These are the results most recently tabulated for Virginia's cities:

Class Standing   *Reading Age*

WHITE

Highest 25% . . . . 18 1/6 years
Middle 50% . . . . 13 1/2 years
Lowest 25% . . . . 12 years

NEGRO

Highest 25% . . . . 11 5/6 years
Middle 50% . . . . 10 7/12 years
Lowest 25% . . . . 9 1/3 years

Thus it was made clear that the lowest quarter of the white students was further advanced than the highest quarter of the Negroes.

This result was not unexpected. Similar answers were obtained from the standard psychological examination of the American Council on Education, generally designated as **IQ** tests, given to all high school seniors. These were the scores obtained in the Virginia cities:

Class Standing	*Score*
WHITE	
Highest 25%	103.2
Middle 50%	89.9
Lowest 25%	71.2
NEGRO	
Highest 25%	63.9
Middle 50%	50.3
Lowest 25%	34.0

How can the gap be bridged? Is it practicable to mix everyone together and have one teacher instructing children whose levels of attainment are as diverse as reading ages of 18 and 9? Will it benefit the children in the schools for this to be required?

This is a very practical measure of difficulties to be encountered in ending segregation.

2. *Standards of Health:* Statistics for Virginia as a whole indicate that tuberculosis is almost twice as prevalent among the Negroes as among the whites. Similarly, in Virginia, where Negroes constitute 22% of the population, 78% of the cases of syphilis and 83% of the cases of gonorrhea occur among Negroes. No white parent will welcome Negro students into the white schools when to do so would increase his child's exposure to such contagious diseases.

3. *Standards of Morality:* In Virginia, one white child out of every 50 is illegitimate; one Negro child out of every 5 is illegitimate. The background of parental morality indicated by these figures dismays Virginia's white parents.

4. *Source of Teachers:* Virginia employs as many Negro teachers as do all the unsegregated States. But Virginia is not prepared to place Negro teachers in charge of white pupils. The need for additional teachers is urgent; the source is not immediately apparent.

It does no good to discuss the cause of the conditions that we have mentioned; cause is irrelevant when the facts exist and must therefore be taken into account. These facts present very practical justification for the position taken by Virginia that integration under present conditions is impossible at this time . . . .

V

CONCLUSION

Neither Prince Edward County nor Virginia come before this Court convicted of a crime; we recognize neither a sense of guilt nor a feeling of inferiority. We feel a sense of bewilderment that traditions and systems that have operated with judicial approval since 1870, and, in fact, since 1619, can be so readily swept away.

In looking at the days ahead, Virginia thinks first of her children. Education is important and it must be preserved. When this Court swept away the traditions and systems of many generations, it did not change the way that Virginians think and believe. How Virginians think and believe is an important factor in determining the future course of Virginia schools. To require integration in Virginia's public schools now will result only in their collapse. As the years go by, conditions may change; if education is to prosper in Virginia, this Court must permit a now indeterminable period to elapse before requiring integration of the races in Virginia's public schools.

3. ARGUMENT OF EMORY ROGERS, REPRESENTING SCHOOL BOARD OF CLARENDON COUNTY, SOUTH CAROLINA

MR. ROGERS: . . . . [W]e must remember that in the very statement that was filed by the appellants, called a social science statement in the original causes, attention was called to the fact that the question of desegregation involved problems that were as they [saw] them, in the frontiers of scientific knowledge. We realize that very much in this district because we have had a biracial society for more than two centuries. As this Court called attention to the fact that we could not turn the clock of progress back to 1895 or even 1868, using the basis that we are now doing— [we]are now exploring the frontiers of scientific knowledge—I do not believe that in a biracial society, that we can push the clock forward abruptly to 2015. We can help . . . .

Whether we like it or not, there is a feeling in the district that the desegregation of the elementary and the high school does affect the social life of the community, and for that reason, we have to remark that to say that the decision is [un]popular in the area is the understatement of the year, but we would wish to work within the framework of the decision. But we do know that we are faced with problems that cannot be solved except with a change of attitude and those attitudes will have to be changed slowly, not quickly.

As a result, we are asking that the cases be sent back without instructions, but to be sent back to the lower court for action in conformity with the provisions of the decision . . . .

THE CHIEF JUSTICE: Is your request for an open decree predicated upon the assumption that your school district will immediately undertake to conform to the opinion of this Court of last year and to the decree, or is it on the basis—

MR. ROGERS: Mr. Chief Justice, to say we will conform depends on the decree handed down. I am frank to tell you, right now in our district I do not think that we will send—the white people of the district will send their children to the Negro schools. It would be unfair to tell the Court that we are going to do that. I do not think it is. But I do think that something can be worked out. We hope so.

THE CHIEF JUSTICE: It is not a question of attitude, it is a question of conforming to the decree. Is there any basis upon which we can assume that there will be an immediate attempt to comply with the decree of this Court, whatever it may be?

MR. ROGERS: Mr. Chief Justice, I would say that we would present our . . . problem to the district court and we are in the Fourth Circuit . . . . I feel we can expect the courts in the Fourth Circuit and the people of the district to work out something in accordance with your decree.

THE CHIEF JUSTICE: Don't you believe that the question as to whether the district will attempt to comply should be considered in any such decree?

MR. ROGERS: Not necessarily, sir. I think that should be left to the lower court.

THE CHIEF JUSTICE: And why?

MR. ROGERS: Your Honors, we have laid down here in this Court the principle that segregation is unconstitutional. The lower court we feel is the place that the machinery should be set in motion to conform to that.

THE CHIEF JUSTICE: But you are not willing to say here that there would be an honest attempt to conform to this decree, if we did leave it to the district court?

MR. ROGERS: No, I am not. Let us get the word "honest" out of there.

THE CHIEF JUSTICE: No, leave it in.

MR. ROGERS: No, because I would have to tell you that right now we would not conform—we would not send our white children to the Negro schools.

THE CHIEF JUSTICE: Thank you.

JUSTICE BURTON: Mr. Rogers, that might not mean that you would violate the decree—

MR. ROGERS: No, sir.

JUSTICE BURTON: —it would mean that you would send your children to some other school, some other than public school?

MR. ROGERS: Yes. We do not want to say that we would violate it. We are trying to work within it. We hope the Court will give us a decree that we can work within.

JUSTICE FRANKFURTER: May I ask one more question? Am I right—I am not asking a leading question—in thinking that you have said or implied, are you asking this Court to reconsider the declaration of unconstitutionality of last May?

MR. ROGERS: No. We are asking the opportunity to work the matter out at the local level.

JUSTICE FRANKFURTER: You are not inferentially or remotely coming before this Court and saying that decision was a mistake and what went on before should be continued?

MR. ROGERS: I am certainly not saying that in my argument, no, sir.

JUSTICE FRANKFURTER: All right.

II. *BROWN II*: INTIMATIONS OF NEUTRALITY

Speed of compliance, was, to be sure, the dominant concern of the litigants in *Brown II*, but obtruding from their arguments are hints that neutral geographic zoning, and no more than that, was the goal of desegregation. Besides Marshall's exchanges with Justice Frankfurter, there are instructive dialogues along this line between the Court and opposing counsel in the District of Columbia desegregation case, James Nabrit and Milton Korman. These concerned, in large part, the District's modification of its geographic zoning plan to make it possible for students to remain in their present schools until graduation, and the appellants' contention that such a provision subtly reintroduced the element of race into school assignment.

The United States government brief also anticipates a neutrality standard. Even more emphatic, perhaps, are the memoranda written by Justice Frankfurter. One of them despairs that a court could even deal with deliberate gerrymandering of geographic zones to preserve segregation, though the formal desegregation decree which Frankfurter suggested to his colleagues is more optimistic on that score.

1. BRIEF OF UNITED STATES GOVERNMENT

2. Because local school authorities have considerable discretion respecting many facets of school administration, and because there is a wide variety in local conditions, it can be expected that, even within the same state, no two school districts will

be faced with precisely the same problems in accomplishing an effective transition to nonsegregated school systems.

(a) In districts where there is more than one school, adjustments in the method employed for allocating students to particular schools may have to be made. In the majority of such districts, children are given little, if any, choice as to the school they are to attend. Instead, each school in the district is assigned a particular attendance area and the pupil must enroll in the facility within whose attendance boundaries he resides.

Many factors are taken into consideration in drawing these boundaries, foremost among them being the size and character of the school, the geographical distribution of the school population in the district, and the ease and safety of public travel to and from school. In the case of segregated school systems, boundaries are formulated separately for white and colored facilities, with the result that the overall objective of making the maximum use of total school facilities and minimizing travel difficulties is seldom achieved . . . .

The extent of the boundary alterations required, in the reformulation of school attendance areas on a non-racial basis, will vary. This is illustrated by the recent experience in the District of Columbia in recasting attendance boundaries on a wholly geographical basis. *In the neighborhoods where there is little or no mixture of the races, and where school facilities have been fully utilized, it was found that the elimination of the racial factor did not work any material change in the territory served by each school* . . . .

If the program for desegregation formulated by the defendants will remove, as expeditiously as possible, state-imposed or state-supported racial classifications of pupils in public schools, the lower courts should not substitute their judgment respecting the administrative features of the program for that of the school authorities. The Constitution prohibits the maintenance of segregated school systems. It does not compel the adoption of any specific type of nonsegregated system. The decisive inquiry is whether race or color has been entirely eliminated as a criterion in the admission of pupils to public schools. The essence of the Court's decision in these cases is that there be no governmental action which enforces or supports school segregation.

2. COMMENTS BY JAMES NABRIT AND MILTON KORMAN—DISTRICT OF COLUMBIA SCHOOL CASE

JUSTICE REED: Mr. Nabrit before you sit down, ... [a]re you familiar with the problems of choice [in this case?]

MR. NABRIT: . . . . In the District of Columbia there is a system of administration and operation of the school which is known as the Districting Plan . . . . That is the basis on which the school board says children shall be assigned, and they voted a policy that it would be done, and only the hardship or necessary situation of overriding necessity would permit any departure from that.

Now that was the policy.

JUSTICE REED: The Board policy?

MR. NABRIT: Yes. Now when the plan was proposed which the Board adopted, there was a difference between the policies and this plan, and it is that difference to which we call the Court's attention, that is, that in this plan which provided for this forthright imposition of the boundary or district system, there was set up inside the system, a system which provided that all of the pupils in all of the schools could stay right where they were until they graduated, . . . unless your remaining there prevented student[s] who lived in that district from getting into [those schools if they chose to].

So that takes some . . . of the sting out of it. But we consider that bad because, looking at the Labor Relations cases and others, where this Court has said where you have a choice regarding a union or not, here is a company union, here is another union, that the choice is not a choice. You do not have freedom of choice. And where you come out of a segregated system where everybody in the system is segregated and you say to the Negro child, sure, you have a choice . . . . I mean that is not choice. So that we simply point it out because it goes for five years and there is nothing that we have found that indicates that at the end of the fourth year the Board would adopt another plan with that in there.

JUSTICE REED: That is in it—

MR. NABRIT: I think it is on page 10 of our brief, Mr. Justice Reed . . . . "All pupils at present enrolled in a given school may remain until graduation provided the school is not overcrowded and provided the priority rights of pupils within the new boundaries of the school are not denied." . . .

Now in [our decree] we said, do not deny any child the right to go to . . . school . . . , on the grounds of race or color, within the normal limits of your districting system.

In other words, you have this districting system here. Now, we say in that system, let children go to the schools . . . within that system.

JUSTICE REED: Within that district.

MR. NABRIT: That is right.

And do not assign them on the basis of race or color, and we have no complaint. If you have some other basis, all boys, all girls, sixteen or fourteen, any other basis, we have no objection. But just do not put in race or color as a factor. And on that basis, we do not complain . . . .

THE CHIEF JUSTICE: Thank you, Mr. Nabrit. Mr. Korman. . . .

MR. KORMAN: [W]hether we like it or not, . . . when neighborhoods change, there are no longer white children going into the neighborhoods where colored now live, but colored children are coming into the neighborhoods that were formerly occupied by white.

So, it is only logical that, when people graduate from one level of a school, we find that colored children may go to schools formerly occupied by white, but it is not likely that the other will occur, that the white children will go into schools formerly occupied by colored because the neighborhoods have been changing the other way.

That is the only answer to that. We cannot read race into that as something that the school system is putting on for these children. It is just not so.

JUSTICE REED: What is your explanation for several all-white schools?

MR. KORMAN: Just that in certain areas in the District, there are no Negro residents. [This is true of grade schools] and in certain areas of high schools . . . . [W]e [do] have two teachers colleges. Those are now open to pupils of both races.

3. FELIX FRANKFURTER— MEMORANDUM ON DISTRICTING

Four principal criteria enter into the establishment of school districts and/or attendance areas:

1. nearness to a school. Certain districts have been worked out over time as to how far children should have to walk to school at certain age levels (or how far they should have to travel by bus).

2. geographic and man-made boundaries. These include rivers, railroad lines, main traffic arteries, and, more subtly, the wrong and right sides of the tracks.

3. community. A school should serve as a focal point of a community or neighborhood . . . . This, of course, may serve as a mask for segregating the rich from the poor, the newer immigrants from the older stock, or negroes from whites, but still is a recognized basis for drawing lines . . . .

4. available facilities. Self-explanatory . . . .

Use of these criteria means that the establishment of attendance areas is a quite discretionary function and subject to considerable manipulation. It is conceded, for example, that wherever negroes live in large concentrations, school lines tend to result in segregated schools; and housing patterns interplay on school zones . . . . However, assuming that the districts thus drawn are "compact and contiguous" (and not a group of isolated pockets patched together) and that one or more of the above criteria are mobilizable in support of the administrative decision, it would be difficult for a court to upset a school board determination, even tho [though] gerrymandering is present.

This is not as bad as it might appear. Non-segregation does not mean compulsory mixing, and as a mode of social adjustment, it is likely that at least at the elementary school level, the typical pattern of [a] desegregated school district will show that most schools are almost wholly of one race or the other . . . . This does not, however, account for haphazard housing arrangements . . . , for shifting populations, or for marginal areas where the races are interspersed . . . .

The result of this situation is that negro children and white children will be mixed in the schools, though not in proportion to population, but rather as the proportion appears in given neighborhoods under the segregated housing pattern. Moreover, at the junior high and high school level, the homogeneity of some of the lower schools will break down . . . .

As we have seen, the range of districting practices . . . points against any one rule for districting in compliance with the court's decision that segregation is unconstitutional. Local practices are both diverse and ordinarily defensible. Certain maneuvers, however, can be detected in the light of sound educational practice . . . . [An] example would be a plan of arbitrary assignment of pupils to schools without regard for proximity, contiguity or the other factors [just] enumerated [,] and resulting in monoracial schools. The more subtle forms, widely practiced in the "enlightened" North, will be more difficult to overcome, and at this point it should perhaps be concluded that the best for which one can hope is a situation in which at least a few negroes will attend white schools and thus promote the educating of both races to live together.

4.FELIX FRANKFURTER— "MEMORANDUM ON THE SEGREGATION DECREE" AND SUGGESTED DECREE

II . . . .Platitude though it be, it does become relevant to say that we do not propose to operate as a super-school board. But the Court can say that school districts must be "geographically compact and contiguous." The experience with political gerrymandering should be drawn upon. The term "gerrymandering" carries sufficient meaning to justify its inclusion in our decree.

This would not, however, prevent a biracial school district containing more than one school from continuing segregation school by school. Thus, it should be considered whether our decree should also exclude [among other things] setting up of attendance areas on grounds other than such relevant educational factors as distance, hazards and facilities.   —F.F.

* * * * * * * * * * * * *

DECREE #2

4. Insofar as reorganization may be necessary in the school districts affected by our judgment, so as to make effective this decree that no student shall be denied

admission to any public school because of his race, the respective lower courts are to require that any new or reorganized school districts to be established by local authorities shall be geographically compact, contiguous and non-gerrymandered. And it shall further be made incumbent upon local authorities that within a given school district Negro students be not refused admission to any school where they are situated similarly to white students in respect to (1) distance from school, (2) natural or manmade barriers or hazards, and (3) other relevant educational criteria.

5. DECISION

These cases were decided on May 17, 1954. The opinions of that date, declaring the fundamental principle that racial discrimination in public education is unconstitutional, are incorporated herein by reference. All provisions of federal, state, or local law requiring or permitting such discrimination must yield to this principle. There remains for consideration the manner in which relief is to be accorded.

Because these cases arose under different local conditions and their disposition will involve a variety of local problems, we requested further argument on the question of relief . . . .

These presentations were informative and helpful to the Court in its consideration of the complexities arising from the transition to a system of public education freed of racial discrimination. The presentations also demonstrated that substantial steps to eliminate racial discrimination in public schools have already been taken, not only in some of the communities in which these cases arose, but in some of the states appearing as amici curiae, and in other states as well. Substantial progress has been made in the District of Columbia and in the communities in Kansas and Delaware involved in this litigation. The defendants in the cases coming to us from South Carolina and Virginia are awaiting the decision of this Court concerning relief.

Full implementation of these constitutional principles may require solution of varied local school problems. School authorities have the primary responsibility for elucidating, assessing, and solving these problems; courts will have to consider whether the action of school authorities constitutes good faith implementation of the governing constitutional principles. Because of their proximity to local conditions and the possible need for further hearings, the courts which originally heard these cases can best perform this judicial appraisal. Accordingly, we believe it appropriate to remand the cases to those courts.

In fashioning and effectuating the decrees, the courts will be guided by equitable principles. Traditionally, equity has been characterized by a practical flexibility in shaping its remedies and by a facility for adjusting and reconciling public and private needs. These cases call for the exercise of these traditional attributes of equity power. At stake is the personal interest of the plaintiffs in admission to public schools as soon as practicable on a nondiscriminatory basis. To effectuate this interest may call for elimination of a variety of obstacles in making the transition to school systems operated in accordance with the constitutional principles set forth in our May 17, 1954, decision. Courts of equity may properly take into account the public interest in the elimination of such obstacles in a systematic and effective manner. But it should go without saying that the vitality of these constitutional principles cannot be allowed to yield simply because of disagreement with them.

While giving weight to these public and private considerations, the courts will require that the defendants make a prompt and reasonable start toward full compliance with our May 17, 1954, ruling. Once such a start has been made, the courts may find that additional time is necessary to carry out the ruling in an effective manner. The burden rests upon the defendants to establish that such time is necessary in the public interest and is consistent with good faith compliance at the earliest practicable date. To that end, the courts may consider problems related to administration, arising from the physical condition of the school plant, the school transportation system, personnel, revision of school districts and attendance areas into compact units to achieve a system of determining admission to the public schools on a nonracial basis, and revision of local laws and regulations which may be necessary in solving the foregoing problems. They will also consider the adequacy of any plans the defendants may propose to meet these problems and to effectuate a transition to a racially nondiscriminatory school system. During this period of transition, the courts will retain jurisdiction of these cases.

[T]he cases are remanded to the District Courts to take such proceedings and enter such orders and decrees consistent with this opinion as are necessary and proper to admit to public schools on a racially nondiscriminatory basis with all deliberate speed the parties to these cases.

CHAPTER ONE

THE FAILURES OF NEUTRALITY

Desegregation proceeded in a remarkably orderly fashion in the large cities of border states such as Maryland, Kentucky, and Missouri. The process brought results thought highly commendable at the time, though, by later standards, these results would be found totally inadequate.

Even before *Brown II* came down, Baltimore adopted a policy giving students the free choice to go to any school in the system at their grade level, unless the school was overcrowded. During the plan's first year of operation, 3% of African-American students chose to attend school with whites; the number more than doubled in the second year. Still, in 1960, more than 50% of all schools were attended solely by students of one race or the other.[1]

St. Louis, which set up geographic zones for its entire school system in September, 1955, did much better, though scarcely satisfying later definitions of "desegregation." By 1956–57, six of the seven formerly white high schools had mixed enrollments. Almost 70% of the elementary school students were attending interracial schools. By 1962, things were reversing themselves, however. About 85% of African-American elementary school pupils now attended schools almost 100% black. (Only 15 or so of these schools out of 136 were significantly integrated.) Approximately 70% of the African-American high school students were in schools 90 to 100% black.[2]

Similar zoning arrangements for Louisville commenced in September, 1956. A status report five years later showed that half of the elementary schools were integrated to some degree. Yet 70% of the African-American junior high students went to three all-black institutions; 73% attended a single high school, which had one white pupil.[3]

Nonetheless, this did represent compliance. But in the old confederacy, the fears expressed by Justice Hugo Black at the initial conference on *Brown* quickly materialized. Every United States Senator from those states, save for Albert Gore and Estes Kefauver of Tennessee, and Lyndon Johnson of Texas, joined 77 members of the House of Representatives in March of 1956 to issue the Southern Manifesto. The document denounced *Brown* as an "unwarranted exercise of power by the [Supreme] Court," as "contrary to the Constitution," and as likely to "creat[e] chaos and confusion in the States principally affected."[4] The manifesto appealed to southerners "to scrupulously refrain from disorder and lawless acts," but its commendation of "the motives of those States which have declared [their] intention to resist forced integration by any lawful means"[5] clearly applauded the revival in the South during this time of ante-bellum constitutional theories. Indeed, nine southern states flourished declarations of interposition between 1956 and 1959, claiming that as sovereign entities they did not have to comply with the *Brown* decision until three-fourths of the union approved a constitutional amendment abolishing segregated schools.[6] Generally, though, these pronouncements served more as a form of psychic release than as a serious program of action, since federal authorities paid no attention to them.

Louisiana, Arkansas, and Virginia, however, instituted more tangible defiance of national authority. Louisiana's legislature sought to countermand *Brown* through a series of bizarre statutory maneuvers, ranging from state seizure of schools which tolerated desegregation to denial of school lunch programs in such institutions. Firm action by the federal courts forestalled these efforts,[7] but in Virginia and Arkansas authorities actually shut down schools rather than obey court orders. Governor Lindsay Almond ordered the closing of schools in Warren County, Virginia, in Charlottesville, and in Norfolk in September, 1958. These actions were quickly declared illegal and the schools resumed operation, but the well-known sequel to Governor Almond's move was played out in rural Prince Edward County, where local officials kept the schools shuttered for five more years, until forced by the Supreme Court to reopen and desegregate them.[8]

Meanwhile, in 1957, Arkansas had experienced the antics of Governor Orval Faubus—his direct use of state force to try to prevent a handful of African-American students from attending Little Rock's Central High School, the atmosphere of mob rule which this perversion of executive authority produced, and the dispatch of federal troops to Little Rock by President Eisenhower, after fruitless attempts to appease the governor. Faubus followed up this display by closing Little Rock's high schools during the 1958–59 school year, until the school closure law he had pushed through the Arkansas legislature was invalidated by a three judge federal panel.[9]

These are oft-told stories, brilliantly recounted in works such as Tony Freyer's *The Little Rock Crisis* and Raymond Wolters' *The Burden of Brown*.[10] Our principal concern here is with another matter, the elaborately conceived alternative to defiance which emerged in the South in the late 1950's, even as that defiance was gradually being quelled.

II

This alternative was the approach, pioneered in North Carolina, of offering to the courts token compliance with *Brown*, by allowing a few carefully selected students to enroll in formerly white schools. The methods for ensuring this glacial movement were embodied in the pupil placement laws, adopted, by 1962, in all of the southern states save Georgia.[11] Under pupil placement, prior zoning assignments keyed to race were supposedly discontinued, and all youngsters assigned to schools based on a number of ostensibly non-racial, though obviously suspect, standards—such as the psychological qualifications of pupils, their morals, health, and personal behavior, and the possibility that assignment of pupils to certain schools might provoke breaches of the peace or economic retaliation by employers.

In practice, of course, such massive sifting of individual records was impossible, and students were actually sent to the same schools they had attended prior to 1954; dual zones, in effect, remained. African-American youngsters who wanted to go to school with whites must then apply for transfer to white schools, and run the gauntlet of the aforementioned educational and psychological hurdles in order to gain admission. This produced a lengthy and, in all but a few cases, a foredoomed consideration of each individual application by the local school board.

Students refused transfer by a local board could ask for reconsideration, or, in some states, could appeal to a county or to a statewide placement authority. If further rebuffed, as was almost always the case, they must seek redress in the state courts before becoming eligible to go to a federal district court. Even on the federal level, they were required to proceed individually or in small clusters; the placement laws prohibited the bringing of class action suits. This racially rigged system applied to entering first graders as well as to students already at school.

That the system aspired to tokenism, at best, was openly acknowledged in many of the placement statutes. The "particular genius" of these statutes, noted one contemporary observer, "derives from the provisions designed to individualize consideration of requests for transfers. Local school boards are not only instructed that they have the right to refuse to make any general reallocations of pupils, but are in fact prohibited . . . from authorizing the transfer of any individual or group without separate consideration of each application . . . . In short, the statutes, functioning as intended, make mass integration almost impossible . . . ."[12]

Some saw the pupil placement laws as a temporary holding action, providing a way for the South to adjust to the shock of desegregation before having to move on to really acceptable versions of it. This contrivance, felt Professor Daniel Meador of the University of Virginia Law School, "is at least a step toward a working solution . . . . Perhaps under such a plan, for a while anyway, the schools can find shelter from the storm. And possibly by this means life and law may in time adjust so that in the South, universal, publicly supported education will survive and peace will return."[13]

In a moving "interview with myself," the great southern author and critic, Robert

Penn Warren, while not endorsing any particular desegregation plan, spoke of the need for gradualism.

Q. Are you for desegregation?

A. *Yes.*

Q. When will it come?

A. Not soon.

Q. When?

A. When enough people, in a particular place, a particular county or state, cannot live with themselves any more. Or realize they don't have to . . . .

Q. Are you a gradualist on the matter of segregation?

A. If by gradualist you mean a person who would create delay for the sake of delay, then no. If by gradualist you mean a person who thinks it will take time, not time as such, but time for an educational process, preferably a calculated one, then yes. I mean a process of mutual education for whites and blacks. And part of this education should be in the actual beginning of the process of desegregation. It's a silly question, anyway, to ask if somebody is a gradualist. Gradualism is all you'll get. History, like nature, knows no jumps. Except the jump backward, maybe.[14]

Unlike Meador or Warren, however, many southern authorities viewed schemes such as pupil placement as a device for *permanently* reducing desegregation to an occasional nuisance, when compliance became unavoidable. "Hopeful liberal observers," wrote Benjamin Muse of the Washington *Post*, "saw in [these laws] a means of effective selective gradualism in adjusting to the Supreme Court ruling; but the object of most of their proponents was to make it possible to deny Negroes admission to white schools or to hold desegregation to a minimum when it could no longer be prevented."[15] In the deep South, the combination of fear on the part of prospective plaintiffs, opposition by local authorities, and the sympathetic ministrations of some federal judges, kept the more pristine alternative alive into the sixties. As late as the 1962–63 school year, not a single student in South Carolina, Mississippi, or Alabama was going to a desegregated school. (The schools in Clarendon County, South Carolina, site of one of the companion cases argued with *Brown* v. *Board of Education*, did not commence desegregation until 1965.)[16]

If North Carolina seemed a model by comparison, it was a model of how little desegregation southern communities could get away with. Charlotte, for instance, enrolled three African-American students in formerly white schools in 1957–58, four in 1958–59, and one in 1960. May, 1964 found barely half of one per cent of North Carolina's African-American students in integrated schools.[17]

From the outset, southern plaintiffs saw nothing "hopeful" about pupil placement. They repeatedly challenged the constitutionality of these laws, but, in the atmosphere created by Little Rock and Norfolk, lower federal courts, and even the Supreme Court, initially upheld them. Judge John J. Parker of the Fourth Circuit set the pattern in 1957 when he sustained the North Carolina placement law, though he denied North Carolina's power to prevent the bringing of federal class action suits by claimants who had exhausted their state administrative and judicial remedies.[18]

Judge Parker rendered his decision in the confidence that the law was producing some actual desegregation in North Carolina schools, a confidence piggy-backed upon by authorities in Alabama when they successfully defended their state's law before a three judge panel of the Fifth Circuit the next year. "Judge Parker himself told me two days before he died," said Alabama's counsel, "that . . . there had been admissions of some colored people to the schools of North Carolina and . . . that is perfectly possible under the laws of Alabama as they are now written."[19] The federal panel found the situation in Alabama somewhat "analogous to that in North Carolina," and upheld the statute.[20] Later in 1958, the Supreme Court affirmed this judgement in a narrowly-cast opinion.[21]

Meanwhile, the Alabama superintendent of education had written a revealing letter to the adult plaintiffs in the case, exposing the fact that the state was not ready for even token integration. Commenting on recent improvements in black educational facilities, the superintendent warned the parents, "I think you will destroy what you already have if you refuse to cooperate with the decision of the local board . . . to place your child in the school they think will be best . . . ."[22] No one successfully questioned these judgements in Alabama for the next four years.

Overall, statistics from the first decade following *Brown* seemed to bear out the views of those southerners who believed that tokens were the most expensive coin of the realm they would ever have to pay in order to comply with the decision. On May 17, 1954, 1.17% of the African-American children in the former confederacy were attending previously all-white schools. Alabama and South Carolina had finally begun minimal compliance, but the percentage in Mississippi remained at zero.[23]

Some observers defended this barren record as a necessary prelude to progress. Most prominent among them was the great constitutional scholar, Professor Alexander Bickel of Yale Law School, who had served as law clerk to Justice Frankfurter in 1952–53, when the "all deliberate speed" formula was promulgated. Bickel conveyed, with his characteristic subtlety and grace, a sense of how fragile judicial supremacy is in a democratic culture, the strongest reason for understanding sympathetically the position on relief taken by courts which seriously feared defiance of a decision unprecedented in its sweep and in its potential for unloosing violence.

Contrary to popular belief, Bickel argued, a judge-made rule like the one in *Brown*, which was enforceable only through the initiative of private litigants, did not carry with it the automatic guarantee of obedience, especially when resisted by a determined, at times fanatical, majority. That *Brown* was finally being established as the rule of law in the South by 1965—even Mississippi "cannot long maintain [its] posture entirely alone"—was "an enormously important achievement; without it, nothing else would have been possible."[24] It was an achievement, Bickel felt, which might not have been realized had judges demanded faster progress in desegregation from the outset.

But veterans of the *Brown* remedy litigation did not agree. The puny results of the immediate post-*Brown* period extinguished any optimism they had allowed themselves to entertain about the gradualist approach to desegregation. Writing in 1968, Robert Carter declared all deliberate speed "a grave mistake," a clear indication that the Supreme Court "failed to realize the depth or nature of the [compliance] problem."[25] The justices "apparently believed that [their] show of compassion and understanding of the problem facing the white South would help develop a willingness to comply. Instead, the "all deliberate speed" formula aroused the hope that resistance to the constitutional imperative would succeed."[26]

In an essay the following year, Kenneth Clark noted the irony inherent in *Brown II*. The same Court which pointedly took note of social science findings in arriving at the original decision outlawing school segregation ignored such findings in articulating its views on remedy. "There is no evidence that a more direct, specific, and concrete implementation decree would have resulted in any more tension, procrastination, or evasion than the seemingly rational, statesmanlike deliberate speed decision of the Court. It does not seem likely that the pace of public school desegregation could have been slower."[27]

As early as 1957, Charles Black had eloquently denounced a policy of what he regarded as segregative appeasement, feeling that it weakened the hand of moderates in the South, while doing nothing to mollify extremists.

> [Some] hope that a soft approach [to desegregation] will somehow placate opposition, and thus ease the way to desegregation by consent. I think this a vain hope, both as regards the decent, law-abiding people and as regards the mob. As to the former, . . . [by] adopting a permissive approach you make irrelevant two of the strongest motives that could press Southerners to compliance: respect for law and desire for peace. But beyond that you take the whole issue off the plane of principle, and pitch discussion on the level of community convenience and preference. And that is a fatal mistake. Community preference means, of course, white preference, and I am afraid that white preference for a long, long time is going to be predominantly segregationist. Some day this may no longer be so; it is impossible to think that so stupid a mis-

take as racism can survive indefinitely. But if you await the spontaneous dwindling of prejudice, I think you'll wait until the segregation decision is just a stale joke . . . .

Now as to the fire-eaters and die-hards, and the political batteners thereon: The soft approach is supposed to throw them a sop, to appease them. Speculation here is unnecessary. We know that the policy of giving these people rope has been a dismal failure; we know from their own mouths that they are not faintly interested in gradualism, in reasonableness, in compromise. They want racism entire and racism forever . . . .

We have seen the result. The people who made trouble in Little Rock cannot be appeased. The beady-eyed race crank and his swamp-brained financial angel, the nutty "Minister" spouting Noachian genealogy, the disturbed truant who thinks this is lots more fun than gigging frogs, the clabber-headed footsoldier in the mob who breathes at last the pure ozone of hate after which he has quested all his life, the virago ridden with fear of dark men breaking in, the garbage-pail politician who waves these troops into the breach—how could you hope to satisfy these people just by going slow? They read moderation as weakness and fear, having never even thought of being moderate . . . . And if you doubted this, Little Rock should convince you. If you are going to delay integration until these people are pacified, you are never going to have it. That is the simple choice. If you go slow, they will make trouble. If you go fast, they will make trouble. Total abandonment of desegregation is their price of peace. And they have frankly said so.[28]

This, then, was the curious situation which first obtained in American desegregation law. Neutrality in pupil assignment, a goal which from our perspective today scarcely qualifies as a radical, or even as a legitimate, one, was the optimum standard derived by the courts from *Brown* during the first decade following its promulgation. Yet no one could suppose that pupil placement represented a serious attempt to realize this ideal, even aside from the shady practices the system nourished. The most well-intentioned defenders of the placement scheme, indeed, were the first to admit that its tokenist aspirations, even if pursued in absolute good faith, comprised only a tenuous foothold on the climb to conformity with *Brown*.

Whatever their ultimate views on remedy, therefore, counsel for southern plaintiffs were expending their energies during the late 1950's and early sixties battling mere caricatures of compliance. In a phrase they shared with litigants bringing suits in other areas of anti-discrimination law, they argued that, no matter what *Brown II* finally required, pupil placement manifestly failed to satisfy the "affirmative and positive duty"[29] placed upon school boards by that decision to eliminate dual systems.

None of these early legal battles, as noted, lead to the actual invalidation of the placement laws. But they produced on occasion a curious, and, as it turned out, a doctrinally significant outcome: an inversion of the very neutrality principle in student assignment which pupil placement was designed to evade, and the first sporadic demands for integration. Here was the initial step toward the situation which would develop by the mid-1960's, when the concept of affirmative duty advanced by southern plaintiffs questioned the very notion of neutrality itself. This development was certainly bound to a more general impatience with the non-discrimination principle displayed by civil rights leaders in that decade, and their growing demand for positive outcomes.[30] Yet the decisive factor in fermenting doctrinal change in school desegregation law was the congenital failure of neutrality, as revealed by the litigation of the 1959–1965 period.

III

It was true that under the standards announced in *Briggs* v. *Elliott* a desegregation plan could not be judged on the amount of racial mixing it did or did not effect, only on its structural and administrative features; the "normal geographic zoning" mentioned in preparation for *Brown II* constituted the perfect example, presumably, of a plan which passed muster. Yet the very gap which separated pupil placement from any pretense, even, of genuine neutrality led southern plaintiffs, and a few adventurous lower court judges of the late fifties, toward a refreshingly subversive notion: that a bargain was a bargain, even if a bad bargain, and that pupil placement schemes could be found inadequate per se if they failed to produce the tokens expected of them. Under concededly suspect arrangements, in other words, integration comprised the only proper measure of compliance.

Failure to achieve any integration, of course, often resulted from blatantly illegal maneuvers by school authorities, actionable in themselves. But blended into some of the briefs and court decisions of the early years of school litigation is the suggestion that officials invited an unbearable weight of suspicion simply because no African-American youngsters were attending a previously all-white school. The pupil placement structures might represent a temporarily tolerated masking of the status quo, but if they did not yield a minimum amount of racial mixing, it was argued, the mask would be ripped away.

This result-oriented, "integrationist" standard peeks through for the first time in a 1958 case, *Holland* v. *Board of Public Instruction*.[31] A panel of the Fifth Circuit, headed by Judge Richard Rives, and including Judge John Minor Wisdom, reversed a lower court ruling and struck down a desegregation plan concocted by Palm Beach County under the Florida Pupil Placement Law. Ostensibly, the circuit court took its action because county officials, while appearing to move forward to a geographic zoning pattern, were perpetuating school boundary lines which formed an exact parallel with residential areas segregated by a municipal ordinance (surprisingly, not called into question in the case). Therefore, it remained as much of a legal impossibility for an African-American child in Palm Beach County to attend an integrated school after *Brown* as before.

Still, the tone of the court's opinion suggests that the mere existence of total segregation in the county was enough to justify its action. It was "not necessary," said Judge Rives, "to review piecemeal the district court's findings," for everyone knew a completely segregated school system remained in Palm Beach, "and the courts simply cannot blot it out of their sight."[32] The palpable reality, as plaintiffs had pointed out, was that African-American children were arranged exactly as they were when segregation was declared "contrary to the Constitution," and this very situation proved that the school board had not made "'a prompt and reasonable start'" toward compliance.[33]

In 1959, another Fifth Circuit panel, also headed by Judge Rives, affirmed plaintiffs' contention that standing alone the Florida placement law did not represent a guarantee of freedom from racial discrimination, where the school system of Dade County remained totally segregated "at the time of trial."[34] As in Palm Beach, there was evidence of hanky-panky in the administration of the desegregation program, focusing this time on the fraudulence of the claim that school officials had impartially "reassigned" all students to schools under the placement statute. It was manifestly clear to the judges, despite resolutions of the Dade County School Board trumpeting compliance, and the distribution of preference cards to all students, that the reassignment process was form rather than substance, that African-American youngsters were automatically sent to their old schools, and were not "afforded a reasonable and conscious opportunity to apply for admission to any school" they wished to attend.[35]

Yet the stark numbers themselves were enough to carry great weight. "For all practical purposes," noted Judge Rives, school segregation remained in Dade County. "That being true, we cannot agree . . . that the Pupil Assignment Law, . . . in and of [itself], . . . constitute[s] a 'reasonable start toward full compliance' with the Supreme Court's May 17, 1954 ruling."[36] Unless some "legally non-segregated schools" existed, the court felt, "there can be no constitutional assignment of a pupil to a particular school."[37] A "legally non-segregated school," officially, was one in which transfer requests by minorities were entertained on an impartial basis under the placement law. The tone of Judge Rives' opinion, however, made it doubtful that schools would qualify as "legally non-segregated" if they remained physically non-integrated.

This "bottom line" approach to desegregation was stated most openly by the plaintiffs in *Dove* v. *Parham*, which turned out to be one of the most revealing controversies of the pupil placement era.

The case arose because, unlike Dade County authorities, officials in the tiny Dollarway, Arkansas school district had not even gone through the charade of individually assigning students in the district to the same schools they attended before *Brown*; nor did they set up any mechanisms under the state's pupil placement act for transfers. They simply maintained the prevailing situation and assumed no troublemakers would materialize. In 1957, though, three African-American students did ask for admission to Dollarway's only comprehensive white school (serving grades 1–12), and were peremptorily rejected.

Lawyers for the children appealed to the federal district court for relief from the school board's discriminatory actions, arguing that the matter had gone beyond the point where relief was possible simply by ordering a non-discriminatory application of Arkansas' pupil placement statute. Clearly, authorities' actions indicated that they would employ the law only as "a discriminatory device,"[38] and in these circumstances the court must issue an order enrolling the three children immediately in Dollarway's white school.

But the plaintiffs' brief struck a deeper chord. The very existence of complete segregation in Dollarway, counsel suggested, itself justified an edict transferring the children. *Brown II* imposed upon school authorities an obligation to "take affirmative steps on their own *to eliminate segregated schools*," and when they failed to do so, for whatever reason, the "burden" fell on them to show why African-American students should not be admitted at once to white schools.[39] The reality of complete racial separation, in short, demanded the corrective of integration.

The district court ordered the children transferred,[40] but an Eighth Circuit panel held, in traditional fashion, that local authorities must be given an opportunity to operate under the pupil placement law before they could be charged with discrimination.[41] The circuit court soon got into the spirit of the plaintiffs' approach, however, when Dollarway officials actually put the loaded game plan which was pupil placement into effect. The authorities frankly indicated their tolerance for student transfers only in "exceptional circumstances,"[42] and set up a forbidding battery of tests and interviews for those who insisted on applying for admission to white schools. Entering first graders who wished to make this switch were supposed to be treated more indulgently, yet were also subjected to intensive screening.

An opinion by Eighth Circuit Chief Judge Harvey Johnsen invalidated this set-up, ruling that Dollarway officials could not subject applicants for transfer—"which . . . here simply means . . . Negro students"[43]—to tests and interviews not required of white students already enrolled in the schools those applicants wished to attend.

Judge Johnsen thought the problem went deeper, though. The district's version of pupil placement failed to meet constitutional standards, he argued, less because of its structural inequity than because it disappointed the expectations reasonable people held for such plans, that they would make a genuine break with the pattern of segregated education. Placement standards having "the effect in application" of perpetuating the racial status quo failed "to constitute a sufficient remedy" for past discrimination.[44] A valid desegregation plan was one which produced tangible integration, and no assignment method could stand if it left "the previous racial situation existing just as before."[45]

By 1962 and 1963, federal courts were finally gutting the pupil placement schemes. A series of decisions ripped the veil from these thinly-disguised replicas of the pre-1954 era.[46] Judges had little trouble demonstrating, once they set out to do so, that the persistence in most southern school districts of dual zoning, and the automatic assignment of students on the basis of race, were inherently unconstitutional. In this course, they were encouraged by the Supreme Court, which finally indicated in 1963 that its patience was wearing thin. While deciding a case involving racial segregation in public parks, the justices issued a warning that, "Given the extended time which has elapsed, it is far from clear that the mandate of the second Brown decision requiring desegregation with 'all deliberate speed' would today be satisfied by . . . plans . . . for desegregation of public educational facilities which eight years ago might have been deemed sufficient."[47] By 1964, after some backsliding by the Fifth Circuit,[48] all southern school desegregation plans were required to move toward the abolition of dual zones.

But while it was natural for the decisions killing pupil placement to focus on the derelictions of a system contrived to produce only tokens, at most, one also finds in some of these opinions condemnation of the system as constitutionally defective *because* it could yield only tokens, because of its results. The admission to white schools of thirteen African-Americans who made application for transfer under the Tennessee pupil placement law was not "the institution of a plan for a non-racial organization of the Memphis school system," said a Sixth Circuit panel in 1962, "*nor*" was it "desegregation."[49] Judge Simon Sobeloff of the Fourth Circuit pronounced it "too late in the day" for a school board "to say that merely by the admission of a few plaintiffs . . . it is satisfying the Supreme Court's mandate for 'good faith compliance.'"[50] Judge Wisdom in the Fifth Circuit characterized pupil placement as a ploy frankly utilized by southern officials "to maintain segregation by allowing a little token desegregation."[51]

A later phase of *Dove* v. *Parham* had already moved on to this result-oriented rejection of tokenism. In 1961, the Dollarway board instituted a plan under the pupil placement law giving all entering first graders of both races a standard aptitude test, and allowing everyone who scored at the national average to go to the school of his or her choice. An Arkansas district court disapproved the plan, because in its first year the testing program wound up placing only two African- American youngsters in previously all-white schools. Though such a program might be acceptable in other districts, Judge Smith Henley acknowledged, "it . . . is not going to produce at Dollarway anything other than token integration."[52]

IV

The notion that desegregation could prove itself only by contributing to some acceptable level of racial diversity reasserted itself even more strongly in the next phase of the compliance controversy. By 1964 and 1965, many southern communities were replacing the pupil placement schemes with a seemingly unassailable principle of educational organization, the freedom of choice option pioneered in Baltimore. Under these plans, which were gradualist variations on Baltimore's approach, dual assignment was discontinued in single grades, or in clusters of grades, and students in the desegregated grades simply selected the school within a district, or a geographic zone within that district, they wished to attend. Under a completed plan, students normally got several opportunities for choice during their education—at the beginning of elementary school, of junior high, and of senior high school. Only logistical factors such as the unavailability of space or of school buses limited these choices. Tests, interviews, and psychological criteria played no part in determining assignment.

The whole enterprise breathed an equalitarian spirit to which no one, presumably, could object. If African-American students wanted to attend previously all-white schools, or whites to go to previously black schools, it would happen. If they did not, that was the American way. "Freedom of choice," enthused one southern judge,

> means the unrestricted, uninhibited, unrestrained, unhurried, and unhurried right to choose where a student will attend public school . . . . [Yet] [i]mplicit in freedom of choice is the right to choose to remain in . . . the school heretofore attended. That in itself is the exercise of a free choice.[53]

Agencies such as the United States Civil Rights Commission quickly exposed freedom of choice as a fraud, the Jeffersonian rhetoric which accompanied its promulgation notwithstanding. The commission (established under the Civil Rights Act of 1957) reported a rash of incidents in which parents enrolling their children in white schools were the victims of employer blackmail, social ostracism, and physical assault. Investigators recounted a typical experience of two families in Webster County, Mississippi. The families had

> selected formerly all-white schools for three children scheduled to enter the first grade in September 1965. In each instance, it was related, within hours after the form had arrived at the office of the superintendent, the families were visited by a white citizen of the county who wondered whether a "mistake" could not have been made. Both families stated that as a result of these visits they altered their "choice" and selected a Negro school. Nevertheless, they assert, within a short time they were told by their white landlords to move out of their houses.[54]

The NAACP Legal Defense Fund cited evidence of "threats and acts of intimidation, economic reprisal and violence . . . throughout the South—sometimes to terrorize Negroes before the registration period; sometimes to discourage the Negroes who had become identified when they registered their children; sometimes to force the withdrawal of Negro pupils after schools had been desegregated."[55] Furthermore, the choice option involved myriad administrative complexities, which explains why it had rarely been preferred to geographic zoning.

Freedom of choice might seem, nonetheless, a structurally sound means to desegregation, if authorities could manage it successfully and contrive to quell official and unofficial coercion. It exhibited a deeper flaw, however. In actual practice, the free choice method was too closely tied to the heritage of past discrimination to serve as a truly equitable mechanism.

Dual zoning might be effaced under these plans, but they could not efface the ingrained racial identity of southern schools, especially black schools. And such vestiges of apartheid, it turned out, exerted a decisive influence, even upon ostensibly unfettered selections. African-American children frequently wished to remain in schools where they felt secure, and which they regarded as "theirs." White students, on the other hand, would not go near a black school. Their exercise of freedom never extended to the choice of institutions so recently stigmatized as the untouchable portion of an educational caste system.

This dilemma was symbolized for the Civil Rights Commission by a plaque in the lobby of a Missouri high school operating under an approved free choice plan: "1932—Hayti Negro School." All of the students and faculty at the school, the commissioners noted, " are Negro."[56]

Those who did want to attend white schools were usually quite reticent about saying so, whether they had experienced intimidation or not. "Many Negro children and parents in Southern States," said the commission, "having lived for decades in positions of subservience, are reluctant to assert their rights."[57] Past racial categories, it was being discovered, were decisive forces in shaping the present under freedom of choice, guaranteeing, certainly, that choice would go in only one direction. Not unexpectedly, patterns of enrollment did not change materially in the South, although the choice option did end outright tokenism in some school districts.

Southern plaintiffs, of course, felt that the paucity of racial mixing under freedom of choice was its obvious objective. In any event, they argued, such schemes were congenitally incapable of measuring up to the "affirmative duty" imposed upon school officials to eliminate dual systems, for they placed the entire burden of desegregation upon African-American parents and children, whereas "the burden should be placed upon the school system to desegregate the schools which they have so long maintained in an unconstitutional manner."[58] Some plaintiffs even suggested that freedom of choice violated *Brown*'s proscription of laws "requiring *or permitting*" school segregation,[59] since allowing African-American youngsters to choose all-black schools was a form of sanctioning racial categories.

By this time, other parts of the executive branch had joined the Civil Rights Commission and the Justice Department in backing up those who were fighting for desegregation in the South. Most notable among them was the Department of Health, Education, and Welfare. Title VI of the landmark Civil Rights Act of 1964 guaranteed that, "No person . . . shall, on the ground of race . . . be denied the benefits of, or be subjected to discrimination under any program . . . receiving Federal financial assistance,"[60] and pursuant to Title VI, HEW's Office of Education issued its first set of school guidelines in April, 1965, setting forth the non-discriminatory standards districts must meet in order to be eligible for federal aid.

The office harbored definite suspicions about freedom of choice. In a letter to an Arkansas school superintendent, written two months before the guidelines were issued, Professor George Foster, a legal consultant to the office, stated explicitly that free choice plans would be judged by their effectiveness.[61] The guidelines themselves made no such demand. They sought merely to guarantee equitable procedures in the administration of the plans, stipulating, among other things, that entering students in a system who indicated no choice of a school must be impartially "assigned to the school nearest their homes or on the basis of non-racial attendance zones."[62]

The whole guideline enterprise, however, communicated doubts about the efficacy of a voluntaristic approach to *Brown*. "Desegregation plans based on freedom of choice," Foster wrote in an article interpreting the guidelines, "are perhaps no more than transitional devices . . . ."[63] In theory, freedom of choice was "unobjectionable"; the "practical difficulty is that the choice . . . may not in fact be free."[64]

Southern judges rarely accepted the invitation of plaintiffs to strike down freedom of choice,[65] but otherwise they were sharply divided in evaluating it. Some believed plans operating without coercion fully satisfied the test of fidelity to *Brown II*. Others maintained that where so many factors, overt and subtle, operated to keep the races apart in southern society, integration provided the only acceptable proof that past racial categories and attitudes were no longer dominant.

A Fourth Circuit decision in the Richmond case of 1965 reflected both points of view. The majority opinion of Judge Clement Haynsworth hewed to the Briggsian line. No suspicion attached to Richmond's desegregation plan, Judge Haynsworth argued, under which "each pupil, in effect, assigns himself to the school he wishes to attend."[66] In no way, felt Haynsworth, could free choice be construed as illegally permitting segregation. "It has been held again and again . . . that the Fourteenth Amendment prohibition is not against segregation as such. [It] is against discrimination." There was "nothing in the Constitution which prevents [a student's] voluntary association with others of his race."[67]

Judges Simon Sobeloff and J. Spencer Bell, by contrast, expressed grave reservations about freedom of choice. It remained to be seen, in their view, whether adoption of the "so-called" free choice principle signified a true change in Richmond's "attitude toward [its] constitutional duty," or represented only "a strategic retreat" to a new type of recalcitrance.[68] The acid test, felt the two judges, lay in the manner in which Richmond officials administered freedom of choice, whether "duty . . . translate[s] . . . into affirmative and sympathetic action."[69]

This concept of affirmative duty, however, seemed inseparable in practice from a result-oriented standard of evaluation. Thus, in acquiescing reluctantly to the Richmond plan, the judges allowed themselves to wonder whether "it will in fact achieve the *desired result*," and "*undo* . . . segregation" in the city.[70] It was hard to see how officials could prove they were undoing segregation under a free choice plan except by producing a noticeable amount of integration.

The Eighth Circuit, like the Fourth, articulated diverse views on freedom of choice, although in the Eighth the split occurred in separate majority opinions written by the same judge. *Kemp* v. *Beasley*, the work of Judge Floyd Gibson, found free choice plans acceptable only if they produced concrete results, if they "prove practical in achieving the goal of a nonsegregated school system."[71] Judge Gibson struck down segregated assignments for students who failed to indicate a choice of school, not only because the practice illegally perpetuated dual zoning, but also because of its outcome. "[T]he present plan has resulted . . . in only four Negroes enrolling in the first grade . . . in previously all-white classes . . . . This constitutes only tardy and inadequate recognition of constitutional rights . . . ."[72]

The next year, though, the judge saw *Kemp* in a different light. His prior decision, he now said, merely required freedom of choice to produce "a school system operated on a *non-racial* basis."[73] Consequently, the "mere presence of statistics" demonstrating negligible levels of integration did not "render an otherwise proper plan unconstitutional." The fourteenth amendment "does not require a school system to force a mixing of the races . . . according to some predetermined mathematical formula."[74]

The most widely varying views on remedial expectation occurred in the Fifth Circuit. In February, 1965, a panel approved freedom of choice plans for rural Georgia without any mention of the need for integration.[75] Then, from the Jackson, Mississippi (*Singleton*) decisions of June, 1965 and January, 1966, came the views of Judge John Minor Wisdom, who pushed skepticism about Briggsian values to the breaking point.[76] Judge Wisdom denounced the intolerable delays dogging the compliance process in the deep South. "The time has come for footdragging public school boards to move with celerity toward desegregation."[77] He enthusiastically endorsed the 1965 Office of Education guidelines.

But Judge Wisdom and his colleagues went beyond the guidelines, demanding that school officials take actions designed to produce concrete results; they required, for instance, that pupils in grades not yet reached by the Jackson freedom of choice plan, slated for completion in 1967, must have the absolute right to transfer to all-white schools.

This approach flowed in large part from the suspicions about freedom of choice which Wisdom shared with Judge Sobeloff and Judge Bell. Other language in *Singleton*, however, poised on the brink of a quantum leap in desegregation law: toward the notion that non-discrimination in student assignment could *never* have any meaning, could never wipe away past harms, aside from actual integration, regardless of the structure of an assignment plan. Thus, at one point in the first *Singleton* decision, Judge Wisdom asserts as a general proposition that school authorities must "mak[e] the transition from . . . segregated to . . . integrated" schools,[78] and in an accompanying footnote he openly rejects *Briggs* v. *Elliott*. Judge Parker's celebrated dictum, he stated, "should be laid to rest . . . . In retrospect, the second *Brown* decision *clearly imposes* on public school authorities *the duty to provide an integrated school system.*"[79] The very existence of all-black schools, *Singleton* implies, is unacceptable per se, though Judge Wisdom's evocation of a post-Briggsian jurisprudence was fleeting and sketchy at this point.

V

In any event, most observers in 1965 and 1966 still saw neighborhood schools as the paradigm of neutrality in pupil assignment, the final port to which the entire southern compliance process was heading. Through the device of geographic zoning, the way most school systems were organized in the North and West, racial classifications, and the harm ascribed to them by *Brown*, would finally be replaced by genuine neutrality. "Presumably, what most of us visualize as the end result of desegregation," felt Alexander Bickel, "is a school system in which there is residential zoning, either absolute or modified by some sort of choice or transfer scheme . . . ."[80] Professor Foster, noting that "[t]hroughout the country geographic zoning is the common means for assignment of pupils to school," believed freedom of choice "ultimately will give way to unitary zoning."[81]

For the previous five years, however, southern plaintiffs had been exposing the less than idyllic nature of the neighborhood school arrangement as a remedy for segregation. While not as blatant a dodge as freedom of choice, residential zoning plans, it was pointed out, offered abundant opportunities for cheating by those resistant to genuine non-discrimination. Several of the earliest neighborhood schemes, for example, were weighted down with the infamous minority to majority transfer provision, which allowed students zoned into integrated schools to return to lily-white institutions (or African-American students to return to the safety of all-black schools). Quite obviously, as the plaintiffs in the Knoxville school case pointed out, such provisions enshrined "racial factors as conditions to support . . . transfer, and the racial factors are designed and necessarily operate to perpetuate racial segregation."[82] Responding to such arguments, the Supreme Court invalidated minority to majority transfer in 1963, in *Goss* v. *Board of Education of Knoxville*.[83]

Zoning arrangements also invited subtle, and not so subtle, forms of gerrymandering to retain segregated schools. The fact was that many zone lines could be drawn in such a way as to reduce racial mixing to an absolute minimum, and southern school boards frequently indulged this temptation. An expert witness, called by plaintiffs in an early phase of the Memphis desegregation case, noted that half of the elementary schools in the city were "so situated that there was a possibility of zoning them so as to get either a maximum or minimum amount of desegregation." The witness felt "that the Board's lines . . . had the appearance of gerrymandering so as to preserve a maximum amount of segregation."[84]

In 1964, the circuit court in the Memphis case held that, "[w]here challenged," a school board must "demonstrate that . . . zone lines . . . were not drawn with a view to preserve . . . segregation."[85] But by this time, southern plaintiffs were moving toward a more fundamental challenge to neighborhood schools, a challenge aimed ultimately at any remaining distinction between "desegregation" and "integration." Between 1962 and 1965, a number of pathbreaking briefs focused on the implications of an obvious but deeply unsettling truth. For most African-American youngsters, especially in urban areas, the end product of a neighborhood zoning system was the very arrangement of schools which existed prior to *Brown*.

Under the dual system, after all, school officials, building on the prevailing patterns of residential segregation, normally placed black schools in black neighborhoods and white schools in white neighborhoods. Customarily, the two races did live in close proximity in one or two areas of an urban community, and this had necessitated some peculiar educational arrangements. Undersized white schools might be placed right next to black schools in order to serve small numbers of whites living adjacent to black pockets of population (or vice-versa); alternately, such students, of either race, were sent out of a neighborhood to more distant schools. In genuinely "mixed" areas, schools could not be located so as to guarantee, in true neighborhood fashion, that the maximum number of students would travel the minimum distance. Their locations were usually skewed away from the natural center of a neighborhood configuration, to accommodate such racial concentrations as did exist.[86]

Generally, however, the web of public and private discrimination in housing did its work well in the pre-1954 era, tying neighborhood schools intimately to the heritage of racial classifications. Physically, neighborhood schools *were* those racial classifications, and the legacy they represented in a Jim Crow society, to such an extent that school segregation laws were barely needed in many southern states, which, as the plaintiffs in Oklahoma City noted, had a "fifty years' history of using all of the state's resources to maintain a segregated school system (as well as segregation generally)."[87]

In the post-*Brown* era, of course, geographic assignments could not rest on an overtly discriminatory basis. And since residential segregation was not monolithic in the South, the small amount of racial separation artificially contrived under the old school systems gave way to some degree of diversity. Still, for vast numbers of African-American students, neighborhood zoning meant that the practical effect of *Brown I* was limited to "simply wiping the laws that enforced [segregation] off the books."[88] The reality of life at their neighborhood school was the same as it had been before the historic decision. Such schools, especially in inner-city areas, were predominantly pre-*Brown* schools, even through the late 1960's.

In this context, it was asserted, the "affirmative duty" of a school board to right prior wrongs went far beyond the avoidance of racial gerrymandering, and even beyond the duty of drawing impartial zone lines. School authorities must take steps to dismantle the physical manifestations of past separation and harm. They must draw boundaries which actively promoted integration when they could reasonably do so. The plaintiffs in the Hopewell, Virginia school case, heard on the same day as *Bradley* v. *School Board of Richmond*, articulated aptly this notion of compliance.

The approved plan employs school zones only slightly different from those used before . . . .

[Thus] [w]hatever might be said of Hopewell's geographic zoning plan for assigning pupils if it were appraised hypothetically in another context where there was no history of compulsory segregation, this case should be decided in its factual context against the background of school planning and manipulation to foster segregation. Against that background it is reasonable to judge the plan by its results. A plan which leaves the four all-Negro schools completely segregated, and allows only about 50 Negro pupils to attend two of four white schools, plainly has not been adequate to eliminate the segregated situation created by past practices . . . . The continuance of segregation cannot be justified by topography or alleged natural barriers such as railroad tracks which were ignored frequently in constructing zones to accomplish segregation prior to the lawsuit. Nor can school segregation be passed off as an inevitable consequence of residential patterns where schools have been deliberately established so as to conform exactly to the segregated housing pattern.[89]

The first expression of such a remedial logic occurred, apparently, in the summer of 1962, in connection with the Delaware desegregation controversy, one of the cases argued alongside *Brown* v. *Board of Education* almost a decade earlier. Louis Redding, who signed the 1955 brief in *Brown II* accepting color blind zoning as an appropriate remedy, had come to an understandable change of mind—along with his colleague and law partner, Leonard Williams.

[Cross-Examination] by Mr. [Leonard] Williams [of Mr. Harry Eisenberg—Delaware school official]:

Q. I understood your [previous] answer[s] to be in terms of standards used in setting up or directing attendance areas. [They were] adequacy and availability of facilities, and access roads, and these are the general rules that are applied throughout the country?

A. There are others over and beyond, such as size . . . .

Q. Was there any consideration given to the distinct possibility of providing an integrated education for the student within this district? . . .

A. I would say only so far as development that might take place would bring white people into [an] area, the same as any other, because when we originally set up our lines we could easily have gerrymandered them around and—

Q. We are not talking about gerrymandering.

A. We could easily have done that and created a nasty situation; instead of that we drew straight lines.

Q. What I am asking you is: Isn't there a distinction in terms of standards used when you are supplying attendance areas pursuant to the compliance with the Brown decision, and attendance areas generally? When setting up a new district wouldn't it have been a primary objective of yours to have considered this item as one of the primary things to be used?

A. It might have been . . . .

Q. Then I ask you again: Was this consideration made, the provision for integrated education for students . . . .

A. Provision was made for adequate use of facilities by whatever children reside within the attendance area.

Q. You don't answer my question.

A. I am trying to.

Q. Was there any consideration given to the provision for integrated education for students . . . along with these other . . . principles which you have so clearly presented to us?

A. We tried to avoid making any distinction as to race or color in setting up the areas.[90]

Integration, then, was held up as the only way of achieving the goals of *Brown I* and *Brown II*, the only way to truly end racial classifications in education, and the continuing "feelings of inferiority" they were said to inflict (or, in the language of Professor Black, to end the tradition of racial subordination they embodied).

Up through the middle of 1965, no federal court endorsed this activist approach to residential zoning. On the contrary, judges almost invariably approved any neighborhood plan unmarred by overt gerrymandering or minority to majority provisions, regardless of how little actual integration resulted.[91] While the Hopewell plan would produce a minuscule amount of racial mixing, Judge Clement Haynsworth admitted, this stemmed wholly from "the residential segregation that exists," and school authorities bore no responsibility for the situation.[92]

Delaware's district judges, however, constituted somewhat of an exception to this pattern of acquiescence, viewing neighborhood plans with at least a dollop of skepticism. Indeed, one intrepid jurist in the state could be said to have anticipated, in a rudimentary sense, the rationale for integration advanced by Louis Redding and Leonard Williams.

In April of 1959, District Judge Caleb Layton was reviewing a state-wide desegregation plan, a mixture of the geographic zoning and free choice techniques later used in parts of the South. While perusing the plan, Judge Layton came across a manifestly rigged provision. It gave students affected by desegregation the option of attending the school nearest their homes, or the school they "would have attended" prior to the promulgation of the plan—a way of allowing white students zoned into predominantly black neighborhoods to escape integration.[93]

But the judge did not dwell on this obvious structural defect. Instead, he looked at the other side of the matter, the fact that for the majority of youngsters in Delaware, particularly in urban settings, the schools referred to in the provision were actually identical. As the Delaware plan operated for them, most significantly for African-American students, it was synonymous with a neighborhood zoning arrangement, without choices. And such an approach to desegregation did nothing to change the pre-1954 racial identity of the state's schools. The physical and institutional fruits of dual zoning would remain untouched. This, Judge Layton decided, was the real reason the provision must go.

> [I]n Georgetown [Delaware], for example, the majority of the Negroes live in a community known as The Hill. The colored school is close by. The white school is at a much greater distance.[I]n the light of these facts, it would seem to result that no Negro student whose family resides on The Hill may ever enter the white school.[94]

Consequently, "*Whatever may have been the reasons for this provision*, it strikes me as unfair and is ordered to be stricken."[95] The judge reiterated this naive sounding but potentially explosive attack on the efficacy of neighborhood zoning when asked to reconsider the provision. "Read against a background of geographical facts of which judicial notice may be taken, it provide[s] that in many localities no colored student could ever attend a white school unless his parents . . . changed their residence . . . ."[96]

When actually confronted by Redding and Williams three years later, Chief Judge Caleb Wright appeared to reject their arguments completely. He hauled out *Briggs* v. *Elliott* and aimed it point-blank at the plaintiffs. "[I]f races are separated because of geographic or transportation considerations or other similar criteria, it is no concern of the . . . Constitution. [D]iscrimination is forbidden but integration is not compelled."[97]

Yet having paid obeisance to Judge Parker, Wright manifested some doubts about the geographic criteria he had just endorsed, for the case in front of him concerned a situation in which Delaware authorities had contrived to create a totally segregated school district, surrounded entirely by all-white ones. No evidence of gerrymandering or of other foul play was cited, but Judge Wright, despite his Briggsian pronouncements, found the plan putatively invalid—because it could produce no actual integration.

Requiring local officials to "intentionally gerrymander"[98] school boundaries in order to increase racial mixing was one thing, he noted. Quiet a different situation arose when African-American youngsters attended completely segregated schools, immediately adjacent to all-white areas. "[A] presumption of unconstitutionality arises," and the authors of the zoning plan bore a heavy burden in justifying their actions.[99]

It fell to a judge of the Western District of Oklahoma to launch the South's first frontal assault on neighborhood schools. The case was *Dowell* v. *School Board of Oklahoma City* (1965)—one of the most significant controversies in the history of school desegregation law.[100] The judge was Luther Bohanon, just beginning a career as one of the most forceful, most "activist" district court judges of his generation.

The seventh of ten children, Judge Bohanon was raised in southeastern Oklahoma, where he and his brothers would attend school from September to March of each year, then take off until November to help on the family's 480 acre farm. Working his way through the University of Oklahoma Law School, Bohanon eventually established himself, by the 1940's, as one of the leading corporate lawyers in the state. He earned over $100,000 a year, and did a good deal of legal work for the Kerr-McGee oil and natural gas corporation.

Senator Robert Kerr, the corporation's dominant partner, and the "uncrowned King of the Senate" in the early sixties, proposed Bohanon as a federal judge for the Western District of Oklahoma in 1961. The nomination stalled when the American Bar Association's Standing Committee on the Federal Judiciary gave him an "unqualified" rating, and Attorney General Robert Kennedy urged Senator Kerr to withdraw the nomination. With important tax legislation pending in the Senate Finance Committee, on which Kerr was the ranking Democrat, the Senator requested an appointment with President Kennedy on August 16, 1961. The next day the White House issued a press release announcing Kennedy's intention to nominate Bohanon to the federal bench. The Senate promptly confirmed him.[101]

The Oklahoma City school case fell to the new federal judge by lot in 1962. The next year he issued an opinion declaring the school system illegally segregated and demanding "a complete and comprehensive plan for the integration" of the city's schools.[102]

Authorities eventually complied, using the same kind of geographic zoning plan recently found satisfactory in Hopewell, and in other cities such as Charlotte, North Carolina. But Judge Bohanon was not buying it. After examining the record in the case and listening to the plaintiffs' witnesses, "I failed to see how the action of the school board was in good faith. Instead, they were taking advantage of housing segregation to maintain school segregation."[103]

Accordingly, the judge's pathbreaking decision in *Dowell II* took extensive "judicial notice"[104] of what he saw as the state responsibility for housing segregation in Oklahoma City, focusing on its prior enforcement of residential segregation statutes and restrictive covenants, as well as its continuing tolerance for discrimination by real estate agencies and banks. This pattern of residential discrimination dovetailed with the laws requiring educational separation to produce schools irrevocably designated as black schools.

To now substitute neutral zoning for statutory dualism, Bohanon felt, would impermissibly perpetuate racial categories wrought out of the multiple forms of prior discrimination. Pupils assigned to schools which "remained 100% Negro," even if those schools were presently part of a uniracial zoning system, would "continue to suffer . . . the same psychological and constitutional harm as set forth in the *Brown* opinion."[105] The few integrated schools that were created by the new assignments had the ironic effect of exacerbating housing segregation. "[I]ntegrated schools and areas" were being quickly "destroyed because uncorrected racial restrictions in the housing field enable whites to move to areas served by all white . . . schools, secure in the knowledge that housing segregation and the neighborhood school policy will not enable Negroes to follow them."[106] The judge concluded that the Oklahoma City board "has failed to desegregate the public schools in a manner so as to eliminate . . . the tangible elements of the segregated system," and thus was perpetuating "the violation of the constitutional rights of the plaintiffs."[107]

A neighborhood approach to desegregation, then, like any other, fell short if its want of genuine neutrality rendered it "insufficient to bring about more than token [integration]."[108] School officials in Oklahoma City must undertake "affirmative action,"[109] therefore, to achieve better results. Judge Bohanon did not demand all-out integration. He limited himself to ordering a majority to minority transfer plan and a number of zone line changes, though he suggested this might not be the end of the matter.

Having debunked the most well-regarded approach to neutrality in student assignment, Judge Bohanon's opinion leaves genuine doubt about whether neutrality was ever possible in the first place. For if retaining the "tangible elements of the segregated system" (the segregated neighborhood schools) perpetuates the "psychological and constitutional harm . . . set forth in . . . *Brown*," it might, or might not, matter why these schools continue to exist. *Dowell* officially holds that neighborhood zoning in Oklahoma City has failed to provide a proper remedy for past segregation because of the discriminatory housing policies with which it was associated. But if residential separation were entirely voluntary, the decision intimates, schools once segregated racially by law still could not be segregated in fact and constitute part of an acceptable remedial plan.

Judge Bohanon's opinion in the earlier installment of *Dowell* strengthens the belief that he viewed integration as the only way to cure educational apartheid. In discussing the racially separate neighborhoods of Oklahoma City, he mentioned some of illicit factors creating them upon which he would dwell further in 1965. But then he invoked a consideration which transcended the matter of whether school assignment in the city was neutral or not. African-Americans, he felt, were bitterly disappointed by the prospect of a neighborhood desegregation plan, because *Brown* held up "before them a new day—new rights which had for years been denied—new hopes and new expectations."[110] Any assignment scheme which frustrated these hopes of transcending past subordination and humiliation was unsatisfactory, the first *Dowell* decision implies. "The Negroes live in great anticipation *of mixed schools of Negroes and whites*, to the extent that the Negro race *will be considered equal in all things . . . to the white race with reference to the education of children.*"[111]

Later in *Dowell I*, while rendering his interpretation of *Brown I*, the judge articulates more explicitly the larger view at which he had arrived: that the racial isolation caused by past racial categories cannot be alleviated merely by creating impartial mechanisms which stop separating by race.

> The [Supreme] Court emphasized [in *Brown*] the necessity of giving . . . minority group children the opportunity for extensive contact with other children at an early stage in their educational experience, finding such contact to be indispensable if children of all ages of all races and creeds were to become inculcated with a meaningful understanding of the essentials of our democratic way of life. The benefits inherent in an education in integrated schools are essential to the proper development of all children.[112]

For Bohanon, as for Judge Wisdom, black schools, it appeared, carried too much of the hurtful legacy of the past to be acceptable in the present.

Bohanon strove to reconcile his decision with those upholding neighborhood schools outside the South. The *Dowell* case, he insisted, had nothing to do with any obligation to achieve racial diversity where dual systems never existed, or where "prior racial policies are deemed corrected," as held in the Gary, Indiana school decision.[113] The judge did not speculate about what decision might have come down in Gary, or New York City for that matter, had courts taken "judicial notice" of the factors he had noted in Oklahoma City.

VI

Despite the judge's denials, the *Dowell* decision, upheld by the Tenth Circuit in 1967, was influenced by and certainly contributed to forces in the mid 1960's which were chipping away at the distinction between de jure and de facto segregation. By 1965, two district court decisions in New York—*Branche* v. *Hempstead*; *Blocker* v. *Manhasset*—and one in Massachusetts, *Barksdale* v. *Springfield School Committee*, had finally broken through the barrier, condemning separation of the races in public schools as inherently unconstitutional, and identifying integration as the only appropriate remedy (though no circuit court decision had yet done so).[114]

As in earlier cases, plaintiffs of the sixties maintained that *Brown* could automatically be extrapolated to all school segregation, but, in *Blocker* and *Barksdale* at least, they also continued to offer data on the diminished educational achievement racial separation allegedly caused.

Indeed, a seminal article of 1965 by Professor Owen Fiss (now of Yale Law School) argued that hard empirical evidence, though not limited to test scores or grade achievement levels, was constitutionally essential in attacking de facto segregation.[115] Professor Fiss offered a reading of the *Brown* decision which was more conservative than the one favored by most northern plaintiffs, for he maintained that Chief Justice Warren's opinion could not be read as pronouncing a nationwide ban on educational separation anymore than it could be read as endorsing the pieties of Judge Parker.

What the chief justice had really done in *Brown* was to announce a broad principle governing education under the fourteenth amendment, "a principle requiring equality of educational opportunity."[116] He accompanied this with a series of "empirical judgements," drawn in part from the *Sweatt* and *McLaurin* decisions, proclaiming that an "open and declared" policy of school segregation harmed its victims and deprived them of equal opportunity.[117] These conclusions held great constitutional significance for the issue of whether all educational segregation was inherently harmful and invalid, but they did not automatically resolve the issue. This matter "can and must be assessed independently of the empirical and normative judgments in *Brown*."[118] Condemnation of racial imbalance could proceed only from detailed adjudication, from the presentation of contemporary "'Brandeis brief[s]'"[119] exposing situations of such imbalance as academically inferior, socially stifling, and psychologically hurtful. Professor Fiss cited a growing body of evidence documenting the comparative effects of segregation and integration.[120]

This collection was critically augmented in mid-1966 with the publication of a massive report on the nation's schools, the product of a team of researchers headed by Professor James Coleman of the Johns Hopkins University.[121] The Coleman Report, mandated by the 1964 Civil Rights Act, found few significant differences among America's elementary and secondary schools in tangible assets such as physical facilities or teacher experience. The decisive factor affecting student achievement, its researchers concluded, was the social and economic status of a student's classmates.

While not concentrating directly on race, the report strongly suggested, therefore, that minority children (often from deprived socio-economic backgrounds) gained measurably from attending school alongside middle class (predominantly white) children, with no regressive effect upon the middle class students. Some scholars questioned the root premise from which Coleman and his associates proceeded, that schools *were* substantially equal except for the students, but the Coleman Report was undoubtedly the most influential educational study of the 1960's.[122]

Blocker and *Barksdale* were argued before the Coleman Report appeared, and both judges subordinated plaintiffs' empirical data to the view of *Brown* which emphasized the social isolation and what they believed to be the self-evident harm flowing from de facto segregation. "The role of public education in our democracy is not limited to . . . academic subjects," said Judge Joseph Zavatt in *Blocker*. "It encompasses a broader preparation for participation in the mainstream of our society . . . . The extent to which this objective is being attained is not measurable by a comparison of [student] achievement . . . ."[123] The situation in Manhasset, Long Island, concluded the judge, generated in African-American youngsters the same "feeling of inferiority" found by the Supreme Court to exist among youngsters in Topeka, Kansas and Clarendon County, South Carolina.

This last, rather subjective point was certainly open to debate. As Professor Kaplan had noted, shortly before *Blocker*, it was not self-evident

> that confinement to overwhelmingly Negro schools [will] "cause feelings of inferiority" in Negro children. Certainly where the state, concededly for no purpose having to do with race, adopts a districting which results in primarily Negro schools in some circumstances and not in others, it is hard to say that it has attached a "badge of inferiority" to the Negro students. It is admittedly possible that a Negro student in a de facto segregated school may not realize that other Negro children differing only in place of residence can attend integrated schools and that the school authorities have determined his school on a basis other than race. On the other hand, it is at least possible that he will appreciate this and be spared psychological harm.[124]

Indeed, a study of academic self-concept, done by Coleman report researchers on over 500,000 pupils in both segregated and desegregated schools, found no significant differences between white and African-American students.[125] Judge Zavatt's analysis derived, it would seem, from broader convictions about the nature of racism in northern society and history.

There also appeared in 1965 a scholarly contribution which attacked the cleavage in school law from another direction. Its author was Judge Skelly Wright, a courageous district judge in New Orleans in the 1950's, removed by this time to the Court of Appeals for the District of Columbia.[126] Judge Wright anticipated *Dowell*'s attack on neighborhood schools, but placed it in the wider venue Judge Bohanon necessarily avoided. Wright zeroed in on the racial separation produced by neighborhood school policies in northern and western cities, and sharply denied that such separation came from voluntary, and innocent, residential choices by private individuals. "State action,"[127] the judge argued, contributed in a very substantial way to one-race schools, in the form of discriminatory public housing policies and state connivance in private acts of prejudice. And this, he suggested, could form the sole and sufficient basis, if necessary, for ordering school integration. Surely, the state should "not be allowed to do in two steps what it may not do in one."[128]

These arguments, later developed by Justice William O. Douglas, largely devastated the notion that any school segregation in America could truly be called "de facto." Yet unless these housing violations of the North and West were considered part of a larger whole, of a more extensive pattern of discrimination against African-Americans, it was doubtful whether the remedy for the school segregation they caused would need to go beyond something like a majority to minority transfer plan between parts of an urban community. Indeed, later in his essay, Judge Wright invoked the racial isolation and the associations with systemic racism which really made all segregated education, in his view, "'inherently unequal.'" "A racially segregated Negro school is an inferior school . . . . No honest person would even suggest . . . that the segregated slum school provides educational opportunity equal to that provided by the white suburban public school."[129]

The housing argument was first utilized in practice by the plaintiffs in the Cincinnati school case, found in the same volume of the federal reports as *Dowell*. They offered evidence of discriminatory conduct by housing authorities as a basis for integration of schools, though they cited violations by school officials as well. The district court, however, later backed up by the Sixth Circuit, consigned these different aspects of state action to the airtight compartments properly deplored by Judge Wright, refusing to allow material on housing to be presented for the purpose of establishing de jure school segregation.[130]

Judge Bohanon explicitly noted the contributions of Professor Fiss and Judge Wright in *Dowell*. He referred several times to the principle of equal educational opportunity, though invocation of this principle was peripheral to the reasoning of his decision.[131] At the close of his opinion, the judge pronounced his remedial demands "educationally sound" as well as "legally appropriate,"[132] and an accompanying footnote frankly admitted: "This conclusion follows despite the similarity of the recommendations to remedies advocated for the correction of problems of racial imbalance. Wright, De Facto Segregation in the Public Schools . . . ; Fiss, Racial Imbalance in the Public Schools: The Constitutional Concepts."[133]

In this altering environment, the Office of Education came forward in March of 1966 with its celebrated revised guidelines, establishing percentage goals for the implementation of freedom of choice.[134] The goals were set up on a graduated basis. If "a significant percentage" of students in a school district, "such as 8 or 9 percent," had chosen to attend integrated schools in the 1965–66 year, the district was expected to double this percentage in 1966–67; if only 4 or 5 percent had chosen to go, the number must triple; where very few students opted for integration in 1965–66, the increase must "be proportionally greater,"[135] though no exact figure was specified. The 1966 guidelines also decreed a mandatory *annual* choice in desegregated grades.

HEW officials denied that they were demanding integration as such. Their "performance criteria," they maintained, amounted to nothing more than a guide for deciding when free choice plans required "further review."[136] Many southerners ventured to predict what the outcome of such reviews invariably would be.[137] Little noticed in all this discussion was a passage in the revised guidelines raising doubts about the automatic acceptability of neighborhood schools. "No single type of [desegregation] plan," the document stated, "is appropriate for all school systems . . . . *In some cases*, desegregation is accomplished by the establishment of nonracial attendance zones."[138]

The 1966 guidelines undoubtedly flowed from administrative frustration at HEW.[139] Yet they also mirrored a growing belief in integration as the only appropriate response to state-imposed segregation. In a article written in late 1966, Mr. James Dunn, legal advisor to the Office of Education, brilliantly summarized the remedial logic which had gradually emerged from a decade of desegregation litigation.[140]

The language of *Brown I*, Dunn argued, was "compelling" for the view that the Supreme Court developed in it a broad "principle of equal educational opportunity."[141] But even if the decision condemned "racial classification alone," it would still direct remedial measures against officials of a dual system who continued to operate schools "segregated in fact."[142] These officials had not eliminated the actions proscribed by the equal protection clause, because "racial classification continues,"[143] until a segregated school system, with the harms it produced, was physically disestablished. "To the degree that the *Briggs* dictum is inconsistent with this conclusion it must be rejected . . . ."[144]

All of this set the stage for "the most important doctrinal change in interpretation of the equal protection clause, as applied to public education, since *Brown* itself"[145]—*The United States* v. *Jefferson County Board of Education*.[146]

I. *DOVE* v. *PARHAM*

Dove v. *Parham* provides a particularly good look at the vicissitudes of litigation in the pupil placement era. The brief filed by the Dollarway plaintiffs (now the appellees) in the Eighth Circuit, unsuccessfully seeking to get the original district court decision upheld, articulates the potentially far-reaching remedial logic which emerged in the late 1950's.

The twisted workings of the pupil placement system, temporarily sanctioned in Arkansas by the first court of appeals opinion, is captured in Robert Carter's memorandum of December, 1959. The spectacle of pupil placement in action led to the landmark circuit court decision of 1960, condemning not only Dollarway's use of the placement act, but any use of such mechanisms which produced a totally segregationist result.

The next year, even a tokenist result was proscribed by District Judge Smith Henley, the judge who had given Robert Carter somewhat of a hard time in 1959.

1. BRIEF FOR APPELLEES

ARGUMENT

I

The Evidence Conclusively Demonstrates That Enforced Racial Segregation Proscribed By the Fourteenth Amendment to the Constitution of the United States Is Maintained in the Dollarway School District.

Dollarway School District operates three schools—the Townsend Park School for Negroes—from the first to the twelfth grade; the Dollarway School for white children—from the first to twelfth grade; and Hardin School for white children— from the first to the fourth grade. There is no evidence that school assignment is based upon residence except as to the Hardin School to which white children living in a certain area are assigned through the first four grades. Negro and white families living in the same district attend separate schools.

The evidence shows that in 1954, shortly after the decision of the Supreme Court in . . . *Brown* v. *Board of Education*, Negro citizens and patrons in the Dollarway School District petitioned the school board to reorganize the school district in compliance with the decision of the United States Supreme Court in that case. In 1955 a group of Negro patrons of the school met with school authorities and requested that they integrate the schools. The board announced that it would study the situation. In 1957 appellee Dove took his children to the Dollarway School, seeking to enroll them. He had a conference with the then superintendent of schools, . . . and the President of the board, Mr. Parham. He was advised that there were no plans for integration, but that they were working on it. In September, 1957, Mr. Dove saw the President of the board and again raised the question with him of the desegregation of the school system. He was advised that they were still studying the proposition.

In September, 1958, adult and minor appellees in this action sought enrollment in the Dollarway School and went to the superintendent's office for that purpose. The superintendent asked the reasons why they sought enrollment in Dollarway and advised them that they had equal or better facilities at Townsend School and told them he had been ordered by the board to maintain the Dollarway School on an all-white basis.

At no time during any of these conversations with any of the school authorities was any mention made of the Pupil Assignment Act; nor was any mention made of any hearing before the board; nor . . . any mention of any qualifications or standards which had to be met warranting refusal to admit the minor appellees and other Negroes to the Dollarway School other than the question of race . . . .

It is clear that here school authorities have enforced a policy of operating segregated schools which is inconsistent with the constitutional requirements as defined by the decisions of the Supreme Court of the United States . . . .

II

The Pupil Placement Act Has No Application to the Present Controversy . . . .

The evidence conclusively established that no assignments to schools in the Dollarway School District were made pursuant to any of the criteria established by this Act. On the contrary, the testimony shows that . . . appellees . . . were not assigned under any criteria set out in this statute.

Mr. Parham testified that he did not feel that the Pupil Assignment Act had application until a Negro applied to attend a nonsegregated school. He did not consider that the board was under any responsibility to do anything independently. Mr. Fallis, the superintendent . . . . admitted that no assignments had been made under the criteria set forth in the Act. According to his testimony Negro and white children went to the schools "voluntarily," and only when they did not "voluntarily" go to segregated schools would his authority under the law have to be exercised. In short, the pupil assignment legislation as applied by the school authorities here has reference only to Negro children seeking admission to nonsegregated schools. As such, it is obviously a discriminatory device, applied with an uneven hand, within the condemnation of *Brown* v. *Board of Education* . . . .

In order for pupil assignment legislation to be valid it must apply to all without racial distinctions . . . . For school authorities to safely rely upon such an Act as a defense in any litigation seeking the vindication of constitutional guarantees of equal educational opportunities, there must be an affirmative showing that the criteria and standards established by the legislation was applied to all children in respect to admission and assignment to the schools in the district . . . .

The language of Judge Parker in *Briggs* v. *Elliott*, 132 F. Supp. 776 . . . to the effect that there is no compulsion on the part of the school board to integrate but only a negative duty not to deny admission to any school based on race, has no application here . . . . [T]hat language does not vindicate the present open and unquestioned discriminatory action of these appellants . . . .

IV

The Appellants Are Under an Obligation to Demonstrate That They Are Proceeding Towards Completion Of Desegregation At The Earliest Practicable Date . . . .

The appellants are under a duty to devote every effort towards initiating desegregation. [The pupil placements acts] are applicable only if it can be found that these statutory provisions provide "arrangements pointed towards the earliest practicable completion of desegregation and that appellants have taken appropriate steps to put their program into operation." [*Cooper* v. *Aaron* 358 U.S. 7.] . . .

These state laws on which appellants rely and their action in this controversy must be scrutinized to determine whether their constitutional obligations to provide nonsegregated education for children in the school district have been met. Having demonstrated, as the evidence conclusively discloses, that segregation still prevails, the burden is on appellants to show within the yardstick established by the United States Supreme Court in *Brown* and *Cooper* that admission of these appellees to the Dollarway School is inappropriate at this time . . . . [The] school authorities cannot hide behind the fiction that Negroes are attending segregated schools because they prefer—a fiction refuted by the record here. They must take affirmative steps on their own to eliminate segregated schools.

2. ROBERT CARTER'S MEMORANDUM OF DECEMBER 22, 1959

My experience in the Dollarway School Case may give some insight into the pattern which defense will take in respect to application of the Pupil Assignment Law. For this reason, I am attempting here a definitive memorandum on the trial and its background . . . .

The Assignment Procedure In This Case

Pursuant to [the Pupil Placement Act of 1959], the local school board assigned the three plaintiffs, Corliss Smith, Ernestine Dove and James Warfield to the Negro school . . . .

The plaintiffs sought reassignment pursuant to the statute and board regulations. They were forced to take a physical examination by a doctor chosen by the board. The hearing before the school board was marked by noise and tumult outside, and our plaintiffs were set upon when they left the hearing. There is no evidence . . . that this was connected to the board although our position was that it could have been avoided by the exercise of prudence and due care by the board.

At the hearing the board had a Dr. Peters, a psychiatrist on the staff of the University of Arkansas and a Mr. Moore, an educational psychologist and Dean of Men, I believe, at the University of Arkansas, attend. They were there to observe the three pupils and their parents.

Thereafter, the children were given various intelligence tests which were administered by the county superintendent. They were given no advance warning of the tests, but were taken out of class one day and given these tests from approximately 9:30–2:45.

Corliss Smith and James Warfield were given the California Mental Maturity Test . . . . A ninth grade class of 29 students at Dollarway, supposedly selected at random, was also given the Mental Maturity Test. It is the testimony of the defendants that based on the test results, the Smith child would rank between 19 and 20 in the class at Dollarway and that the Warfield child would rank between 20 and 21 of this class.

Ernestine Dove, a 12th grade student, was not given the California Mental Maturity Test but was given the Otis Quick Scoring test . . . . She did not score high. In addition each child spent approximately an hour with Dr. Peters who was apparently examining their emotional stability.

Based upon these examinations and the children's scholastic record, the board made specific findings in respect to each of these children . . . .

It found that the scholastic records of Corliss Smith and James Warfield were good, that based on the mental maturity tests, each would place in the low average group and on the basis of tests administered to a similar grade at Dollarway they would rank between 19 and 21 out of a group of 29 whites. Ernestine Dove's scholastic record was not good, and she had done poorly on the tests.

Part VI states that the Smith and Warfield children were hard working and occupied positions of leadership at Townsend Park; that each has had a history of harmonious relationships without being subject to pressures; that reassignments would not be based upon educational needs or the progress of the student; that it was a historically unsound educational practice to transfer students at the higher grades, and that transfer here would have an unquestioned detrimental effect on the progress of each of the children. As to Ernestine Dove, the findings state that she would be incapable of keeping up.

Part VII recites that the real reason to have the children transferred was a desire to have them attend an integrated school, but this desire reflected a lack of consideration of the best interest of the child on the part of the parents. The unanimous conclusions were that the request for reassignment would not be in the best interest of the child or the educational program of the district and that the board was aware of its duty to obey the law in respect to integration and was proceeding with that in due course.

The Results of Test Administered by Persons Selected By Us

We were fortunate enough to have these children tested by a Mr. Talbert, director of testing at A & M College. They were more extensively tested by him than they were tested at the school . . . .

[T]he Dove child's I.Q. was 96, Corliss Smith was 108 and James Warfield was 98 . . . .

The tests were interpreted by Dr. Phillips, who is Director of the Division of Social Science at A & M College and a sociologist. His conclusions were that the children scored average to well, based upon the norm of the region; and that insofar as the public schools were concerned, there was no reason to believe that they would not do as well if transferred . . . .

The Trial

When the trial started, we took the position that the burden of proving that the plaintiffs were not eligible for admission to Dollarway rested on the defendants and it was their duty to go forward. The judge said that this may be true, but that since we were the moving parties he was going to require us to put on our evidence first.

I think the case law gives us a sound basis for making such a point, and it seems to me that in all of our cases this is what we should insist upon and, if overruled, raise the issue on appeal.

At the trial, the President of the board was the first witness and I sought to make inquiry of him concerning each of the statutory criteria which was supposedly administered by the board. I attempted to find out from him what he understood them to mean. The judge was very testy with me about going into this. Yet, I believe it legitimate for us to seek to ascertain from those charged with responsibility for doing various duties to recite what he understood his duties to be . . . .

[W]hen closely questioned about the meaning of various findings, Mr. Parham said that he was unable to testify about them because they were adopted on the recommendation of professional educators and specialists.

Query: Since the board is supposed to administer and apply the criteria, isn't it necessary that representatives of the board show understanding of the criteria and be able to explain findings in which supposedly the criteria are applied?

An item of interest and, I think, importance is that of the board's five members, two have been to college one year (one of whom never attends board meetings), one has completed the eleventh grade, and two finished high school.

Query: Doesn't the limited educational background of the members of the board make them less equipped to exercise the responsibilities which the statute imposes?

Because of the necessity of making out a prima facie case, we put on evidence— the parents, the pupils, results of the tests . . . .

The defendants put on . . . . Dr. Peters, the psychiatrist . . . . His conclusions were that these children would suffer a trauma if they were transferred. The import of his testimony seemed to be that it was psychologically hazardous to make the transfers at the age of these children because at the junior high and high school age, opinions and prejudices are formed and this would make adjustment more difficult. He seemed to feel that transfer should come about at an early age . . . . He did not seem to feel that any change should take place at the present level.

He was not of the impression that the presence of these children in Dollarway would have an adverse effect on the academic progress of white students, but because they would meet hostility, he felt emotional disturbance was likely to result and that it was in the best interests of the children to remain at Townsend Park.

On cross-examination, I think that one thing I was able to establish was the fact that his observation would not apply to transfer of white children or Negro children from School A to School B within the segregated system at the junior high school and senior high school level, assuming equality in the curricula and the teaching staff, but the observations applied solely to a transfer of Negro children to white schools and thus was based upon the racial factor. He placed emphasis on the fact that his views related to this time and to this situation—he was reluctantly forced to agree that what he was talking about was race, and he was also reluctantly forced to agree that he had not projected on the children an in depth psychological or emotional profile . . . .

The educational psychologist whose name was Mr. Moore, I believe, who interpreted the test results, was the Dean of Men at one of the colleges in Arkansas and a Mississippian. He testified that as far as the children were concerned that it would be adverse and educationally unsound to make a change, etc. In the findings of the board there was a statement that it was historically unsound to make this kind of transfer at this stage and educationally unsound. I questioned him as to whether this was a result of his recommendation, and he agreed. I asked him what evidence he had, what studies had been made to support this statement, what authorities could he point to, and he, of course, had to say that the statement merely reflected his own personal views . . . .

The judge asked the witnesses what would be their view as to when it would be desirable from the psychological and educational standpoint to make a transfer since the import of their testimony seemed to be that the transfer was undesirable under all circumstances. There was no satisfactory answer to this. Both men took the view that transfers of Negro children to white schools in the present climate in Arkansas would be bad for the Negro child.

3. CHIEF JUDGE
HARVEY JOHNSEN'S DECISION
(282 F.2d 256: 1960)

[I]n its announced climate of principles for using the [pupil] placement statute, the [Dollarway] District has . . . made its processes of application of the statute consist in having applicants for transfer subjected to such devices as the California Mental Maturity Test, the Iowa Silent Reading test, the Otis Quick Scoring Test of Mental Ability, the California Language Tests, the Bell Adjustment Inventory, and other such things—which, at least in the elementary area of public education, are new adornments upon the entrance doors to school houses and class rooms.

Again, in what the District has done and proposes to continue doing, application of these devices is not going to be made to the students generally of the system but only to such individuals as undertake to engage in application for . . . transfer—which in the realities of the District here simply means, to Negro students seeking to enter a white school.

The District admittedly has no intention to engage in any such general application of these devices as to enable it to effect a reconstruction or reorganization of its school system or its class rooms on the basis of the levels that might be arrived at from such individual scorings. Nor can it be said to intend to make the statute serve as a means for making a choice or selection among Negro students in relation to each other, for purposes of some initial, limited, transitional step in effecting the disestablishment of its segregation system—because the plan does not contain any definitive expression of indicated opening at any point for the admission . . . of some contemplated number of Negro students, by a particular time, at a designated grade-level.

The plan does engage in a use of some general softening language in respect to first-grade students . . . .

[But] the board has presented no objective plan for the admission of any Negro students to the first grade of its two white schools, as a step in the process of effecting desegregation in its educational system . . . . Nor has it stated that it is ready to make any such desegregating assignments. Instead, it in effect says that, before it can answer that question, it must, even as to first graders, delve into such things as "emotional stability, readiness ability, adjustment potential, and related matters" . . . .

[A]fter a lapse of six years, we think a board should be required to come forth with something more objectively indicative as a program of aim and action than a speculative possibility wrapped in dissuasive qualifications . . . .

Standards of placement cannot be devised or given application to preserve an existing system of imposed segregation. Nor can educational principles and theories serve to justify such a result. These elements, like everything else, are subordinate to and may not prevent the vindication of constitutional rights. An individual cannot be deprived of the enjoyment of a constitutional right, because some governmental organ may believe that it is better for him and for others that he not have this particular enjoyment . . . .

In summary, it is our view that the obligation of a school district to disestablish a system of imposed segregation, as the correcting of a constitutional violation, cannot be said to have been met by a process of applying placement standards, educational theories, or other criteria, which produce the result of leaving the previous racial situation existing, just as before. Such an absolute result affords no basis to contend that the imposed segregation has been or is being eliminated. If placement standards, educational theories, or other criteria used have the effect in application of preserving a created status of constitutional violation, then they fail to constitute a sufficient remedy for dealing with the constitutional wrong.

Whatever may be the right of these things to dominate student location in a school system where the general status of constitutional violation does not exist, they do not have a supremacy to leave standing a situation of such violation, no matter what educational justification they may provide, or with what subjective good faith they may have been employed . . . .

Placement standards and educational doctrines are entitled to their proper play, but that play . . . is subordinate to the duty to move forward, by whatever means necessary, to correct the existing constitutional violation with "all deliberate speed".

4. JUDGE SMITH HENLEY'S DECISION

(196 F. Supp. 944: 1961)

As to pre-school students who will enter the first grade in September, the Board reported that 158 of such students of both races were registered during late spring. Eighty-one of those students were white and were assigned automatically to the Dollarway School at which school they had been presented for registration. Of the 77 Negro students who were registered, only two were presented at Dollarway, the remaining 75 being presented at Townsend Park. All 75 of the students presented at Townsend Park were automatically assigned to that school.

All of the children were administered the Metropolitan Readiness Tests and the California Test of Mental Maturity, Pre-primary. Of the 75 Negroes who had registered at Townsend Park, 22 scored average or better on the tests, but the two Negro children who had applied for admission to Dollarway made scores which were well below average. On the basis of the test results and upon impressions formed in the course of interviews with the children, the Board concluded that the educational program of the District and the educational needs of the two Negro children in question would be served best by assigning them to Townsend Park, which was done. A number of white students made lower scores on the tests than did the two Negro applicants for enrollment in the first grade at Dollarway, but since the tests were not used as assignment criteria for white students, the grades made by the white children just mentioned did not affect their assignment to Dollarway . . . .

II

The Board's plan in operation having been considered by the Court in the light of earlier opinions of the Court of Appeals in this case, the Court is of the opinion that insufficient progress has been made to justify the Court in giving its full approval to the plan at this time as a permissible plan of transition . . . .

[I]t is clear that the validity of the plan from a constitutional standpoint depends primarily upon its application at the first grade level. And it is at that level that the plan in action has failed with respect to 1961–62 to produce satisfactory progress.

The problem stems from the fact that there appears to be very little demand for integration among the Negro patrons of the Dollarway District, and consequently very few Negro applicants for assignment to the Dollarway School . . . .

In giving the Board's supplemental plan tentative and facial approval the Court anticipated that there would be a substantial number of applications by Negroes for initial assignment to the Dollarway School at the first grade level, and that a substantial number of the applicants would be able to meet the objective intelligence and mental maturity standards prescribed by the Board, which standards are not in themselves unreasonable, as is indicated by the satisfactory scores made on the pre-school tests by 22 of the Negro students who applied for enrollment at Townsend Park. As things developed, however, there were only two of such applications for enrollment at Dollarway and neither applicant was able to score within the average or better range of the pre-school tests.

Certainly, the Board cannot be blamed for the apparent lack of demand for desegregation in the District, or for the failure of the two applicants to score satisfactorily on the tests, or for adhering to its own objective criteria which it adopted at the urging of the Court. But, the fact remains that as the situation now appears the use by the Board of its objective intelligence and mental maturity criteria as an assignment standard at the first grade level, however well it might work in some other school district, is not going to produce at Dollarway anything other than token integration . . . unless the number of Negro applications at the first grade level increases substantially and unless the intelligence of the applicants is substantially higher than that of the two children who applied this spring. [S]uch token integration is not a sufficient compliance with *Brown*.

II. FREEDOM OF CHOICE

Southern judges took varying views of the desirability and effectiveness of freedom of choice. But the harsh realities behind it are graphically exposed in a 1966 report of the Civil Rights Commission.

1. UNITED STATES COMMISSION ON CIVIL RIGHTS:

SCHOOL DESEGREGATION IN THE SOUTHERN AND BORDER STATES, 1965–66

2. Factors Retarding Integration Under Free Choice Plans

Negroes in the South have occupied for decades a subservient status to which many are strongly conditioned. It is difficult for many of these Negroes to exercise the initiative required of them by free choice plans. In many cases the long history of subservience has eroded the motivation they might otherwise have to alter their way of life. In addition, there are other factors identified by the Commission which have retarded integration under free choice plans.

a. Continued Racial Identity of Schools
Under freedom of choice plans, schools tend to retain their racial identification. Such plans require affirmative action by parents and pupils to disestablish the existing system of dual schools . . . . [Thus it] is rare for a white pupil to choose voluntarily to attend an identifiably "Negro" school. In only one of the districts visited by Commission attorneys (Lexington, Ky.) did a white child choose a Negro school, and that school subsequently became fully segregated when the child moved out of the State three months later. Racial identification of schools strengthens and is perpetuated by normal school ties, which render students reluctant to leave the schools which they presently attend. This is true of Negro students as well as white students. The Lexington, Ky., school superintendent pointed out that there is a strong attachment to the Negro high school by the Negro community even though the Negro high school has known inadequacies. He said that the all-Negro Dunbar School has won or been runner-up in the State basketball tournament several times; that in 1965–66 a senior girl at Dunbar was a national merit scholarship finalist, and that several Dunbar students have won State debating and other scholastic awards in integrated competitions. Such achievements, he suggested, tend to increase the Negro student's identification with his school.

A Negro school board member in Charlottesville, Va., told staff attorneys that Negro students could transfer from all-Negro Burley High school to formerly white Lane High School but that many were primarily interested in the Burley football team and band, both of which had won honors. A Negro student in Americus, Ga., told staff attorneys that he did not choose a white school because he wanted to play football for the Negro school and graduate with his friends . . . .

Negro school administrators and teachers frequently have an interest in maintaining the dual school system. A report of a task force study financed jointly by the National Education Association and the Office of Education—issued in December 1965—stated:

> . . . when Negro pupils in any number transfer out of Negro schools, Negro teachers become surplus and lose their jobs. It matters not whether they are as well qualified as, or even better qualified than other teachers in the school system who are retained. Nor does it matter whether they have more seniority. They were never employed as teachers for the school system—as the law would maintain—but rather as teachers for Negro schools.

The task force found that from May 1965 to September 1965, at least 668 Negro teachers were displaced by desegregation.

Some Negro educators are opposed to desegregation wholly apart from any fear that they will lose their employment. One Mississippi Negro principal interviewed by a Commission investigator reasoned that Negro youngsters should be realistic about their employment opportunities, and that Negro high schools that emphasize trades are more suitable than white high schools. He also stated that because of economic and cultural deprivation many Negro children enter school much less prepared for education than white children. Until this gap is repaired, he thought, dual schools would be advantageous. The attitudes of such educators are relevant because they frequently are among the most respected members of the Negro community and their opinions influence the choices made by Negro parents and children.

b. Fear, Intimidation, and Harassment

A substantial factor in the reluctance of Negro parents and children to select "white" schools is fear . . . . Frequently, . . . the fear is based upon actual instances of harassment and intimidation of Negro parents and pupils.

For example, in Webster County, Miss., where Negroes constitute 28 percent of the student population, school desegregation began in 1965 under a plan providing free choice for all students in grades 1, 7, 10, and 12 only. The plan was published on July 22, 1965. A local newspaper editor told a staff attorney that on or about July 1, 1965, a cross was burned in the front yard of the sheriff of Webster County and that a few weeks later near midnight crosses were fired at the county courthouse and on highways near three county towns. Negroes told staff attorneys in October 1965 that Ku Klux Klan literature had appeared in their mailboxes or on the front steps of their houses for several months. A former Negro school teacher reported that on August 12, near midnight, about 60 shots had been fired into his home . . . . About a mile from this house staff attorneys saw a sign announcing a Klan rally on August 27, the day school registration had been scheduled . . . .

Staff investigators talked to 16 Negro families in Webster County. These families were aware that the white community did not want desegregation; feared for their safety and that of their children; believed freedom of choice would only work if there were Federal protection and if a sufficient number of Negroes were involved; and doubted that any Negroes would choose a white school next year....

Sumter County, Ga., this year has been operating four all-Negro schools that serve 1,943 pupils, 66 percent of the county enrollment. Four all-white schools complete the system. Under the Sumter County desegregation plan approved by the Office of Education, all 12 grades were to be desegregated. All of the Negro children who had designated white schools on their freedom of choice forms changed their choice. Some of the Negro parents who had chosen white schools said to staff attorneys that they had received threats of physical violence to themselves or their children. The father of one Negro student stated that within 48 hours of submitting the choice form designating a white school he was told by his employer, who also was his landlord, that he would lose his job and home if his child attended the white school. The mother of a Negro student who selected a white school was fired from her job as a maid within 24 hours after submission of the choice form. Other Negro parents electing white schools for their children said that they were threatened with loss of employment. Sumter County Negro families are vulnerable to economic pressure. According to a survey of students by school authorities conducted on October 28, 1965, 73 percent of the Negro pupils were from families with incomes of less than $2,000 per year.

Americus, Ga., which is located in Sumter County but has a separate school system, first desegregated in 1964 when the school board accepted the applications of four Negro children to attend Americus High School. Life was not the same thereafter for these children or their families. One of the families reported to staff attorneys that after they had elected the white school for their daughter their house had been attacked repeatedly . . . . Members of the family said that bottles, stones, toilet paper, and paint had been thrown at the house and that there had been many threatening and obscene phone calls. The girl student—then aged 15—was convicted of a morals charge before the school year ended. The girl's father, an Americus school teacher for 19 years, feared he would be fired. Notwithstanding these facts, the girl returned to Americus High School in 1965 and was joined by her 14-year-old brother.

The family of another of the four students to desegregate Americus last year informed staff attorneys that they have lived in armed vigil for more than a year. Guns were observed in nearly every room of their modest house by a staff attorney.

The mother said that the house has been assaulted frequently by bricks, bottles, and rocks thrown from passing cars. She stated that five or six attacks had been reported to the police, and that the reports had specified the license tag numbers of the cars. Although the chief of police confirmed that rocks had been thrown at the house, he said that no arrests have been made. He blames the race troubles of Americus on "outside agitators." . . .

The Department of Justice has investigated at least 80 alleged incidents of intimidation and harassment of Negro families and students in eight States in connection with desegregation for the 1965 school year. Thirty of the investigations were conducted in Mississippi, 14 in South Carolina, 11 in Georgia, 7 in North Carolina, 6 in Alabama, 5 in Tennessee, 4 in Arkansas, and 3 in Louisiana . . . .

On January 11, 1966, the Department of Justice filed lawsuits against three school districts . . . . One case involves a district operating under a . . . freedom of choice plan approved for Franklin County, N.C. The complaint alleges that after 31 free choice applications . . . had been filed by Negroes . . . , the [School] Board had the names and addresses of these . . . Negroes published in a local newspaper. After the publication, . . . the students and their families were "threatened and intimidated by various means, including cross burnings and the shooting of firearms at homes of Negroes . . . ." The complaint alleges that 20 of the 31 children withdrew their choices and are enrolled in all-Negro schools . . . .

Harassment of Negro students who attend formerly white schools is another deterrent. In Americus, Ga., ...[n]inety Negro pupils chose "white" schools at spring registration in May 1965. All requests were granted but when school opened at the end of August, only 40 of the original 90 Negroes entered such schools. At the time of the Commission's staff investigation in November, only 26 remained. Staff attorneys interviewed eight of the students who had transferred back to all-Negro schools. One student declared he could not study because buckshot, books, and BB-gun pellets had been thrown at him by white students and he had received threatening telephone calls at home. Another Negro boy related that he had been subjected to similar treatment and had been suspended for three days when a fight developed after a white boy had called him "nigger."

Of the 26 Negroes still enrolled in integrated schools, 12, and the families of 4 others, were interviewed by Commission staff. Information disclosed in these interviews indicates that a pattern of harassment and violence in the secondary schools had developed, accompanied by a lack of supervision and enforcement of discipline by high school officials. It was alleged that white students had struck Negro students with their fists and thrown rocks and books at them. It was stated that Negro students had been called derogatory names, had had their books thrown on the floor and knocked from their hands, and had been tripped, spat upon, and nearly run down by cars in the parking lot . . . . One Negro boy stated that he had been the repeated target of a missile consisting of two long needles, bound to wooden pegs and propelled by a rubber band, and that one such weapon had lodged in his clothing. A Negro girl asserted that she had been pushed down a flight of stairs and later hit on the head by a rock.

These Negro students complained of this treatment but felt that little or nothing had been done to prevent it or punish those responsible . . . .

In Calhoun County, Miss., ... [t]wenty-three Negro students elected white schools but . . . . [by] October [1965], only three were enrolled . . . .

Investigators talked to the three Negro students still enrolled. One seventh grade girl stated that she was the only Negro in her homeroom class of 48 students. She declared that none of these students nor any other white pupil had befriended her, but that students had called her "nigger and other things" and had hit and teased her. She had never eaten lunch at school, she said, because she was afraid to enter the lunchroom and had been insulted when she had attempted to purchase food from a nearby store. At recess, she reported, she sat alone. She said she feared she would not be safe on the bus and therefore had never used it. According to this girl, school officials had never helped or asked how she was getting along. The girl, although still enrolled, had stopped attending the integrated school in late September. In January 1966, she still was not in school. The school board refused to let her transfer back to the Negro school and she remained at home. The superintendent said that the policy of the school board was that once a choice is made, no transfer to another school will be allowed and that this policy was required by the Office of Education. The girl had stated she had been first in her class the previous year and had selected the white school in the hope it would provide her with a better education.

The other two Negro pupils, a 10th grade girl and a 12th grade boy, told staff investigators they were determined to stay the entire year. The boy, who stated he had been threatened several times by a band of 10 white students, nevertheless expressed determination to graduate from the white school. In November the superintendent telephoned the Office of Education to report that shots had been fired into the houses of the two Negro students and threatening notes had been left from the Klan. Both students withdrew.

III. THE ATTACK ON DE FACTO SEGREGATION

The district court decisions in *Blocker* v. *Board of Education* and *Barksdale* v. *Springfield School Committee* deal with two separate, if related, rationale used to deny the constitutional validity of the supposed distinction between de jure and de facto segregation—integration as a national command of law flowing directly from the logic of *Brown I*, or integration as the outgrowth of empirical studies showing that racial imbalance deprived African-American youngsters of the equal educational opportunity mandated by *Brown*. *Blocker* rejects the second rationale, while *Barksdale* basically credits it, but both deny flatly that racial imbalance can be consistent with equal protection of the laws.

The first attack on racial imbalance to be appealed to the Supreme Court, in *Bell* v. *School City of Gary Indiana*, adopts the "legalistic" approach. It also articulates openly, however, the deeper criticism bound up with this view of *Brown*, that integration of schools was a constitutionally imperative remedy for the rampant, systemic racism of American society.The justices, however, were not yet ready to tackle this issue.

1. *BLOCKER* v. *BOARD OF EDUCATION OF MANHASSET*

(226 F. Supp. 208: 1964)

JUDGE JOSEPH ZAVATT

The Basic Contentions of the Parties
    The plaintiffs contend that the racial imbalance in the Valley School is segregation in the constitutional sense and within the decision of the Supreme Court in *Brown* v. *Board of Education*; that segregated schools, be they segregated de jure or "de facto," are inferior per se and deprive children of minority groups of equal educational opportunities. This segregation, they contend, is the result of the defendant District's rigid neighborhood school policy . . . . While the plaintiffs contend that damage flows from separate but equal school facilities as a matter of law, they contend further that they have proven damage in fact. Under either theory they claim a deprivation of rights guaranteed by the Fourteenth Amendment.

    The defendants deny that *Brown*, supra, is controlling as a matter of law. They maintain that the neighborhood school policy of the District is color blind; that it operates equally upon all children within each attendance area, regardless of race or color; that the racial imbalance in the Valley area is a fortuitous circumstance due solely to the pattern of housing within the District for which they are not responsible; that, therefore, they are under no duty to change attendance area lines or modify their present attendance rules. They contend, further, that the plaintiffs and the class they represent are not being injured by the continuance of the Board's attendance rules . . . .

Have The Plaintiffs Been Injured By This Segregation?
    In order to obtain relief the plaintiffs must establish that they have been injured as a result of the state action complained of . . . . Many days, hundreds of pages of

testimony and numerous exhibits centered around the question as to whether or not the underachievement of the Valley children is attributable to the segregated character of the Valley School. The plaintiffs did not establish by a fair preponderance of the evidence that their underachievement . . . is due solely to the racial composition of their school. A study by the New York State Department of Education, the Quality Measurement Project, supports the thesis that there is a correlation between scholastic achievement and socioeconomic level. It should be noted, however, that this study did not include race as a possible factor . . . .

Psychologists are not as knowledgeable about intelligence as some might expect. They are not certain as to what intelligence is, much less how to measure it with any degree of accuracy. Nor is there agreement as to whether intellectual potential (IQ) as measured is capable of improvement or is a fixed characteristic; or whether IQ tests are culture dominated and, thereby, underestimate the intellectual potential of children in the low socioeconomic stratum . . . . But, despite the infirmities and uncertainties of presently available means of measuring estimated intellectual potential and scholastic achievement, the evidence in this case falls short of establishing a causal relation between the scholastic achievement of the Valley children and their separation from practically all of their white contemporaries.

[Yet the] denial of the right not to be segregated cannot be assuaged or supported by evidence indicating that underachievement in the three R's may be due in whole or in part to low socioeconomic level, home influence or measured intelligence quotient. The role of public education in our democracy is not limited to these academic subjects. It encompasses a broader preparation for participation in the mainstream of our society. Public education "is the very foundation of good citizenship." [*Brown I*, at 493.] The extent to which this objective is being attained is not measurable by a comparison of achievement in the 3 R's to IQ, or to socioeconomic level . . . .

In *Brown* the Court emphasized "intangible considerations." The opportunity "to study, to engage in discussions and exchange views with other students" at the graduate level was found to "apply with added force to children in grade and high schools." It also adverted to the psychological effect of segregation with and without the sanction of law. It quoted with approval the finding of the lower court that "Segregation of white and colored children in public schools has a detrimental effect upon the colored children. The impact is *greater* when it has the sanction of the law." The Court made its own finding as to the psychological effect of that type of segregation before it in *Brown*:

"To separate them from others of similar age and qualifications solely because of their race generates a feeling of inferiority as to their status in the community that may affect their hearts and minds in a way unlikely ever to be undone." . . .

We are dealing with children in grades K through 6, i.e., from age 5 to 11. They see themselves living in an almost entirely Negro area and attending a school of similar character. If they emerge beyond the confines of the Valley area into the District at large, they enter a different world inhabited only by white people. They are not so mature and sophisticated as to distinguish between the total separation of all Negroes pursuant to a mandatory or permissive State statute based on race and the almost identical situation prevailing in their school district. The Valley situation generates the same feeling of inferiority as to their status in the community as was found by the Supreme Court in *Brown* to flow from substantially similar segregation by operation of State Law. This harmful effect, like pain and suffering in a tort action, is not susceptible of precise measurement.

2. *BARKSDALE* v. *SPRINGFIELD SCHOOL COMMITTEE*

(237 F. Supp. 543: 1965)

JUDGE JOHN SWEENEY

I find that there is no deliberate intent on the part of the school authorities to segregate the races. If segregation exists, it results from a rigid adherence to the neighborhood plan of school attendance . . . .

However, segregation in the sense of racial imbalance, exists in the Springfield school system . . . .

[And] [f]rom the evidence, I find that those schools in which the vast majority of negro students are enrolled consistently rank lowest in achievement ratings based on the Iowa Test of Basic Skills. Those students, when transferred to other schools, had difficulty keeping abreast with their contemporaries. Special programs in science and French for gifted children who have attained a high achievement level had had few, and sometimes no, negro participants.

While it is not possible to determine how much of this is the result of home environment and how much is attributable to schools and teachers, these facts, nonetheless, bear out the testimony of the plaintiffs' expert, Dr. Thomas F. Pettigrew, that racially imbalanced schools are not conducive to learning, that is, to retention, performance, and the development of creativity. Racial concentration in his school communicates to the negro child that he is different and is expected to be different from white children. Therefore, even if all schools are equal in physical plant, facilities, and ability and number of teachers, and even if academic achievement were at the same level at all schools, the opportunity of negro children in racially concentrated schools to obtain equal educational opportunities is impaired, and I so find.

The defendants argue, nevertheless, that there is no constitutional mandate to remedy racial imbalance . . . . But that is not the question. The question is whether there is a constitutional duty to provide equal educational opportunities for all children within the system. While *Brown* answered that question affirmatively in the context of coerced segregation, the constitutional fact—the inadequacy of segregated education—is the same in this case, and I so find. It is neither just nor sensible to proscribe segregation having its basis in affirmative state action while at the same time failing to provide a remedy for segregation which grows out of discrimination in housing, or other economic or social factors. Education is tax supported and compulsory, and public school educators, therefore, must deal with inadequacies within the educational system as they arise, and it matters not that the inadequacies are not of their making. This is not to imply that the neighborhood school policy per se is unconstitutional, but that it must be abandoned or modified when it results in segregation in fact . . . .

I cannot accept the view . . . that only forced segregation is incompatible with the requirements of the Fourteenth Amendment, nor do I find meaningful the statement that "[t]he Constitution does not require integration. It merely forbids discrimination."

3. APPEAL TO THE SUPREME COURT: PETITIONER'S BRIEF IN

BELL v. SCHOOL CITY OF GARY (1964)

Reasons for Allowance of the Writ . . . .

1. . . . In *Brown* v. *Board of Education*, this Court determined that separate educational facilities are inherently unequal, particularly since the separation of white and Negro children by the state in the public schools generates pervading and injurious feelings of inferiority in the minority group children.

What *Brown* and the decisions which have followed sought to accomplish was the transition from a segregated to a non-segregated society, in which race is not a barrier to the enjoyment of advantages espoused under a democratic system . . . .

School systems which are administered so that all or nearly all the Negro children attend schools, separate and apart from all or nearly all the white students, are no less segregated than those systems where separate Negro schools are mandated by state constitution or statute. A public school system is operated by the state through a local administrative agency. The responsibility of the state is the same whether the legislature decrees that there be a separation of the races in public schools, or that separation occurs by means of attendance zone lines or school board policy evolved by school authorities. In the latter instance as stated in *Blocker* v. *Board of Education*, "It is segregation by law—the law of the school board." [at 226] . . .

When a school system is comprised of attendance areas, the delineation of which inevitably results in "Negro schools," the result is constitutionally objectionable whether achieved adventitiously or intentionally. A line which outlines or confines a Negro community, restricting it within the boundaries of a limited area, is not relieved of its illegal character because a clear intention to segregate is lacking. The constitution reaches the resultant discrimination . . . .

If the *Brown* decision is to be meaningful and viable, . . . it must deal with and proscribe all racial discrimination and segregation in education, not merely that form of discrimination explicitly mandated by a state legislature. [A] biracial school system that results from school board zoning practices and policies, whether described as "neighborhood schools" or by some other euphemism, cannot be consonant with *Brown*, unless *Brown* is to be reduced to sterile abstraction, incapable of dealing with reality . . . .

2. The court of appeals has decided an important question of federal law which has not been, but should be settled by this Court. The court below determined that since the respondent had not intentionally segregated public school students, it was not obligated to remedy the discrimination despite its awareness that in administering the school system, racial imbalance was maintained and perpetuated. In so holding the court relied upon dicta in . . . *Briggs* v. *Elliott*.

The observation of the court in *Briggs* v. *Elliott*, that the "constitution does not require integration, it merely forbids discrimination," has been cited by so many subsequent decisions that it is erroneously viewed as an authoritative construction of *Brown* . . . . The difference between desegregation and integration is irrelevant to whether the principle of *Brown* is to be realistically applied.

The issue is not, as the court below stated, whether the constitution requires an intermingling of the races as some abstract exercise, but whether the constitution tolerates a school board's acquiescence in the operation of a school system which is segregated in fact, merely because it did not intentionally or overtly create it . . . .

The view adopted by a court depends on whether the terms racially imbalanced or de facto segregated schools and segregated schools are used as interchangeable. Those courts which impose a duty on boards to modify policies which result in racially imbalanced schools see no qualitative difference between segregated education created by statute, court decision or intentional state action, and that flowing . . . from a neighborhood school policy. They construe *Brown* as implying that inequality inheres in segregated education no matter what its cause . . . . Courts, like the one below, which distinguish segregation from the racial imbalance which results from school administration which perpetrates that concentration construe *Brown* as relating only to state decreed segregation . . . .

This profound confusion in concept requires resolution by this Court . . . .

The adverse effect of segregated education is not confined to the Negro in the South. Nearly one-half of the Negro population of the United States live outside of the South and the great majority are thrust into segregated neighborhoods. The myth of the inherent inferiority of the Negro is accepted as true by three-fourth of the white community. This attitude is reflected in all aspects of life and is continuously conveyed to the Negro in many ways. The Negro school is regarded as a low status school . . . . It is not attractive to the community, and where possible, is avoided by both teachers and students.

The Negro in the predominantly Negro school in the North is as psychologically and educationally disadvantaged as his counterpart in the South. He is not immunized from the effects of segregation by reason of geography and his color prevents his assimilation into the community. The situation of the Negro student is accurately defined in *Blocker* v. *Board of Education* . . . .

The opinion in the district court and of the court below were predicated upon the thesis that the delineation of school zones, and selection of sites for new schools pursuant to criteria used in the "neighborhood school system", absolved the school board of responsibility for the severe racial imbalance in the Gary system. Examination of the cases where racial imbalance is sought to be excused, by the existence of the "neighborhood school" demonstrates that term to include any school produced as the result of the partition of any school district into attendance areas. Because such factors as distance, safety, school capacity, topographical features and other variables determine the location of a school, the "neighborhood plan" is a fluid concept which takes whatever form a board decrees . . . .

It follows, therefore, that a school board may, within the concept of the neighborhood school plan . . . , implement its rules, regulations and policies to maintain a pattern of separate schools or to accomplish racial integration. The result of its action generally reflects the board's philosophy as to the desirability of multi-racial schools.

With *Brown* v. *Board of Education*, this Court launched a new era wherein segregation in public education was required to be discontinued and eradicated. It recognized two important principles: the basic constitutional inequality of segregated education and the obligation of school authorities to provide a remedy . . . . It is, therefore, incumbent upon a school board to mitigate segregation in education where possible. A board may not contend a lack of responsibility for a constitutionally inadequate school system when perpetuation of that system has occurred by administrative policies or acquiescence in pre-existing administrative practices. Transition to a racially nondiscriminatory school system "with all deliberate speed" was ordered to remedy the inherent inadequacy of segregated education. Accordingly, that transition must remove the harm sought to be prevented without regard to how it occurred. To view the problem otherwise is but superficial recognition of form rather than substance.

IV. THE CINCINNATI CASE: THE HOUSING ISSUE

Deal v. *Cincinnati* offered another twist in the attack on the Briggsian distinction in school law, an attempt by the plaintiffs to tie discriminatory actions in housing, especially by public officials, to racial separation in schools. The trial brief in the district court presented such evidence, but, despite the strenuous arguments of plaintiffs' counsel Robert Carter and Norris Muldrow, Judge John Peck ruled the evidence inadmissible. The Cincinnati plaintiffs brought the issue to the Supreme Court for the first time in late 1965, but again the Court was not ready to act.

1. TRIAL BRIEF: *DEAL* v. *CINCINNATI BOARD OF EDUCATION*

(244 F. Supp. 572: 1965)

HOUSING SEGREGATION

Housing in the City of Cincinnati is segregated as the result of policies of both private and public agencies. This is the conclusion of a report made by the Ohio Civil Rights Commission . . . . This report is substantiated by the record in this case.

Joseph Murphy, Supervisor of Relocation for the City of Cincinnati, Department of Urban Development, testified that he was responsible for family relocation, planning as well as execution, for all governmental projects. He was asked:

Q. Well, let me ask you, is there any practice against sending Negro families into White neighborhoods, in your department?

A. We refer families to units that have been made available. Now, the units are made available to us on a racial basis, and we are also aware of the fact that there are areas in which Negroes are not accepted.

Q. And is it a practice not to send Negro families to those areas?

A. Correct.

Dean Clark of the same agency testified that she did not "block bust," a term which she defined to mean, "a person goes into a neighborhood that has been restricted, either White or Negro, and attempts to integrate by bringing in another race."

Exhibits . . . further make clear that it is common knowledge in the City of Cincinnati that housing has been segregated by public and private interests.

Knowledge of this fact was admitted by Calvin Concliffe, a member of the Board of Education. He was asked:

Q. And don't you mean that the housing pattern in Cincinnati is such that it is segregated?

A. From the standpoint that there are areas in which Negroes have not been able to obtain housing, yes.

Q. When you say have not been able to obtain houses, don't you mean areas where they have been restricted from obtaining housing, sir?

A. Yes, I think that is a fair statement.

Every member of the board and of the school administration who was asked testified that he or she knew where the Negro residential areas were in Cincinnati. Assistant Superintendent Shreve also had in his files reports prepared for the Cincinnati Board of Education by the Bureau of Government Research, Inc. from 1960 to 1962 which clearly showed where Negroes lived in Cincinnati and what type of housing they occupied.

2. COLLOQUY IN THE DISTRICT COURT

(244 F. Supp. 572: 1965)

JUDGE JOHN PECK

[MR. NORRIS MULDROW]: One other evidentiary area [is] denied plaintiffs, and . . . reflects a ruling consistent with the position indicated by the Court during early conferences. Plaintiffs called one Dean Clark, a relocation representative for Urban Redevelopment in the employment of the City of Cincinnati (The City is not, of course, a party to this action.) . . . . She . . . identified a proffered exhibit as "a listing from an investment corporation of both White and non-White vacancies in the city." Following objection to the exhibit, the following colloquy appears: . . . .

"THE COURT: How does it become material, Mr. Muldrow?

"MR. MULDROW: It becomes material, sir, from the viewpoint of Negroes being segregated in public housing by public officials.

* * * * * * * * * * * *

"THE COURT: The only public officials named in this suit are members of the Cincinnati Board of Education, and the Board. Even conceding that there may have been improper action taken by the City of Cincinnati, or the governor of Arizona, or some other public authority, how do we here become concerned with that?

"MR. MULDROW: We become concerned, Your Honor, because the Board of Education is a public body, and the City of Cincinnati is a public body, being a part of the State of Ohio. And here we have state action which is practicing segregation upon Negroes, and in that respect it is pertinent to the question of whether or not Negroes are segregated in the Cincinnati Public School System, and whether or not they are receiving equal educational opportunities.

"THE COURT: Mr. Muldrow, how could any order that might issue from this Court be binding on any person, private or public, who is not a party to this action and has not had an opportunity to respond, in either a public or private capacity?

"MR. MULDROW: Our position, Your Honor, on that particular question is that we have before this Court an agency of the state, the Cincinnati Board of Education, which is segregating against Negro children; and further that Negro children are segregated in housing, and that one part of the state cannot segregate, which will affect another part.

"THE COURT: Mr. Muldrow, I don't want to debate with you what some other agency may or may not do. I am only asking how this Court is empowered to take any action with reference to any individual, private or public, who is not a party to this lawsuit?

"MR. MULDROW: The action would be taken against the Cincinnati Board of Education, because we are saying the fact that even though another agency might discriminate, as far as in housing, that this could not be used as a scapegoat for the Cincinnati Board of Education furnishing equal educational opportunity to Negro children.

"The Cincinnati Board has to adjust to segregated housing in order to make equal educational opportunities available to all of its citizens.

"Therefore, an order would be directed to the Cincinnati Board of Education to correct whatever segregation is practiced upon Negro children, even though it might be brought about by another agency. [T]he Board has to deal with education, and segregated housing affects education. And . . . you cannot get an equal educational opportunity by being confined or restricted to a particular section, and that the Board has power, or can do something about it to correct that segregation.

* * * * * * * * * * * *

"THE COURT: Mr. Carter, in the one or two sessions which you have helpfully participated in, the pretrial conferences, you contributed very substantially to the forwarding of this matter . . . .

"If you care to offer anything on the question I have asked Mr. Muldrow, I would be pleased to hear it.

"MR. CARTER: I would, if it please the Court.

"What is being attempted to elicit from this witness is the fact that in a city agency relocating families, . . . that the agency uses as a part of its information for relocation, lists in which properties are restricted on the basis of race, in assisting persons in finding houses.

"Now, this we think—we think, Your Honor, that this is a part of—we are attempting to show to the Court in some measure the participation of a public agency, not the Board of Education, but another public agency, in the residential segregation which exists in the City of Cincinnati, and on the basis of which the School Board indicates that this is reason, because of housing segregation, geographical segregation, is the reason for the maintenance of the schools which we say are segregated schools . . . .

"This is the purpose or the intent of this testimony.

"THE COURT: Mr. Carter, the difference between us, and the point that I was attempting to make a few moments ago, is that I fail to see how it becomes material and proper evidence in this case to indicate transgressions or wrongdoings that may have been perpetrated by some other individual or agency.

"For example, I think it might be even entirely arguable that the actions of the governor of Alabama may have had some influence on some people in this district. We recently had within the Southern District of Ohio a national meeting of the Ku-Klux-Klan. I am sure that you would not suggest that any evidence with reference to that matter could be brought into this courtroom.

"I strongly suggest to you, gentlemen, that the difference is only one of degree. You are picking an agency of the City of Cincinnati, which is entirely separate legally and factually, from the individual Defendants, as well as the defendant entity of the Board in this case.

"I suggest that the fact that there is some geographical proximity does not mean there is any reason for permitting whatever this lady's agency may or may not have done improperly come into this case . . . .

"MR CARTER: I understand that, Your Honor . . . . However, it is my feeling in terms of the whole evidence of what produces, or what causes or what is the basis of what we call segregated schooling here, that this is part of the evidentiary facts which we think we should present to the Court. And particularly we think it is a part of the evidentiary fact, that a part of this is produced by an agency of the City of Cincinnati.

"We respectfully submit that this isn't the same case as the governor of Alabama. I think that the governor of Alabama's action, or the Ku-Klux Klan is more tenuous action. We think here we have a direct agency involved, which is a public agency in the same city as the School Board, which helps create this situation. And this is the reason we want this evidence in.

"THE COURT: Gentlemen, I permitted this to be gone into a little more fully at this time than might otherwise be justified, but I wanted the counsel to understand the Court's position. I think that I understand your position.

"The objection to the Plaintiff's Exhibit Number 1 for identification at the present time will be sustained, subject to the right of the Plaintiffs to reoffer the exhibit when and if it is shown to have some connection with the Defendants in this case."

3. APPEAL TO THE SUPREME COURT

II. Whether Evidence Designed to Prove That the Housing Patterns in Cincinnati Are Segregated and That This Has Been Accomplished by the Actions of Both Public and Private Agencies Should Be Considered in a School Segregation Case? The Court Below Answered, "No". Appellants Answer, "Yes".

Appellants have proven by admission that housing patterns are segregated in the City of Cincinnati, and that public housing agencies have been and continue to be responsible for this fact. Illegal state action was also taken in that restrictive covenants have been judicially enforced in the State of Ohio. The court of appeals [of Ohio] held that it was "a matter of common knowledge that [use of racial occupancy restrictions] is a frequent and extensive practice throughout the state." 70 N. E. 2d at 491. The fact that such covenants can no longer be enforced does not undo the damage done. There can be little doubt that the segregated housing patterns which came into being prior to 1948 still exist today. Moreover, the conclusion of a recent report by the Ohio Civil Rights Commission, entitled, *Discrimination in Housing in Ohio*, states that there is a consistent pattern of discrimination against Negroes in housing which is the result of the practices and policies of both private interests and public governmental housing agencies. The report, erroneously excluded from evidence, was the result of public hearings held throughout the State of Ohio and Cincinnati was one of the cities studied.

All of the appellees and board officers questioned indicated knowledge of racial housing patterns. Appellees, therefore, have with knowledge, drawn district lines in such a manner so as to reflect in the school population the patterns of segregation in housing. This fact alone should entitle appellants to relief.

In *Holland* v. *Board of Public Instruction of Palm Beach County, Florida*, the court predicated its entire decision on the fact that the schools reflected the patterns of segregation caused by housing ordinances. In *Dowell* v. *School Board of the Oklahoma Public Schools*, the court used the connection between housing and school segregation as the starting point of its factual analysis. Further, the court made it explicit that the results of the past patterns of housing segregation have to be dealt with by the school board, no matter how difficult the task . . . .

It is therefore irrelevant that the board of education is not responsible for housing segregation in Cincinnati. Housing segregation exists, and the board may not close its eyes to this reality; the board may not duplicate in the schools what has already been done in housing. The responsibility to draw district lines must therefore be exercised in such a manner so as to create racially balanced schools in so far as is possible and consistent with sound educational practices.

The court below's ruling that evidence of housing segregation is not admissible in an action against a school board is clearly contrary to precedent and the opinion of legal authorities.

CHAPTER TWO

JEFFERSON AND *GREEN:* THE GREAT TURNING

Just as few members of the Supreme Court shaped American law in general as did Judge Learned Hand of the Second Circuit Court of Appeals, so few have shaped school desegregation law as has Judge John Minor Wisdom of the Fifth Circuit.

A life-long resident of New Orleans (born in 1905), a member of the most exclusive segments of the city's aristocracy, Judge Wisdom rebelled against conventional respectability at an early age, joining the Republican party while still a student at Tulane Law School. In February, 1952, he helped organize and served as chairman of the Southern Conference for Eisenhower, part of a national draft movement for the general. At the Republican Convention in July, he successfully urged the seating of a pro-Eisenhower delegation from his state, which had been illegally steamrollered by the party regulars.

Wisdom's nomination by the President to the Fifth Circuit Court of Appeals in 1957 required some delicate handling, due to his position as a board member of the bi-racial New Orleans Urban League. This aroused the suspicions of arch-segregationist Senator James O. Eastland, chairman of the Senate Judiciary Committee, who quizzed the candidate during confirmation hearings about the league's possible interest in "the segregation question, the school integration question."[1] Wisdom's reassuring, if somewhat disingenuous, answers to these inquiries, and the support proffered the nomination by other Fifth Circuit judges, convinced Eastland to drop his opposition. When asked in later years if he had been mislead, the senator "clamped his mouth tight on his cigar, hesitated, then said, 'I don't have any comment on that.'"[2]

Once on the bench, Judge Wisdom moved promptly to the cutting edge of school law, demanding, in *Holland*, that tokenism produce the tokens it promised, helping, in the New Orleans school case, to dismantle the tokenist structure of the pupil placement laws, and, in *Singleton*, calling the dictum of *Briggs* sharply into question. Furthermore, while ruling in a different area of civil rights enforcement, the judge suggested strongly that non-discrimination was an inadequate remedy for past sins.

In the *United States* v. *Louisiana* (1963),[3] a federal panel headed by Judge Wisdom struck down the so-called "understanding and interpretation" section of the Louisiana Constitution—a provision giving election registrars unlimited discretion to debar from voting citizens unable to explain to the registrar's satisfaction any passage in the state or national constitution. This device had emerged in the 1950's as the principal way of disenfranchising African-American voters in Louisiana, after the Supreme Court's interment of the white primary. Wisdom, joined by District Judge Herbert Christenberry, easily dispatched the understanding test as discriminatory in origin, unconstitutionally vague because of the unbridled power it vested in election officials, and unrelated in any rational way to the qualifications needed for voting.

A thornier issue arose, however, while the case was in process. To replace the soon to be voided constitutional provision, Louisiana enacted a new and facially unassailable prerequisite for voting, a straightforward citizenship test composed of objective questions about the workings of government. Here was a neutral, impartial method of assessing voter qualifications from that time forward, the apparent solution to the problem of discrimination.

But Judge Wisdom thought it clear that the citizenship test could not really wipe the slate clean, could not dissipate the effects of the earlier injustices visited upon African-American voters. In fact, the test "froze in" prior constitutional violations, for unless Louisiana conducted a complete re-registration of the electorate, illiterate whites who had no hope of passing the new test would remain registered, while African-Americans, disenfranchised in the past by lawless registrars, must nonetheless survive the examination. "The cessation of prior discriminatory practices," argued Judge Wisdom, "cannot justify the imposition of new . . . requirements, theoretically applicable to all, but practically affecting primarily those who bore the brunt of previous discrimination."[4] While reserving judgment, therefore, "on the constitutionality of the new examination," the panel ordered it suspended until parishes in the state which had relied on the "understanding" provision undertook "a general re-registration of all voters."[5]

A neutral assessment of citizenship skills might be unobjectionable per se, the panel concluded, but the "promise of evenhanded justice in the future does not bind our hands in undoing past injustices."[6]

II

The themes sounded by Judge Wisdom between 1958 and 1966, indeed by all of those who had questioned the orthodoxies of *Briggs*, came together in grand convocation in the *United States* v. *Jefferson County Board of Education*[7]—a case which consolidated on appeal seven controversies involving free choice plans from Alabama and Louisiana. Officially, *Jefferson County* provided judicial endorsement for the revised HEW guidelines on freedom of choice, firming up their integrationist leanings and fashioning out of them a model desegregation decree for the Fifth Circuit. In its deeper thrust, however, Judge Wisdom's majority opinion completed a process of basic constitutional redefinition.

The central premise of *Jefferson County* is stated plainly at the outset. *"The only desegregation plan that meets constitutional standards is one that works,"*[8] because *"the only adequate redress for a previously overt system-wide policy of segregation directed against Negroes as a collective entity is a system-wide policy of integration."*[9] In his decision, Judge Wisdom pointed out, "we use the words 'integration' and 'desegregation' interchangeably."[10]

The necessity for integration flowed from a rationale equally applicable to North and South. "[P]sychological harm and lack of educational opportunities to Negroes may exist whether caused by de facto or de jure segregation."[11] *Brown* unquestionably pointed "toward the existence of a duty to integrate de facto segregated schools,"[12] as a way of providing equal educational opportunity.

Yet even if *Brown* demanded only that officials get rid of state-imposed racial classifications, it still mandated integration as the remedy for these violations, since the "central vice" of de jure segregation was dual zoning, and "[d]ual zoning persists,"[13] so long as the racially identifiable schools created by those zones persist. African-American children continue to be subjected to racial categories and the harms *Brown* ascribes to them while the state continues to operate, for any reason, "schools identified as Negro, historically," and where "the faculty and students are Negro."[14] The matter goes deeper, however. One-race schools are inherently unconstitutional, *Jefferson County* asserts, because, by their very nature, they perpetuate an entire social order based on hurt and humiliation. "Denial of access to the dominant culture, lack of opportunity in any meaningful way to participate in political and other public activities, the stigma of apartheid condemned in the Thirteenth Amendment are concomitants of the dual educational system."[15]

Thus, *"no matter what view is taken of the rationale in Brown I,"* *Brown II* still decreed the same remedy for official segregation, "the state's correcting its discrimination against Negroes . . . , through separate schools, by initiating and operating . . . integrated school[s]."[16] The racial classification theory of the first *Brown* decision, no less than broader interpretations, imposed upon school officials "the affirmative duty"[17] to efface racial separation.

Judge Wisdom does not spell out the exact degree of integration required to redress past evils, but he shied away from any demand for racial balance. He was convinced at this point in his constitutional development that the "law does not require a maximum of racial mixing or striking a racial balance accurately reflecting the racial composition of the community or the school population. It does not require that each and every child attend a racially balanced school."[18] His concern was the elimination of racially identifiable black schools. Compliance fell short, he felt, when schools with disproportionate concentrations of African-American students continued to exist unnecessarily. As long as school officials made every possible effort to eliminate these concentrations, it was alright, presumably, for the racial composition of most schools in a district to vary from the overall racial composition of that district, even for all-white schools to remain intact.

Officially, *Jefferson County* concerned only freedom of choice. Yet no one doubted that the broad rationale of the decision swept geographic zoning plans into its wake if they perpetuated disproportionately black schools, as their structure almost always did. Like Judge Bohanon, Judge Wisdom exposed the stacked deck which were neighborhood schools, the opportunity they gave school boards to preserve a segregated system "by using the neighborhood plan"[19] to take advantage of prior residential discrimination. Indeed, past actions by school officials, he suggested, played some role in shaping these discriminatory patterns, since compulsorily segregated schools reduced such residential mobility as African-Americans might otherwise have exercised, further guaranteeing that they would cluster in compact neighborhoods. "Cause and effect [come] together."[20] This led the judge to some cross-sectional speculations on "whether tolerance of de facto segregation" based on housing patterns did not comprise "an unsubtle form of state action."[21]

But even more urgently than *Dowell*, the *Jefferson* opinion labored to open up space between the northern and southern methods of linking residential with educational separation. Despite surface congruities, the similarities were "more apparent than real" between what Judge Wisdom regarded as the "actual de facto segregation" of the North and the "pseudo de facto segregation" of the South.[22] Though northern authorities were scarcely without fault, racial separation in their schools could genuinely be described, in many cases, "as an unfortunate fortuity,"[23] coming about because of a legitimate devotion to the neighborhood school.

In the South, however, the overriding commitment had always been to racial apartheid and all that it signified in southern life; the original decision to put black schools in black neighborhoods and white schools in white neighborhoods hardly qualified as an innocent judgment. This pattern followed from a devotion to the "dual zoning system,"[24] the very system which must see its physical and psychological structure torn down. To "continue" much of that system, out of a sudden zeal for "pure" neighborhood zones, represented nothing less than "racial gerrymandering," and "[s]egregation resulting from racially motivated gerrymandering is properly characterized as 'de jure' segregation."[25]

Judge Wisdom's reasoning was clearly open to question, since he raised but failed to explore the possibility that "actual de facto segregation" was not "actual" at all, because northern communities were accomplishing "in two steps" what they dared not accomplish "in one." But his exposure of neutrality at the remedy phase took precedence, at this point, over pursuing a new basis of violation. Furthermore, establishment of a sharp division between types of segregation aided the judge in the formidable task of reconciling *Jefferson County*, and the guidelines they endorsed, with some rather pointed language found in the 1964 Civil Rights Act. The 88th Congress had added several amendments to the act expressing a Briggsian distaste for the notion that desegregation plans must produce sizable amounts of integration. Foremost among them was an addition to Title IV. This title gave the Attorney General of the United States extensive new powers to bring school desegregation suits. But Section 401(b) attempted to place limits on the whole litigation process.

> "Desegregation" means the assignment of students to public schools and within such schools without regard to their race, color, religion, or national origin, but "desegregation" shall not mean the assignment of students to public schools in order to overcome racial imbalance.[26]

The author of the last part of 401(b), beginning with the "but," was Representative William Cramer of Florida. His purpose, thought the congressman, was straightforward, to prevent executive or judicial interference with the "de facto segregation"—the legal segregation, he believed—certain to manifest itself in southern schools as compliance with *Brown* took effect. As Cramer said during debate, "De facto segregation is racial imbalance," and he wanted to guarantee that Congress did not "include in the definition of 'desegregation' any balancing of school attendance."[27]

Essential to Representative Cramer's achieving his purpose, of course, was his assumption that such a thing as innocent, adventitious racial separation could exist in the South, after a district adopted a court-ordered desegregation plan. He was plainly intent upon preserving the racial disparities which would manifest themselves in Mississippi or in Florida as freedom of choice or neighborhood zoning took hold. And during the Judiciary Committee hearings on the Civil Rights bill, he expressed fear that it gave the attorney general the power to institute suits against school districts already operating under non-discriminatory plans, if racial disproportions still existed.[28]

> Mr. Cramer. [T]he Attorney General could bring a suit on behalf of a person living in a Negro area and state that the student is still being discriminated against in that there are not enough whites to Negroes . . . .[29]

By amending section 401(b), Representative Cramer felt he had foreclosed this possibility, and avoided the danger of a much vaunted "double standard" between regions.

Judge Wisdom merely legitimized the possibility by excising Representative Cramer's categories. By denying that "actual de facto segregation" could exist in the South, the judge was also denying that the HEW guidelines could ever have the purpose of eliminating racial imbalance as Representative Cramer conceived it—since, after all, *de facto segregation* is racial imbalance. The imbalances, however, which were the "consequence of past segregation policies"—which could never qualify as "an unfortunate fortuity"—were quite another matter. They could, and must, be remedied as part of the process of desegregation, "the organized undoing"[30] of the discriminatory effects of the past.

The judge blandly dichotomized the Cramer amendment, stripping it of any significance.

> The affirmative portion of [section 401(b)], down to the "but" clause, describes the assignment provision necessary in a plan for conversion of a de jure dual system to a unitary, integrated system. The negative portion, starting with "but," excludes assignment to overcome racial imbalance, that is acts to overcome de facto segregation.[31]

Such a construction obviously subverted Representative Cramer's purpose, yet followed consistently the architecture of *Jefferson County*. Judge Wisdom simply disallowed the congressman's root assumption: that schools created by law and sanctified by tradition as "black" could still become part of a truly non-discriminatory system for assigning students. This was decidedly less chancy than loosing the storm certain to erupt if *Jefferson County* declared Cramer's amendment an unconstitutional interference with the equity powers of federal courts.

The opinion gave equally short shrift to an amendment added in the Senate, stipulating that

> Nothing herein shall empower any official or court of the United States to issue any order seeking to achieve a racial balance in any school by requiring the transportation of pupils or students from one school to another . . . .[32]

Senator Hubert Humphrey had defended this amendment during a lengthy colloquy with Senator Robert Byrd. The Senator from West Virginia, then very much in his segregationist incarnation, wanted, like Representative Cramer, to protect what he thought to be legitimate de facto segregation in the South. Senator Humphrey hastened to reassure him, and while he did so by quoting from the district court decision in the Gary case, his tone and language, to say nothing of the senator he was assuaging, indicate his belief that the amendment applied to all sections of the country.

> Mr. Byrd . . . .Can the Senator from Minnesota assure the Senator from West Virginia that school children may not be bused from one end of the community to another . . . to relieve so-called racial imbalance in the schools?

> Mr. Humphrey. I do . . . . As the law in the Federal Court now stands,

while intentional gerrymandering of school districts to perpetuate segregation has been held to be a violation of the 14th amendment, normal
residential zoning resulting in de facto school segregation will apparently be upheld by the courts. As to racial balancing, [the district court]
opinion in the Gary case is significant in this connection. [I]t was decided to write the thrust of the court's opinion into the proposed [amend-
ment].[33]

Later, Senator Humphrey declared, "This case makes it quite clear that while the
Constitution prohibits segregation, it does not require integration."[34]

Judge Wisdom easily discounted the relevance of this legislation to the issues
raised in *Jefferson County.* Senator Humphrey spoke "several times in the language
of *Briggs,*" the judge admitted, but "his references to *Bell* indicate that the restrictions in the Act were pointed at the Gary, Indiana de facto type of segregation."[35]
Congress "was well aware of the fact that *Bell* was concerned with de facto segregated neighborhood schools—only."[36] It was also clear that the Congress did not
think such schools incapable of ever existing in the southern states.

Judge Wisdom's reasoning in *Jefferson County* scarcely muted the cry of double
standard, either in Congress or among his colleagues on the Fifth Circuit Court of
Appeals. In early 1967, the entire membership of the court reheard the *Jefferson*
case and not only affirmed the original decision, but hinted at an even broader standard of compliance, one directed at all racially identifiable schools. "Expressions in
our earlier opinions distinguishing between integration and desegregation must
yield to [the] affirmative duty we now recognize . . . . [O]fficials administering public schools in this circuit have the affirmative duty . . . to bring about an integrated
. . . school system in which there are no Negro schools and no white schools—just
schools."[37] Four judges out of twelve dissented, however, and the dissenters took the
occasion to comment bitterly on the regional injustices they felt were being perpetrated. The only way to avoid such injustice, they argued, was either for southern
judges to return to the principles of *Briggs* or for northern judges to abolish the de
jure—de facto distinction. "All children . . . in the nation," wrote Judge Walter
Gewin, "are protected by the Constitution, and treatment which violates their constitutional rights in one area of the country, also violates such constitutional rights
in another area . . . . [E]qual protection will not tolerate a lower standard, and surely not a double standard."[38] Judge Griffin Bell thought it appropriate, in light of the
majority's action, to "disavow the de jure-de facto doctrine as being itself violative
of the equal protection clause . . . . It is reverse apartheid."[39]

III

Jefferson County reigned as the law of the Fifth Circuit by mid-1967, but the
other circuits dealing with school desegregation did not agree. The Fourth Circuit,
sitting *en banc,* upheld freedom of choice plans for the "black belt" of Virginia in

language reaffirming *Bradley*. Judge Clement Haynsworth flatly rejected the plaintiff's contention "that compulsive assignments to achieve a greater intermixture of the races . . . is their due."[40] Judges Simon Sobeloff and Harrison Winter registered a vigorous dissent.

The Sixth Circuit accepted a plan for Jackson, Tennessee, combining geographic zones with a variation on freedom of choice. Students were initially assigned to their neighborhood school, then could exercise the unrestricted right to transfer to any other school in the city. Naturally, white students zoned into black schools quickly took advantage of the transfer provision. But a Sixth Circuit panel saw nothing wrong with this procedure, since "the Fourteenth Amendment [does] not command compulsory integration of all of the schools."[41] Furthermore, it noted, the Supreme Court had endorsed such an open transfer plan, free of the taint of minority to majority provisions, in *Goss* v. *Board of Education of Knoxville*.

The Eighth Circuit again divided. No less than four panels in the circuit sustained Judge Wisdom's freedom of choice standards, including one (without Judge Floyd Gibson as a member) which decided a later phase of *Kemp* v. *Beasley*.[42] Two panels, both with Judge Gibson on them, held to the Briggsian criteria.[43] (The Tenth Circuit, as noted, approved Judge Bohanon's post-Briggsian formulations in a geographic zoning context.)

One of the Eighth Circuit cases decided in the old-fashioned way concerned the tiny Gould School District in rural Arkansas. The Supreme Court picked the Gould case, along with the ones in Virginia and Jackson, Tennessee, for consideration at its October, 1967 term. Officially, the cases went by the names of *Green* v. *School Board of New Kent County, Virginia, Raney* v. *Board of Education of the Gould School District,* and *Monroe* v. *Board of Commissioners of the City of Jackson, Tennessee*.[44] In determining the direction school desegregation law would take, the *Green* trilogy posed the most important questions faced by the justices since *Brown II*.

Indeed, attorneys for the three school boards (now the appellees) based their legal strategy on the alleged difference between the moderate teachings of 1954–55 and the unwarranted radicalism of 1967. The *Brown* decisions, they asserted, were never meant as "a command for racial mixing." The Court simply said: "Stop segregation, compulsory segregation, and establish a system of admissions to your schools based on some other factor than race."[45] Predictably, school board lawyers quoted the Thurgood Marshall of Legal Defense Fund days to the formidable figure now sitting on the bench above them. "Mr. Justice Marshall was the distinguished counsel [in the original case of *Briggs* v. *Elliott*]. And . . . at one point he said: 'My emphasis is that all we are asking for is to take off the state-imposed segregation.'"[46]

Defense Fund counsel (the appellants), working as always with local attorneys, countered by taking two interlinked legal tracks. On the one hand, they articulated a general remedial logic mandating integration as the necessary end product of any desegregation plan, whether involving freedom of choice, geographic zoning, or anything else. The doing of equity—restoring the victims of a wrong to the position they would have occupied but for that wrong—required the perpetrators "to do more than cease unlawful activities." Equity compelled them "to take affirmative steps to undo [the] effects of their wrongdoing."[47] And picking up on the Fifth Circuit's sentiments, the Defense Fund lawyers argued that the only acceptable integration plan was indeed one which eliminated all racially identifiable schools (though they did not elaborate on the issue at this point). Such plans "should be judged by whether they are reasonably designed to convert dual systems into unitary systems. Adequate plans should desegregate both formerly all-white and formerly all-Negro schools."[48]

The advocates of this remedial position inevitably made use of *Brown's* references to harm in criticizing approaches to compliance which fall short of integration. But their discussion in this area drew on history and common sense, not experimental psychology. "The fundamental premise of *Brown I,*" noted the *Green* brief,

> was that segregation in public education had very deep and long term effects. It was not surprising, therefore, that individuals reared in that system and schooled in the ways of subservience (by segregation, not only in schools, but in every other conceivable aspect of human existence) when asked to "make a choice," chose, by inaction, that their children remain in the Negro schools . . . .

> [S]chool officials adopted, and lower courts condoned, free choice knowing that it would produce fewer Negro students in white schools, and [thus] less injury to white sensibilities than under [other approaches].[49]

The Gould school district, said the *Raney* brief,

> adopted a method whose success depended on the ability of Negroes to unshackle themselves from the psychological effects of the dual system of the past, and to withstand the fear and intimidation of the present and future. Only the "choice" plan selected by the board . . . gives undue weight to the very psychological effects of the dual system that this Court found unconstitutional in *Brown* v. *Board of Education.*[50]

The *Green* trilogy provided the occasion, then, for a bold advance in desegregation jurisprudence by the appellants. Yet it was not clear that such intricate remedial contentions were necessary to the resolution of at least two of the cases at bar. For as any informed observer knew, and as the Defense Fund lawyers did not forebear to point out, freedom of choice, notwithstanding its ingenious capacity to hurt, was nothing more at bottom than another version of the old southern shell game, an absurdly contrived method for dodging effective compliance with *Brown.*

The Virginia and Arkansas situations certainly strained credulity. There were only two schools in each district, and no pattern of residential segregation. Nonetheless, when officials were forced to go beyond pupil placement, they eschewed the simple zoning arrangement used in so many southern communities before *Brown*, and certain, in both New Kent and Gould, to produce considerable integration. They set up instead a mechanism which continued duplication of many facilities, and entailed far greater administrative problems, but preserved an all-black school. In presenting the Gould case to the Supreme Court, Defense Fund counsel Jack Greenberg underscored these absurdities of freedom of choice.

> Now, it might be argued that . . . freedom of choice was perhaps justified as the best available alternative to reach desegregation; or, it might be argued that freedom of choice was more economical or simpler to administer, but the record indicates quite the contrary.

> They are running two sets of science rooms. They're running two auditoriums and gymnasiums; two sets of cafeterias under the new system. It would be far more economical to divide . . . the school facilities . . . .[51]

Louis Claiborne, arguing for the United States government, amicus curiae, also came down hard on the incongruities presented by the choice option.

> It seems to be educational nonsense. It's a pure haphazard system. And, of course, it is an administrative nightmare, if it works as it should, in theory, because not only do you have form letters to send out, receive, tabulate, count—all of which would be unnecessary if the school board simply assigned, as it used to, on the basis of residence—but the results are unpredictable from year to year.

> Of course, the fact is that freedom of choice is not supposed to work toward desegregation. If it did, it would be self-defeating, from the point of view of its authors, because pretty soon the white school to which all the Negroes would transfer would become overcrowded. The Negro school would have to be closed. And the whole theory of freedom of choice would be ended and there would be no free choice.

> There would then have to be compulsory assignments on the basis of proximity to schools. This fact alone shows that freedom of choice is not supposed to work, in the sense of achieving desegregation. It is calculated on the theory that the whites will all choose to attend the white schools, and that very few Negroes will overcome the burden and have the courage to take the adventure into a school where they have been shunned, where they don't expect to be welcome.[52]

The Jackson geographic zoning and free transfer scheme was ostensibly more plausible, and in arguing that case counsel James Nabrit took care to stress the shortcomings even of unsullied impartiality.

> [T]he policy of neutrality is not good enough to undo what they've done in a community like this. After all, Tennessee school segregation laws, when you think about them, were really significant. They were criminal statutes in Tennessee. It was a crime. You could get six months in jail for running an integrated school. A policy like that is significant to the public, and it can't be uprooted by a "hands-off," laissez-faire attitude.[53]

Not that Nabrit was prepared to concede the Jackson plan's fairness. He admitted that the free transfer option displayed "a gloss of neutrality,"[54] but argued that previous findings of discrimination in administering it confirmed its obvious intent: at an earlier phase of the controversy, District Judge Bailey Brown had found that the school board denied African-American children the right to transfer from all-black to majority white schools, while allowing white students to escape majority black institutions. Beyond that, however, Nabrit suggested that the transfer scheme should stand or fall, as should any desegregation provision, by the results it produced. And from that perspective, it was "a segregationist plan," because, in its implementation, "it groups all Negroes together."[55] Acceptance of such remedial logic, it seemed, would require the Court to repudiate *Goss.*

IV

The justices displayed curiosity about the larger issues contested in the *Green* trilogy. They questioned counsel on both sides about the requirement of "compulsory integration." Justice Black even raised the issue, at some length, of whether denying students freedom of choice in school selection did not deprive them of equal protection of the laws, a conclusion which would have invalidated thousands of neighborhood plans throughout the country.

Yet the Court's inquiries conveyed, above all, an unappeasable skepticism about the honesty of the plans before them. This was accompanied by a brusque impatience with the authorities' tardiness in offering relief for past discrimination, an attitude intensified, most likely, by a belief that the Court itself shared in the responsibility for the stalling. At any rate, counsel for the school boards bore the brunt of repeatedly tough questioning. A few of the exchanges with Jackson school counsel Russell Rice catch the tone of the oral proceedings.

> MR. JUSTICE MARSHALL: [Y]ou realized that this [transfer plan] was allowing for the individuals on their own to use their racial prejudice to determine which school they would go to?

MR. RICE: I don't know that I realized that at all, Your Honor.

MR. JUSTICE MARSHALL: Didn't you realize that there were some white people living next door to that Negro high school that wouldn't go there?

MR. RICE: I had no idea. We didn't know what would happen . . . .

MR. JUSTICE MARSHALL: What do you think happened, if there are none there?

MR. RICE: They didn't wish to go there, Mr. Justice Marshall? . . .

MR. JUSTICE MARSHALL: You didn't realize that a white citizen in Jackson, Tennessee, might not want to go to the Washington-Douglass School, did you?

MR. RICE: I was reasonably sure—

MR. JUSTICE MARSHALL: Especially if it was Booker T.?

MR. RICE: —I was reasonably sure that the white people wouldn't want to go there, yes, sir.

MR. JUSTICE MARSHALL: And you knew that when you adopted the plan?[56]

✳ ✳ ✳ ✳ ✳ ✳ ✳ ✳ ✳ ✳ ✳ ✳

MR. CHIEF JUSTICE WARREN: Is there any reason why you couldn't have divided the City a little differently, so it wouldn't find all the Negroes, or most of the Negroes in one district, and most of the whites in another?

MR. RICE: I assume not; yes, sir.

MR. CHIEF JUSTICE WARREN: Why did they [not] do that, then?[57]

In conference, the justices voted 8-1 to nationalize the law of the Fifth Circuit. Justice Black originally favored affirmance of the lower court decisions, but went along with his colleagues in the end.[58]

Chief Justice Warren assigned Justice William Brennan to write the opinions, and Brennan sought to cast them, particularly the lead one for *Green* v. *New Kent*

County, in the mold of *Brown I*—"short, pungent, and to the point."[59] His language, however, was more reminiscent of Judge Wisdom and Professor Black than of his chief.

> The stigma of inferiority which attaches to Negro children in a dual system originates with the State that creates and maintains such a system. So long as the racial identity ingrained, as in New Kent County, by years of discrimination remains in the system, the stigma of inferiority likewise remains.[60]

Such language evokes less the emotions internalized by children because of segregation than the humiliating disparagement segregation represents in its very essence. Justice Brennan sketches more a portrait of that racial insult which is the most urgent reason for integration, than a picture of psychological deprivation.

The justice articulated the same view in the Jackson case. "Only by dismantling the dual system, to purge the racial identity ingrained in the system by years of discrimination, can the stigma of inferiority that works to deny the Negro child equal educational opportunity be effectively eliminated."[61]

This distinction between types of harm, if such is what Justice Brennan intended, carried no significance for Justices Byron White and John Harlan. They saw the Brennan draft as echoing the psychological conclusions of *Brown I*, and they refused to go along with it. "White . . . said that in his view modern sociological and psychological data did not support" the analysis in *Brown*, "and that, had he been on the Court in 1954, he would not have agreed with the opinion's famous footnote 11."[62] Chief Justice Warren, however, indicated distaste for any "fooling around"[63] with Brennan's original effort; he "preferred the first version, with its stronger references to *Brown*"[64] (as, apparently, he interpreted his colleague's language). But the chief justice acquiesced in Brennan's eventual decision to delete the disputed passages because he continued to hold strongly to the view that there must be no break in the Court's unanimity in school cases. The only echo of footnote 11 retained in any of the final drafts is a reference at 391 U.S. 438 to the "harm . . . compounded" by "perpetuation of the unconstitutional dual system."

Unanimity exacted its price in *Green* v. *New Kent County*. Drained of its most meaningful language, the Court's unanimous opinion possesses the brevity of *Brown I*, but none of Warren's directness. *Green's* tone is tortured, even disingenuous, as would befit a product from which something essential has been deleted. The decision ultimately leaves no doubt that lower courts can now accept only desegregation plans resulting in substantial integration, and that this command is not limited merely to freedom of choice plans. "The burden on a school board today," the opinion decrees, "is to come forward with a plan that promises realistically to work, and promises realistically to work *now*."[65] Local officials, it holds, in language cribbed from the Fifth Circuit affirmance in *Jefferson*, must "convert promptly to a system without a 'white' school and a 'Negro' school, but just schools."[66]

Yet *Green* never acknowledges openly that "integration" and "desegregation" are being "use[d] interchangeably." It is markedly reluctant to face up to the revolution in constitutional law it has sanctioned. Indeed, Justice Brennan sharply rebuts the school board's charge that he is demanding compulsory integration. Such an argument, he proclaims, "ignores the thrust of Brown II," which called for "the dismantling of well-entrenched dual systems," imposed upon local officials "the affirmative duty . . . to convert to a unitary system in which racial discrimination would be eliminated root and branch . . . .The constitutional rights of Negro school children articulated in Brown I permit no less than this; and it was to this end that Brown II commanded school boards to bend their efforts."[67]

The problem with such language, however emphatic, is that none of it clarifies what is actually going on in *Green* and its companions. None of it confronts and exorcises the Briggsian notion of remedy. We simply learn from *Green* a few paragraphs after these assertions that New Kent County has flunked the test of compliance, because 85% of its African-American children continue to attend the county's all-black school. "In other words, the school system remains [an unconstitutional] dual system."[68] Clearly, this can be true only if a "dual system" now means a system marked by insufficient racial mixing, but nowhere does Justice Brennan come out and say so.

Similarly, in dispatching the plan for Jackson, Tennessee, which involved the free transfer provisions, Justice Brennan managed to recast the language of *Goss* to suit the Court's new mood. In *Goss*, the justices had struck down a minority to majority transfer provision, but suggested that a neutral transfer option, free from any racial taint, would pass muster. As the opinion phrased it,

> [W]e would have a different case here if the transfer provisions were unrestricted, allowing transfers to or from any school regardless of the race of the majority therein. But no official transfer plan or provision of which racial segregation is the inevitable consequence may stand under the Fourteenth Amendment.[69]

A rule "the inevitable consequence" of which was "racial segregation" referred, presumably, to the kind of rule invalidated in the case—a rule structured on race and designed solely to advance segregation.

In *Monroe*, however, this passage from *Goss* is now taken to refer to results, not structure. Since the Jackson transfer provision "operates as a device to allow *resegregation* of the races,"[70] it is invalid, because increased racial separation will be its "inevitable consequence." That inevitability, though, was a matter of outcome, not of legislative design—much unlike the rule struck down in *Goss*. In fact, some African-American students had transferred to white schools under the Jackson provision. What the Court really said in *Monroe* was that no transfer device which fails to advance integration is permissible. But it is not openly said.

The entire performance in the *Green* trilogy is captured aptly in the words of Professor Lino Graglia. "The Supreme Court . . . .found no need to speak, as had the Fifth Circuit, of requiring 'integration'; requiring only 'desegregation' and the 'disestablishment of the dual system' would serve as well . . . . Humpty-Dumpty, of Lewis Carroll's *Through the Looking-Glass*, who insisted that when he used words they meant exactly what he intended them to mean, no more and no less, would have approved."[71]

The decisions come across, like the oral arguments, mainly as a cry of exasperation against dilatory southern school boards. If there is any rationale at all stated for integration in the *Green* trilogy, it is as a prophylactic measure, the only way to guard against the South's incessant tendency toward evasion and cheating.

In the lead case, Justice Brennan noted pointedly that he and his colleagues were considering a "first step" toward compliance from New Kent County, which "did not come until some 11 years after Brown I was decided and 10 years after Brown II directed the making of a 'prompt and reasonable start.'"[72] He also dwelled on how effortlessly the segregated system in the county "would vanish with non-racial geographic zoning."[73]

In *Monroe* too, Brennan recounted Tennessee's persistent efforts under pupil placement to "continue . . . pupils in their assigned [segregated] schools,"[74] and pointed out the ease with which Jackson authorities could have increased integration by not insisting on the transfer provision. "The Court's holding," said Alexander Bickel, "was tied to evidence of foot dragging and bad faith on the part of the school board[s]."[75]

The new remedial standards decreed in *Green* also lacked specificity. The words directing officials to create "a system without a 'white' school and a 'Negro' school, but just schools," suggests that all racially identifiable institutions must be eliminated, not just black schools. But, as usual with *Green*, the matter is not explored.

Whatever school officials must accomplish, however, they must accomplish it "now." The justices made this quite apparent the next year, when they brushed aside a Fifth Circuit decree granting a sixty day delay in implementing desegregation plans in Mississippi. "Under explicit holdings of this Court," said the one paragraph decision in *Alexander* v. *Holmes County Board of Education*, "the obligation of every school district is to terminate dual school systems at once . . . ."[76]

V

Meanwhile, the Court had moved decisively in an area of school law less publicized than student assignment, but vital to the remedial process: desegregation of educational personnel, especially of teachers. In this area, its orders were blunt and precise.

The demand for such desegregation did not arise in the earliest lawsuits brought after *Brown II*. By about 1960, though, plaintiffs were arguing regularly that the racial division of southern teachers and school staff must end as part of legitimate compliance. The first full-dress exploration of this issue found in the federal reports occurred before Judge Harold Carswell in the northern district of Florida. Thurgood Marshall, among others, maintained that while *Brown II* made no direct reference to faculty or staff desegregation, the decision clearly implied the need for action, in its emphasis on dismantling dual school *systems*, and in its specific mention of "personnel." But *Brown I* supplied even more potent support for ending segregation of personnel, Marshall believed. His elaboration of this point contained one of the frankest meditations found in early school law on what African-Americans saw as the palpable, quite uncomplicated evil which really lay behind segregation.

Like racial assignment of students, Marshall asserted, "[a]ssignment of school personnel on the basis of race and color" was also "predicated on the theory that Negroes are inherently inferior to white persons."[77]

> The plaintiffs, and members of their class, are injured by the policy of assigning teachers, principals and other school personnel on the basis of the race . . . of the children attending a particular school . . . . [This practice rests on the view] that Negro teachers, Negro principals and other Negro school personnel are inferior to white teachers, white principals and other white school personnel and, therefore, may not teach white children.[78]

Such assertions made it clear that the aims of the plaintiffs in this area left little room for fine-spun distinctions between "desegregation" and "integration." The only way to end the policy of "assigning teachers, . . . and other school personnel on the basis of race," quite obviously, was to send African-American teachers to teach white students.

Predictably, Judge Carswell brushed aside plaintiffs' arguments, especially the one about the "irreparable injury"[79] students suffered because of the racial placement of teachers. The students could "no more complain of injury" from these assignments, he felt, than from "the assignment . . . of teachers who were too strict or too lenient."[80] The judge also ruled that student plaintiffs possessed no legal standing to bring a suit affecting the rights of teachers, and he struck the entire personnel section of the complaint before trial even began.

A Fifth Circuit panel found Judge Carswell's action unduly peremptory.[81] He should at least have considered at trial the relation of personnel desegregation to the aims of *Brown I* and *Brown II*, it held. Judges in the Sixth Circuit agreed, ruling in 1962 that while pupils might not formally possess standing to "assert . . . [the] constitutional rights of . . . teachers and others,"[82] courts must allow them to claim "that continued assigning of teacher personnel on a racial basis impairs *the students' rights* to an education free from any consideration of race."[83]

None of these decisions actually required desegregation of faculty and staff. On the contrary, they yielded to the trial judge total authority to grant or withhold relief. "Within his discretion," said a Sixth Circuit panel, "the District Judge may determine when, if at all, it becomes necessary to give consideration to [personnel deseg-regation]."[84]

The situation changed somewhat with the promulgation of the first set of HEW guidelines, pressuring school boards to "provide assurance that steps will be taken to remove racial discrimination in assignment of teaching personnel."[85] Judge Wisdom gave general endorsement to these guidelines in *Singleton I*, though saying nothing directly about faculty, and, in the first incarnation of *Kemp* v. *Beasley*, Judge Gibson recognized "the validity of the plaintiffs' complaint regarding the Board's failure to integrate the teaching staff."[86] He assured them "that this is a sit-uation which will be corrected,"[87] without supplying any specifics.

The Richmond freedom of choice decision, however, stuck to the beaten path, upholding a relief plan in which the trial judge ignored contentions of faculty and staff segregation. The district court, felt Judge Haynsworth, obviously preferred to concentrate on "direct measures . . . to eliminate all . . . discrimination in the assign-ment of pupils," and possessed "a large measure of discretion" in determining the propriety of additional steps, especially since there had been no detailed inquiry in the lower court "as to the possible relation, in fact or in law, of teacher assignments to discrimination against pupils."[88] The matter "need not be determined" while it remained "speculative."[89] At this point in 1965, faculty and staff desegregation could best be described as reposing in a pre-*Brown* state.

On November 15 of that year, however, the Supreme Court finally brought teachers, and, by implication, other staff, into the post-1954 era.[90] Officially, the Court merely forced the district judge in Virginia to rescind his action approving desegregation plans for Richmond, "without considering, at a full evidentiary hear-ing, the impact on those plans of faculty allocation on an alleged racial basis."[91] The justices went on, however, to sharply delimit the scope of the required hearing, and, in the process, to significantly broaden the reach of school desegregation law. "There is no merit," said the brief opinion, "to the suggestion that the relation between faculty allocation on an alleged racial basis and the adequacy of the deseg-regation plans is entirely speculative."[92] In other words, whether faculty segregation disadvantaged African-American students and sabotaged the compliance process no longer qualified as an open question. Upon remand, therefore, the district judge was empowered only to ascertain if "faculty allocation on [a] . . . racial basis" happened to exist in Richmond, and to correct the situation. The Fourth Circuit quickly pro-vided a definitive gloss on this phase of *Bradley*. "We read the decision," said Judge Albert Bryan, "as authority for the proposition that removal of race considerations from faculty selection and allocation is, as a matter of law, an inseparable and indis-pensable command within the abolition of pupil segregation in public schools . . . ."[93]

Southern courts reacted in varying ways to the new dimension of compliance with *Brown*. The remarkable Judge Bohanon, later backed up by the Tenth Circuit, pushed the command quickly to its ultimate limit: assignment of teachers should result in the racial composition of each faculty in a school system being approximately equal to the system's overall racial composition.[94]

Another district judge, in Virginia, provided a most incisive justification for this remedy. If state authorities had assigned teachers to schools on a neutral, non-racial basis in the first place, Judge Thomas J. Michie argued, those teachers, unlike their students, might "have been as evenly distributed throughout the various schools in the system as, for want of a better analogy, those teachers with blue eyes or cleft chins."[95] Consequently, a requirement of approximate racial balance, while not able to restore the precise, and unknowable, situation which would have prevailed but for discrimination, represented a reasonable form of redress, and no educational value of overriding importance stood in the way of it. "Unlike the pupil situation," Judge Michie noted, there were no unrestricted "'freedom of choice' plan[s]"[96] for teachers. (Nor did neighborhood residential patterns create a justification for racially skewed teacher assignments, as they might in the assignment of students.)

Judge Michie's superiors on the Fourth Circuit Court of Appeals, opted, however, for a quasi-Briggsian view of *Bradley's* demands concerning faculty desegregation. An *en banc* gathering in early 1967 approved a consent decree for Charles City County, Virginia, laying down criteria for non-discrimination in teacher hiring and placement, and even indicating a willingness to move toward positive integration of faculties. But the decision required no definite outcomes.[97] Several district judges, including the one in Richmond, accepted similar plans.[98] (Five years later, 45 schools in Richmond still had virtually all-black or all-white faculties.)

Decisions in the Fifth Circuit displayed similar caution at first, contenting themselves with demands that faculties and staff not be exclusively "composed of members of one race."[99] But by 1967, the circuit was governed by the *Jefferson County* decree, which hewed to HEW's revised guidelines, and to new provisions they had formulated on faculty desegregation.[100] Though silent on the exact amount of racial diversity required, these new directives were interpreted by Judge Wisdom to mean that authorities must immediately reassign teachers "so that more than one teacher of the minority race (white or Negro) shall be on a desegregated faculty."[101] The decree stressed that the tenure position of many teachers, and the preference in assignment it often gave them, "shall not be used as an excuse for failure to comply with this provision."[102]

More important, Judge Wisdom ordered establishment of a long-term program for dealing with faculty which went beyond the proscription of only identifiably black schools he had decreed for student assignment. School boards, he held, "shall establish as an objective that the pattern of teacher assignment to any particular school not be identifiable as tailored for a heavy concentration of *either* Negro or white pupils in the school."[103]

Meanwhile, the Eighth Circuit was exploring the ground charted by the Tenth. Two complementary opinions of 1967 endorsed "[n]umbers and percentages"[104] as an approach to faculty desegregation "which comports with *Brown*,"[105] even though neither opinion saw fit as yet to impose such numbers. They "are not the ultimate answer," said Judge Harry Blackmun, "but, up to a point, they touch upon realities."[106]

The next year, District Judge Frank Johnson of Alabama decided to take the plunge. After three years of frustration in dealing with the school officials of Montgomery, Judge Johnson concluded that indefinite criteria encouraged evasion of faculty desegregation, particularly since many of the school administrators expressed perplexity as to their proper course in the absence of concrete direction. The judge unmistakably provided direction in March of 1968.

> The school board will accomplish faculty desegregation by hiring and assigning faculty members so that in each school the ratio of white to Negro faculty members is substantially the same as it is throughout the system. At present, the ratio is approximately 3 to 2.[107]

This numerical distribution need not come about at once; "gradualism" was "contemplated by this Court in accomplishing [the] 'ultimate objective.'"[108] For the 1968–69 school year, the decision demanded only that schools with fewer than twelve faculty have on them "at least two full-time teachers"[109] of the race in a minority at the school (later reduced to one), and that schools with more than twelve faculty attain a one-sixth minority representation. (It did order immediate implementation of the 3–2 ratio for substitute and student teachers.)

A Fifth Circuit panel overturned the long-range aspect of Judge Johnson's order, rejecting what Judge Walter Gewin referred to as the "fixed mathematical ratio"[110] it employed. The majority on the panel still thought it wise not "to tinker with the model decree" in *Jefferson County*.[111] Judge Homer Thornberry, who had joined Judge Wisdom in the *Jefferson County* opinion, dissented. A petition for *en banc* rehearing was turned down on a tie vote; among those favoring the rehearing were Judge Wisdom and Chief Judge John Brown.[112]

In a unanimous decision of June 2, 1969, the Supreme Court overruled the Fifth Circuit, reinstated Judge Johnson's complete order, and definitively settled the matter of faculty desegregation.[113] Justice Hugo Black's opinion in the *United States* v. *Montgomery County Board of Education* exhibited more precision than *Green*, because of the nature of the issues involved. Yet it too breathed a remote, unrevealing air, for Justice Black never touches the matter of how requiring numerical equality in teaching assignments comports with the past violations being addressed. The Courts' action, as in *Green*, seemed largely a response to the recalcitrance of Alabama school officials. Two-thirds of the opinion reviews Judge Johnson's tribulations in seeking compliance. The judge is mentioned by name throughout, an unusual occurrence in Supreme Court reports, and is understandably praised for his "patience and wisdom."[114] The result in *Montgomery County* represents a vindication of this courageous jurist as much as anything else.

Otherwise, Justice Black pronounced it sensible for the district court order to use numbers in a situation where "school officials themselves indicated the need for more specific guidelines,"[115] and denied that Judge Johnson was imposing any "fixed mathematical ratio" upon the Montgomery faculties. His long-term order represented merely a target, which the judge would, and had, adjusted to accord with educational or logistical realities. To dispense with the order would take from the trial court "some of its capacity to expedite, by means of specific commands"; and certainly, Judge Johnson was not proposing racial balance as a general constitutional requirement "in every single school under all circumstances."[116]

So began, at the Supreme Court level anyway, the debate in school desegregation law over the supposed distinction between "quotas"—defined specifically in this area as "racial balance"—and mere "goals" tending toward that end. The discussion in *Montgomery County* illustrated the shortcomings on each side of the argument. Justice Black was surely correct in maintaining that Judge Johnson's ratios were not "absolutely rigid or inflexible,"[117] as the Court of Appeals implied; and obviously they did not point to any constitutional duty beyond complying with *Brown*. But perfect proportions would seldom materialize in a real-life educational situation such as this one, and as a basic remedial guide racial balance was exactly what was being required, and approved, in *Montgomery County*. As Judge Harvie Wilkinson notes, "The justices, in effect, had sanctioned minimum racial quotas in the public workplace without any independent discussion of the merits of such a course."[118]

United States v. *Montgomery County Board of Education* constituted the last word on faculty desegregation. In the more explosive realm of student assignment, the riddles of *Green* remained unsolved.

I. *JEFFERSON COUNTY*

The Fifth Circuit's affirmance of Judge Wisdom's seminal opinion boiled his analysis down to a few simple commands, which hinted at goals more ambitious even than he had projected. Judges Walter Gewin and Griffin Bell expressed, in dissent, their incredulity at this remedial demarche.

1. THE FIFTH CIRCUIT'S AFFIRMANCE (380 F. 2d 385: 1967)

School desegregation cases involve more than a dispute between certain Negro children and certain schools. If Negroes are ever to enter the mainstream of American life, as school children they must have equal educational opportunities with white children.

The Court holds that boards and officials administering public schools in this circuit have the affirmative duty under the Fourteenth Amendment to bring about an integrated, unitary school system in which there are no Negro schools and no white schools—just schools. Expressions in our earlier opinions distinguishing between integration and desegregation must yield to this affirmative duty we now recognize. In fulfilling this duty it is not enough for school authorities to offer Negro children the opportunity to attend formerly all-white schools. The necessity of overcoming the effects of the dual school system in this circuit requires integration of faculties, facilities, and activities, as well as students. To the extent that earlier decisions of this Court . . . conflict with this view, the decisions are overruled . . . .

Freedom of choice is not a goal in itself. It is a means to an end. A schoolchild has no inalienable right to choose his school. A freedom of choice plan is but one of the tools available to school officials *at this stage* of the process of converting the dual system of separate schools for Negroes and whites into a unitary system. The governmental objective of this conversion is—educational opportunities on equal terms to all. The criterion for determining the validity of a provision in a school desegregation plan is whether the provision is reasonably related to accomplishing this objective.

The percentages referred to in the Guidelines and in this Court's decree are simply a rough rule of thumb for measuring the effectiveness of freedom of choice as a useful tool. The percentages are not a method for setting quotas or striking a balance. If the plan is ineffective, longer on promises than performance, the school officials charged with initiating and administering a unitary system have not met the constitutional requirements of the Fourteenth Amendment; they should try other tools.

2. JUDGE WALTER GEWIN, DISSENTING

I

De Facto and De jure Segregation

The thesis of the majority, like Minerva (Athena) of the classic myths, was spawned full-grown and full-armed. It has no substantial legal ancestors. We must wait to see what progeny it will produce.

While professing to fashion a remedy under the benevolent canopy of the Federal Constitution, the opinion and the decree are couched in divisive terms and proceed to dichotomize the union of states into two separate and distinct parts . . . .

By a process of syllogistic reasoning based on fatally defective major premises the opinion has distorted the meaning of the term segregation and has segmented its meaning . . . . The South is heavily condemned . . . . This area of the nation is variously characterized as "The eleven states of the Confederacy," . . . "wearing the badge of slavery", and "apartheid". [T]he opinion concludes that the two types of segregation are different, have different origins, create different problems and require different corrective action . . . .

It is undoubtedly true that any problem which reaches national proportions is often generated by varying and different customs, mores, laws, habits and manners. [But] differences in the causes which contributed to the creation and existence of the problem in the first instance, do not justify the application of a fundamental constitutional principle in one area of the nation and a failure to apply it in another.

While all the authorities recognize the existence and operation of different causes in the historical background of racial segregation, there are also marked similarities. This fact is noted in the recently released study by the United States Commission on Civil Rights, RACIAL ISOLATION IN THE SCHOOLS, 1967, Vol. I (pp. 39, 59–79) . . . . :

> "Today it [racial isolation or segregation] is attributable to remnants of the dual school system, methods of student assignment, residential segregation, and to those discretionary decisions *familiar in the North*— site selection, school construction, transfers, and the determination of where to place students in the event of overcrowding." (Emphasis added). . . .

The Negro children in Cleveland, Chicago, Los Angeles, Boston, New York, or any other area of the nation which the opinion classifies under de facto segregation, would receive little comfort from the assertion that the racial make-up of their school system does not violate their constitutional rights because they were born into a de facto society, while the exact same racial make-up of the school system in the 17 Southern and border states violates the constitutional rights of their counter-parts, or even their blood brothers, because they were born into a de jure society. All children everywhere in the nation are protected by the Constitution, and treatment which violates their constitutional rights in one area of the country, also violates such constitutional rights in another area . . . . Basically, all of them must be given the same constitutional protection. Due process and equal protection will not toler-ate a lower standard, and surely not a double standard. The problem is a national one . . . .

IV

Percentages, Proportions and Freedom of Choice

Freedom of choice means the unrestricted, uninhibited, unrestrained, unhurried, and unharried right to choose where a student will attend public school subject only to administrative considerations which do not take into account or are not related to considerations of race. If there is a free choice, free in every sense of the word, exer-cised by students or by their parents . . . in accordance with a plan fairly and justly administered for the purpose of eliminating segregation, the dual school system as such will ultimately disappear . . . . If the completely free choice is afforded and nei-ther the students nor their parents desire to change the schools the students have heretofore attended, this Court is without authority under the Constitution or any enactment of Congress to compel them to make a change. Implicit in freedom of choice is the right to choose to remain in a particular school, perhaps the school heretofore attended. That in itself is the exercise of a free choice. The fact that Negro children may not choose to leave their associates, friends, or members of their families to attend a school where those associates are eliminated does not mean that freedom of choice does not work or is not effectively afforded. The assertion by the majority that "[t]he only school desegregation plan that meets Constitutional standards is one that works" . . . simply means that students and parents will not be given a free choice if the results envisioned by the majority are not actually achieved. There must be a mixing of the races according to majority philosophy even if such mixing can only be achieved under the lash of compulsion . . . . Accordingly, while professing to vouchsafe freedom and liberty to Negro children, they have destroyed the freedom and liberty of all students, Negro and white alike . . . . Such has not been and is not now the spirit or the letter of the law . . . .

There is no constitutional requirement of proportional representation in the schools according to race. Furthermore, since there can be no exclusion based on race, proportional limitation is likewise impermissible under the Constitution . . . .

V

Enforced Integration . . . .

If the alleged *Briggs* dictum is so clearly erroneous and constitutionally unsound, it is difficult to believe that it would have been accepted for a period of almost twelve years and quoted so many times . . . . If the majority is correct, it is entirely likely that never before have so many judges been misled, including judges of this Court, for so long by such a clear, understandable, direct, and concise holding as the language in *Briggs* which the opinion now condemns. The language is straightforward and simple . . . .

It is interesting also to observe that the Supreme Court has never disturbed the *Briggs* language, although it has had numerous opportunities to do so . . . .

The majority rule requiring compulsory integration is new and novel, and it has not been accepted by the Supreme Court or by the other Circuits.

3. JUDGE GRIFFIN BELL, DISSENTING

The plain intent of the [*Jefferson*] opinions is to establish a uniform law for the school systems of this circuit. Thus, the opinions must be tested as laws . . . .

It is fundamental in law making that laws should be fair as between people and sections. The requirement that laws be clear in meaning is also a fundamental. We cannot be expected to obey the law if we cannot understand it. Caligula kept the meaning of the laws from the Romans by posting them in narrow places and in small print—it is no different today when the law is couched in vagueness.

Then there is the matter of personal liberty. Under our system of government, it is not to be restricted except where necessary . . . to give others their liberty, and to attain order so that all may enjoy liberty. History records that sumptuary laws have been largely unobserved because they failed to recognize or were needlessly restrictive of personal liberty. Our experiments with sumptuary-like laws are exemplified by the *Dred Scott* decision, Reconstruction, and the prohibition laws. All failed.

The majority opinions, considered together, fail to meet the tests of fairness and clarity . . . . [They] exceed what is constitutionally permissible under the Fourteenth Amendment. They cast a long shadow over personal liberty as it embraces freedom of association and a free society. They do little for the cause of education . . . .

The mandate of the Supreme Court in *Brown II* can be carried out by the assignment of faculty and students without regard to race, and by affording equality in educational opportunity from the standpoint of buildings, equipment, and curriculum . . . .

But this approach is too simple for the majority. Their view is that something more is required—a result which brings about substantial integration of students.

The mandatory assignment of students based on race is the method selected to achieve this result. This is a new and drastic doctrine. It is a new dimension in constitutional law and in race relations. It is new fuel in a field where the old fire has not been brought under control . . . .

THE DE JURE-DE FACTO DOCTRINE IS UNFAIR

The unfairness which inheres in the majority opinion stems [further] from the new doctrine which the original panel fashioned under the concept of classifying segregation into two types: de jure segregation, called apartheid, for the seventeen southern and border states formerly having legal segregation; and de facto segregation for the other states of the nation. This distinction, which must be without a difference and somewhat hollow to a deprived child wherever located, is used as a beginning. The original opinion then goes on to require affirmative action on the part of the school authorities in the de jure systems . . . . The neighborhood school systems of the nation with their de facto segregation are excused. The Constitution does not reach them . . . .

We should disavow the de jure-de facto doctrine as being itself violative of the equal protection clause. It treats school systems differently. It treats children differently. It is reverse apartheid. It poses the question whether legally compelled integration is to be substituted for legally compelled segregation. It is unthinkable that our Constitution does not contemplate a middle ground—no compulsion one way or the other.

The de jure-de facto doctrine simply is without basis. Segregation by law was legal until the *Brown* decision in 1954. Such segregation should hardly give rise to punitive treatment of those states employing what was then a legal system. The Supreme Court has never so indicated. Moreover, the Supreme Court holding in *Brown* was based on the finding that segregated education was unequal. How can it be unequal in one section of the country and not another? Does *Brown* interdict only segregation imposed affirmatively by law, or does its rationale also include the state action of holding to neighborhood assignments thereby perpetuating de facto segregation? . . .

The real answer is that no such new doctrine or theory is necessary. The schools of the South and border states must do what the Supreme Court has ordered—convert dual school systems into unitary nondiscriminatory school systems. The constitutional power already exists in the courts to see that this is done. This newly discovered source of power tends only to disturb settled doctrine . . . .

The Supreme Court has not said that every school must have children from each race in its student body, or that every school room must contain children from each race, or that there must be a racial balance or a near racial balance, or that there be assignments of children based on race to accomplish a result of substantial integration. The Constitution does not require such. We would do well to "stick to our last" so as to carry out the Supreme Court's present direction. It is no time for new notions of what a free society embraces. Integration is not an end in itself; a fair chance to attain personal dignity through equal educational opportunity is the goal. My view, however, is now lost in this court; hence this DISSENT.

II. THE *GREEN* TRILOGY

While *Green* v. *New Kent County* was the lead case of the 1968 trilogy, the briefs filed in *Monroe* v. *Jackson* tackled more interesting and far-reaching constitutional issues, for *Monroe* concerned whether the obligation to integrate overrode the pieties connected with geographic zoning. The school board brief, predictably, invoked the fleeting authority of *Briggs* v. *Elliott*.

Green was obviously a simpler case than *Monroe*, and if the justices gave Jackson counsel Russell Rice a going-over at oral argument, they were even tougher on New Kent County's attorney, Frederick Gray. Yet they also probed, at times suspiciously, the new logic of compliance offered by veteran Defense Fund counsel James Nabrit and Jack Greenberg. This was the logic the Court ultimately accepted in the *Green* trilogy, though its articulation would have been less opaque had Justice Brennan's original language been accepted.

1. APPELLEES' BRIEF: *MONROE* v. *BOARD OF COMMISSIONERS*

IV

ARGUMENT

a. RELIEF SOUGHT OPENS NEW CONSTITUTIONAL FIELD . . . .

The appeal before . . . this Court is the culmination of nationwide efforts by the real plaintiff in all of these school proceedings to have the Federal Courts command "compulsory integration." The phrase "affirmative duty to disestablish segregation" has been especially coined for the hoped-for purpose of changing by semantics a prohibition into a positive command . . . .

The Plaintiffs in this case are proceeding in the hope this Court will determine that the "end justifies the means," and the exercise in semantics set out above is an ingenious but transparent effort to provide this Court blinders with which to look the other way and declare compulsory integration a constitutional requirement.

The relief sought in the lower Court was an end to actions taken "solely because of race or color." The relief sought by this appeal is compulsory assignment of students based on no other factor except race. This presents a new Constitutional question . . . .

b. IS THERE A CONSTITUTIONAL DUTY TO MIX THE RACES IN PUBLIC SCHOOLS? . . .

The Plaintiff's position is sustainable only if the Fourteenth Amendment requires Negro children to attend schools with whites and requires that they may be made to do so by compulsory racial assignments. This Court and every other Federal appellate court case, except one, have held that this is not required by the Fourteenth Amendment . . . .

[T]he discussions between counsel and members of [this] Court during the argument in the original *Brown* cases . . . clearly indicate that they [were] concerned only with the elimination of discrimination and that free choice and lack of compulsion may result in all Negro or all white schools without condemnation.

The fact that separation of races could constitutionally exist even after segregation based on law is removed was clearly recognized by the parties involved in the original *Brown* cases . . . .

c. JEFFERSON COUNTY . . . .

It is plain that the Plaintiffs in *Jefferson County*, as in this case, were complaining not about State action, they were complaining about the action of the individual members of the class which they claimed to represent. These Plaintiffs arc complaining because individual Negro families are not electing to do with their own children those things which are freely available to them. This is not a Constitutional violation, it is the exercise by a free American of a free choice . . . .or right guaranteed by the . . . Fourteenth Amendment to the Constitution of the United States.

The paternalistic attitude of the Plaintiffs in this case, as evidenced by this appeal, is that they know what is best for every single Negro family in these United States and that these families should not have the legal right to make their own determination . . . .

d. IS THE CONSTITUTION SUBJECT TO REGIONAL APPLICATION?

The Plaintiffs have conceived the rationale that the alleged Constitutional command of integration applies only to States which had a current segregation statute prior to *Brown* . . . . The Fifth Circuit seemingly agreed to this double standard of law in *Jefferson County*.

How do plaintiffs draw [such a] line . . . ? This Court could not say in *Brown* at exactly what point in time segregation became unconstitutional; apparently the development of the art of psychology was related in some way to such point in time. All States had segregation statutes to some extent at one time or another . . . . Until 1949 [for example] Indiana had such a statute . . . . Who is to say that statute did not lay the ground work for present day de facto segregation? . . .

Is this Country ready for a federal system of regional law? Is one State to be judicially declared a "good" state and the other a "bad" state? Are States which today are lawfully carrying on their affairs to be punished tomorrow if this Court declares a new concept of Constitutional law thereby invalidating such State action? We think Mr. Justice Thurgood Marshall expressed the proposition about as well as it can be expressed in argument to this Court while serving as counsel for the plaintiffs in the original *Brown* case, wherein he stated:

> "The next point I want to make . . . is the need for uniform application of our Constitution and all of its provisions throughout the Country . . . . It has never been said on any . . . right that I know of that special exceptions should be made as to one state or the other." [Argument, p. 525]

We concur with Mr. Justice Marshall on that point.

The theory that the "South" must pay its price for having, pursuant to what was then recognized without question as the law of the land, segregated the races in its schools [should be rejected] . . . .

e. COMPULSORY INTEGRATION IS EDUCATIONALLY DAMAGING TO UNDERPRIVILEGED GROUPS AND TO SCHOOL SYSTEMS GENERALLY . . . .

The attempt to legally compel white children to attend [formerly black] schools will produce one immediate result, the white people will leave, to private schools or anywhere else available to them.

The Court can simply look out of the window at the Washington, D.C. schools to see what happens when desegregation places white students in predominantly Negro schools or forced integration occurs—where are the white students in Washington, D.C. schools? . . .

Jackson does not believe it can compel or otherwise force integration . . . . There is no real way out of this dilemma . . . .

The argument can be made that all white children cannot afford private schools and that is true. The poverty area white and the underprivileged white—the Negro has no monopoly in these fields—will remain and there will then be created an integrated school [system] composed of all classes of Negroes and a few underprivileged whites.

2. APPELLANTS' BRIEF: *MONROE* v. *BOARD OF COMMISSIONERS*

I

The Courts Below Applied an Erroneous Legal Standard in Reviewing the Adequacy of the Jackson Desegregation Plan . . . .

Because the Jackson school officials have established an unconstitutional dual system of segregated schools, it is their affirmative duty to abolish the dual system. Abolishing the dual system involves desegregating the all-Negro schools as well as the all-white schools . . . . It is not sufficient for a court to consider merely the abstract constitutionality or reasonableness of a desegregation plan's provisions. The Court should judge whether, when viewed in a practical context, the provisions are reasonably calculated to abolish the dual system of white and Negro schools speedily and effectively and to the greatest extent feasible in the circumstances. [T]he plan must be tested in actual operation "by measuring the performance—not merely the promised performance—of school boards in carrying out their constitutional obligation 'to disestablish dual, racially segregated school systems and to achieve substantial integration within such systems'". (*Jefferson County*, 895.) . . .

The contrary position of the courts below should be repudiated. The essence of the matter is that the courts below have declined to accept the argument that the school board has an affirmative duty to disestablish the segregated system.

The [lower courts] emphasized the well-known dictum enunciated by Judge Parker in *Briggs* v. *Elliott*, six weeks after the second *Brown* decision, that the Constitution "does not require integration". *Briggs* sounded the call for resistance to *Brown*. It was an attempt to narrow the scope of the opinion so as to almost deprive it of meaning. *Briggs* has been argued as the supporting foundation for almost every evasive effort to subvert *Brown* which has come before the courts . . . .

If [a School] Board's duty is to "devote every effort toward initiating desegregation" (*Cooper* v. *Aaron*, 358 U.S. at 7), surely this duty must include something beyond merely refraining from drawing dishonest, plainly arbitrary, or segregationist zones. There is a duty to make a reasonable effort to actually desegregate those schools which the state previously established and maintained for one race only.

Pupil transfer rules adopted as part of a desegregation plan should also be required to meet a similar test. In this case the trial court . . . . left it open to the Jackson system to continue a transfer arrangement by which every white pupil zoned into a Negro school area transferred out of his zone to a white school and thus perpetuated the all-Negro schools . . . . Everyone—all the parties and the courts below—fully understood and expected that this pattern, which has held true throughout the south, would continue and that the all-Negro schools would remain all-Negro, notwithstanding the fact that white pupils did live in the zones designated for these schools. It was error, we submit, for the courts below to approve a transfer arrangement which was thus manifestly designed and expected to defeat the objective of eliminating the dual system . . . .

In the second *Brown* decision, this Court directed that "in fashioning and effectuating the decrees [requiring desegregation], the courts will be guided by equitable principles." The general equity principle is that there is no wrong without a remedy, and therefore equity courts have broad power to provide relief and are obligated to do so. The test of the propriety of measures adopted by such courts is whether the required remedial action reasonably tends to dissipate the effects of the condemned actions and to prevent their continuance. *Louisiana* v. *United States*, 380 U.S. 145 (1965). An example of the application of this equitable principle is in the antitrust area, where it has been held to require the complete dissolution of large national business enterprises which had been created by illegal monopolization, when there was no other way to counteract the effects of such illegal monopolization. *United States* v. *Standard Oil Co.*, 221 U.S. 1 (1910); *Schine Chain Theatres* v. *United States*, 334 U.S. 110 (1948). Similarly, it has been held to require that federal courts supervise the redrawing of state legislative districts when there is no other way to counteract the effects of population disparities in existing state legislative districts. *Reynolds* v. *Sims*, 377 U.S. 533 (1964).

[T]his equitable doctrine, as applied to the problem of remedy for the unconstitutional creation and operation of a segregated public school system, requires a school board to undertake affirmative action purposed to disestablish segregation completely, and that the standard for determining the completion of desegregation is that the formerly Negro schools must cease being identifiable as Negro schools. The creation and operation of separate schools for Negroes was the condemned action, and the test of the propriety of remedial action to be required by a court is thus whether it will disestablish the existence of the Negro schools, i.e. integrate Negro students.

3. ORAL ARGUMENT OF FREDERICK GRAY

MR. JUSTICE MARSHALL: Mr. Gray, was [the freedom of choice plan] adopted with any purpose other than to perpetuate as much segregation as you could?

MR. GRAY: Mr. Justice Marshall, let me answer you in this manner if I may. As I conceive the situation in New Kent County, . . . prior to the *Brown* decision with two schools one at each end of the County, . . . there was a fence. There was a legal fence across that County, and the law of the State of Virginia said to the white children, "You go to school A. You may not climb that fence and go to school B." And it said to the colored children in the County, "You go to school B, and you may not climb the fence and go to school A."

And this Court, sir, said to the County: "Take down that fence." And it was taken down by the *Brown* decision. And the School Board said to the children, and says to the children: "There are two schools in this County. Look them over. Regardless of whether you are white or colored, look them over and go to the one that you choose." . . .

MR. CHIEF JUSTICE WARREN: Has there ever been a white child admitted to the colored school?

MR. GRAY: No white child has applied to go to the colored school, no sir.

MR. CHIEF JUSTICE WARREN: Isn't the net result, then, that although they took down the fence they put booby traps in the place of it?

MR. GRAY: No, sir.

MR. CHIEF JUSTICE WARREN: So there won't be any white children going to a Negro school.

MR. GRAY: No, sir.

MR. CHIEF JUSTICE WARREN: Isn't the experience of three years in that County, where there never has been a white child go to a Negro school, isn't that some indication that it was designed for the purpose of having a booby trap there for them, that they couldn't—didn't dare to go over?

MR. GRAY: If Your Honor please, if the free choice of American citizens is a booby trap, then this plan has booby traps.

MR. CHIEF JUSTICE WARREN: Yes. Didn't we say in *Brown* that we couldn't let the feelings of the community delay this "deliberate speed" that we spoke of?

MR. GRAY: But deliberate speed to what, Your Honor? Deliberate speed to the granting of equal protection of the law?

MR. CHIEF JUSTICE WARREN: That's right.

MR. GRAY: Not to the integration of the school system. Not to the integration of the school system.

I ask you, sir, who is the plaintiff in this lawsuit? I think you get to the question there. Who is the plaintiff? Who can stand before the bar of this Court and say to this Court: "I am being denied my equal rights"?

MR. CHIEF JUSTICE WARREN: If I was a Negro in Kent County, I would say so.

MR. GRAY: But, sir, by signing this piece of paper, you may go to either school that the County offers.

MR. CHIEF JUSTICE WARREN: But the social and cultural influences, and the prejudices that have existed for centuries there, are by themselves written into that piece of paper.

✳ ✳ ✳ ✳ ✳ ✳ ✳ ✳ ✳ ✳ ✳ ✳

MR. CHIEF JUSTICE WARREN: When you say to us that there are no community attitudes . . . which would militate against the Negro child saying that he wanted to go to the white school, can you say that to us, honestly?

MR. GRAY: I think, Your Honor, that I can . . . . Race relations in New Kent County . . . are excellent . . . .

MR. CHIEF JUSTICE WARREN: But aren't we entitled to take into consideration what has happened in that County for 100 years before?

MR. GRAY: I don't know what you mean by what has happened in the County for 100 years before.

MR. CHIEF JUSTICE WARREN: I mean you actually had segregation in all things, not only in schools but in everything—your buses, and your trains, and everything else. Where you segregate the races, aren't we entitled to . . . take those things into consideration in determining whether this was an honest effort to desegregate these schools?

MR. GRAY: I think they did take that into consideration . . . . It was a matter of law up until the *Brown* decision, that it was constitutionally permissible to have separate facilities; and this Court had put its stamp of approval on it. I think that what you should do is look at what has happened under this plan.

MR. CHIEF JUSTICE WARREN: Without relation to anything that's gone before?

MR GRAY: To see if this plan is working fairly, look at what has happened under this plan.

MR. CHIEF JUSTICE WARREN: Is it accomplishing the purpose of *Brown* or its progeny, when there hasn't been a single white child going to that school that is entirely Negro? Is that accomplishing any purposes for *Brown*?

MR. GRAY: As I understand *Brown*, its purpose was to strike down compulsory segregation. That has been totally and completely accomplished.

4. ORAL ARGUMENTS OF JAMES NABRIT AND JACK GREENBERG

MR. JUSTICE WHITE: Where there's been official segregation, it should be followed by official integration?

MR. NABRIT: Yes.

MR. JUSTICE WHITE: That is your submission?

MR. NABRIT: Yes, sir. That the policy of neutrality is not good enough to undo what they've done in a community like this. After all, Tennessee school segregation laws, when you think about them, were really significant. They were criminal statutes in Tennessee. It was a crime. You could get six months in jail for running an integrated school. A policy like that is significant to the public, and it can't be uprooted by a "hands-off," laissez-faire attitude . . . .

MR. JUSTICE WHITE: You're apparently—your principle, then, would be limited to those areas where there has been legal segregation?

MR. NABRIT: Well, I think I [could] make an argument in other areas that is consistent with that one, but the argument I make [here] is addressed to such a community.

MR. JUSTICE WHITE: It's a matter of remedy. It's an issue of remedy.

MR. NABRIT: Yes. I think looking at it as an issue of remedy is very illuminating.

✳ ✳ ✳ ✳ ✳ ✳ ✳ ✳ ✳ ✳ ✳

MR. JUSTICE HARLAN: Do you read *Brown* to require, in certain circumstances, compulsory integration?

MR. GREENBERG: I read *Brown* to require disestablishment of the dual school system. There has been, in some of the Court of appeals' decisions, some debate over integration, or desegregation, or compulsory integration. I think that becomes, after a while, a semantic morass. I think the issue is: What are the available alternatives? What are the options a school district may exercise to end up with a school system which is, as far as possible, different in terms of racial composition and racial allocation, than the school system they had before 1954? . . .

And we think the option which produces the greatest departure from the pre-existing situation, should be used rather than the option which produces the least especially where the option which produces the least was adopted with that expectation in mind.

MR. JUSTICE BLACK: Why would it not violate a man's right to enjoy the equal protection of the laws, contrary to the Fourteenth Amendment, to compel him to go to a school that he was against going to . . . ?

MR. GREENBERG: Mr. Justice Black, the typical method of assigning students to schools, before the *Brown* decision . . . , [was] to just assign students to school. And no one has ever questioned that being assigned to a school, even though one might object to going to that school, is a denial of a constitutional right . . . .

MR. JUSTICE WHITE: [Y]our position is that it's perfectly permissible to draw a school line based on racial considerations?

MR. GREENBERG: Oh, yes. I don't think—since the case is all about race—I don't think you can put race out of your head.

MR. JUSTICE WHITE: It was bad to draw school zone lines based on race to segregate, but it is all right—to eliminate that—to draw school zone lines based on race in order to integrate . . . ?

MR. GREENBERG: I would say, as a matter of remedy, yes . . . .

MR. JUSTICE WHITE: Of course you could say that in order to desegregate you should draw school zones on neutral factors, without regard to race at all, but you say: "No, you may draw the zone lines based on race"?

MR. GREENBERG: Just to take a simple hypothetical case, in desegregating a school system, you could draw a north-to-south, or an east-to-west line. One would keep you as segregated as before. The other would substantially integrate. Given those two options, you have to make a choice, and I assume you would take the one—

MR. JUSTICE WHITE: There are a lot of school districts where there are no racial problems at all . . . . And the zone lines are drawn without regard to race. They are based on all sorts of other things, I suppose, such as capacity, geographical factors. And I suppose that even in a city where there are racial problems, where there has been segregation, you could draw school zone lines based on those so-called "neutral" factors?

MR. GREENBERG: Yes.

MR. JUSTICE WHITE: But you think that that would not be permissible, against a background like this? That the school zone lines must be drawn with a racial consideration in it?

MR. GREENBERG: I think you cannot ignore the racial consideration. And I don't think that anyone doing it actually does ignore it. To me it is inconceivable that someone facing a situation in which he's trying to redraw school zone lines, somehow or other puts the consideration of race out of his head. I have heard children play the game in which one tells another, "Don't think of an elephant." And . . . of course—all they do is think of an elephant. Well, you can't say, "Integrate the school system, but don't think about race." You have to think about it.

MR. JUSTICE WHITE: I know, but that assumes you are going to integrate the school system.

5. *GREEN* v. *NEW KENT COUNTY* (391 US 430: 1968)

(With Justice Brennan's Original Language in Bold)

The [New Kent County] School Board contends that it has fully discharged its obligation by adopting a plan by which every student, regardless of race, may "freely" choose the school he will attend. The Board attempts to cast the issue in its broadest form by arguing that its "freedom-of-choice" plan may be faulted only by reading the Fourteenth Amendment as universally requiring "compulsory integration," a reading it insists the wording of the Amendment will not support. But that argument ignores the thrust of Brown II. In the light of the command of that case, what is involved here is the question whether the Board has achieved the "racially nondiscriminatory school system" Brown II held must be effectuated in order to remedy the established unconstitutional deficiencies of its segregated system. In the context of the state-imposed segregated pattern of long standing, the fact that in 1965 the Board opened the doors of the former "white" school to Negro children and of the "Negro" school to white children merely begins, not ends, our inquiry whether the Board has taken steps adequate to abolish its dual, segregated system.

Brown II was a call for the dismantling of well-entrenched dual systems . . . . School boards . . . then operating state-compelled dual systems were . . . clearly charged with the affirmative duty to take whatever steps might be necessary to convert to a unitary system in which racial discrimination would be eliminated root and branch . . . . The constitutional rights of Negro school children articulated in Brown I permit no less than this [.] **[Each child's right to an education in the public schools is "a right which must be made available to all on equal terms." [Brown I, at 493.] Brown I held that purposefully racially segregated public schools denied that right because "separate educational facilities are inherently unequal." The Court stated in plain language why this is so. "To separate [school children] from others of similar age and qualifications solely because of their race generates a feeling of inferiority as to their status in the community that may affect their hearts and minds in a way unlikely to be undone." And this is the very evil of the dual system which must be eliminated:**

> **"'Segregation of white and colored children in public schools has a detrimental effect upon the colored children. The impact is greater when it has the sanction of the law; for the policy of separating the races is usually interpreted as denoting the inferiority of the negro group. A sense of inferiority affects the motivation of a child to learn. Segregation with the sanction of law, therefore, has a tendency to [retard] the educational and mental development of negro children and to deprive them of some of the benefits they would receive in a racial[ly] integrated school system.'"**

The stigma of inferiority which attaches to Negro children in a dual system originates with the State that creates and maintains such a system. So long as the racial identity ingrained, as in New Kent County, by years of discrimination remains in the system, the stigma of inferiority likewise remains. Only by reorganizing the system—extending to pupils, teachers, staff, facilities, school transportation systems, and other school-related activities—can the State redress the wrong of depriving Negro school children "of some of the benefits they would receive in a racial[ly] integrated school system."] [I]t was to this end that Brown II commanded school boards to bend their efforts.

In determining whether [the New Kent County] School Board met that command by adopting its "freedom-of-choice" plan, it is relevant that this first step did not come until some 11 years after Brown I was decided and 10 years after Brown II directed the making of a "prompt and reasonable start." This deliberate perpetuation of the unconstitutional dual system can only have compounded the harm of such a system. Such delays are no longer tolerable . . . . Moreover, a plan that at this late date fails to provide meaningful assurance of prompt and effective disestablishment of a dual system is also intolerable. "The time for mere 'deliberate speed' has run out," Griffin v. County School Board, 377 US 218, 234 . . . . The burden on a school board today is to come forward with a plan that promises realistically to work, and promises realistically to work *now* . . . .

We do not hold that a "freedom-of-choice" plan might of itself be unconstitutional . . . . Although the general experience under "freedom of choice" to date has been such as to indicate its ineffectiveness as a tool of desegregation, there may well be instances in which it can serve as an effective device . . . . On the other hand, if there are reasonably available other ways, such for illustration as zoning, promising speedier and more effective conversion to a unitary, nonracial school system, "freedom of choice" must be held unacceptable.

The New Kent School Board's "freedom-of-choice" plan cannot be accepted as a sufficient step to "effectuate a transition" to a unitary system. In three years of operation not a single white child has chosen to attend Watkins school and although 115 Negro children enrolled in New Kent school in 1967 (up from 35 in 1965 and 111 in 1966) 85% of the Negro children in the system still attend the all-Negro Watkins school. In other words, the school system remains a dual system. Rather than further the dismantling of the dual system, the plan has operated simply to burden children and their parents with a responsibility which Brown II placed squarely on the School Board. The Board must be required to formulate a new plan and, in light of other courses which appear open to the Board, such as zoning, fashion steps which promise realistically to convert promptly to a system without a "white" school and a "Negro" school, but just schools.

6. *MONROE* v. *BOARD OF COMMISSIONERS* (391 US 450)

(With Justice Brennan's Original Language In Bold)

The principles governing determination of the adequacy of the plan as compliance with the Board's responsibility to effectuate a transition to a racially nondiscriminatory system are those announced today in Green v. County School Board, supra. Tested by those principles the plan is clearly inadequate. Three school years have followed the District Court's approval of the attendance zones for the junior high schools. Yet Merry Junior High School was still completely a "Negro" school in the 1967–1968 school year, enrolling some 640 Negro pupils, or over 80% of the system's Negro junior high school students. Not one of the "considerable number of white pupils in the middle and northern parts of the Merry zone" assigned there under the attendance zone aspect of the plan chose to stay at Merry. Every one exercised his option to transfer out of the "Negro" school. The "white" Tigrett school seemingly had the same experience in reverse. Of the "considerable number of Negro pupils in the southern part of the Tigrett zone" mentioned by the District Court, only seven are enrolled in the student body of 819; apparently all other Negro children assigned to Tigrett chose to go elsewhere. Only the "white" Jackson school presents a different picture; there, 349 white children and 135 Negro children compose the student body. How many of the Negro children transferred in from the "white" Tigrett school does not appear. The experience in the junior high schools mirrors that of the elementary schools. Thus the three elementary schools that were operated as Negro schools in 1954 and continued as such until 1963 are still attended only by Negroes. The five "white" schools all have some Negro children enrolled, from as few as three (in a student body of 781) to as many as 160 (in a student body of 682) . . . .

Plainly, the plan does not meet [the Jackson school board's] "affirmative duty to take whatever steps might be necessary to convert to a unitary system in which racial discrimination would be eliminated root and branch." Only by dismantling the state-imposed dual system can that end be achieved. [Justice Brennan's original version of the previous sentence reads: **Only by dismantling the dual system, to purge the racial identity ingrained in the system by years of discrimination, can the stigma of inferiority that works to deny the Negro child equal educational opportunity be effectively eliminated.**] [M]anifestly, that end has not been achieved here . . . . [T]he Board has chosen to adopt a method achieving minimal disruption of the old pattern . . . .

Like the transfer provisions held invalid in Goss v. Board of Education, 373 US 683, 686, "[i]t is readily apparent that the transfer [provision in Jackson] lends itself to perpetuation of segregation." While we there indicated that "free-transfer" plans under some circumstances might be valid, we explicitly stated that "no official transfer plan or provision of which racial segregation is the inevitable consequence may stand under the Fourteenth Amendment." Id., at 689. So it is here; no attempt has been made to justify the transfer provision as a device designed to meet "legitimate local problems," ibid.; rather it patently operates as a device to allow *resegregation* of the races to the extent desegregation would be achieved by geographically drawn zones. [The school board's] argument in this Court reveals its purpose. We are frankly told in the Brief that without the transfer option it is apprehended that white students will flee the school system altogether. "But it should go without saying that the vitality of these constitutional principles cannot be allowed to yield simply because of disagreement with them."

CHAPTER THREE
THE WAY TO *SWANN*

Between 1968 and 1971, the South struggled with the meaning and implications of *Green*, as judges, plaintiffs, and government lawyers debated the degree of integration required for compliance with the decision. Yet this very struggle tore away at the gap between de jure and de facto segregation—a distinction also challenged at this time by other forces in the society.

I

Southern judges, including Judge Wisdom himself, initially read the commands of *Green* as being in harmony with *Jefferson County*, directed predominantly to the elimination of all-black schools. If, in a school district, wrote Wisdom in 1968, "there are still all-Negro schools, or only a small fraction of Negroes enrolled in white schools, . . . then, as a matter of law, the . . . plan fails to meet constitutional standards as established in *Green*."[1] This spelled the doom of freedom of choice plans; circuit courts regularly ordered them scrapped and replaced by geographic zones.[2] The neighborhood schools usually produced by such zoning were not an end in themselves, however. "[L]ike any other attendance plan," neighborhood plans remained unacceptable if they "tend to . . . reinforce the dual system."[3] A Fourth Circuit opinion, issued just after *Green*, held that this was true even of a plan based wholly upon private housing discrimination. "If residential racial discrimination exists," ruled Judge John Butzner, "it is immaterial that it results from private action. The school board cannot build its exclusionary attendance areas upon private racial discrimination."[4]

In practice, however, a compromise evolved, particularly in urban areas, between elimination of the black schools and the use of neighborhood arrangements. School officials were expected to produce such integration as resulted from a neighborhood zoning scheme, bent to yield racial diversity, yet by no means broken. Boundary lines must be juggled in mixed residential areas, and new schools supposedly constructed at spots propitious for promoting racial diversity, but no upheaval of school systems was demanded.

District Judge William Miller, writing in the Nashville case, summarized the alterations in remedy law thought by most southern judges to flow from *Green*. A reading of the decision, he allowed, "shows the lack of vitality of the oft-quoted language in *Briggs* v. *Elliott*."[5] Still, courts had "retreated somewhat" from Judge Wisdom's command that every black school be eliminated, so long as authorities took "affirmative action to maximize integration in all feasible ways."[6] School boards must manipulate attendance areas, to be sure, or pair the zones of contiguous elementary schools—sending the first three grades to one school, and grades 4–6 to the other—when these tactics produced favorable results. But "compulsory bussing of pupils . . . is not required by decisions of the Supreme Court."[7] The exertions of southern defendants were limited to "the area of [geographic] zoning," and to making therein "a conscious effort to change zone lines . . . which tend to preserve segregation."[8] If they fulfilled this obligation, courts could not ask for more, in Judge Miller's view, when "segregation is purely the unavoidable result of *de facto* housing patterns."[9]

Indeed, a Fifth Circuit panel headed by Griffin Bell came up with an improved integration level for Orange County, Florida (Orlando) by insisting on the ultimate neighborhood plan. It forced school officials to discontinue an arrangement allowing variances from strict contiguity for such things as traffic conditions, and to adopt, instead, a "true neighborhood . . . system," one rigidly "assigning students to the school nearest the student's home."[10] Revising the plan in this way, the panel proudly noted, eliminated eight of the eleven all-black elementary schools tolerated under the board's plan.

These manifold variations on the neighborhood theme in 1969 and 1970 brought uneven results to the South, especially as between small and large communities. Thus, the desegregation plan for Clarksdale, Mississippi, where black enrollment totaled 60%, left only one all-black school, and percentages ranging otherwise from 34% to 87% (the next highest was 74%).[11] The sole dispute in Iredell County, North Carolina centered around the maintenance for one year of a single all-black elementary school. The other schools ranged from 6% to 48% black (the next highest was 38%), in a district with a 23% black enrollment.[12]

In the Orange County system, however, 82% white and 18% black, the court's "pure" neighborhood plan sanctioned a more lopsided result. Only three all-black schools remained, but five more were over 90% black, six other schools majority black. Meanwhile, in many parts of Orlando, mere handfuls of African-American students attended schools which were well over 90% white.

In the Memphis case, District Judge Robert McRae responded to *Green* by approving some minor zoning changes which barely put a dent in a system where 55 of the 166 schools were all-black.[13] The equidistant zoning plan accepted by a district court for Houston schools (69% white-31%black) left four of them all-black and 27 more over 90% black.[14] Judge Smith Henley in Little Rock refused to touch elementary schools at all.[15] Obviously, no significant increases in busing characterized such plans. "[T]ransportation of pupils to overcome the racial imbalance caused by residential patterns is not constitutionally required," held Judge McRae, "nor is it a feasible method of desegregation . . . ."[16]

Some federal panels stretched the remedial obligation of school authorities to include pairing of non-contiguous schools and grouping of three or more schools at similar grade levels—clustering, as it was called. The Fifth Circuit touched up the Houston plan in this way.[17] The plan for the Miami area (Dade County) also relied upon such techniques.[18] But neither plan strayed very far from the neighborhood; neither posited cross-district busing. Its modifications, said the Houston panel, lay "well within any reasonable definition of a neighborhood school system."[19] The decision in the Dade County case rejected busing on the secondary school level because of distances of three miles in one instance and five miles in another. Both cities continued with large-scale segregation. A quarter of Miami's African-American students remained in virtually all-black schools, in Houston one-sixth. An overwhelming number of African-American pupils in both cities languished in majority black institutions.

Plaintiffs naturally attacked the failure to eliminate black schools, but their objections often went beyond such blatant shortcomings. They continued to argue for the elimination of all racially identifiable schools. And this position soon shaded into the demand which pushed integrationist ideals to their furthest reach. The attorneys of the Legal Defense Fund began to set out in the late 1960's and early 1970's (though not in every case) the notion that the humiliations of the past could only be counteracted by school systems where the percentage of black and white in each school would approximate the racial percentages of the system as a whole.[20]

The United States Justice Department, now under the stewardship of Richard Nixon and John Mitchell, preferred the more conservative interpretation of *Green* articulated by southern courts. In briefs filed amicus curiae, and in cases the department itself brought, Justice Department lawyers stressed the limits on remedies involving integration as much as their necessity. Even this position represented a shift to the left. During the presidential campaign of 1968, Nixon had vigorously attacked busing, and, in his early days as attorney general, Mitchell told a group of Republican congressmen that he saw nothing wrong with an amendment to the HEW appropriation bill requiring the agency to accept freedom of choice plans as being in full compliance with 1964 Civil Rights Act.[21]

The amendment, proposed repeatedly during these years by Representative Jamie Whitten of Mississippi, died in the Senate, however, and under the influence of Assistant Attorney General Jerris Leonard, head of the Civil Rights Division, the department moved at least toward Judge Miller's position, though no further.

Only "two options" existed in dismantling dual systems, claimed Leonard. "One is racial balance . . . The other is a kind of hybrid neighborhood zoning . . . ."; faced with this somewhat overdrawn dichotomy, Leonard and his colleagues opted for the latter choice, soft-pedaling the option of a more determined assault on all-black schools. "What I am saying is that an honest measure of the compliance . . . effectuated by the Department of Justice and HEW is not tested by a determination of how many black children are in racially balanced schools . . . ."[22]

Southerners were not mollified by these evidences of executive and judicial moderation. Post-*Green* desegregation plans still meant the proscription of attendance patterns tolerated in the North; they institutionalized the dreaded "double standard." Not all southerners reacted with as much fire and brimstone as did Georgia's Governor Lester Maddox. Writing to Justice Brennan in October of 1970, Governor Maddox denounced those judges "who have made, and continue to make, . . . un-American and blantantly [sic] communistic demands upon the helpless and poor." Desegregation ukases, the governor was certain, constituted a principal cause in contemporary society of "deaths, robberies, extortions, beatings, stabbings and shooting."[23]

The governor's social analysis left something to be desired. Nonetheless, *Green* and its aftermath did feed the notion, in both north and south, that no difference now existed between de jure and de facto segregation of school children. Technically, *Green* had no doctrinal application to areas outside the South, for it dealt with the remedial implications of past racial categories. But its practical implications, and those it spawned in the realm of what might be termed social psychology, were potent. In a celebrated speech on the floor of the Senate in February, 1970, Senator Abraham Ribicoff of Connecticut accused the North of "monumental hypocrisy" for tolerating its own forms of racial separation. "[If] segregation is wrong in the public schools of the South, it is wrong in the public schools of all other States."[24]

Senator Ribicoff's jeremiad came in support of an amendment to the Elementary and Secondary Education Act offered by his colleague from Mississippi, John Stennis, which sought to use northern uneasiness to southern advantage. The amendment provided that Justice Department and HEW enforcement of desegregation "shall be applied uniformly in all regions of the United States in dealing with conditions of segregation by race in the schools . . . without regard to the origin or cause of such segregation."[25] While not applying to the federal courts, Stennis' effort did mean that unless the executive branch "was prepared to move out in front of the . . . courts and require desegregation in the North, nothing could be done in the South."[26] The senator's entire enterprise, of course, flowed from the conviction that any distinction between types of segregation was meretricious. "[T]he public schools in many areas of the South are . . . being destroyed," mourned Stennis, while "through a legal fiction only—there is virtually nothing . . . being done in the other States of this Nation."[27]

In opposition, some senators pointed out that northern and southern school segregation were not identical. "Let us remember," noted Senator Jacob Javits of New

York, "that separate but equal was the social order in the South for nearly a hundred years before 1954."[28] The thoughtful Senator John Sherman Cooper of Kentucky, however, hit on the real reason why the South was crying "double standard," and why some northern consciences were guilty.

> There is no holding by the Supreme Court yet, whether de facto situations fall under the 14th amendment and come under the jurisdiction of the courts . . . . In the North, several courts have held . . . —notably in the case of Deal against School board of Cincinnati—that they will not take jurisdiction in a de facto situation . . . . But in the South it has been argued in the lower courts, that because Southern States had before the Brown decision . . . enforced segregation by law, such States and school districts have an affirmative duty to act in situations, which would certainly be de facto districts in the North.

> I would say that the correct interpretation of the [Stennis] amendment, and it should be of the courts, [is] that if they are to move into a de facto situation in the South, [they] must move that way all over the land. If the court holds that a de facto situation is outside the 14th amendment in the North, then the holding should apply to North and South as well.[29]

The Stennis amendment passed the Senate, but was gutted in a House-Senate conference committee; its final, sanitized version defined uniformity as referring "to one policy applied uniformly to de jure segregation wherever found," and another policy "applied uniformly to de facto segregation wherever found."[30] A disgusted Senator Stennis resigned himself to the continuation of the double standard. Mississippi "would be condemned on all fours, all over the State," while New York and Pennsylvania "could not be touched, just because of a legalism."[31]

The congressional debate generated some sparks, though. District Judge Damon Keith quoted Senator Ribicoff's reference to "monumental hypocrisy" in an important decision of early 1970, declaring school segregation in Pontiac, Michigan unconstitutional. Reigning precedent allowed such action by northern courts only if school officials had committed palpable acts of discrimination, so Judge Keith attained his result by collapsing, in effect, the distinction between varieties of segregation. He condemned Pontiac authorities for de jure violations. Yet their principal offense consisted of a disposition to run a neighborhood school system, and failure to make good on promises of integration. "[T]he testimony clearly reflects that the Board of Education *never* considered achievement of racial balance as a factor in setting the original [attendance] boundaries," nor had it ever moved "toward modification, alteration or realignment of boundaries" for that purpose. "When the power to act is available, failure to take the necessary steps so as to negate or alleviate a situation which is harmful is as wrong as is the taking of affirmative steps to advance that situation."[32] Judge Keith directed the Pontiac Board of Education to present "a comprehensive plan for the complete integration of the entire school system."[33]

At about the same time, Judge Manuel Real took a similar, if more aggressive, stance in deciding the first phase of what turned out to be a highly significant desegregation controversy in Pasadena, California. The "racial segregation" condemned in *Brown*, felt Judge Real, and what was often dismissed as "racial imbalance," were actually but "two names for the same phenomenon, racial separation."[34] The two terms, he indicated, were "used interchangeably" in his opinion, since the *Brown* Court had "made no distinction as to Northern segregation or Southern segregation. [It] held, simply, that segregated education is inherently unequal, that it deprived Negro children of the educational opportunity to fulfill all their dreams in this country."[35] Not surprisingly, Judge Real condemned the segregation in the Pasadena system.

II

Meanwhile, other forces were congealing in pursuit of a "single standard" for school desegregation. For one thing, advocates of such a standard gained a prominent national forum with the establishment in 1970 of the Senate's Select Committee on Equal Educational Opportunity, headed by Senator Walter Mondale of Minnesota.

The Coleman Report, for another, had handed considerable ammunition to those who sought empirical proof that all segregation denied equal opportunity. Coleman's conclusions, it was true, related to class rather than to race per se. A complex reanalysis of the data, however, in a 1967 Civil Rights Commission report, *Racial Isolation in the Schools*, suggested the possibility that racial integration could be separated out as a positive factor in academic achievement.[36] Some experts argued that distinctions between race and class made little practical difference in charting school policy. As Professor Thomas Pettigrew, who headed the reanalysis team, told the Mondale committee, "I think . . . that an all black school can be a good school, . . . but the strong element there [would be] social class, and there are simply not enough middle-class blacks to go around."[37] Professor Coleman implicitly endorsed this contention when he noted "that from an achievement point of view" the optimum student population of a school was around "50 percent advantaged in terms of background."[38]

Both Pettigrew and Coleman dismissed the notion of a differentiation between segregations. "From the point of view of effects on children," Coleman told Senator Edward Brooke of Massachusetts, "there is no distinction between de facto or de jure segregation . . . . The effect of segregation on children is quite independent of its origin, that is, whether it arises from law or from residence."[39]

This insight applied, of course, to the South as well as to the North. Indeed, it was in a case skirting the regions, in 1967, that Judge Skelly Wright first centered attention on judicial application of the Coleman Report, using Professor Coleman's

direct testimony, and evidence based upon his research, to order further desegregation efforts in Washington, D.C.[40] Professor Coleman also testified in the early
stages of the *Keyes* case in Denver.[41] His testimony was instrumental (as we shall
see) in a decision invalidating segregation in the black ghettos of the city.

Coleman's report could be pointed in the other direction, though. In Norfolk,
where student enrollment totaled 60% white and 40% black by 1969, school officials decided that the only way to raise minority achievement was to arrange for an
optimum white enrollment of 70% at each school; in a 60–40 system, this would
leave one-third of the African-American students in all-black neighborhood
schools. District Judge Walter Hoffman blessed this concept anyway, thinking the
plan might deter middle class "white flight" from Norfolk, and stressing that
Professor Pettigrew had spoken favorably of it.[42] The Fourth Circuit, while eschewing any exploration of educational philosophy, reversed Judge Hoffman, because,
as the great enterprise worked out in practice, almost 90% of the district's African-
American elementary pupils wound up attending schools more than 90% black, as
did three-quarters of the junior high students.[43]

One of the judges who heard the Norfolk appeal had definite opinions about its
pedagogical aspirations, however. Writing in a case involving Clarendon County,
one decided after *Norfolk* was heard, but before the decision came down, Judge
Sobeloff bitterly attacked the views of Professor Pettigrew. It was an effort revealing of the fact that integrationist philosophies could collide on occasion, for in
Sobeloff's estimation the scheme for creating enhanced educational opportunity in
Virginia ran afoul of the views inspired by Professor Black. The "inventors" of the
Norfolk plan, Sobeloff charged, "grossly misapprehend the philosophical basis for
desegregation."[44] It was "not founded upon the concept that . . . . black children will
be improved by association with their [supposed] betters," though many legitimately hoped that "members of each race will benefit from unfettered contact."[45] But
educational separation by law "is forbidden simply because its perpetuation is a living insult to . . . black children and immeasurably taints the education they receive.
This is the precise lesson of *Brown*."[46] To accept the "Pettigrew rationale" would
"do explicitly what compulsory segregation laws did implicitly."[47]

In any event, controversy continued to swirl around the Coleman Report in the
early 1970's, especially over the complex question of whether resources in
America's schools were in fact substantially equal. A number of scholars maintained that Coleman and his associates had focused too narrowly on physical facilities and teacher qualifications, while paying scant attention to such things as curriculum content and academic standards; this rendered questionable their conclusion
that school characteristics exerted no effect on educational outcomes. The dispute
over this matter, and over other issues raised by the Coleman Report, were thoroughly gone over at a Harvard symposium in 1971, and the results were published
the next year, as *On Equality of Educational Opportunity*.[48]

Like many scholarly controversies, the debate over Coleman's work involved
abstruse questions of interpretation, and much technical data, and if many plaintiffs

and lawyers seized upon his conclusions nonetheless in the late 1960's and early 1970's, other civil rights advocates warned that such recondite and endlessly disputed material could not anchor a solid constitutional case for integration. "[T]here is a great deal in dispute," Professor Paul Brest of Stanford told the Mondale Committee, "as to the accuracy of the Coleman and Racial Isolation Studies," and "I would hesitate to have any constitutional rights turn on evidence one way or the other that is as unclear or as tentative as those reports . . . ."[49] Gary Orfield of Princeton agreed. "Although the evidence does suggest that racial or socioeconomic isolation adversely affects achievement," Coleman's studies raised so many interpretive questions, "that it would be premature to give them much weight."[50]

Professor Brest, and others, leaned toward the view that it was housing discrimination which rendered the distinction between de jure and de facto segregation meaningless. Former Attorney General Ramsey Clark, in league with Senator Mondale, gave the Senate committee a particularly forceful statement of this approach.

> MR. CLARK . . . .In fact, there is no de facto segregation. All segregation reflects some past actions of our governments. The FHA itself required racially restrictive covenants until 1948 . . . .
>
> SENATOR MONDALE . . . .Others also have said . . . that if you probe deeply enough into the alleged de facto situation you find very quickly an official basis for the separation. You invariably can point out . . . several . . . kinds of public acts which provide the constitutional basis for legal action.[51]

The plaintiffs in Cincinnati tried again, in late 1968, to use discrimination by housing authorities as the basis for a de jure case of school segregation, but again the courts rebuffed them.[52] Judge Real in Pasadena, however, refused to accept the approach in *Deal*, and included deliberate housing segregation as part of the case against school authorities.[53]

This rationale for integration, like equal educational opportunity theories, called into question the sanctity of the line between city and suburb. In Professor Brest's opinion, the courts possessed the "power to say, 'You can call this one school district and this another school district, but for [the] purpose of desegregation, we are going to consider them one' . . . . In terms of legal remedies, I think the courts have the power . . . ."[54] The only way, felt Ramsey Clark, to attack the school segregation flowing from "black-minority central cities," and the "white suburbs around them," was "by slicing up these jurisdictions so that they make sense and serve people."[55] Professor Orfield, too, believed school district boundaries "vulnerable to constitutional attack."[56]

Professor Kenneth Clark still felt that it was on the basis of "modern psychological knowledge" that the Court of 1954 had effectively condemned all segregation in public schools, because all segregation "damag[es] Negro children; and [the justices were] specific in the nature of this damage—educational damage and psychological damage."[57] But those insights, he told the Mondale committee, were closely related, as they always had been, to viewing "racially segregated schools from a total concept of a racially segregated society, and to [dealing] with . . . segregation and cruelty in the context of other forms of racial injustice which affect society."[58] Having published, in 1965, a searing historical and sociological study entitled *Dark Ghetto*, Professor Clark sought, in his testimony before the committee, to tie the evils of school segregation very explicitly and very angrily to the deeper currents of racism in America. He felt that as the nation moved from an exclusive preoccupation with southern segregation toward a concern about segregation in northern urban ghettos, "we find an intensification of white backlash in northern communities, black separation, . . . and the phenomenon of an increased intensity and frequency of urban ghetto disruptions."[59] Such developments "may be seen as . . . intensely focused forms of the socially detrimental conditions of segregated schools in a segregated society . . . . Segregated schools and cruelty in American ghettos are . . . the institutionalized and inescapable morality of American racism . . . ."[60].

By 1970, then, it was clear that any Supreme Court pronouncement clarifying *Green* for the South would reverberate in the rest of the country.

III

The controversies the Supreme Court chose for its exercise in elucidation concerned Mobile, Alabama and Charlotte, North Carolina.

Davis v. *School Commissioners of Mobile County* followed the dominant pattern of southern cases since *Green*, indeed since *Brown II*. Mobile authorities, scarcely a model of cooperation, commenced desegregation only in 1963, and their initial plan gave students in desegregated grades the option of "attendance at the school in the district of their residence, or the nearest school *formerly attended exclusively by their race.*"[61] The courts disallowed this stratagem, and after a number of false starts the district drew up new attendance zones, which, in accordance with *Green*, made " a conscious effort . . . to desegregate."[62] The effort was limited, though, by the neighborhood school concept, and the resultant notion that cross-district busing was not required across a major interstate highway dividing the majority of African-Americans in the city from whites. In June of 1970, a Fifth Circuit panel modified, then approved, a Justice Department desegregation plan for Mobile also treating the highway as a legitimate barrier. The plan left eight elementary schools all-black, and two approximately 70% black, serving almost one-third of the younger African-American children. Two of the middle schools were 72% and 84% black respectively; three others hovered at two-thirds. Two high schools ranged at about two-thirds black. Meanwhile, six elementary schools, three middle schools, and two high schools were more than 90% white. This in a city with a student enrollment 58% white and 42% black. "The all Negro student body schools," noted Judge Griffin

Bell, "which will be left after the implementation of the Department of Justice plan as modified, are the result of neighborhood patterns."[63]

A different situation developed in the Charlotte-Mecklenburg school system, 43rd largest in the nation, covering 550 square miles. The school board adopted a geographic zoning plan in 1965, replete with free transfer provisions. This brought racial diversity to the county areas of the system, but the city of Charlotte remained massively segregated. In 1968, over 14,000 of the city's 24,000 African-American students attended all-black or nearly all-black schools. Three months after *Green* and *Monroe* were decided, the plaintiffs in *Swann* v. *Charlotte-Mecklenburg Board of Education* filed a motion for further relief, the plan operating in Charlotte being substantially the same as the one struck down in Jackson, Tennessee.[64]

District Judge James McMillian, a contemporary at Yale of Justice Potter Stewart, admitted that the Charlotte-Mecklenburg board had "achieved a degree and volume of desegregation . . . apparently unsurpassed in these parts."[65] However, the "difference between 1965 and 1969 is simply the difference between *Brown [II]* and *Green* v. *New Kent County* . . . . The rules of the game have changed . . . ."[66] McMillan ordered a new desegregation plan submitted, pointing out that "Counsel for the plaintiff" wanted a pupil percentage in each school approximating the 71/29 white-black ratio of the entire system.[67] The judge then noted cryptically, "This court does not feel that it has the power to make such a specific order"; yet, "if this could be done, it would be a great benefit to the community."[68]

The Charlotte school board found out what Judge McMillan was driving at, when it responded halfheartedly to his urgings. The board promised to close seven all-black schools in the center of the city and transport the students to white schools in outlying areas, but allowed most of them to transfer instead to predominantly black institutions. By the judge's calculations, this left 16,197 of Charlotte's 24,714 African-American pupils attending majority black schools at the start of the 1969–70 school year (the same 14,000 in overwhelmingly black schools). And while this situation was McMillan's primary concern, he also noted that almost 48,000 students were still going to "schools readily identifiable as white," meaning that they had white enrollments of 85% or more.[69]

Unlike the judges in Mobile, and other cities, Judge McMillan was determined to get rid of both identities. Consequently, when further board suggestions failed to go beyond the usual expedient of juggling attendance lines a bit, he issued an order in December, 1969, directing the plaintiffs' consultant, Dr. John Finger of the College of Rhode Island, to prepare a desegregation plan designed to rid Charlotte, once and for all, of its racially identifiable schools. Since a school became "identifiable," under McMillan's definition, when its attendance pattern varied only twenty percentage points from the system's 71–29 ratio, it did not seem entirely unreasonable, though it was not absolutely essential, perhaps, for him to "start with the thought . . . that efforts should be made to reach a 71–29 ratio in the various schools," even if "variations from that norm may be unavoidable."[70]

The Charlotte board did finally submit a completed plan in early 1970, desegregating all high schools but one, and creating in those schools a range of 17%–36% black. At a hearing on February 5, Judge McMillan accepted this part of the plan with one significant modification; he ordered 300 African-American students bused to the high school on the outskirts of Charlotte having only a 2% black enrollment. Noting, however, that the board's approach to the rest of the schools "relies almost entirely on geographic attendance zones, and is tailored to the Board's limiting specifications,"[71] the judge adopted Dr. Finger's plans for the elementary and junior high schools. They relied on pairing and clustering of non-contiguous schools, and, of course, on extensive cross-district busing. By resorting to these methods, Finger got rid of all majority black institutions: the highest black percentage in any elementary school was 41%, in any junior high, 33%. Only a few identifiably white schools remained—one junior high at 91%, two elementary schools at 97% and 91%. For the most part, pupils were "assigned in such a way that as nearly as practicable the various schools at various grade levels have about the same proportion of black and white students."[72]

McMillan made it clear that he was not requiring exact racial balance for Charlotte, which everyone knew from the outset would be impossible to achieve. Nor did he lay down even the goal of racial balance as a substantive constitutional requirement, indispensable to desegregation, as had Judge Johnson. But as a practical matter, eliminating all racially identifiable schools to the extent possible required a pretty good facsimile of such balance in Charlotte. And only if white schools, as well as black schools, fell under the plan, Judge McMillan argued, could the latter preserve their integrated identity—the primary end, after all, of any desegregation remedy. Holding all-white clusterings to a minimum, in his view, was essential in order to avoid the resegregation which came from whites "shopping around for schools."[73] This concern about resegregation explains the order busing the 300 African-American students to the system's only all-white high school.

To carry out Dr. Finger's plan, the district court estimated, would necessitate the busing of 13,300 additional pupils and the acquisition of 138 new buses, at a cost of just over $1,000,000. School authorities claimed they would need 422 new buses to transport over 19,000 additional students, at a cost of almost $3,500,000. All of this arguing assumed that busing for such purposes was permissible, but during the midst of the *Swann* litigation the North Carolina General Assembly passed legislation prohibiting school transportation "for the purpose of creating a balance or ratio of race."[74] (In April of 1970, a three judge federal panel invalidated the law and issued an injunction against its enforcement, pending appeal.)[75]

Judge McMillan justified his busing order by articulating two familiar rationale for integration. The residential separation in Charlotte did not stem from innocent, neutral forces, he contended. Restrictive covenants, as well as discriminatory real estate and banking practices, sanctioned by the state, had trapped African-Americans in a ghetto in Charlotte's northwest corner. Others were relocated there by urban renewal projects, heavily financed by the federal government. Onto this pattern of housing segregation, the school board engrafted its 1965 zoning plan, supplemented by free transfer. These pupil assignments perpetuated and "accentuated patterns of racial segregation in housing"; the transfer plan manifestly resulted in "resegregation" of schools temporarily integrated.[76] "There is so much state action embedded in and shaping these events that the resulting segregation is not innocent or '*de facto*,' and the resulting schools are not . . . desegregated."[77]

But Judge McMillan focused even more urgently on the harmful effects of segregation upon minority student achievement. He cited statistics showing that African-American students in all-black schools in Charlotte scored one to three grades lower on achievement tests than students in all-white schools, but that minority students attending integrated schools scored comparably to the ones in all-white environments. The judge mentioned trial testimony based on the Coleman Report, with its emphasis on "socio-economic-cultural background"[78] as the determinant of academic performance. Yet he blamed racial separation itself for the tragic situation in Charlotte. The terrible disparities in achievement could not be understood "solely" by looking at class, "without honestly facing the impact of segregation."[79] In any event, until segregation ended, it was "idle to speculate" on whether the gaps in performance "can be charged to racial differences or to 'socio-economic-cultural' lag."[80]

The Fourth Circuit Court of Appeals stayed full implementation of Judge McMillan's busing order until it could hear the case, a stay which the Supreme Court refused to disturb.[81] The circuit court's *en banc* opinion, issued on May 26, 1970, paid little attention to Judge McMillan's discussion of educational philosophy, but endorsed his analysis of the "interplay" between segregation in housing and in education, pointedly emphasizing the national implications of this insight. "The fact that similar forces operate in cities throughout the nation," noted Judge John Butzner, "under the mask of *de facto* segregation provides no justification for allowing us to ignore the part that government plays in creating segregated neighborhood schools."[82]

Judge Butzner then announced that in evaluating the district court's plan the Fourth Circuit would adopt a test of reasonableness, a standard resting, it seemed, midway between Judge McMillan's criterion and the one which the Fifth Circuit utilized in Mobile. If a school board put forth "every reasonable effort" to create a unitary system, "an intractable remnant of segregation" should not invalidate its proposals.[83] Under this test, McMillan's substitution of the Finger plan for Charlotte's elementary schools was pronounced excessive, because of the extra busing involved. The circuit court sent the case back to him for reconsideration of the matter, approving the rest of the plan.

Judges Simon Sobeloff and Harrison Winter dissented on the issue of the elementary schools. *Green*, they argued, set feasibility, not reasonableness, as the standard by which to evaluate desegregation efforts. And they thought the plan for elementary school youngsters eminently feasible. Unlike Judge Michie in Virginia, Judge Winter saw no distinction between using arithmetical ratios for faculty and using them for students. If such ratios were employed to bring about faculty integration, he contended, "I know of no reason why the same should not be true to achieve pupil integration, especially where, as here, some wide deviations from the overall ratio have been permitted . . . ."[84]

On remand, Judge McMillan staunchly defended his elementary school orders as reasonable. More than half of all school children in North Carolina already rode buses, he revealed, including 70.9% of those in grades 1–8. In the Charlotte-Mecklenburg district, bus routes for four and five year olds reached 39 miles in some instances; the average one-way trip in the school system totaled an hour and fifteen minutes. Under his plan, those transported to achieve integration would undertake an average trip of seven miles and 35 minutes. The judge stuck to his estimate that 138 additional buses were enough to do the job (90 of them for the elementary school children), and called attention to new testimony from the school system's transportation superintendent, admitting the system had 107 extra buses at its disposal for the 1970–71 school year, and could get 75 more from the state.

His plan most emphatically did not require "racial balance," McMillan claimed, since the desegregation order "expressly contemplated wide variations in permissible school population."[85] This was not a quest for exact numerical congruence, but for "racial diversity. The purpose is not some fictitious 'mix,' but the compliance of this school system with the Constitution by eliminating the racial characteristics of its schools."[86] The judge's defense was accurate, though there is good reason to think that if a 71–29 ratio for every school in Charlotte could easily have been devised, Judge McMillan would have ordered it.

Before remand proceedings commenced, the plaintiffs in Charlotte had appealed the circuit court's refusal to approve the elementary school plan; the school board appealed the circuit's acceptance of the high school and junior high school schemes. The Supreme Court granted certiorari in the Charlotte case, setting it down for argument with the one from Mobile, and with an appeal from the invalidation of North Carolina's anti-busing law. Charlotte posed the most critical controversy, because it tested Judge McMillan's actions moving desegregation remedy law to a higher plateau.

The cases were argued on October 12, 1970. Appearing for the United States government, Solicitor General Erwin Griswold expressed views on busing and its supposed doctrinal justification which may well have squared with his personal convictions, but which were certainly *de rigueur* for an official of the Nixon administration. Griswold approved of Judge McMillan's plan for the high schools and junior highs, but felt that in rearranging the elementary schools the judge arguably sought an improper goal, a conclusion the Solicitor General arrived at largely by conflating the judge's aim and his method. McMillan "may well have acted on the assumption that he was required to produce . . . 'racial balance' *or* what is defined as 'no student may be assigned to a racially identifiable school.'"[87]

On the other side of the issue was an amicus brief submitted by a number of diverse organizations, including the United Negro College Fund and the League of Women Voters. Written by Marian Wright Edelman and Joseph Rauh, among others, it was probably the most systematic statement ever composed of what remains the most compelling justification for integration in the post-*Brown* South.

> In the American historical context, the system of segregation was no less than a massive government-sponsored racial insult to the black people subjected to it, based on assumptions of their intellectual and moral inferiority to white people. The system of segregation, and the official insult it carried with it, was most damaging as applied in the schools, for there it was directed at children of unformed minds and developing personalities, in the public institutions most crucial to their growth. The system was unconstitutional because the history of the Fourteenth Amendment made clear that the framers meant to forbid all official action which injured or degraded black people because they were black . . . .
>
> Thus the black schools of today, identified by their all-black or predominantly black student bodies and by their location in black neighborhoods, retain for the white community which seeks so hard to avoid them the stigma originally conferred by the underlying segregationist assumption that they are for inferior children. But if they still bear that stigma for the white community, so do they for the black community and for the black children who attend them. This being so, assignment to these schools must have for these black children the same ineradicable effects upon their hearts and minds which this Court condemned as the central vice of state-imposed segregation in *Brown I*.[88]

IV

The Supreme Court's consideration of the *Swann* cases, brilliantly recounted in Bernard Schwartz's *Swann's Way*,[89] revealed a group of justices not too sharply divided on outcome, yet all over the lot in terms of the basic principles they wished to see governing school remedies. Indeed, as might be expected in a controversy with obvious national implications, the draft opinions and memoranda circulated in *Swann* rehearsed nearly all of the constitutional rationale in desegregation law previously articulated by lower court judges, by public officials, and by scholars. Some of these rationale inevitably breached the wall between de jure and de facto segregation.

Swann was deemed sufficiently important for Chief Justice Warren Burger to suggest it be discussed at a special Saturday conference on October 17, 1970. As in the original conference on *Brown*, the Court would take no formal vote. The justices followed this procedure at the October 17 meeting, and at another one, held on Thursday, December 3. The discussions revealed, however, a solid majority for affirmance of Judge McMillan's order. Justices Brennan, John Marshall Harlan, Thurgood Marshall, and William O. Douglas strongly favored this course. Potter Stewart, Byron White, and Harry Blackmun seemed willing to go along, with a few modifications. Only the chief justice and Senior Associate Justice Hugo Black expressed disapproval of the district court's actions.

Despite this, Chief Justice Burger took the lead in framing an opinion. On December 8, 1970, he sent his colleagues a draft, accompanied by a memo emphasizing "the importance of our attempting to reach an accommodation and a common position."[90] Burger's draft scarcely represented the vehicle, though, for such a consensus. It came closer to approving the Charlotte board's advocacy of neighborhood schools than Judge McMillan's rearrangement of the system. In many ways, the draft was a last echo of *Briggs* v. *Elliott*.

In setting down general guidelines for desegregation remedies, the chief justice unmistakably revealed the drift of his thinking. "It may well be," he asserted, "that some of the problems we now face arise from viewing *Brown I* as imposing a requirement for racial balance, *i.e.*, integration, rather than a prohibition against segregation."[91] This observation was reinforced by a footnote containing a radical reinterpretation of *Green*. The *Green* opinion, Burger felt, "seem[s] to have been read *over broadly by some as a mandate for integration.*"[92] Actually, it reflected only the fact that "fully desegregated schools will, of course, tend to bring about integration"; but only the *"former is constitutionally required."*[93] Since "racial balance" was equated with "integration," the chief implied strongly that setting up such balance as a remedial standard in achieving pupil desegregation was impermissible, shrewdly contrasting it with faculty desegregation. "Whatever the legal foundations of the mandate to achieve a 'racial balance' in the faculties of each school it is readily apparent . . . that the movement . . . of teachers by reassignment presents very different problems from those concerning pupils. In metropolitan school systems there is no nexus between the neighborhood . . . residence of teachers and the schools to which they are assigned" (the very reason why African-American plaintiffs had demanded faculty integration as the goal of desegregation before they demanded student integration).[94]

These constitutional predilections conditioned the chief's answers to what he saw as the unresolved issues facing the Court in *Swann*: (1) Whether the Constitution did indeed authorize courts to demand a particular racial balance in desegregating a school system. (2) Whether all one-race schools must be eliminated. (3) What limits there might be on remedial altering of attendance zones. (4) What limits there were on busing as a remedial tool.

His treatment of the first issue made explicit the position forecast in the *Green* footnote. "Neither the Constitution nor equitable principles grants to judges the power to command that each school in a system reflects, either precisely or substantially, the racial origins of the pupils within the system."[95] The chief justice feared Judge McMillan had done just that in Charlotte, despite disclaimers, with his talk of variations from a *"norm,"* and, if so, his actions were unconstitutional. The judiciary could not compel school authorities "to construct a system . . . to offset . . . the imbalances resulting from the residential patterns of the area served."[96]

Nor was there any compulsion to eliminate the one-race schools produced by these patterns. Such schools, particularly all-black schools, would inevitably persist in large urban ghettos, "[d]espite the most valiant efforts of school authorities and courts."[97] A majority to minority transfer provision must be available for those African-American students who regarded attendance at identifiably black institutions as a "'badge of inferiority.'"[98] Otherwise, "[u]ndesirable" as the situation might be, "we find nothing in the Constitution . . . that precludes the maintenance of schools, all or predominantly all of one [race] . . . , so long as the school assignment is not part of state-enforced school segregation."[99]

The next section, however, seemed to contradict Burger's favorable references to the neighborhood setup and his equanimity in the face of one-race schools. The chief showed a surprising receptivity to the remedial altering of attendance zones, and even to busing, as tools of the compliance process. "Absent a history of a dual system," school officials were perfectly free to assign students to the schools nearest their homes, or in any other convenient manner.[100] "But all things are not equal in a system that has been deliberately constructed to enforce racial segregation."[101] And repairing the damage could involve sacrifices. "The remedy for such segregation may be administratively awkward, inconvenient and even bizarre in some situations and may impose burdens on some."[102]

Orders for busing, Burger held, at the beginning of the next section, also fell within the permissible scope of a court decree. Objections to it might be valid, he admitted, "when the time or distance of travel is so great as to risk either the health of the children or impinge on the educational process."[103] Still, the "search for solutions is not aided by simplistic slogans for or against 'busing,' as though the term described a uniformly invidious course of action."[104]

As the section on transportation unfolded more fully, however, it became clear that the contradictions in the chief justice's position were more apparent than real. For those "inconvenient and even bizarre" departures from the neighborhood pattern he had spoken of earlier were necessitated, it turned out, only by the gross manipulations of that pattern which were the special province of Jim Crow education: things such as the building of tiny schools to house black minorities in overwhelmingly white neighborhoods, or the deliberate failure to place schools in the center of "mixed" residential areas, since the schools could serve only one race. *This* was what Burger meant by "a system . . . deliberately constructed to enforce racial segregation," and it was transgressions of this sort alone which justified altering of attendance zones.

Thus, in his discussion of busing, the chief justice asserted once again that courts would not give "blanket approval" to racially impartial zoning plans.[105] Then he gave the real reason why. "[S]uch plans may fail to counteract the continuing effects of past segregation *resulting from discriminatory location of school sites or distortion of school size in order to achieve or maintain an artificial racial separation.*"[106]

After the words "artificial racial separation," Burger engrafted an extremely significant footnote, stipulating that "[a]n artificial racial separation *is to be distinguished
from separation flowing normally from residential patterns.*"[107] The entire critical
paragraph read:

> The objective should be to achieve as nearly as possible that distribu-
> tion of students and those patterns of assignments that would have nor-
> mally existed had the school authorities not previously practiced dis-
> crimination. This is not to be read as blanket approval of all "racially
> neutral" assignment plans proposed by school authorities to a district
> court, for such plans may fail to counteract the continuing effects of past
> segregation resulting from discriminatory location of school sites or dis-
> tortion of school size in order to achieve or maintain an artificial racial
> separation. [An artificial racial separation is to be distinguished from
> separation flowing normally from residential patterns.][108]

The sentence introducing this discussion repeated, of course, the oft-cited definition of the purposes judges should seek in ordering equitable remedies. ("The
objective should be to achieve as nearly as possible that distribution of students . . .
that would have existed." . . .) Burger's analysis pointed unmistakably toward the
"distribution of students" existing in 1970 in Chicago or New York.

Why non-contiguous zoning or extensive busing would even be needed to correct purely artificial separations by school officials is not explained, but Burger's
draft held that the web of complicity in creating illegal segregation went no further
than those officials. Constitutional violations by housing authorities, or by state-reg-
ulated banks and real estate agencies, did not figure into the remedial equation.
School cases, he had asserted earlier in the draft, could not "embrace all the residential problems, employment patterns, location of public housing, or other factors
beyond the jurisdiction of school authorities that may . . . contribute to some disproportionate racial concentration in some schools . . . . Too much baggage can
break down any vehicle."[109]

Burger's first draft closed by remanding the *Swann* case to the district court for
"further action not inconsistent with this opinion."[110]

The chief's effort did not go over well with his colleagues. Before he even circulated his draft, two justices had set forth strikingly different constitutional visions.
In a memorandum sent to Burger on November 3, 1970, Justice John Marshall
Harlan supported affirmance of Judge McMillan on the basis of a brilliantly articulated statement of the prophylactic, or guarantee, theory of integration implied in
Green. With the thoroughness and acuity typical of this great jurist, Justice Harlan
expounded the view that a neighborhood system of zoning, producing numerous
racially identifiable schools, could not satisfy the demand for good faith compliance
with *Brown*. The designing of such a post-*Brown*, allegedly neutral system, he
pointed out, involved endless administrative complexities, and endless opportuni-

ties for perpetuating the segregated system, especially the black institutions so pivotal to the old system of educational apartheid. Judicial supervision of this process of desegregation, therefore, would entail the grueling and imponderable task of evaluating "the expression of official policy in the innumerable day-to-day choices which go into the task of administering a local school system, as well as the manifestation of that policy in expressly racial judgments."[111] The only realistic alternative to this assessment of the "motivations" of officials who left pre-*Brown* neighborhood schools intact was "testing compliance by the results of [their] proposed changes," as measured by actual integration.[112]

Consequently, "two considerations—the central role played by the racially identifiable school in the former dual system and the necessity for definite remedial criteria for measuring school board compliance with the Constitution—" required the Court to reject neutral neighborhood zoning as evidence of a "school board's . . . contention that their affirmative duty to disestablish the former dual system is met."[113] Instead, the justices must insist on the elimination of identifiably black schools as the overriding task of desegregation, and where officials tolerated a school with majority black enrollment, they bore "a heavy burden of justifying such assignments."[114]

Yet the persistence of all-white schools, Harlan believed, was also highly relevant in evaluating desegregation plans, largely because such schools could serve as the cutting edge of resegregation. Judge McMillan was fully justified, therefore, in striving to eliminate white schools as well as black schools, and in adhering to his racial balancing scheme for the purpose of doing so. "[T]o the extent that . . . resegregation truly threatens the stability of a desegregation plan, the proper remedy can only be to assign students in substantially similar proportions throughout [a] school system."[115]

Justice Harlan's rationale for demanding integration cut off any attempt to distinguish between de jure and de facto segregation in Charlotte or Mobile, but was not applicable to the problems of the North and West. The justice did not send his memorandum to any of his other colleagues, but, as Professor Schwartz notes, it "put Chief Justice Burger on notice" from the beginning "that [he] could not expect any support from the Justice whom he might ordinarily consider his natural ally."[116]

Justice William Brennan sent Burger a memorandum at approximately the same time as Harlan, persisting in the views he had expressed so eloquently in *Green*. "Separation of the races," he reiterated "was found to be unconstitutional in *Brown* because it stigmatized members of the Negro race . . . .The only way to remove the stigma . . . is to achieve substantial integration."[117] Judge McMillan unquestionably sought this essential end.

Justice Brennan's constitutional standard did not cut directly across regional boundaries. Indeed, in an earlier memorandum on *Swann*, written when the Court refused to vacate the Fourth Circuit stay of Judge McMillan's order, he expressed skepticism about the constitutional principle of equal educational opportunity, spurred, most likely, by the judge's heavy reliance on empirical data. "[T]hough it is possible to read *Brown* as establishing a general principle of equal educational opportunity, which would apply without regard to [deliberate] racial segregation, I do not think such a reading is necessary or even preferable as a guide to deciding school segregation cases."[118] Brennan's own standard, however, could not help but raise severe doubts about whether he would countenance northern segregation, though on grounds extrapolated more from Professor Black's essay than from Professor Coleman's report.

Harlan and Brennan were among those unhappy with the neo-Briggsian cast of the chief justices' initial effort. Brennan sent in a critique on December 30, repeating many of the points made in his memo, and sharply countering the premise from which much of chief's argument proceeded, that the Court's earlier decisions on desegregation left many issues unresolved. "I feel that the cases following *Brown*, particularly *Green* v. *County School Board*, travelled far down the road, so that all we are . . . required to do here is fill in the outline constructed by *Green*."[119] Brennan defended Judge McMillan's order on racial balance as a "rule of thumb," not "an inflexible quota," though in doing so he essentially admitted that the order displayed some of the normative quality the chief justice detected. "Strict compliance with the goal" was not required, yet *"all deviations must be adequately justified by the school board."*[120]

Justice William O. Douglas had also responded negatively to the chief's draft. He wrote on December 10, indicating complete approval of Judge McMillan's actions. Thurgood Marshall did the same on December 22. He sent Burger a draft opinion justifying the district court's remedy by use of the residential discrimination approach, a theory with obvious national implications. In devising its relief, Justice Marshall stressed, the "Court was . . . bound to become aware of the influence of non-school board governmental action on [housing] patterns. It would be . . . hollow . . . indeed . . . to provide a remedy that removed all traces of direct school board action designed to maintain the dual system and to ignore other governmental action, which dramatically affected the schools."[121]

The most significant response to Burger's draft turned out to be the one registered by Justice Potter Stewart. On December 14, 1970, Stewart sent the chief justice a note, saying he harbored "serious reservations about your treatment of some of the problems" in *Swann*. Accompanying it was a draft opinion laying out a justification for integration which had much in common with Justice Harlan's views. Like his colleague, Justice Stewart rejected the proposition that a "'color blind neighborhood zoning plan' . . . is immune from constitutional attack," partly because the problems posed in evaluating such complex plans defied judicial competence, but even more because the attitudes which shaped the formation of a dual system "acquire a formidable stability and imperviousness to change . . . . strong enough . . . [a]t times . . . to survive conscious decisions for change by those in positions of responsibility."[122] The only way to guarantee genuine compliance with *Brown*, therefore, was to "hold that where . . . 'color blind' neighborhood zoning would result in a pattern of school attendance essentially similar to that which existed under the dual system . . . , it is not enough to meet the affirmative remedial duty of the local board."[123]

In a later section of the memorandum, Stewart took up on a point alluded to by Judge Wisdom in *Jefferson County*—the reciprocal relationship which the justice felt existed between school segregation and residential isolation of African-Americans. Construction policies, Stewart argued, both past and present, determined not only the racial composition of schools; they also determined, in some measure, the racial composition of neighborhoods. "[C]onstruction and abandonment of schools influence as much as they respond to movements of population."[124] Judge McMillan found, not surprisingly, that the dual system in Charlotte had been established, and its essence now maintained, by "locating and controlling the capacity of schools so that there would usually be black schools handy to black neighborhoods and white schools for white neighborhoods." But "[s]uch a policy," in Stewart's view, "does more than simply influence the short-run composition of the student body of a new school. It may well promote segregated residential patterns which, when combined with 'neighborhood zoning,' further lock the school system into the mold of separation of the races."[125]

Justice Stewart concluded, however, that many factors besides school board actions, or governmental actions of any kind, created housing patterns. Therefore, it was "not incumbent on the district judge in a school case to alter or even to remedy . . . [these] patterns," as such.[126] Partly for this reason, Stewart could not accept a definition of desegregation mandating the elimination of all racially identifiable schools. Instead, he opted for a standard "less precise," and less demanding, though still certain, in many instances, to disrupt neighborhood arrangements. A school board must "achieve the greatest possible degree of actual desegregation, taking into account the practicalities of each of the means employed."[127] Since Judge McMillan, by contrast, "may have felt compelled"[128] to adopt a racial identity test, Stewart's memorandum closed with an order remanding *Swann* for further consideration of this matter. The ambiguous ending did not obscure Justice Stewart's sympathy for his fellow Yale man's approach. The overall flow of his memorandum represented "a direct challenge to the Chief Justice's draft opinion."[129]

The beleaguered chief sent a revised draft of *Swann* to his colleagues on January 11, 1971, claiming to have taken "into account the views expressed by several of you."[130] Despite these assurances, the second draft differed little from its predecessor, exhibiting the same traditionalist approach to desegregation. Burger endorsed Justice Stewart's discussion of school construction, adding it word for word to his opinion as a new section. He also added material squaring the Court's actions with the 1964 Civil Rights Act. Nonetheless, the heart of Burger's remedial position remained: the reinterpretation of *Green*, the tolerance for one-race schools, and the operating standard which justified that tolerance—the need to correct only contrived racial separations. Indeed, Burger moved the paragraph on contrasting species of separation, with its explosive footnote, from the section on transportation to the section on remedial altering of attendance zones, where, logically, it belonged.[131] Now the warning about remedial measures which might have to be "awkward, inconvenient and even bizarre" is followed almost immediately by the assurance that such concoctions would come into play only to counteract the "discriminatory location of school sites or distortion of school size in order to . . . maintain an artificial racial separation," so clearly "to be distinguished from separation flowing normally from residential patterns." The second draft also persisted in dismissing housing violations by state officials as irrelevant to school desegregation.

The chief's limited revisions did nothing to quell the revolt building against him. On January 12, 1971, Justice Marshall submitted his memorandum to the rest of the justices, defending use of housing violations in formulating school desegregation remedies. The next day, Justice Douglas distributed a draft dissent, articulating a position which reinforced and amplified the one Marshall had taken. While Douglas saw no need to treat de jure violations by non-school officials in a state long supporting "the historic separate school system for the two races," he objected to Burger's outright denial of their applicability, and, if the matter was to be explored, he felt that discriminatory acts by state officials, "by themselves and apart from the dual school system," might well be "relevant to a school board's task" in assigning students and faculty.[132]

Eventually, Justices Brennan and Douglas persuaded Justice Stewart to turn his memorandum of December 16 into an opinion dissenting from Burger and affirming Judge McMillan's order. The Stewart opinion, circulated shortly after a February 16 meeting with Douglas and Brennan, now credited McMillan with framing "a final decree which was fully within his discretionary power."[133] On the same day as the meeting, Justice Harlan sent Burger a letter indicating his continued disagreement with the chief's position. A majority was forming at this point for the Stewart opinion.

Accordingly, Chief Justice Burger commenced a strategic retreat, resulting in a sharply altered third draft. Dated March 4, 1971, the revision went some distance toward meeting the myriad objections of the Court majority. Above all, Burger affirmed Judge McMillan's order. To do so, he rewrote the section on racial balance, emphasizing the obstreperousness of the Charlotte school board, and concluding, rather grudgingly, that "reading [the district court's] language in context . . . we cannot say it abused its discretion in formulating the remedy."[134]

Gone too was the footnote reinterpreting *Green*, and the accompanying text proclaiming the distinction between "integration" and a "prohibition against segregation." But the section on racial balance now contained a defiant restatement of this conviction. "The Constitution, of course, does not command integration; it forbids segregation."[135] More important, the basic remedial scaffolding of the original opinion had yet to be pulled down. The critical passage in "Remedial Altering of Attendance Zones" was untouched. So was the endorsement of one-race schools, except for a cautionary, but in the context largely meaningless, directive to lower courts to "closely scrutinize" such "racially identifiable" institutions.[136] Still included as well was the admonition against worrying about "racial prejudice in residential patterns, . . . location of public housing, or other factors beyond the jurisdiction of school authorities"[137] (now moved to the end of the section on racial balance). The result at which the chief justice arrived in his third draft warred with his reasoning.

Justice Brennan remonstrated with the chief about the resurrection of Judge Parker.

> I think this would be a most unfortunate statement for us to make at this juncture in the struggle to gain compliance with *Brown*. That statement . . . was the rallying cry of the massive resistance movement in Virginia, and of die-hard segregationists for years after *Brown*. It calls to mind Judge Parker's opinion which caused so much trouble for so long a time. To revive it again would I think only rekindle vain hopes.[138]

Justice Douglas criticized the latest Burger draft for continuing to deny the "relevan[ce] to school problems [of] both restrictive social covenants and racial public housing," though suggesting that if this matter was smoothed over, "I could . . . [t]hen . . . join *Swann*."[139]

The most important player, however, in trying to remold the chief's eclectic offering was Justice Harlan. In a letter of March 11, Harlan proposed revisions designed to eviscerate Burger's remedial logic and substitute Harlan's own reasoning, bringing the opinion's outcome and its substance into harmony.

First, Harlan offered a rewrite of the section on racial balance, excising the allusion to *Briggs*, and eliminating the less generous references to Judge McMillan. Of even greater significance was the suggestion that the section on attendance zones drop its discussion of "artificial racial separation," its footnote, and its hornbook definition of equity. Such a definition, claimed Justice Harlan, "asks . . . school boards and district courts to imagine the pattern of community life that would have emerged if . . . there had never been dual systems and then devise desegregation plans accordingly. I feel that this standard cannot offer any real guidance."[140] From the perspective of the scholarly, disciplined Harlan, this argument undoubtedly made sense. In fact, the standard proposed by Burger would have offered very real guidance to southern judges who did not see why the post-*Brown* educational structure of the region couldn't look just like the ghettoized school systems of the North and West.

In any case, Justice Harlan wanted the entire passage removed, and, with it, Burger's essential justification for tolerating one-race schools. Harlan suggested new and much tougher language for the section on those schools, language which would make it almost impossible for racial identification to survive.

Harlan's proposed language is worth quoting in full.

> "[A]lthough the presence of 'one-race' schools—like the presence of racial imbalance—does not in and of itself establish the system as 'dual' within the meaning of *Brown I* and *Green*, the amount of actual deseg-

regation of the races is certainly an appropriate consideration in assessing the claim of a school board to have converted a system of school board decision-making from one premised on state-enforced racial separation to one in which 'no person is . . . effectively excluded from any school because of race or color.' *Alexander* v. *Holmes County Board of Education*, 396 U.S. 19, 20 (1969). And, the need for remedial criteria of sufficient specificity to enable a district court to assure the good-faith discharge of the school board's duty to convert forthwith to a unitary system warrants establishment of a presumption in favor of the maximum degree of actual desegregation possible in all the circumstances. In a school district of mixed population, where the school board's proposed plan for conversion from a dual system to a unitary system contemplates the continued existence of schools all or predominantly of one race, a reviewing court must closely scrutinize all such schools in order to assure that their racial composition truly reflects compelling countervailing considerations of educational policy or pupil welfare unrelated to community resistance to desegregation."[141]

The chief justice obliged Harlan, though by no means completely, in a fourth draft circulated on March 16. He accepted most of his colleagues' discussion of one-race schools, if in words borrowed from Justice Stewart's draft opinion. ("The greatest possible degree of actual desegregation" was substituted for "the maximum degree of actual desegregation.")[142] He also accepted Harlan's reorganization of the racial balance section, and its more positive references to Judge McMillan's actions. The judge's percentages were "no more than a starting point" in devising a remedy, the chief now concluded.[143]

Furthermore, the revised portion on racial balance softened Burger's injunction against considering other types of discrimination in school suits, although he certainly did not endorse doing so. Harlan's alternative dropped the references to employment practices and to location of public housing projects, and simply noted that the Court's objective in *Swann* "does not and cannot embrace all the problems of racial prejudice," even when they contributed "to disproportionate racial concentrations in some schools."[144] The chief modified the language to read, "We are concerned in these cases with the elimination of the discrimination inherent in the dual school systems, not with myriad factors of human existence which can cause discrimination in a multitude of ways on racial, religious or ethnic grounds . . . . One vehicle can carry only a limited amount of baggage."[145] This alteration, however, did not satisfy Justice Douglas, who still felt "[y]our opinion decides that . . . other kinds [of official segregation] are not relevant . . . in working out a school integration program,"[146] and who responded on March 19 with a draft dissent which unmistakably crossed regional lines. "Segregation is not *de facto* simply because it is not the result of perceptible discriminatory acts by the *school* board."[147]

Nonetheless, the alterations in draft four went some way toward building a majority in *Swann*, what with the chief accepting Harlan's endorsement of Judge McMillan, and much of his colleague's language about one-race schools. Burger did not accept, however, the last sentence of Harlan's draft in this section. ("[W]here the school board's proposed plan for conversion from a dual system to a unitary system contemplates the continued existence of schools all or predominantly of one race, a reviewing court must closely scrutinize all such schools in order to assure that their racial composition truly reflects compelling countervailing considerations of educational policy or pupil welfare unrelated to community resistance to desegregation.") In its place, the chief wrote, "Where the school authority's proposed plan for conversion from a dual to a unitary system contemplates the continued existence of some schools that are all or predominantly of one race, a reviewing court must give close scrutiny in order to assure that their racial composition is not the result of present or past discrimination."[148]

This was an extremely important change, because it combined with the fact that the fourth draft's section on remedial alteration of attendance zones contained no alterations at all. The paragraph spelling out the hornbook definition of equity, the reference to "artificial racial separation," and the Briggsian footnote remained firmly in place.[149] This meant that when the new draft proscribed the existence of one-race schools resulting from "present or past discriminatory action," it could still be interpreted as limiting those proscriptions to the fruits of artificial, as opposed to normal, racial cleavages, particularly since the purpose of remedial action was but to restore the "distribution of students . . . that would have normally existed."

Brennan quickly supported Harlan in calling for deletion of this entire paragraph, and, at a conference on March 18, the chief agreed to drop all mention of the equitable objective of desegregation remedies, as well as to get rid of the disputed footnote about the "separation flowing normally from residential patterns." Still, the reference which the footnote qualified remained—to those prior segregative acts creating "an artificial racial separation," acts such as "discriminatory location of school sites or distortion of school size." But with the footnote now excised, such references seem to take on an altered meaning. They are no longer contrasted with anything, but serve as illustrations, merely, of the "past discrimination" referred to in the section on one-race schools, the "discrimination" which required a court to give "close scrutiny" to such schools.

That terminology remained, despite Justice Brennan's plea that Burger adopt Justice Harlan's discussion of the unirace issue. "I am still seriously troubled about the formulation of the standard for assessing the constitutionality of one race schools," he told the chief, and "urgently" requested "adoption of John's formulation," requiring that black schools "truly reflect compelling countervailing considerations of educational policy or pupil welfare unrelated to community resistance to desegregation."[150]

The chief justice would not budge on his wording. The sentence continued to read, "Where the school authority's proposed plan . . . contemplates the continued existence of some schools that are all or predominantly of one race, a reviewing court must give close scrutiny . . . to assure that their racial composition is not the result of present or past discrimination." Burger did agree, however, to an addition in the final draft which won over Justice Douglas, by explicitly reserving the question Douglas had treated so aggressively in his proposed dissent. "We do not reach in this case the question whether a showing that school segregation is a consequence of other types of state action, without any discriminatory action by the school authorities, is a constitutional violation . . . ."[151] While not overruling *Deal*, the chief's words cast doubt on Judge Peck's cavalier dismissal of housing arguments in a school case.

Some more eleventh hour revisions were necessary to satisfy Justice Hugo Black, who wrote to the chief on March 25, detailing his objections to the proposed opinion. Black accompanied the memorandum with the draft of a possible dissent, which sounded in places like the opinion the chief justice would like to have promulgated in the first place.

Justice Black was unhappy from the time of oral argument. At the original conference on *Swann*, he expressed a marked preference for neighborhood schools. "I have always had the idea that people arrange themselves . . . to be close to schools. I never thought it was for the courts to change the habits of the people in choosing where to live."[152] Since then, he had not been involved in the Court's give and take, but after reading the supposed final version of the decision, he registered a number of protests. The justice wanted the entire section on remedial altering of attendance zones removed, as well as the statement placing the "burden" on local authorities to justify one-race schools. He also took issue with the inclusion of Judge McMillan's statement about "locating schools" so that they would be "handy" to black or white neighborhoods. "This sounds," Black noted, "as though there can be something unconstitutional about sending pupils to a school in their neighborhood, closest to their homes."[153]

The chief obliged Justice Black by removing Judge McMillan's comment, and one on busing which had survived since the first draft. "The search for solutions is not aided by simplistic slogans for or against 'busing,' as though the term described a uniformly invidious course of action." Burger would not budge on the "burden" issue, but Justice Black finally agreed to go along with his colleagues. The decision in *Swann* v. *Charlotte-Mecklenburg Board of Education*, and in its companion cases, came down on April 20, 1971.

The Court vindicated Judge McMillan's actions, and Mobile, quite naturally, went the way of Charlotte. The justices found the interstate highway dividing Mobile's racial population an insufficient barrier to achievement of the maximum amount of integration, "taking into account the practicalities of the situation."[154] School officials, they held, gave "inadequate consideration . . . to the possible use of bus transportation and split zoning."[155] The Court also peremptorily disposed of the notion that North Carolina, or any other state, could forbid busing designed to advance racial balance. Such a "flat prohibition . . . must inevitably conflict with the duty of school authorities to disestablish dual school systems."[156]

V

Swann and *Davis* were indeed the Supreme Court's "busing decisions." Their warnings against identifiably black schools and their calls for maximum integration opened a new round of litigation in the South. Some judges quickly ordered communities to adopt plans on the Charlotte or Mobile model. Nashville, in the process of implementing Judge Miller's restrained version of integration, was now required to redo its plan in light of *Swann*. Officials rearranged the city's student population of 75% white and 25% black so that three-fourths of the elementary schools would have a 16%–41% black enrollment; 22 schools in outlying areas would have a black ratio of 0%–22%; 82–84 additional buses joined the transportation fleet.[157]

But as Professor Orfield points out, *Swann* "still insisted that federal district judges had wide discretion" in evaluating desegregation plans, and "[i]n a number of cases, the [lower] courts failed to follow the *Swann* model."[158] Intractable racial separation in urban areas, and judges sympathetic to local interests, led to approval of many plans leaving considerable segregation untouched. Twenty-five all-black or nearly all-black schools remained in Memphis in 1973.[159] The plan accepted for Knoxville, with a 16.5% black student population, produced a system with less than a fifth of the schools having black enrollment between 10% and 30%.[160] Judge Smith Henley in Little Rock stuck initially to his refusal to desegregate elementary schools, *Swann* notwithstanding, until the Eighth Circuit forced him to do so.[161] On the whole, however, the *Swann* decision effected another transformation of southern school systems. Most "[f]ederal courts in the South rapidly updated old desegregation plans to conform to their interpretation of . . . new requirements," and, while not absolutely required to use racial balance as a yardstick, often found it difficult to achieve maximum desegregation unless they "imposed [plans] requiring approximately proportional enrollment at all schools."[162]

Yet on what doctrinal basis did this transformation rest? Why had a unanimous Court taxed school authorities with achieving "the greatest possible degree of actual desegregation"? *Swann* never exposes its constitutional underpinnings to clear inspection. The decision's strictures certainly do not flow from Justice Douglas' belief that violations by housing officials alone might call for integration of schools, as Chief Justice Burger's disclaimer, endorsed by Douglas himself, clearly indicates. Nor was the decision inspired by Justice Marshall's view of independent housing violations serving as the justification, at least, for wide-sweeping school remedies in a de jure system. Though the Court technically accepted Judge McMillan's findings of collateral discrimination by upholding his decision, there is no actual discussion of the relationship between Charlotte's Housing Authority and its school board. As in *Green*, Justice Brennan's theory of segregation as racial insult received no significant articulation. The Court was not wholly oblivious to the emotional aspects of enforced racial separation. In demanding that desegregation plans include a majority to minority transfer provision, Chief Justice Burger noted that the "[p]rovision . . . is . . . indispensable . . . for those students willing to transfer to other schools in order to lessen the impact on them of the state-imposed stigma of segregation"[163]—an updating of his earlier reference to segregation as "a badge of inferiority." But his decision does not emphasize such concerns. And neither the circuit court nor the Supreme Court opinion dwells at all on test scores or comparative achievement levels.

Not even the views of Justices Harlan and Stewart, the prime reshapers of the opinion, finally prevail in Chief Justice Burger's final draft. "There is no indication," argues Professor Frank Goodman, " . . . that [the] prophylactic rationale is in fact the basis" of the Court's decision.[164] Much of Justice Harlan's reasoning shows through, no doubt. Identifiably black schools must almost certainly be eliminated, and maximum integration achieved, because a school board's past transgressions dictate "the need for remedial criteria of sufficient specificity to assure a school authority's compliance with its constitutional duty." But in the final version of *Swann*, these demands on school authorities flow less from suspicion of their motives than from the suspected effects of their prior decisions. In order to preserve segregation in any of their schools, they must satisfy a court not that the racial make-up of a school "truly reflects compelling countervailing considerations of educational policy or pupil welfare," but that its "racial composition is not *the result* of present or past discriminatory action."

In short, *Swann* posits not an attitudinal connection between prior discrimination by school authorities and present racial separation, but a causal connection. The Court's focus is on the instrumental role a school board has played, through its various manipulative devices, in shaping the neighborhood patterns so resistant to racial diversity. The key inquiry in determining whether a racially identifiable school can continue to exist centers on how crucial have been the board's actions in accounting for the fact that neutral geographic assignment of students does not result in integration.

But how decisive an influence can a school board possibly have exerted on a phenomenon as massive and as complex as neighborhood segregation? Justice Stewart, for one, had indicated that he did not think the influence was fundamental. But the Court was never forced to attack this thorny empirical question, for here is where the language adapted from Justice Harlan becomes critically important, though not in the way Harlan originally intended. Harlan's guarantee theory of integration asserted that the need for specific remedial criteria warranted a strong "presumption" against black schools, which officials could overcome only by proving their intentions were pure. *Swann* winds up asserting, instead, a theory of demographic causation to challenge such schools. But faced with the varied problems posed by that theory, the opinion falls back on Justice Harlan's words to finesse these problems, by creating a "presumption" that the past prejudicial actions of school officials constitute *in fact* the source of current neighborhood patterns and school enrollments. As Professor Fiss notes, *Swann* overcomes the difficulties of determining the "causal connections between past discrimination and present segregation" through announcement of an "evidentiary presumption," directed "against the school board," which "in effect resolves all [causal] uncertainties against" them, and effectively charges them with creating the interlocking segregated patterns of a community.[165]

In the official, negotiated language of *Swann*, the prior existence of a dual system of education justifies "a presumption against schools that are substantially disproportionate in their racial composition," and the precise "burden" placed on school authorities because of that presumption is to demonstrate there is no demographic connection between "past discriminatory action on their part" and a current condition of segregation. The burden is virtually insurmountable, for a school board must prove that its conduct is no part of the causal chain resulting in segregated schools. If authorities fail to carry their burden, they are held responsible for all of the segregation currently existing in a school system, and must achieve, therefore, "the greatest possible degree of actual desegregation." In Professor Fiss' words,

> Although the existence of past discrimination cannot be denied, the Court made no serious attempt [in *Swann*] either to determine or even to speculate on the degree to which it contributes to present segregation. Nor did the Court attempt to tailor the remedial order to the correction of that portion of the segregation that might reasonably be attributable to past discrimination. The Court moved from (a) the undisputed existence of past discrimination to (b) the *possibility* or *likelihood* that the past discrimination played *some* causal role in producing segregated patterns to (c) an order requiring the complete elimination of those patterns. The existence of past discrimination was thus used as a "trigger"—and not for a pistol, but for a cannon.[166]

Pre-1954 black schools would obviously be swept into this web; post-1954 schools in traditionally white neighborhoods would not fare any better.

Eventually, this assumed link between past sins and present realities would break. Burger closed *Swann* by assuring school authorities that "[a]t some point," they would "have achieved full compliance with this Court's decision in Brown I. The systems would then be 'unitary' in the sense required by our decisions . . . ."[167] For the time being, however, the authorities must work off the evidentiary presumptions resolved against them.

The doctrinal outcome of *Swann* did not represent the deliberate intention of any of the justices. It is best described as a cross between the partially thwarted goals of Justice Harlan and the decisively thwarted aims of the chief justice. Almost from the beginning, in fact, Burger harbored second thoughts about his handiwork. This is indicated by his actions a few months after *Swann*, when, sitting in his recess capacity as Circuit Justice for the Fourth Circuit, he received a request from the school board of Forsyth County, North Carolina, asking him to stay a court order directing adoption of a new desegregation plan for the county.

Forsyth County's school system was experiencing the same fate as others in the

South following *Swann* and *Davis*. In 1970, District Judge Eugene Gordon had approved a school plan based on geographic zoning and majority to minority transfers, but the Fourth Circuit remanded the case to him in April of 1971, since it was "now clear, we think, that in school systems that have previously been operated separately as to the races . . . , 'the district judge or school authorities should make every effort to achieve the greatest possible degree of actual desegregation, taking into account the practicalities of the situation.'"[168]

Judge Gordon complied. He believed that it was "as 'practicable' to desegregate all the public schools in the Winston-Salem/Forsyth County system as in the Charlotte-Mecklenburg system and that [in this situation] the appellate courts will accept no less. Consequently, this Court can approve no less . . . ."[169] Gordon induced the school board to submit a revised desegregation plan, employing extensive cross-district busing.

Local officials raged at this altered situation. Their appeal for a stay indicated they felt themselves being forced to "accomplish the *required objective* of achieving a racial balance in the public schools."[170]

The chief refused to grant the stay because county officials were intolerably tardy in submitting their request. (It arrived at the Court on August 26, with the school year due to start on August 30). Still, Burger found quite "disturbing" any reference to racial balance, since it indicated a definite "misreading of the opinion of the Court in the Swann case."[171] If either "the Court of Appeals or the District Court read this Court's opinion as requiring a fixed racial balance or quota, they would appear to have overlooked specific language . . . in . . . Swann . . . to the contrary."[172] To clarify matters for the future, Burger repeated the part of *Swann* containing its disclaimer on racial balance. He had a copy of his opinion in *Forsyth* sent to every district and circuit judge in the country.

But, of course, the problem with Burger's whole effort was that neither the Fourth Circuit nor Judge Gordon had made any reference to racial balance. They stuck to the argot of achieving "the greatest possible degree of actual desegregation." The "required objective of . . . racial balance" represented strictly the conception of a hostile school board. The thing that really bothered the chief justice, one would surmise, was the "disturbing" similarity between what *Swann* mandated and what it formally forbade. As Professor Graglia notes

> [Burger] apparently believed that, despite the decision he was required
> to reach [in *Swann*], he would be able to establish meaningful limits on
> the balancing requirement . . . . The lower-court decisions in *Winston-
> Salem/Forsyth*, however, made clear that any such strategy . . . had not
> succeeded. [The chief justice], evidently, then sought to nullify on his
> own the busing requirement that he in *Swann* and *Davis* had greatly
> assisted the Court in imposing.[173]

VI

If *Green* produced no sustained remedial logic, *Swann* produced a logic which was markedly strained and artificial; the price of unanimity here was any real coherence. School board actions under de jure segregation had likely exerted an influence over residential developments in some instances, most obviously when to move to a white neighborhood meant for an African-American family that their youngsters could no longer attend a neighborhood school. But no evidence yet existed on the precise interrelationships between school segregation and residential segregation. And no demographer or urban sociologist seriously contended that pre-compliance student assignments played the dominant role in shaping subsequent neighborhood patterns in southern cities, all the way to the lily-white suburbs far from the central ghettos.

The evidence on housing segregation presented at trial, and in briefs, by the *Swann* plaintiffs made no such sweeping claim. The plaintiffs focused, quite naturally, on the policies of public housing authorities, realtors, and banks, arguing, as did Justice Marshall, that a remedy which ignored this discrimination was denying reality. But the *Swann* presumptions and the all-encompassing power they imputed to school authorities rendered this evidence superfluous.

The justices were facing, to be sure, what Professor Robert Sedler has called a "remedy dilemma" in the case, because of the very point noted so emphatically by Chief Justice Burger, the distorted arrangement of numerous schools in the Charlotte system, or in any urban school system shaped by de jure segregation. A "school map" in such cities, Sedler pointed out, "would look very different today were it not for [the previous] requirements" of dual zoning.[174] In this situation, Professor Sedler felt that the conclusion in *Swann* technically credited to the chief justice was the correct one. The Court could not "ignore the influence of state-imposed segregation on the structure of [a] school system and uphold 'neighborhood school' assignment."[175] On the other hand, it was difficult "to 'sort out' the schools that would not have been racially identifiable in the absence of . . . segregation."[176] This made more understandable the decision to "treat the school *system* as being racially segregated, and require its dismantling by a plan that would achieve the 'greatest possible degree of actual desegregation.'"[177]

Yet the oddly constructed and positioned schools in a southern system were found only in neighborhoods where some integration had taken place, and the residential segregation index of Charlotte had surpassed 90% from 1940 into the 1960's.[178] In the extensive all-black and all-white areas of the city, and of virtually all cities in the South, a school map at any time would have looked very much like a map in Cleveland or Philadelphia.

Thus, in terms of demographic realities, Judge Miller's notion of maximum integration, but within an approximate neighborhood context, seemed to represent as coherent a solution to the Court's "remedy dilemma" as did the commands of *Swann*; the more capacious version of Judge Miller's view, adopted in Houston and

Dade County, would do even better, presumably. For the inescapable fact remained that no other school system in the country in 1971 looked anything like the Charlotte and Mobile school systems were now going to look. Despite its veneer of urban sociology, the decision in *Swann* could not help but nourish the suspicion that it was educational segregation per se which actually met with the justices' disapproval. The import of the opinion remained puzzling, concluded Professor Fiss, "unless the primary concern of the Court is the segregated patterns themselves, rather than the causal relation of past discrimination to them" (though the exact rationale for integration which nourished this concern was certainly not made clear).[179]

Swann's strictures proceeded from a foundation of educational apartheid unique to the South, but its "significance for northern school segregation" stood to be considerable, Fiss believed. The decision might serve "as a way-station to the adoption of a general approach to school segregation which, by focusing on the segregated patterns . . . , is more responsive to the . . . segregation of the North . . . . [T]he Court [after all] will want to avoid the appearance of picking on the South."[180]

Professor Fiss' analysis overestimated, perhaps, the degree of clarity emerging from the justices' wranglings in *Swann*, but their equivocal end product understandably encouraged the notion that the de jure-de facto distinction no longer contained any potency, and introduced a fundamental ambiguity, therefore, into the decision's remedial conclusions. At some point, *Swann* proclaims, the causal chains foisted upon school boards will break and judicial supervision will cease. But if racial separation itself was the problem crying out for remedy, why should "compulsory integration" be ended anytime in the foreseeable future?

I. *SWANN* IN THE SUPREME COURT: THE BRIEFS

The petitioners in *Swann*, not cognizant of the magical powers which the final decision would give to school boards, based their case on the residential discrimination perpetrated by the whole range of government agencies in Charlotte. The amicus brief, composed, among others, by Marian Wright Edelman and Joseph Rauh, took a more philosophical approach to remedy. Senator Sam Ervin of North Carolina, soon to embark upon his Watergate adventure, sounded a last call for adherence to *Briggs* v. *Elliott*

1. BRIEF FOR PETITIONERS

ARGUMENT

I

The Public Schools of the Charlotte-Mecklenburg School System Are Racially Segregated in Violation of the Equal Protection Clause of the Fourteenth Amendment as the Result of Governmental Action Causing School Segregation and Residential Segregation . . . .

B.Governmental Agencies Created Black Schools in Black Neighborhoods by Promoting School Segregation and Residential Segregation.

The findings of the district court make it plain that the existing pattern of school segregation in Charlotte-Mecklenburg is the deliberate result of state action designed to create a segregated school system. The court found that all the school segregation in Charlotte was illegal and that there was no aspect of possibly innocent or adventitious segregation. Each and every black school in the system was held to be segregated in violation of the constitutional prohibitions against racial discrimination . . . .

The court heard extensive evidence about the extent of residential segregation in Charlotte and the governmental responsibility for the existing pattern of almost total residential separation. About 98% of the black inhabitants of Charlotte reside in the northwest quadrant of Charlotte. Judge McMillan summarized the findings about how this extensive segregation came about in these words:

> The black schools are for the most part in black residential areas. However, that does not make their segregation constitutionally benign .

. . . Briefly summarized,[the] facts are that the present location of white schools in white areas and of black schools in black areas is the result of a varied group of elements of public and private action all deriving their basic strength originally from public law or state or local governmental action. These elements include, among others, the legal separation of the races in schools, school busses, public accommodations and housing; racial restrictions in deeds to land; zoning ordinances; city planning; urban renewal; location of public low rent housing: and the actions of the present School Board and others, before and since 1954, in locating and controlling the capacity of schools . . . .

(PETITIONERS' SUPPLEMENTAL BRIEF SUPPLIES A DETAILED ANALYSIS, AS FOLLOWS)

2. *Urban Renewal* . . . . The [district] court characterized this practice as follows:

Under the urban renewal program thousands of Negroes were moved out of their shotgun houses in the center of town and have relocated in low rent areas to the west. This relocation of course involved many ad hoc decisions by individuals and by city, county, state and federal governments. Federal agencies (which hold the strings to large federal purses) reportedly disclaim any responsibility for the direction of the migration; they reportedly say that the selection of urban renewal sites and the relocation of displaced persons are matters of decision ("freedom of choice"?) by local individuals and governments. This may be correct; the clear fact however is that the displacement occurred with heavy federal financing and with active participation by local governments, and it has further concentrated Negroes until 95% or so of the city's Negroes live [in one small area of Charlotte].

The record demonstrates, [moreover], that . . . this relocation did not afford the affected families a "free" choice for . . . homes in other areas were simply not available to black families . . . .

3. *Public Housing.* Consistent with the city's zoning practices of locating multifamily and low income housing in black residential areas, all public housing, built principally since 1960 and now generally occupied by blacks, has been located in black residential areas. Even projected public housing has been designated for black residential areas . . . .

4. *City Zoning.* City zoning has influenced separation of the races by marking out and designating by land usage those areas of the city occupied by blacks and those occupied by whites. Beginning in 1947, the city enacted its first zoning ordinance and in effect delineated the black and white residential areas. All white residential areas were zoned residential with restricted land usage. All black residential areas,

with the exception of two small pockets adjacent to white residential areas, were zoned industrial for multi-land usage, including heavy industry, multi-family homes and high density areas. Even the two excepted black areas were zoned for higher density use than the white residential areas. This difference in zoning practices for black and white residential areas has been carried forward to the present day in the major revisions of the zoning ordinance in 1962 . . . .

It delineates for governmental and private developers, school officials and home buyers and renters those areas of the city for blacks and those for whites . . . .

6. *Streets and Public Highways.* Streets and public highways have perpetuated barriers between the races. Streets have been designed to provide ease of communication only within the separate white or black residential areas with little means of communication between them . . . .

7. *Private Discrimination.* Private discrimination has been pervasive in establishing and perpetuating the racially segregated housing that exists in the city. Blacks simply have been denied access or the right to purchase or rent in white residential areas. Construction firms and real estate agents and banking institutions, including the federal government, have planned and developed racially segregated areas. As the court below noted, such developments were perpetuated by racially restrictive covenants which were enforced by the North Carolina Supreme Court until this Court's decision in *Shelley* v. *Kraemer*, 334 U.S. 1 (1948) . . . . Limitations on the ability and freedom of blacks to purchase and rent homes in other areas of the city continue today.

The school board now proposes to engraft on this segregated system, district and housing pattern zones which would leave the majority of the black and white students in racially segregated schools . . . . The pervasiveness of the state practices in creating and perpetuating the housing patterns and segregated schools is no different [from] the former constitutional provisions compelling racial separation in public schools. It is clearly illusory to contend otherwise—for the black students in the all black and predominantly black schools would be locked into those schools just as effectively and with as much state control as they were under the former compulsory system rejected in *Brown* . . . .

(THE MAIN BRIEF RESUMES)

The [Fourth Circuit] accepted the finding of the trial court that the schools in Charlotte were illegally segregated. Judge Butzner wrote:

> The fact that similar forces operate in cities throughout the nation under the mask of *de facto* segregation provides no justification for allowing us to ignore the part that government plays in creating segregated neighborhood schools . . . .

It does not matter, for purposes of judging the constitutionality of the resulting school segregation, that agencies of the state, other than the local school board, are in part responsible for the residential segregation pattern. As this Court made plain in *Cooper* v. *Aaron*, 358 U.S. 1, 16–17 (1958), school boards are agents of the state and will not be excused from their duty to guarantee the constitutional rights of Negro children because the "vindication of those rights was rendered difficult or impossible by the actions of other state officials." Nor is the local board's responsibility relieved by the fact that private as well as governmental discrimination in housing has contributed to the segregated residential pattern. As Judge McMillan has found, the board has made choices in locating schools, fixing the sizes and grade structures of schools, determining the transportation patterns, and adopting the policy of assigning pupils by residences. The board has defined the relevant school "neighborhoods" by its own decisions. Housing segregation results in school segregation only in the context of these choices by the school board—an agency of the state. Thus, a situation which has the appearance of inevitability—school segregation in Charlotte's black ghetto—is revealed as the product of governmental decision-making.

2. AMICUS BRIEF: MARIAN WRIGHT EDELMAN AND JOSEPH RAUH

I

Disestablishment of a dual school system requires that, unless demonstrably unfeasible, pupils be assigned so that no school has a student body which is all black or so disproportionately black as to make the school identifiable as a "black school."

These cases raise the question whether school officials who have been operating separate systems of schools based upon race can be said to have disestablished those systems when they continue to assign pupils so as to maintain schools with all-black or disproportionately black student bodies. We submit that the answer is "No"-at least where there exist feasible alternative methods of assignment which would desegregate those schools.

The issue is not whether as an abstract matter the Constitution requires any particular racial balance in public schools generally, or even whether the Constitution generally forbids all-black or predominantly black schools whatever their historical background. Rather the issue is the narrower one of what remedy is required to eliminate the last vestiges of a particular historical practice, long since judged to be unconstitutional, namely the official and mandatory assignment of black children to separate schools set aside for their race.

The underlying rationale of *Brown* v. *Board of Education of Topeka*, 347 U.S. 483 (1954) (*Brown I*) and the specific principles pronounced in *Green* v. *Board of School Commissioners of New Kent County*, 391 U.S. 430 (1968), require the abolition of schools identifiable as black by the makeup of their student bodies, wherever this can be accomplished by feasible techniques of student assignment . . . .

A. The Rationale of *Brown I.*

In the first *Brown* decision, this Court held that racial segregation of the public schools violated the equal protection rights of black children. In the American historical context, the system of segregation was no less than a massive government-sponsored racial insult to the black people subjected to it, based on assumptions of their intellectual and moral inferiority to white people. The system of segregation, and the official insult it carried with it, was most damaging as applied in the schools, for there it was directed at children of unformed minds and developing personalities, in the public institutions most crucial to their growth. The system was unconstitutional because the history of the Fourteenth Amendment made clear that the framers meant to forbid all official action which injured or degraded black people because they were black.

Thus *Brown I* rested firmly on the finding of the Kansas district court: "Segregation of white and colored children has a detrimental effect upon colored children. The impact is greater when it has the sanction of the law; for the policy of separating the races is usually interpreted as denoting the inferiority of the Negro groups." 347 U.S. at 494. That was sufficient to establish the constitutional violation; official segregation meant official imputation of racial inferiority, and hence official injury to black people because of their race.

B. The Principles Declared in *Green* . . . .

In *Green*, the Court addressed itself in detail to the standards governing . . . implementation [of *Brown I* and *II*], and laid down three essential guidelines which govern these cases.

First, the Court stated that the constitutional goal was "the abolition of the system of segregation and its effects." 391 U.S. at 440. The Court, in referring to the *system* of segregation and its *effects*, recognized that the dual school system constituted and supported a set of social practices, practices which by their existence and maintenance conveyed and continued the racial insult condemned in *Brown I*. The job of the courts in remedying the wrong of segregation was not merely to undo the formal legal arrangements of the dual system, but also more broadly to dismantle the institutions in which those arrangements found fruition.

Second, the Court specified what a unitary system was: it was one "without a 'white' school and a 'Negro' school, but just schools." 391 U.S. at 442. Here the Court dispelled any notion that a system might somehow be desegregated while its schools retained their former racial identification.

Third, the Court placed upon officials who had operated dual school systems "the affirmative duty to take *whatever steps might be necessary* to convert to a unitary system in which racial discrimination would be eliminated root and branch." 391 U.S. at 437–438 (emphasis added) . . . . Thus no excuse would be heard that the means required might be too onerous; the school officials were to take "whatever steps might be necessary," to adopt "any alternatives which may be shown to be feasible." . . .

C. Schools With Black Student Bodies Which Could by Feasible Assignment Techniques Be Desegregated Are Remnants of the System of Discrimination Condemned in *Brown I.*

Where a school in a dual system is attended exclusively or very largely by black children, and where school officials maintain this attendance pattern in the face of feasible alternatives which would produce an integrated student body, that school is as a practical matter the equivalent to the "colored school" of the pre-*Brown* system of segregation. The very difficulty of persuading southern school officials, southern judges, and even federal bureaucrats to do the job of integrating these schools is the best evidence for this fact. White school officials and parents feel a peculiar horror at the idea of assigning white children to these schools, as the records in these cases attest . . . .

Thus the black schools of today, identified by their all-black or predominantly black student bodies and by their location in black neighborhoods, retain for the white community which seeks so hard to avoid them the stigma originally conferred by the underlying segregationist assumption that they are for inferior children. But if they still bear that stigma for the white community, so do they for the black community and for the black children who attend them. This being so, assignment to these schools must have for these black children the same ineradicable effects upon their hearts and minds which this Court condemned as the central vice of state-imposed segregation in *Brown I.*

Black schools are inferior not only because of the racist assumptions upon which they are founded and the consequent psychological harm they do, but also in a more tangible sense. These schools receive less of the resources available for education than do schools attended by the children of the dominant white community, and provide correspondingly inferior facilities and services. For example, the Civil Rights Commission found that, in a sixteen-county area of Alabama, white-attended school buildings and their contents were worth an average of $981 per pupil, compared with an average of $283 per pupil at black-attended schools. Test scores reveal the stark results of this kind of disparity—black twelfth grade pupils in the urban South score 3.5 grade levels behind their white counterparts on standard reading comprehension tests.

It is a fact of political life in the South that the power and influence needed to improve the quality of schools resides in the white community. That community would not long tolerate for its children the kind of education which has typically been supplied to black children in their separate schools. Only when there are no

more black schools as such, when the children of the white community attend every school, will every school receive its fair share of available educational resources
. . . .

[T]his means that school officials must adopt any *feasible* plan of pupil assignment which promises to leave no school's student body identifiably black . . . .

The limitation of feasibility is meant only to deal with those few isolated situations where existing techniques do not make full desegregation a practical possibility. It is meant to exclude all other excuses for the continued maintenance of black schools in dual systems . . . .

We have not argued that every school with an all-black or predominantly black student body represents a violation of the equal protection clause. Such an argument could be made; there is substantial evidence that isolation of black children in schools, wherever and for whatever reason it occurs, correlates highly with inferior education. United States Commission on Civil Rights, *Racial Isolation in the Public Schools*, 202–204 (1967). However, no such substantive constitutional doctrine need be advanced in order to decide these cases according to the rule we have argued for.

3. AMICUS BRIEF: SENATOR SAM J. ERVIN

ARGUMENT

I

The Charlotte-Mecklenburg Board of Education has complied with the Equal Protection Clause of the Fourteenth Amendment and the Supreme Court decisions interpreting it by establishing and operating a unitary public school system, which receives and teaches students without discrimination on the basis of their race or color. Any racial imbalance remaining in any of the schools under the jurisdiction of the Board represents de facto segregation, which results from the purely adventitious circumstance that the inhabitants of particular areas in and adjacent to the city of Charlotte are predominantly of one race.

The Equal Protection Clause of the Fourteenth Amendment, which was certified to be a part of the Constitution on July 28, 1868, forbids a state to "deny to any person within its jurisdiction the equal protection of the laws." . . .

If it faithfully observes this limitation upon its power, a public school board has the right to assign children to the schools it operates in any non-discriminatory fashion satisfactory to itself.

The School Board exercised this right when it created non-discriminatory attendance districts or zones and assigned all children, whether black or white, to neighborhood schools in the districts or zones of their residence without regard to race.

Since the children are similarly situated and the School Board treats them exactly alike, its action is in complete harmony with the Equal Protection Clause. It accords, moreover, with the implementing decision in the second *Brown Case*, 349 U.S. 294 (1955), which expressly recognizes that a school board may employ non-discriminatory geographic zoning of school districts "to achieve a system of determining admission to the public schools on a nonracial basis."

As is true in respect to virtually every city of any size in our land, the different races are concentrated to a substantial degree in separate residential areas in Charlotte, and for this reason the School Board's non-discriminatory geographic zoning and assignment program necessarily results in some racial imbalances in some schools.

Notwithstanding this, the order of the District Court commanding the School Board to exclude thousands of children from their neighborhood schools and to bus them long distances to other schools to overcome these racial imbalances is without support in the Equal Protection Clause.

This is true for an exceedingly plain reason. The Equal Protection Clause does not prohibit any discrimination except that which is arbitrary or invidious . . . .

Despite the fact that the Charlotte-Mecklenburg School System is in the South, racial imbalances produced in its schools by de facto residential segregation are just as innocent as racial imbalances produced in the public schools of the North by the same cause, and are equally exempt from federal interference, whether legislative, executive, or judicial, under the Equal Protection Clause . . . .

The amicus curiae is confident that the Supreme Court will so adjudge. Indeed, it must do so if the United States is truly one nation under one flag and one Constitution.

It no longer comports with intellectual integrity to call all racial imbalances in the public schools of the South de jure, and all racial imbalances in the public schools of the North de facto.

There is now no de jure school segregation anywhere in our land. Racial imbalances in public schools are either arbitrary or invidious and, hence, constitutionally impermissible, both North and South, or innocent and, hence, constitutionally permissible, both North and South. Racial imbalances resulting from de facto residential segregation or non-discriminatory districting or zoning, whether in the North or in the South, are clearly innocent and constitutionally permissible.

Moreover, it no longer comports with reality, common sense, or justice to apply one rule to the North and another to the South because the South did not precede the Supreme Court in discovering that the "separate, but equal doctrine" had ceased to be the law of the land.

II. *SWANN* IN THE SUPREME COURT: THE JUSTICES

As we have seen, the justices' draft opinions and memoranda in *Swann* approached desegregation law from virtually every angle—except for the angle displayed in the final product.

1. "MR. JUSTICE STEWART, DISSENTING IN PART" (FEBRUARY, 1971)

III . . . .

B

[It is argued that a school] board found to be in violation of *Brown I* has discharged its affirmative duty to desegregate when it has established a system of school administration which does not "take race into account." The theory put forward is that where the racial composition of student bodies is the product of a "color blind neighborhood zoning plan," it is immune from constitutional attack. This is said to be true even where such a "desegregation plan" results in practice in the same basic pattern of attendance that prevailed under the system of state-imposed segregation . . . .

It is said in support of the proposed rule that it is clearly mandated by the language, unaccountably ignored by the courts below, of our decision in *Brown II* . . . .

There is, however, a . . . fundamental consideration which leads me to reject the proposition that a school board found to have maintained a dual system discharges its affirmative duty by establishing a system which does not "take race into account." A public school system is not built in a day; it is not built in isolation from the community around it. As a school system takes shape through innumerable decisions by hundreds of educational and noneducational officials acting in many different capacities, it acquires a formidable stability and imperviousness to change. Practices, predispositions and attitudes build up in administrators, teachers, children, parents, and local noneducational officials, and come to be independent of particular administrative regulations or legal rules. At times, these may be strong enough to survive conscious decisions for change by those in positions of responsibility.

For decades before *Brown I*, and for at least a decade after that decision, the school district involved in these cases subjected *all* of [their] choices to the test of race. Zone lines, construction, capacity, grade structure, teacher assignment, extracurricular activities, transportation policy, even the naming of schools—all of these decisions and many more like them played their part in the construction of the dual system. When they are taken together with more general patterns of discrimination in the community, they constitute a structure which, as 16 years of litigation have shown, cannot be rendered "color blind" simply by the repeal of those local ordinances or regulations that made overt racial distinctions.

Viewed as a remedy for decades of state-imposed segregation, colorblind neighborhood zoning . . . is closely analogous to the "freedom of choice" plans that were before us in the *Green* trilogy. The considerations that led us in those cases to hold freedom of choice plans inadequate of themselves to discharge a local board's affirmative duty were considerations of *effectiveness* . . . .

So today I would [also] reject colorblind neighborhood zoning, not in the abstract, but as an inadequate remedy in the particular situation of the cases at bar. I would not hold that such a technique can have no place in a desegregation plan. I would not hold that a plan based on this technique might of itself be unconstitutional. But I would hold that where, as here, it appears that "color blind" neighborhood zoning would result in a pattern of school attendance essentially similar to that which existed under the dual system to be disestablished, it is not enough to meet the affirmative remedial duty of the local board.

IV . . . .

B . . . .

In the case before us, it was . . . clearly correct for the District Court to order that the school board make student-assignment decisions in such a way as to achieve a higher degree of actual desegregation than would have resulted from "color blind" neighborhood zoning . . . .

In so ordering, it was, in my opinion, altogether appropriate for the court to pay special attention to the problems of "resegregation" which may occur when the schools within a system differ markedly in the degree of actual desegregation achieved. The danger of resegregation may justify the requirement of a higher degree of actual desegregation of particular schools than would be necessary given a likelihood that populations will remain stable. Where a decree creates a disparity between schools or between areas which invites the migration of white parents from one school zone to another, it does not adequately perform its function of disestablishing the dual system . . . .

C

It is implicit in what I have said above that the goal of local boards and district courts in fashioning remedies under *Brown II* should be to use the techniques available to achieve the greatest possible degree of actual desegregation, taking into account the practicalities of each of the means employed. I would adopt this standard fully aware that it is considerably less precise than that strenuously urged upon us by some of the parties in these cases. They have argued that a desegregation plan should be judged adequate only if it eliminates, by whatever means necessary, every "racially identifiable school" in the district. A racially identifiable school in turn has been defined as one in which the proportion of Negro children exceeds by some degree (*e. g.* 20%) the proportion of Negro children in the school district as a whole. In rejecting this proposed test, I would also reject *a fortiori* the notion that a desegregation decree must require that every school in the system must have a student racial composition commensurate with that of the student population of the entire district.

From the viewpoint of its proponents, the advantage of the "no racially identifiable school" test is its guarantee that residential patterns will have no impact on the racial composition of school student bodies. Residential patterns are often the product of racial discrimination in housing. It is argued that insofar as such housing discrimination is reflected in school attendance patterns, it is an element of official segregation in the school system.

It is of course true that officially imposed residential segregation violates the Fourteenth Amendment. *E. g.*, *Shelley* v. *Kraemer*, 334 U.S. 1. Private discrimination in the sale of housing has been prohibited by Congress . . . . But there obviously exist situations in which racially identifiable residential areas are the product of private, nondiscriminatory choice or economic conditions. It is plain that many of the difficulties encountered in achieving a high level of school desegregation arise from the existence of residential patterns reflecting *all* of these elements.

In these circumstances, the function of a district judge acting in his equitable discretion to frame a school desegregation decree is of necessity a limited one. He must be aware of the actual patterns of residency, since they form the basis for the application of techniques like benevolent gerrymandering, split zoning, pairing and grouping. But it is not incumbent on the district judge in a school case to alter or even to remedy the effects of patterns of housing segregation. This responsibility must fall on officials and private individuals and on courts in proper cases, acting through the great variety of legal means available to them. The concern of the judge in framing a school decree must be with the creation of a *school system* administered without a trace of discrimination based on race, a system in which no child is effectively excluded from any school because of race or color.

In light of the above, it should be clear that the existence of some small number of all-Negro, or virtually all-Negro, schools within a district is not in and of itself the mark of a system which still practices segregation by law. The district judge or local board working to achieve the greatest possible degree of actual desegregation will necessarily be vitally concerned with the elimination of all-Negro schools. But no *per se* rule of results can adequately summarize the difficult process boards and courts must go through in reconciling the conflicting interest involved.

V . . . .

I would affirm those parts of the Court of Appeals' opinion which upheld the District Court's plans with respect to junior and senior high schools . . . . As to the elementary schools I believe that the means used by the District Court . . . in redrawing the Charlotte-Mecklenburg Board of Education's desegregation plan so as to achieve a greater degree of actual desegregation were altogether appropriate means. None of them was in itself offensive to the Constitution, and so far as appears on this record, none of them was used in such a way as to contravene the principles I think should guide the equitable discretion of a district court.

2. MEMORANDUM OF JUSTICE JOHN MARSHALL HARLAN (NOVEMBER 3, 1970)

II . . . .

[W]e begin our analysis . . . with a consideration of two related questions: First, does the adoption of a non-racially gerrymandered geographic zoning plan for assigning students satisfy the school board's affirmative duty with respect to this aspect of the process of disestablishing a former state-sponsored dual school system? Second, assuming a school board can be compelled to go further than adopting such a zoning plan, is the degree of actual race mixing in the school system a proper criterion for assessing compliance by the school board with its constitutional duty to disestablish such a racially dual system? . . .

A

In *Brown I*, this Court held that enforced separation of the races in the public schools violated the Equal Protection Clause of the Fourteenth Amendment . . . .

The policies of state government which *Brown I* condemned encompassed not merely the enactment of public laws which in terms discriminated between the races, but also the implementation of those laws through the maintenance by state officials of two separate systems of public education, one for black and one for white . . . .

The role that racially identifiable schools played in this dual system obviously was not a peripheral one; indeed, the official status of the schools attended by the children as "white" and "black" (or "colored") schools was manifested in every significant feature of local school board policy. Thus, as *Green* noted, black teachers were assigned to the "black" schools, inter-school extracurricular activities were arranged according to the school's identity as a "black" school or a "white" school, and geographic attendance zones were separately devised according to the school board's decision to designate certain schools as "white" or "black." The racially identifiable school was both a necessary end and the ultimate expression of the state educational policies condemned in *Brown I*. Under the dual school system all considerations of local educational policy—neighborhood proximity, personal safety of children, optimal school size, etc.—were subordinated to the goal of maintaining separate schools for white and black children. Conversely, the existence of schools officially designated as "white" schools and "black" schools structured the local educational decision-making process in its entirety.

In assessing the dimensions of the school board's affirmative duty to extirpate this dual system, we cannot lose sight of the central role the racially identified school played in that system.

B . . . .

The maintenance of a racially dual system of education entailed a complex local governmental decision-making process . . . exercised with absolute priority given at all times to the goal of keeping blacks apart from whites. The "system" which *Brown I* condemns is . . . precisely this process of school board decision-making . . . . Judicial regulation of the process of extirpating that system of official decision-making must take account of the expression of official policy in the innumerable day-to-day choices which go into the task of administering a local school system, as well as the manifestation of that policy in expressly racial judgments.

In taking account of these imponderables, a court must choose between assessing the motivations of local school board officials in leaving some effects of the former dual system intact, or testing compliance by the results of the school board's proposed changes as manifested in actual change in the makeup of faculties and student bodies. The motivations of school board officials are of the essence in assessing the claim of the school board to have finally disestablished the former dual system. But the many difficulties involved in the judicial assessment of motives of governmental officials in choosing among the many legitimate options they face argue strongly for the substitution, where possible, of remedial criteria framed in terms of the results of local governmental efforts to convert from one system of decision-making to another. Of course, any criterion framed in terms of the results, or effectiveness of governmental remedial action, encompasses the risk that otherwise legitimate governmental options will be foreclosed. But to refrain from pronouncing definite standards to guide remedial action is to run the alternative risk that the system of decision-making premised on racial separation will persist at the heart of the local administrative process in forms not susceptible of judicial discernment, yet working the same fundamental deprivation of constitutional rights that were condemned in *Brown I*. In weighing these risks—to legitimate local governmental interests on the one hand and personal constitutional rights on the other hand—we must of course bear in mind the deep-rooted nature of the system of segregation in the public schools, as manifested not merely in the longstanding traditions of enforced racial separation which preceded *Brown I*, but also the continued adherence to dual system policies in the local areas concerned long after *Brown I* condemned them.

C

These two considerations—the central role played by the racially identifiable school in the former dual system and the necessity for definite remedial criteria for measuring school board compliance with the Constitution-require this Court's rejection of the school board's basic contention that their affirmative duty to disestablish the former dual system is met by the adoption of a student assignment plan based on nonracially gerrymandered geographic zones . . . .

III . . . .

The fairest reading of the record below is that Judge McMillan—while forswearing the goal of a mathematical racial balance—did employ a criterion based primarily on the elimination of all schools which were racially identifiable on the basis of student bodies which were either all black or predominantly black in composition . . . .

Under the dual system which *Brown I* condemned, particular schools were racially identifiable not merely because of their actual student body composition, but also because that student body composition was the foreordained result of a process of governmental decision-making which proceeded from the premise that black students were to be forcibly kept apart from white students . . . .

The substance of the constitutional right recognized in *Brown I* is, therefore, the right to attend school in a system where there are no "racially identifiable" schools, in the sense of schools whose racial composition is attributable to governmental pursuit of the goal of enforced racial separation. Today we approve the use of remedial criteria based on actual racial composition as a proper means for determining when the substance of official decision-making comports with that requirement . . . . This is [done] because [of] the thrust of the segregation policies which *Brown I* condemned . . . . Ostensibly justified under the "separate-but-equal" doctrine of *Plessy* v. *Ferguson*, in the interests of all of the State's citizens, in reality segregation was the outgrowth of a political process in which the majority race—having entirely disenfranchised the minority race—forcibly confined the children of the black community to schools designated for their own race. In this circumstance, schools became racially identifiable as "white" primarily because of the existence of schools which were all black; or, to put the point another way, the central institution of the former dual system was really the "colored" school. [Thus the need for] the elimination of such schools in actual fact . . . .

Although we have said that the elimination of racially identifiable schools requires primarily the elimination of predominantly- or all-black schools, the existence of all-white schools is still relevant to judicial assessment of a particular student assignment plan. School board officials placed great emphasis in argument here on the problems of parental resegregation. They raised the spectre of the courts being forever forced to compel the reassignment of students as white parents move from school district to school district in search of a school where their children can avoid contact with children of the black race. Whatever the empirical basis for these representations, to the extent that parental resegregation truly threatens the stability of a desegregation plan, the proper remedy can only be to assign students in substantially similar proportions throughout the school system. We hold, in other words, that mathematical racial balancing may be imposed on a school system where, in the district court's informed discretion, this remedy is necessary to achieve a stable desegregation plan.

IV . . . .

[W]e think the Court of Appeals' standard fails to meet the requirement we spelled out in *Green*: namely, that the school board must demonstrate the unfeasibility of any plan which would be more effective in converting to a unitary school system. We hold, therefore, that the school board's affirmative duty to disestablish a dual system requires the elimination of all racially identifiable schools to the maximum extent feasible.

3. "MR. JUSTICE DOUGLAS" (MARCH 19, 1971)

Segregation is not *de facto* simply because it is not the result of perceptible discriminatory acts by the *school* board. Housing patterns built by restrictive covenants, racial zoning, and other state sanctioned practices certainly constitute *de jure* segregation. And this segregation is no less legally imposed because the overt state practices have been discontinued. Present housing segregation may be the direct result of past enforcement or practices. Housing patterns remain fixed, and people find it difficult to move from ghettos.

It is assumed that if school boards have to take into consideration state-sanctioned restrictive covenants they are sent far afield from their accustomed tasks.

That, of course, is nonsense. Restrictive covenants—like public housing - created racial neighborhoods. It is still racial neighborhoods that school boards deal with, whatever state action created them. The command of the Fourteenth Amendment runs against the States—and state school boards must undo all the segregation problems which the State created. For each state-action—whether a dual school system or judicially enforced restrictive covenants or state financed public housing—had direct impacts on the complexion of public schools maintained under segregated regimes.

I agree that school authorities cannot remedy housing patterns . . . . But it does not follow that children should be made to suffer the disadvantages of a segregated education because it is "caused" by one arm of the state rather than another. Nor is it any answer to say that the burden on the school board is too great, or unfair. The burden is upon the State to provide equal educational opportunity, undiminished by racial segregation . . . . It cannot be that the federal courts are powerless to remedy this violation and provide desegregated education to these victims.

Should a State decide to remedy present problems by a broader attack on housing segregation, it might eventually accomplish much more than is sought in desegregation suits. But it cannot avoid its immediate responsibility to the present victims of racial segregation by claiming each of its agencies is autonomous . . . . Where the State has been instrumental in total separation of the races, both petitioners and the school board may be powerless to entirely remedy the situation. But the Board does have the power, and the responsibility as an agency of the offending State, to remedy the adverse effects on education which result therefrom . . . .

The school board had been following what it called the "neighborhood school" theory. But in Charlotte a neighborhood tends to be a group of homes generally similar in race and income. With a few exceptions "the schools which have been built recently have been black or almost completely black, or white or almost completely white, and this probability was apparent and predictable when the schools were built." 300 F. Supp., at 1369.

There is much talk both legalistic and sentimental about the values of the neighborhood school. If everyone preferred to live in his or her neighborhood, forced bussing would never have become an issue. People normally like their neighborhood with its church, stores, and schools. But the victims of racial prejudice do not. They do not like subhuman housing; they do not like higher prices or usurious interest rates; they are not at all attracted to their overcrowded, understaffed, decrepit schools.

As stated by the District Court: "The quality of public education should not depend on the economic or racial accident of the neighborhood in which a child's parents have chosen to live—or find they must live—nor on the color of his skin. The neighborhood school concept never *prevented* statutory racial segregation; it may not now be validly used to *perpetuate* segregation." 300 F. Supp., at 1360.

4. MEMORANDUM OF JUSTICE WILLIAM J. BRENNAN

Separation of the races was found to be unconstitutional in *Brown* because it stigmatized members of the Negro race; that is, racial segregation involving state action was found to reflect a state policy or judgment that Negroes are inferior to whites. The Court found that as a result of this stigma (this label of officially determined inferiority), Negro school children suffered psychological harm and educational deprivation. However, the gist of the evil of segregation is not the psychological or educational disadvantages; even if there had been no evidence that segregation produces psychological or educational harm, segregation of the races would still have denied equal protection because it labeled one race as inferior. And that a state may not do under the Fourteenth Amendment.

Since, in my view, the evil of segregation was stigma, the goal and purpose of desegregation is the elimination of stigma. A unitary school system is one whose pupil assignment, faculty assignment, school site location, facilities allocation, etc., do not stigmatize any race. A *de jure* segregated system is one whose policies have stigmatized and still stigmatize one race. In each of these cases, despite the repeal of segregation laws and the discontinuance of the practice of gerrymandering school districts so as to create racial separation, the remaining racial separation continues to bear the stigma which was attached to it by the original unconstitutional state action. In that circumstance the school board has an affirmative duty to do whatever is necessary to eliminate that stigma. And it must eliminate the stigma at once.

What is necessary to eliminate the stigmatizing effect of racial separation in a formerly *de jure* segregated school district? Clearly, the mere repeal of segregation laws is not enough if it leaves the situation of racial separation substantially the same as it was before. The only way to remove the stigma of racial separation is to achieve substantial integration. This does not mean that every last Negro child must attend an integrated school; it does not even mean, necessarily, that there cannot constitutionally be an all-black school in a particular district. What it does mean is that there must be enough mixing of the races throughout the public school system that any remaining racial separation is [not] fairly attributable . . . to state policy past or present . . . . Only when a school board has demonstrated its good faith in racial matters by bringing about substantial racial mixing will any remaining separation be fairly interpretable as not reflecting the previous state policy of treating Negroes as inferior. How much integration must there be? No one set of figures will give the answer in all situations, but some rules of thumb are possible. An "integrated school" can be defined as one in which neither race constitutes more than 90% of the student body. And, as a rule of thumb, a school system will be considered presumptively unitary if 70% of the Negro pupils attend integrated schools. However, if conditions are particularly favorable for more integration (as they were in the *Green* case), a higher degree of integration will be required. For, if a higher degree of integration is easily achievable, to stop at a lower degree of integration will be to adopt a state policy that encourages segregation, and such a policy stigmatizes . . . .

How is this integration to be achieved? The Constitution does not prescribe a particular method, and a variety can be used—including: neighborhood school districts gerrymandered to promote integration, bussing, school site location, etc. It is within the discretion of the school boards initially and of the courts ultimately to select in each particular case that method which achieves the constitutionally required degree of integration in the most convenient manner. But there can be no doubt that where bussing is the only way to achieve the required amount of integration, the district judge has the power and the duty to order it.

CHAPTER FOUR

KEYES

Before the year 1971 was out, *Swann* had become a byword for judges in the North and West who chafed at regional differentiations in desegregation law. While the decision admittedly "did relate to [the] southern states," noted Judge Stanley Weigel, in a major case involving the San Francisco schools, "neither the logic nor the force of the ruling is limited by any North-South boundary line . . . .[T]he Supreme Court has never condoned [a] double standard of constitutional compliance based upon geography."[1] If a school board anywhere drew attendance lines that "maintain or heighten racial imbalance, the resulting segregation is *de jure*."[2] Similarly, a Seventh Circuit panel upheld Judge Damon Keith's finding of what the panel called "purposeful segregation"[3] in Pontiac, Michigan, without thinking it necessary to confront Judge Keith's highly capacious view of what was purposeful. The circuit rejected school board protests against the broad remedy Judge Keith had ordered, pointing out in a footnote: "Before the issuance of this opinion, the United States Supreme Court handed down its decision in *Swann* v. *Charlotte-Mecklenburg Board of Education* . . . . We observe that the District Court's order in this case . . . is within the scope of its remedial powers as enunciated by the Court [in *Swann*]."[4]

In another decision in northern California, only a month after *Swann*, District Judge Harold Pregerson issued an edict against the Oxnard school district, because its schools were "segregated in fact"[5]; the judge accepted plaintiffs' contention that "'the imposition of a neighborhood school plan on a racially segregated residential pattern . . . caus[es] racially imbalanced attendance areas and . . . such actions cast *de jure* overtones.'"[6] His holding, Judge Pregerson hastened to point out, "does not conflict with . . . *Swann* v. *Charlotte-Mecklenburg Board of Education*."[7] A few months later, District Judge Stephen Roth of Michigan, espousing a view of liability which had much in common with those put forth in California and in his own state, ordered Michigan officials to submit desegregation plans implicating three counties surrounding Detroit, as part of the process of remedying unconstitutional racial separation in the city.

Swann and its northern progeny also intensified the political reaction against busing for integration, by both the Congress and by the Nixon administration. An obvious given, during this period, was the bitter, potentially explosive opposition to this practice by the vast majority of Americans. Polls consistently showed that three out of every four people were against it.[8] Responding to this sentiment in November of 1971, the House adopted a series of amendments to a higher education bill which went further than ever before in seeking to stifle judicial and executive authority to bus.

One of the amendments, offered by Representative William Broomfield of Michigan, forbade future court orders requiring racial balance to take effect until the defendant school board got a chance to appeal the order to the Supreme Court. Broomfield's creation directly contradicted the Court's 1969 decision in *Alexander* v. *Holmes County Board of Education*, decreeing that desegregation mandates must be implemented "forthwith," even while appeals were pending.

Another amendment, from arch-conservative John Ashbrook of Ohio, prohibited the use of federal funds for busing students in order to achieve desegregation. A third, by Representative Edith Green of Oregon, would essentially have stripped HEW of its power to cut off federal funds to school districts resisting court-ordered segregation.[9]

The Senate staved off this volley by a single vote, and a conference committee eventually adopted only the Broomfield amendment. But President Nixon, grudgingly signing the education measure in June of 1972, made it plain that the busing battle was far from over. The bill's antibusing provisions, he asserted, were "inadequate, misleading, and entirely unsatisfactory . . . . Had these disappointing measures alone come to this office . . . they would have been the subject of an immediate veto."[10]

Nixon pressed the Congress to adopt the antibusing program he had offered the previous March, entitled the Equal Educational Opportunities Act. The critical part of this legislation provided that courts could not order any elementary school student farther away from his or her neighborhood school than to the next closest one, or increase the overall amount of busing in a school district. School boards were entitled to a rehearing on court orders going beyond these standards, an obvious recipe for the resegregation of many districts.[11]

If the Congress did not act on his program, Nixon threatened, "we will have no choice but to seek a constitutional amendment which will put the goals of better education for all of our children above the objective of massive busing for some children."[12] Several versions of such an amendment were kicking around by 1972, the most influential one stating that, "No public school student shall, because of his race, creed, or color, be assigned to or required to attend a particular school."[13] (None of them, though, ever came to a vote on the floor of either the House or

Senate.)

More than 500 law professors signed a statement pronouncing Nixon's scheme *un*constitutional. But the House passed the Equal Educational Opportunities Act on August 17, 1972, after toughening up its provisions by prohibiting the busing of secondary as well as elementary school students beyond the school next nearest to their homes. It took an end of session filibuster by Senate liberals and moderates to keep the bill from passing.

In this superheated atmosphere, the Supreme Court finally moved to examine segregation in schools outside the South.

I

The showdown came in Denver, Colorado, a city with an Hispanic as well as an African-American minority group. Both groups eventually involved themselves in the legal battle. (In a decision appearing just before *Brown* v. *Board of Education* in the Supreme Court reports, the Court had ruled that Hispanic-Americans were a distinct class in the nation, included under the protective scope of the equal protection clause, and able to bring suit under it.)[14]

Between 1950 and 1970, Denver's African-American community grew from 15,000 to 47,000, though this still constituted less than 10% of the total population. Concentrated at first in an area just northeast of the city's center (referred to as the "core" area), the community migrated eastward toward a six-lane highway, Colorado Boulevard, then across the boulevard into a section known as Park Hill. African-Americans comprised 5.6% of the population between the core city and Colorado Boulevard in 1950, 50.6% in 1960, and 69.8% in 1970. The Park Hill area was 98% white in 1960, majority black in 1970. Much of the Hispanic population clustered in the core area, but, on the whole, was more scattered through Denver; it numbered 86,000 in 1970, 16.8% of the total population.

The demographic changes west of Colorado Boulevard, then in Park Hill, meant changes in school enrollment patterns, and a number of disputes erupted in the late 1950's and early 1960's between the school board and African-American parent groups, over allegations that the board was manipulating attendance zones and school construction in order to maintain as much segregation as possible. A study commission of 1962 recommended that Denver modify its professed allegiance to a neighborhood school philosophy and seek greater racial and ethnic diversity. The school board adopted a resolution endorsing this view, but little happened as a result.

In the wake of a further study, the board moved decisively, however, in 1968. It passed a motion submitted by its only African-American member, directing the superintendent to draw up plans for integration in the Denver schools. The essence of this planning was embodied in three board resolutions, aimed at achieving racial balance in Park Hill and the immediately adjacent neighborhood. Approved between January and April of 1969, the resolutions assigned minority junior high and elementary school children in the area to noncontiguous Anglo schools, and Anglo youngsters to ones in Park Hill. Before the school board could implement the resolutions, though, a new election saw the replacement of two of the members who had voted for them. In June of 1969, the reconstituted board rescinded the integration resolutions.

African-American parents immediately filed suit in federal court in the name of their children, claiming that rescission of the resolutions, by itself, violated the childrens' constitutional rights, but also that illegal segregative practices were being perpetrated in Park Hill (and slightly east of it). They demanded that the court immediately implement the resolutions.

There were other claims, however, which brought Hispanic-American plaintiffs into the suit from the outset, for counsel argued that many of the core schools had been illegally segregated by deliberate actions of the board. In addition, they maintained that all minority schools in the Denver system (all of them in the core city, just west of it, or in Park Hill) were grossly inferior to the rest of Denver's schools and denied equal educational opportunity. Most of the core schools were predominantly Hispanic, of course, though significant numbers of African-Americans still attended some of them.

Due to the need for action before the September, 1969 school term began, Judge William Doyle ruled first, at a preliminary hearing, on the constitutionality of the rescission. (There were eventually two hearings, because of a remand from the Tenth Circuit on technical and statutory grounds.) His initial opinions preserved traditional distinctions in school law, for the most part. The rescission was unconstitutional, he held, and the resolutions must be implemented, because their withdrawal *undid* the efforts of Denver authorities to correct identifiable de jure violations which had occurred in Park Hill and environs over the previous decade. "[W]e are not here faced with . . . simple or innocent de facto segregation."[15] During the ten years preceding passage of the resolutions, Denver authorities pursued policies designed to "maintain, encourage and continue segregation in the public schools in the face of the clear mandates of *Brown* v. *Board of Education*."[16] Rescission, Judge Doyle argued, was the "climactic and culminative act" of this drama.[17]

The judge detailed what he saw as numerous instances of "de jure segregation"—open and obvious actions of the school board and school administrators designed to separate the races. In 1959, for example, the board approved construction of a new elementary school, the Barrett school, just west of Colorado Boulevard, when that represented the exact eastern terminus of black population advance in the area. Ignoring the protests of African-American parents, the administration not only built the school, which opened 90% black, but made it of unusually small size, guaranteeing it would not pick up attendance from two overcrowded white schools—Stedman and Hallett—just east of the Boulevard.

As Stedman and then Hallett changed their demographic character during the 1960's, the school board made a number of boundary alterations, which Judge Doyle condemned as racially motivated. In 1962, the board abolished a so-called optional zone between Hallett—still 85% white, but in the process of transformation—and the all-white Phillips school, a zone consisting predominantly of Anglo students. Pupils in this zone had previously chosen which of the two schools they wished to attend. Now, the white students were forced into Phillips.

Two years later, officials abolished an optional zone between the Stedman school, 85% black by this time, and Park Hill, 95% white, giving the zone permanently to Park Hill. The zone was 96% Anglo. They also detached what Judge Doyle claimed was an 80% Anglo section of the attendance area around Hallett, now down to 68.7% white, and gave it to Phillips, a shift involving about 70 students. (The judge also reproved Denver authorities for cutting off, at the same time, an Anglo portion of the Stedman zone and zoning it to Hallett, though if the authorities were subject to censure for sending white students away from Hallett, it was not clear why they were actionable for sending them to the school as well, especially since Stedman was irrecoverably segregated.)

Besides manipulating boundaries in Park Hill, the administration ordered mobile classrooms placed at Stedman and Hallett in 1964–65 "to solidify segregation," by augmenting the schools' "capacity to absorb the additional influx of Negro population into the area."[18] By the time of the *Keyes* hearings, Barrett was 100% black, Stedman 92.4%, Hallett 84.4%. Park Hill, on the other hand, was 71% Anglo, Phillips 55.3%. The other elementary school in Park Hill (Smith) was 95% black. "Between 1960 and 1969," the judge concluded, "the Board's policies with respect to these . . . Denver schools show an undeviating purpose to isolate Negro students . . . ."[19]

When de dure violations were unavailable, however, Judge Doyle used the very existence of the rescission as a deprivation of constitutional rights, and did so in a manner suggesting that he was not as picayune about the de jure-de facto distinction as his discussion of the elementary school irregularities indicated. Thus Smiley Junior High, into which the Park Hill schools, plus Barrett, fed, was segregated, quite naturally, in 1969, but no specific violations were cited in connection with its development. The judge found, nonetheless, that since the school board resolutions "were designed to desegregate Smiley," withdrawing them "was wilful as to its effect" on the school.[20] In this same vein, he later held, at the trial on the merits, that rescission of the resolution affecting another junior high school (Cole) "was unlawful," because it frustrated "ultimate desegregation."[21] The same thing applied to rescinding proposed action at East High School, "allow[ing] the trend toward segregation at East to continue unabated."[22] Judge Doyle's conclusions as to rescission, made at the preliminary hearing and reaffirmed at trial, mixed condemnation of deliberate violations with the belief that racial imbalance per se was proscribed. "The policies . . . of the Board prior to . . . adoption of [the] Resolutions" constituted "de jure segregation," and rescission "was a legislative act which had for its purpose restoration of the old status quo." Yet the "act *in and of itself* was an act of de jure segregation."[23]

At this full-dress trial, which commenced in February, 1970, plaintiffs pressed their claim that some of the core city schools were illegally segregated, and that all of the segregated schools in the city, whether majority black, majority Hispanic, or a combination of the two, "are grossly inferior and provide an unequal educational opportunity for minority students."[24]

In treating the first of these charges, Judge Doyle suddenly altered course, his views on the rescission notwithstanding. He unveiled a far more exacting criterion for assessing de jure violations in the core city than he had used in dealing with Park Hill. To comprise such a violation, he now stated, "the school administration must have taken some action with a purpose to segregate"; a "current condition of segregation must exist"; and, most important, there had to be a significant "*causal connection* between the acts of the school administration complained of and the current condition of segregation"—a connection supported by specific demographic evidence.[25] The burden of proving these offenses still fell on the plaintiffs in Denver. The judge set up, in short, a *Swann*-type inquiry into violation, without benefit of what were to become the *Swann* presumptions.

Armed with these newly forged tools, Judge Doyle rejected allegations of de jure segregation in the core city, although plaintiffs' evidence closely resembled that presented in the earlier phase of the case. In 1952, for instance, school authorities authorized a new building for Manual High School, located in the heart of the black ghetto, though not yet a majority black school. Despite vigorous opposition from community residents, they constructed the building at exactly the spot where the old one stood. As the black population moved east toward Colorado Boulevard, officials moved the Manual boundary line with them, abolishing, in 1956, the optional zone the high school shared with a predominantly Anglo school. They made the identical boundary adjustment for nearby Cole Junior High, abolishing its optional zone with then predominantly white Smiley. In 1962, they abolished optional areas around another junior high (Morey), undergoing racial and ethnic transition. In this case, though, the obliterated zones fell overwhelmingly in all-white areas, the students were compulsorily zoned into white schools, and the next year the Anglo population of Morey went down from 65–80% to 45–49%. In this connection, plaintiffs pointed accusingly at the reverse action taken by administrators a decade earlier, with regard to a core city elementary school in transition (Columbine). Here, authorities *established* optional zones with Anglo schools, zones "apparently employed by Anglo students as a means of escaping from Columbine."[26]

Yet none of these maneuvers satisfied Judge Doyle's altered notion of de jure segregation. Surprisingly, the judge denied the presence of any segregative intent in these actions. With regard to Manual, he noted, "It should . . . be kept in mind that prior to *Brown* v. *Board of Education*, it was apparently taken for granted by everyone that the status quo, as far as the Negroes were concerned, should not be disturbed . . . ."[27] But regardless of intent, he denied liability, because it was obvious to him that the school board's prior actions could not have contributed significantly to the segregated condition of the core schools in 1969. Most of the minority concentration at Cole and Manual "occurred long after" the disputed sitting and boundary decisions took place. "The . . . situation then cannot be placed at the administration doorstep; if cause or fault has to be ascertained it is that of the community as a whole in imposing . . . housing restraints."[28] Similarly, official actions with regard to Columbine, "as in the case of Manual and Cole, . . . appear in retrospect to have had little to do with the present minority population."[29] And "whether Morey is presently a segregated school remains a question," the judge declared, though its black enrollment in 1969–70 was 52.4%.[30] Overall, he felt, "it would be inequitable to conclude *de jure* segregation exists where a *de jure* act had no more than a trifling effect on the end result which produced [a given] condition."[31]

Had this general approach been followed in evaluating Park Hill, it is hard to see how Judge Doyle could have come up with any de jure violations. On whatever side of Colorado Boulevard Barrett School stood, and whatever its capacity, it was destined to be an overwhelmingly black school by 1968. No evidence existed as to how many Anglo children actually chose to attend Hallett in 1962 and were forced into Phillips by abolition of the optional zone between them, though it cannot have been a great number. There was a comparable lack of evidence with regard to the Stedman-Park Hill zone, abolished two years later. The sad truth, however, is that had the zones existed into the late 1960's, no white student would have opted for Hallett or Stedman. Furthermore, sending 70 or so white students from Hallett to Phillips in 1964, offset, in some measure, by the whites sent to Hallett from Stedman, could not explain, by Judge Doyle's revised standard, why Hallett lost 175 Anglo students in that year, and numbered over 80% black by 1968. (Denver's lawyers maintained, in fact, that 50 of the 70 students sent from Hallett to Phillips in 1964 were African-American.)[32] Mobile classrooms made their appearance at Stedman and Hallett only after the schools were well on their way to becoming overwhelmingly black, and the students kept there because of the mobiles would not otherwise have gone to the white schools in Park Hill, for those schools too were overcrowded.

The two segments of Judge Doyle's analysis diverged so widely as to cause Denver's attorneys to maintain that he had not meant to find de jure segregation in Park Hill at all. His initial opinions, they argued, rested on the "finding . . . that the rescission, per se, was the operative act" of discrimination.[33] The references to "state-imposed segregation . . . at Barrett, Stedman, Hallett, and Smiley were not, . . . we submit . . . , the basis for the Court's order directing the implementation of the rescinded resolutions."[34] Judge Doyle had dealt with these segregated conditions in the Park Hill area only insofar "as they were probative" of the purpose behind the board's rescission actions: to retain the "racial imbalance" already existing in the area, whatever the reason for it.[35]

There was certainly force to this argument, considering the judge's perambulations on the matter of segregative intent. Yet the earlier pair of decisions do close with the explicit assertion that, "[T]he policies and actions of the [Denver] Board *prior to* the adoption of [the] Resolutions . . . constitute de jure segregation."

II

It was in dealing with the plaintiffs' final contention that Judge Doyle's most deeply-held values about school law made their appearance. Having rejected accusations of de jure segregation in some of the core schools, he decisively crossed the line between de jure and de facto he had just drawn. All segregated schools in the city, he ruled, were offering an inferior education to their students, and denying them, therefore, the constitutional right to an equal educational opportunity. This was due partly to actions censurable even under *Plessy*, and not calling necessarily for integration as a remedy. The judge cited assignment to the minority schools of less experienced teachers, and constant teacher turnover, all of which helped to produce lower achievement scores and higher dropout rates among minority students.

"[B]ut we cannot ignore the overwhelming evidence to the effect that isolation or segregation per se is a substantial factor in producing unequal educational opportunity."[36] It was obvious to Judge Doyle that the African-American community in Denver did not "consider the segregated school as a legitimate institution for social and economic advancement."[37] Because "students do not feel that [such a] school is an effective aid in achieving their goal—acceptance and integration into the mainstream of American life," they did not push themselves to learn.[38] And parents, harboring "similar feelings," often failed to encourage their children.[39] "It strikes one as incongruous that the community of Denver would tolerate schools" so "inferior in quality."[40]

The judge engaged in somewhat circular reasoning to justify his conclusions. Under reigning precedent, he admitted, school authorities were "not constitutionally required" to exalt integration over a neutrally-zoned neighborhood system, so long as they ensured, "at a minimum," equal quality education for all children.[41] Yet how was that possible when "segregated schools are inherently unequal," and "segregation, regardless of its cause, is a major factor in producing . . . unequal educational opportunity"?[42] A footnote at the beginning of the discussion of educational equality took the bark entirely off the matter. "There is no discernible difference in result between the *de facto* and *de jure* varieties [of segregation]. Both produce the same obnoxious results . . . ."[43]

The nature of this second set of constitutional violations precluded compensatory education as a remedy. After hearing the testimony of experts, including Professor Coleman, Judge Doyle ordered a plan designed to make all of the inferior schools majority Anglo. The plan required the busing of 7,000 children, in addition to the 4,000 to be bused in Park Hill. Doyle included in the remedy, however, only those schools having a black *or* an Hispanic enrollment in excess of 70%. He refused to combine the two minority groups to reach 70%.

The Denver defendants appealed to the Tenth Circuit Court of Appeals. They asked for a stay, pending appeal, of the implementation of Judge Doyle's orders concerning equal educational opportunity in the core city. The circuit court initially denied the request, but then granted it on March 26, 1971, concluding that the school board should not be forced into "implementation of the total plan" until the circuit and the various litigants had "the benefit" of the Supreme Court's immanent decision in *Swann*.[44] Exactly a month later, *Swann* having come down, the Supreme Court vacated the stay.[45]

Before anything could happen, though, a Tenth Circuit panel scuttled Judge Doyle's plan for the core city. Doyle's opinion, noted Judge Delmas Hill (who, as a district judge, sat on the original panel in *Brown* v. *Board of Education*), left "little doubt that the finding of unequal educational opportunity . . . pivots on the conclusion that segregated schools, whatever the cause, per se produce . . . an inferior educational opportunity."[46] This assertion, Judge Hill felt, "must rest squarely on the premise that Denver's neighborhood school policy is violative of the Fourteenth Amendment."[47] Yet "[w]e [have] never construed *Brown* to prohibit racially unbalanced schools."[48]

The circuit panel, indeed, removed the core city entirely from judicial supervision by upholding Judge Doyle's rejection of the claims of deliberate discrimination in that area. The burden of proving de jure violations there, it held, had appropriately been foisted on the plaintiffs, in a school system never segregated by law and designed on a neighborhood pattern. Since neighborhood schools were "tolerated under the Constitution, it would be incongruous to require the Denver School Board to prove the non-existence of a secret, illicit, segregatory intent."[49]

The circuit decision did affirm the violations in Park Hill, ignoring any incongruity between this judgment and the clean bill of health given the core city schools. There was "ample evidence . . . to sustain the trial court's findings that race was made the basis for school districting with the purpose and effect of producing substantially segregated schools in the Park Hill area."[50] For this reason, it was "unnecessary to . . . decide whether the rescission . . . was *also* an act of de jure segregation."[51]

The school board appealed the affirmance of Judge Doyle's original decisions on Park Hill. The plaintiffs wanted the charge of deliberate segregation in the core schools approved. They also wanted a finding of unequal educational opportunity in all of the minority schools, including those with combined black and Hispanic enrollments exceeding 70%. The Supreme Court granted certiorari in *Keyes* v. *School District No. 1* on January 17, 1972.

III

The Denver plaintiffs (now the petitioners) offered a variety of arguments on appeal, any one of which justified, in their view, a systemwide remedy. The illegal segregation in Park Hill alone, they asserted, called for such a remedy, at least for the African-American students, since it affected a significant percentage of them (over a third); and the deliberate violations which should have been found in the core schools would extend this remedy to yet other black pupils, as well as to Hispanic youngsters. Petitioners also defended Judge Doyle's findings of unequal educational opportunity. Racial or ethnic isolation, itself, was surely a factor in making the ghetto school "'a symbol' of inferiority and impotency for the minority community."[52] But "[e]ven standing alone," the gross material inequities in Denver "constitute a clear denial of equal protection based upon race and ethnicity, for it is exactly [this] type of invidious, disadvantaging discrimination at which the Fourteenth Amendment was directed."[53]

Feeling, however, that the Court might not want to assault the frontier between de jure and de facto segregation, petitioners placed heavy emphasis on yet another submission, the one which *Swann* and *Davis* now opened to them. They adapted to the northern context the *Swann* presumptions, though using them for liability purposes as well as for remedial ones. Both the district court and the Tenth Circuit, they maintained, had committed the same fundamental error, "misplac[ing] the burden of proof"[54] on the issue of deliberate segregation outside of Park Hill. Because of the extensive violations in that area, the lower courts "should have followed a rule similar to that in *Swann* v. *Board of Education.*"[55] Instead of requiring the plaintiffs to prove the presence of de jure violations in the core schools and to assay their effects, the courts should simply have imputed the imbalances there, and in the rest of Denver's schools, to the discriminatory acts of local officials, unless they could show that current segregation was not the result of any "present or past discriminatory action on their part."[56] Otherwise, all of the racial, and ethnic, separation in the city should be considered de jure, making Denver, in essence, a dual system. A *Swann*-type remedy necessarily followed, therefore, a remedy encompassing the Hispanic minority as well as African-American youngsters (though the violations in Park Hill which sparked this process focused only on the latter).

The same kind of presumption, and the ensuing remedy, applied to the issue of segregative intent on the part of school officials, another area where Judge Doyle had taken a relaxed approach to the core schools. The offenses in Park Hill comprised "a prima facie case" of segregative intent in the entire Denver system, and shifted to the school board the burden of proving that any other racial or ethnic separation found in the system was dictated "by a compelling state interest, which could not be served by less segregatory practices."[57]

The petitioners could succeed, therefore, not only without breaching the barrier between types of segregation, but also without having to document the connection between past segregative acts of the school board and current demographic patterns in Denver. Their brief, in fact, offered some arresting evidence on the interrelationship between residential and educational separation, focusing on the testimony, at trial, of African-American parents who saw gerrymandering by school officials as irrefutable proof "that wherever they move they will be segregated"; such feelings, it was noted, "tend to further impact segregation in established black residential areas."[58] The point was a valid one, though, fortunately for the erstwhile plaintiffs, not part of an analysis essential for victory on appeal.

Those plaintiffs never knew how close the Supreme Court came during this period to striking at the de jure- de facto distinction. But the papers of Justice Hugo

Black, now crucially reinforced by material from the papers of Justice William O. Douglas, tell a revealing story in this regard.

When the request to vacate the circuit court stay in *Keyes* went up to the justices in the spring of 1971, Justice Douglas wrote a memorandum, dated April 6, favoring this course of action, and endorsing Judge Doyle's approach to the minority schools. By the next day, three of his colleagues had joined an expanded version of this document.[59] The memorandum they signed on to threatened regional boundaries in educational litigation, if on a somewhat opaque doctrinal basis.

Officially, Douglas justified the lower court's action as an application of *Plessy*, of the principle merely that "a school board may not channel all the better resources of the system into the white schools even if the racial imbalance in the schools is constitutionally permissible."[60] Whether the fourteenth amendment reached all "types of school segregation is one question . . . . Whether schools are providing an equal educational opportunity for their students is another question. *Plessy* is relevant to this latter question."[61]

That the justice knew Judge Doyle's opinion went beyond these matters, however, and that he sympathized with the extension, is indicated by his addition of an appendix to his memorandum, quoting selected passages from the opinion. "The overwhelming evidence in this case supports the finding . . . that improvement in the quality of education in the minority school *can only be brought about by a program of . . . integration . . . .* [C]ompensatory education . . . without . . . a program of desegregation and integration has been unsuccessful."[62] Justices Brennan and Marshall quickly endorsed the Douglas opinion, not surprisingly in light of the suspicions about the de jure-de facto distinction they had conveyed in *Swann* (though Brennan's endorsement seemed to fly in the face of his earlier reservations about an empirical, "equal educational opportunity" reading of *Brown*). More surprising was the addition of Justice Potter Stewart's name to the Douglas memorandum. With four justices supporting Douglas' position, and with Justice Byron White having removed himself from the Denver case because of past associations with the city school board, this meant one-half of the Court favored an expression of views challenging, though gingerly, the traditional separation in school law.

Still, four was not a majority, and Chief Justice Burger proposed that the Court simply vacate the stay, and say no more. Stewart and Douglas indicated a willingness to accept this disposition of the matter, but, now, Justice Hugo Black weighed in. On April 16, he told the chief that he could not accept such an order, which still seemed to indicate approval of the district court's actions.[63] The next day he circulated a new draft of a dissent he had composed, attacking the logic espoused by Judge Doyle. Black doubted whether the trial judge's findings "actually show that minority students in central city schools are being denied equal educational opportunity."[64] In any event, he asserted, "when the State is not responsible for . . . racial concentrations," as he believed to be the case here, the appropriate remedy for inequities in education "would be an order that the teaching staffs and facilities be equalized, not that the pupils be sent to distant schools to achieve a better proportioned racial balance."[65]

Douglas quickly stated that if Black filed this opinion, he would forget about going along with the chief and publish his own contribution, which he now augmented to rebut Black's arguments. Judge Doyle had thought integration the best remedy for the inequities in Denver, Douglas noted, and while an order simply equalizing faculty and facilities would have been "constitutionally unassailable . . . if it promised to be effective," nothing "limited the power of the District Courts to fashion [the] equitable relief" they felt "appropriate."[66] Finally, though, the justices coalesced around a draft order originally submitted on April 15 by Justice John Marshall Harlan.[67] The order, recast somewhat before being promulgated, vacated the circuit court's stay, while noting explicitly that, "We . . . intimate no views upon the merits of the underlying issues."[68] Yet, clearly, a significant number of justices had expressed a willingness to end all talk of a double standard by the time *Keyes* came up for full consideration in the fall of 1972.

The Court's conference on October 17, however, failed to produce a majority willing to discard the de jure-de facto distinction. Justice Lewis Powell, who had replaced Hugo Black in late 1971, favored a uniform rule, and the end of what he regarded as an invidious discrimination between regions; but he strongly opposed the kind of cross-district busing which usually went with such a position, and specifically went with Judge Doyle's opinion. Justice Brennan contented himself, therefore, with building on already excavated ground. He put together a tentative majority, including Justice Harry Blackmun, by focusing on the lower courts' misallocation of the burden of proof, once violations in Park Hill were proven, and the broad remedial program needed to rectify that error, a program which would achieve the same result in Denver, of course, as the position Justice Douglas had articulated.

Even then, the possibilities of forming a majority around a single standard were not exhausted. Justice Blackmun, now holding back, in early 1973, from giving the fifth vote to Justice Brennan's *Swann*-like draft, sent Brennan a note containing a tantalizing hint. "I am not at all certain that the de jure—de facto distinction in school segregation will hold up in the long run. Segregation may well be segregation, whatever the form."[69] And when Justice Brennan subsequently examined Justice Powell's draft exposition of the views Powell had expressed at conference, he wrote to his colleagues, on April 3, 1973, stating a definite willingness "to recast the opinion and jettison the distinction [between de jure and de facto segregation] if a majority of the Court is prepared to do so," though he did not say exactly on what basis he would do this.[70] He had Powell and Blackmun, and presumably Stewart, in mind.

But Brennan got no positive feedback on his suggestion. Justice Powell, most likely, could not surmount his differences with the majority over busing, though John Jeffries' magisterial biography of the justice suggests that Powell's "surprising ineffectiveness as a Court politician"[71] kept him even from trying.

[W]ould Brennan have been willing to revise his opinion on the de facto-de jure distinction and let Powell go his own way on busing? There is no way of knowing, for Powell never asked. He never tried to accept Brennan's offer on his own terms or approached Brennan to explore the common ground. He never tried to make a deal . . . . Had the situation been reversed, had someone with four votes and good prospect of a fifth offered Brennan half a loaf, he would have jumped at the chance.[72]

Justice Stewart, apparently, made no written response to Brennan's initiative. As for Justice Blackmun, he finally pulled back from the effort to merge de jure and de facto segregation. At least that is what we must make of the note he sent to Justice Brennan on May 30, giving final endorsement to the existing majority opinion. Blackmun admitted to retaining "some unease about the situation, for I am persuaded, as Lewis and Bill Douglas appear to be, that the de jure-de facto distinction eventually must give way."

I take it, from your letter of April 3, that you also are inclined to the view Lewis entertains except for the question of remedy. I feel, however, as apparently you do, that we need not meet the de jure-de facto distinction for purposes of the Denver case. Because I feel this way, I join you.[73]

But the issue was not whether it was possible to resolve *Keyes* without discarding the traditional separation between types of segregation. Obviously, that could be done. The issue raised by Justice Brennan's April 3 letter was whether the Court should deliberately use *Keyes* as the vehicle for doing away with this separation. Justice Blackmun, it appears, simply did not wish to do so.

Blackmun was ready to bring *Keyes* to closure partly because of the clumsy maneuvers being executed at this time by the chief justice. Burger had voted in the conference of October 17, 1972 to uphold the circuit court decision, and, as early as December, 1972, was hinting that the Supreme Court delay final action on Denver until further developments took place in the Detroit case, concerning interdistrict remedies.[74] On May 30, 1973, at the eleventh hour, Burger formally proposed that since Sixth Circuit action in Detroit's controversy was imminent, "I think this case [Denver] should go over to the next term," so that it could be coupled with the Detroit matter. He admitted, though, that the "6th Circuit opinion may alter my view."[75]

Brennan instantly objected to any such proposal, regarding it as a transparent stall. "I most strenuously oppose your suggestion that *Keyes* go over for reargument. If you have canvassed the *Detroit* issues, as I have, you might agree that none of them is even remotely connected with any decided in *Keyes*."[76] A somewhat defensive chief immediately wrote back to Brennan, admitting, "I freely confess I have not canvassed the *Detroit* issues. I have an abundance of work on the cases already here . . . ."[77] Nonetheless, he tartly reminded his colleague, the circuit court analysis of the issues in Detroit "may not correspond with yours and, of course, it will be their opinion we will be asked to review."[78]

This "bickering proved too much for [Justice] Blackmun,"[79] whose letter joining the Brennan opinion was dated the same day as the barrage of missives between Burger and Brennan. His action, however, he diplomatically informed Justice Brennan, was "[w]holly apart from the suggestion of the Chief Justice."[80] Two days before the *Keyes* decision came down, the chief wrote Brennan, "Will you be good enough to show me as concurring in the result."[81]

IV

The decision in *Keyes* v. *School District No.1* was announced on June 21, 1973. Much unlike the Court's product in *Swann*, the majority opinion tracked rather closely reasoning found in the petitioners' brief. Like *Swann*, however, *Keyes* officially maintained, yet in reality blurred, the line between types of segregation.

Justice Brennan eschewed discussion of educational deprivation or minority perceptions of separate schools. He made it clear that this case was about old-fashioned de jure segregation, and "that the differentiating factor between de jure segregation and so-called de facto segregation to which we referred in Swann is *purpose* or *intent* to segregate," the existence of "a current condition of segregation resulting from intentional state action."[82] The Court found "no occasion to consider [here] whether a 'neighborhood school policy' of itself will justify racial or ethnic concentrations in the absence of a finding that school authorities have committed acts constituting de jure segregation."[83]

But Judge Doyle had failed to assess properly the import of the de jure violations in Denver. He had "fractionated"[84] his analysis by making the plaintiffs start over again in proving discrimination in the core city. The fact was that the Park Hill violations "did not relate to an insubstantial or trivial fragment of the school system."[85] Therefore, Justice Brennan asserted, "it is only common sense to conclude that there exists a predicate for a finding of the existence of a dual . . . system."[86]

This was because the violations in Park Hill had undoubtedly exerted a "substantial reciprocal effect,"[87] which spread to nearby schools, keeping them predominantly Anglo. More important, these effects could also have played a decisive role in shaping "the racial composition of residential neighborhoods within [the] metropolitan area," by "earmarking schools" as black or white.[88]

Such a broad ranging hypothesis certainly raised questions, especially in a community not subject to the gross distortions caused by southern-style de jure segregation. It was even more likely here that school separation exerted only a tangential influence on residential separation. A perceptive critic in the *Harvard Civil Rights–Civil Liberties Law Review* pounced on the weaknesses of the majority's analysis. "Many factors other than de jure school segregation downtown keep blacks out of the upper middle class suburbs of American cities. Residential effects stirred up by localized de jure acts may dissipate to imperceptible ripples before reaching the 'nice' bedroom suburbs of a district . . . . The Court's conclusion . . . derives little support from the realities of urban demographic patterns."[89] Indeed, any "reciprocal effects" exerted on Denver's core city by segregation in Park Hill would have been of quite a remarkable nature, since housing segregation in the former manifested itself ten years before the school violations in the latter.

But Justice Brennan's observations were not meant as a definitive discourse on urban sociology, for *Keyes* quickly drew on the logic of its southern predecessor. By means of a "judicially created presumption," the opinion suddenly transformed speculation into constitutional certainty; it abruptly "shifted gear—from an explanation as to how the germ [of illegal segregation] *might* have spread to a conclusion that [it] had *in fact* so spread, . . . throughout [a] school system" such as Denver's.[90]

Thus *Keyes* moves from its musings on "reciprocal effects" to the pronouncement that the only way authorities can keep violations in a significant part of a school system, such as Park Hill, from leading to the determination that they maintain a dual system is by proving their district is one "in which . . . geographic structure . . . or . . . natural boundaries . . . have the effect of dividing the district into separate, identifiable and unrelated units."[91] Such cases, Justice Brennan added, "must be rare,"[92] and, except in such extraordinary instances, presumption automatically becomes proof. A northern school system is adjudged the equivalent of Charlotte or Richmond. Then the *Swann* standard on remedy comes into play. The system must achieve all-out integration, except to the degree that a school board can shoulder the burden of showing that its prior acts in no way caused the existing racial disparities.

Even if Denver officials did manage to show that their district consisted of divisible parts, it still would do them little good, since they faced another hurdle to vindicating themselves. The manipulations in Park Hill, thought Justice Brennan, clearly revealed a segregative intent on the school board's part, relating to a sizable portion of the school system, and this constituted a prima facie case of intentional segregation throughout the system, wherever racial imbalance existed. If Denver's board and administration had cheated, in short, to bring about some of the city's segregated schools, why was not all of the segregation the result of evil design? "[W]e hold that a finding of intentionally segregative school board actions in a meaningful portion of a school system, as in this case, creates a presumption that other segregated schooling within the system is not adventitious."[93]

To carry this second burden, officials must "adduce proof sufficient to support a finding that segregative intent was not among the factors that motivated their actions."[94] Absolution required more than reliance on a facially neutral criterion like neighborhood zoning as the basis of student assignment. A school board and administration must refute the suspicion that racial animus played any part in anyone's decisions. The placing of such a burden was "as a practical matter . . . nearly conclusive on the issue of intent."[95] If, as expected, officials could not rebut the charge of pervasive segregative intent, they are regarded, in effect, as operating a dual system and are thrown back on the rigors of *Swann*. As Justice Brennan put it, "At that stage, the burden becomes the school authorities' to show that the current segregation is in no way the result of . . . past segregative actions."[96] In Denver, he made clear, this burden applied to segregation of Hispanic as well as of African-American youngsters, and to any combinations thereof, and he spelled out why he thought this proper. "We conclude . . . that the District Court erred in separating Negroes and Hispanics for purposes of defining a 'segregated' school."

> [T]here is . . . much evidence that in the Southwest Hispanos and Negroes have a great many things in common . . . . Focusing on students in the States of Arizona, California, Colorado, New Mexico, and Texas, the [United States Commission on Civil Rights recently] concluded that Hispanos suffer from the same educational inequities as Negroes and American Indians. In fact, the District Court itself recognized that "[o]ne of the things which the Hispano has in common with the Negro is economic and cultural deprivation and discrimination." 313 F. Supp, at 69. This is agreement that, though of different origins, Negroes and Hispanos in Denver suffer identical discrimination in treatment when compared with the treatment afforded Anglo students.[97]

The segregative intent displayed in Park Hill had clearly taken place subsequent to the school board actions now putatively condemned because of it in the core area, but the opinion brushed aside any notion of "remoteness in time" being material to the issue, and did not feel obliged to consider how personnel changes on the board might relate to an assessment of the bodies'motivations. Yet it scarcely seemed irrelevant to the situation in Denver that nearly all of the Park Hill offenses, ending with the rescission, were the product of a board almost entirely different in membership from the one which acted on the core schools. It was also unclear how segregative purpose would have entered into the assignment of children to geographic zones in the all-white sections of Denver, assignments made, in most instances, years before the disputes arose in the core city. The Denver system consisted, after all, of 119 schools; the Park Hill schools numbered eight.

The rationale of *Keyes* is strained, like the one in *Swann* with which it joined up. Still, the *Keyes* presumptions reflected an ugly reality, a reality all too common in northern and western cities beset by demographic change. Whether segregative intent could be imputed to all the actions of Denver authorities or not, and no matter how crucial, or how insignificant, those actions in shaping the structure of current segregation, the truth was that the authorities had practiced purposeful discrimination enough times and in enough places to demonstrate vividly to African-Americans what the community really thought of them. These prejudiced actions put on display an attitude of racial superiority, "which," as petitioners' brief pointed out, "inevitably affects all students and schools, white or black, either directly or indirectly," and which could not help but scar and humiliate minority youngsters.[98] Here was a simpler, more cogent justification for integration than the one laboriously constructed in the majority opinion.

The Court remanded *Keyes* to the district judge "for further proceedings consistent with this opinion,"[99] but, self-evidently, the only proceeding consistent with Justice Brennan's strictures would be one resulting in an order for approximate racial balance in Denver's schools.

V

Justice Douglas joined the *Keyes* opinion, while adding some separate words which flayed its logic. "I think it is time to state that there is no constitutional difference between de jure and de facto segregation . . . ."[100] Douglas returned, though, to the views he had expressed in connection with *Swann*, rather than articulating the equal opportunity theme found in his earlier *Keyes* memoranda. When "state action," he argued, working through enforcement of restrictive covenants and manipulation of urban development projects, had defined racial ghettos in the first place, characterizing the schools created therefrom as segregated "de facto is a misnomer."[101]

This raised again the critical issue reserved in *Swann*, whether discrimination by housing officials could serve per se as the basis for school integration. But the logic of *Keyes* rendered the issue largely moot. So long as northern school officials were guilty of a modicum of de jure violations, they were assessed the blame for a community's housing patterns anyway. Only if educational authorities were "clean," or their violations *de minimus*, would housing violations assume any significance.

Keyes produced, however, the first full-fledged dissent in a school desegregation case. Its author was Justice William Rehnquist, who had joined the Court with Powell in 1971 (and became chief justice in 1986). In retrospect, his opinion sounds characteristic—conservative in its constitutional and social leanings, but brilliantly reasoned, aimed unerringly at the weaknesses of the *Swann-Keyes* presumptions.

Unlike at least six of his colleagues, Justice Rehnquist genuinely believed in the validity of the de jure-de facto distinction, essentially as Judge Doyle had sketched it out in dealing with the core city. Consequently, he found it difficult to understand how violations affecting eight schools in northeast Denver laid the evidentiary foundation for cross-district busing. This brace of schools, and a few surrounding ones, might properly have their attendance patterns rearranged. But if the school authorities "had been evenhanded"[102] in drawing other attendance lines in the district, no need arose for action in those areas. "It certainly would not reflect normal English usage to describe [an] entire district as 'segregated' on such a state of facts," unless "the Equal Protection Clause of the Fourteenth Amendment now be held to embody a principle of 'taint,' found in some primitive legal systems but discarded centuries ago in ours."[103]

Justice Lewis Powell's long incubating effort, "concurring in part and dissenting in part,"[104] displayed the balance and thoughtfulness associated with this widely respected jurist. Powell offered a critique of the majority opinion sharing some of

Rehnquist's premises, yet going ultimately in a very different direction. *Swann*, argued Justice Powell, "undercut whatever logic once supported the de facto/de jure distinction," because it required school districts "to alleviate conditions which in large part did *not* result from historic, state-imposed de jure segregation."[105] Rather than import this obsolete distinction to the North, as Brennan was doing, or try to restore its purity, as Rehnquist was seeking to do, Powell proposed dispensing with the distinction altogether.

He would replace the old doctrinal and regional division with a new constitutional right, flowing from *Brown I*, but added, really, as "a significant gloss" to the "original right" in later decisions of the Court. ". . . I would now define it as the right, derived from the Equal Protection Clause, to expect that once the State has assumed responsibility for education, local school boards will operate *integrated school systems* . . . ."[106] Segregation itself would constitute prima facie evidence that authorities were not fulfilling their duty, and in nearly all instances would dictate "an affirmative policy" of creating racial diversity.[107]

Justice Powell followed through, however, on his belief that the courts must place definite limits on this remedial obligation. He took an approach to remedy much in the spirit of Judge Miller's opinion in the Nashville case. School officials must draw attendance zones so as to promote integration, place new schools "with this same objective in mind,"[108] and scrupulously integrate faculties, in accordance with *Montgomery County*. But much of Powell's opinion consisted of a fervent denunciation of cross-district busing, especially when used for elementary school children. To regard extensive busing as a constitutional obligation, he felt, required an "expansive" reading of *Swann*, about which "I record my profound misgivings."[109] The busing controversy "has risked . . . exacerbating, rather than ameliorating, interracial friction and misunderstanding."[110] Powell offered the version of "compulsory integration" which was most likely to have won public acceptance, but one incapable of producing genuine racial diversity in America's schools.

Powell did not articulate a detailed justification for the right to an integrated education. Such hints as he offered, however, suggest an extrapolation from the realities of American history as much as from the language of *Brown*. *All* segregation in public schools, the justice seemed to believe, was harmful to African-American children, because, surrounded as they were by other evidences of racial isolation and discrimination, it made them feel more sharply the stigma of societal contempt. In a footnote, Justice Powell quoted Alexander Bickel on the effects of educational ghettos. "If a Negro child perceives his separation as discriminatory and invidious, he is not, in a society a hundred years removed from slavery, going to make fine distinctions about the source of a particular separation."[111] Powell did not give the impression he thought extensive educational or psychological data was needed to document this insight.

A similar view of de facto segregation pervades Justice Brennan's discussions of statutory separation in *Green* and *Swann*. It was after reading Powell's draft opinion, indeed, that Brennan offered to recast *Keyes* and "jettison the distinction" between types of segregation. The revised opinion Justice Brennan had in mind, we may surmise, would have rested on a broad social analysis of segregation rather than on a piling up of empirical data about test scores or self-esteem.

The fact was that Judge Doyle's views on the educational value of integration were being increasingly disputed as the busing ordered because of such views grew more widespread. "Prior to *Swann*," Professor David Armor has pointed out, "a major limitation common to desegregation studies was that very few reflected the type of comprehensive desegregation policies implemented after 1970, particularly mandatory busing plans . . . . After the onset of large-scale desegregation plans, a much greater cross-section of students was exposed to desegregation, and more rigorous experimental studies became possible."[112]

These studies frequently rebutted the proposition that African-American youngsters fared better in integrated schools, and sparked more scholarly controversy over this endlessly debated issue.[113] In 1972, Professor Armor published a controversial essay in *the Public Interest* evaluating a voluntary city-suburban busing program in Boston, and reviewing six other studies of desegregation. Armor concluded that achievement among minority students had not improved, and that race relations had suffered.[114]

A more comprehensive study of the effects of integration upon African-American students, published in 1975 by Professor Nancy St. John, concluded that "adequate data have not yet been gathered to determine a causal relation between school racial composition and academic achievement. More than a decade of considerable research . . . has produced no definitive positive findings," though it was clear that "desegregation has rarely lowered academic achievement for either black or white children."[115] Professor St. John despaired that convincing proof on the matter would ever emerge. "In view of the political, moral, and technical difficulties of investigation on this question, it is doubtful that all the canons of the scientific method will ever be met."[116]

The evidence was not all on one side. Professor Armor's findings touched off a vigorous dispute in *The Public Interest*.[117] On a broader scale, a 1977 book by Professor Meyer Weinberg reviewed 71 studies of desegregation and found that most of them reported positive effects.[118] But by the late 1970's, the situation regarding empirical evidence about *Brown* was reminiscent of the situation two decades earlier. Observers in the late fifties had rejected a "psychological" interpretation of the decision because of what they regarded as flimsy evidence; now the problem seemed to lie with evidence which, while far more extensive and sophisticated, would always be debatable.

Keyes ended, or should have ended, the cries of "double standard" intensified by *Swann*. Yet, as with *Swann*, the belief necessarily remained "that the predominant concern of the Court . . . is . . . the segregated pattern of student attendance [itself], rather than the causal role played by past discriminatory practices."

VI

The nation's political fires were stoked still further by *Keyes*, and by the Sixth Circuit decision upholding Judge Roth's suburban remedy for Detroit. Representative John Dingell of Michigan even went so far as to propose an amendment to legislation dealing with the Arab oil embargo, which would have prohibited the use of gasoline to bus children away from the school closest to them offering a curriculum appropriate to their grade level.[119]

More serious was the attempt to revive President Nixon's antibusing program in the form of amendments to the 1974 Elementary and Secondary Education Act. Representative Marvin Esch of (again) Michigan proposed such a package in March, replicating the provisions passed by the House in August, 1972, and filibustered to death by the Senate. The House eagerly approved the Esch amendments, and Senator Edward Gurney of Florida took up their sponsorship in the upper house. The Senate initially beat off Gurney's measure by a single vote.

Among those backing the amendments, it should be noted, was the liberal democrat from Colorado, Floyd Haskell, who proclaimed that busing "does not work and has not worked. [It] arouses the passions of both parents and students. It generates hostility and resentment in the community and defiance among school officials. Thus, it stands in the way of education . . . ."[120] Eagerly joining Haskell was his Republican colleague, Peter Dominick.

> I know of parents right now, in fact, one of them called me at midnight last night, wanting to know whom he could telephone or telegraph to urge support of the Gurney amendment . . . .
>
> This busing is going to tear the whole public education system apart in our city, and if the Supreme Court, . . . God forbid, should go ahead and assert the Detroit decision across district lines, we are liable to have a revolution in our own State against the school boards and the court system.[121]

The one vote defeat of the Gurney amendments did not end things in the Senate. Robert Griffin of Michigan (of course) reintroduced the amendments on May 16, 1974, though without the section reopening court orders which transgressed their other provisions, and civil rights advocates knew it was time to back and fill. Senators Hugh Scott and Mike Mansfield, the minority and majority leaders, introduced a substitute containing Griffin's text, but adding the stipulation that nothing in the bill was "intended to modify or diminish the authority of the courts . . . to enforce fully the . . . Fourteenth amendment."[122] The Scott-Mansfield substitute also noted that Congress possessed the power to propose remedies "for the elimination of the vestiges of dual school systems, *except to the extent that such [power] is inconsistent with the requirements of the . . . Fourteenth Amendment . . . with regard to the elimination of such vestiges of dual school systems.*"[123]

The substitute passed by the now familiar one vote margin. Its language survived a marathon House-Senate conference, which beat back attempts by the House conferees to insert the "reopener" section of the Esch-Gurney amendments. Instead, the antibusing provisions would apply only to those school districts not yet under court order to bus.

A disgusted Senator Gurney observed that passage of the Elementary and Secondary Education Act of 1974 "means about as much protection against forced busing as a paper umbrella against a hurricane."[124]

Meanwhile, it was increasingly apparent that the integration mandated by *Swann* and now by *Keyes* for major urban areas throughout the country was taking place in a rapidly altering demographic context. The movement to overwhelmingly white suburbs in America, and the abandonment of the inner cities to African-Americans, was cresting in the 1960's and 1970's, with obvious implications for city schools.

By the end of the seventies, census figures revealed that in the nation as a whole, including the many cities which were still predominantly white, 7.8 million white pupils attended school in the central cities, compared to almost six million African-American and Hispanic youngsters. Outside the central cities, the total was seventeen million white students, less than three million black and Hispanic ones.[125]

Scholars debated the extent to which "white flight" was exacerbated in cities hit with desegregation decrees. Professor Coleman, for one, was convinced by 1975 that busing sharply accelerated the movement to the suburbs.[126] Other scholars, including Thomas Pettigrew, Gary Orfield, and Christine Rossell quickly disputed this contention; they claimed that the evidence did not support Coleman, partly because flight to the suburbs characterized metropolitan areas untouched by racial balance mandates.[127]

But this very point limited the centrality of the entire dispute. White desertion of the urban core, as the critics of *Keyes* had noted, was a phenomenon with many social and economic causes, and its pattern would not be fundamentally altered because of what was done, or not done, about schools. By 1978, New York City, never subjected to a mandatory busing program, was administering a school system over two-thirds black and Hispanic. The Chicago school district, also free from desegregative court orders in the 1970's, was 60% black in 1978. Two years later, only 18% of the district's students were white.

By the time Philadelphia began a desegregation plan in 1978, based largely on voluntary transfers, the city's school population was 62% black. As Cleveland's court-ordered busing plan began in 1979, the schools were already 58% black.

Baltimore, the pioneer of desegregation during the 1950's, was required by HEW to take additional steps in the late 1970's, though these did not include mandatory transportation. The city's school population at the time was 76% black and 24% white.[128]

In this context of impoverished inner cities, increasingly black, and affluent white suburbs, the justices made it plain, shortly before *Keyes*, that poverty was not a category demanding equalization of resources between disparate portions of a state's educational system. *San Antonio School District* v. *Rodriquez* upheld the constitutionality of the unequal funding schemes for education typical of most states.[129]

By the time *Keyes* came down, then, it was clear that if the Supreme Court's doctrinal aim was really directed at segregated patterns of school attendance per se, the justices would have to take the step which, in terms of its capacity to stoke public outrage, would dwarf the step taken in *Brown I*. They would have to breach on racial and ethnic grounds the line between city and suburb they would not breach on economic grounds.

I. *KEYES* AND THE FALLOUT FROM *SWANN*

That *Swann* was thought to have quietly done away with the de jure-de facto distinction is made especially clear in a brilliant essay of January, 1972 by Professor Paul Dimond, extending the "stigma" view of *Brown* to northern ghettos, and articulating a unified standard for judging school segregation cases. Meanwhile, the Supreme Court was moving warily in this direction, as indicated by Justice Douglas' memorandum of 1971, and by Justice Brennan's offer, two years later, to scrap the traditional cleavage in school law. *Keyes*, instead, simply deepened the ambiguity created by *Swann*, but brought forth the opinions of Justice Powell, explicitly rejecting regional distinctions, and of Justice Rehnquist, explicitly upholding them.

1. PAUL R. DIMOND – "SCHOOL SEGREGATION IN THE NORTH: THERE IS BUT ONE CONSTITUTION"

The time has come to scrutinize closely public school segregation everywhere. No longer can an accusing finger be pointed at the South under some regional doctrine of original sin. School segregation is pervasive in all regions of this country, in big cities and small, in suburban and rural areas . . . .

Swann v. *Charlotte Mecklenburg Board of Education* [suggests] that the same practices may be held unconstitutional in North and South . . . .

Unless the Supreme Court is going to place the South under a "judicial Bill of Attainder" by applying the Constitution on a regional basis, that suggestion should . . . become a clear directive when . . . lower court decisions holding school segregation in the North unconstitutional come to the Court for review and decision.

This Article will attempt to show what standards are appropriate for judicial review of school segregation, and what types of action by public school authorities make school segregation violative of the equal protection clause.

II. THE PRIMA FACIE CASE: A PROPOSED STANDARD

In most places, public school authorities are responsible for annually assigning all pupils and teachers, to public schools, and in all but three states, they have the sanction of compulsory attendance laws. Public schools are supported almost exclusively by public tax monies. In such circumstances, wherever school segregation exists, it results from some degree of "state action" and is therefore in some part "state-imposed." There may be an argument that the original sin of explicitly dual schools carries implications of black inferiority not present where a policy of segregation is not openly preached, but just implicitly practiced. Courts, however, would have to be naive (or hostile) not to recognize that (1) patterns of racial discrimination are entrenched throughout this country, (2) all school segregation is largely traceable to such racial discrimination, (3) dominant white majorities everywhere are hostile to association with blacks, especially in schools and residential neighborhoods. The essence of the wrong of segregation—North and South—is the historic political and social expression of white hostility to blacks, and containment of blacks and whites in separate public schools by direct and indirect exercise of governmental authority.

Given these circumstances, where school segregation in fact is substantial, it should be scrutinized by the court as if it amounted to a racial classification: proof of substantial segregation should create a *prima facie* case of "state-imposed segregation". Such a *prima facie* case can be rebutted only if the segregation can be adequately justified by school authorities as necessary to the promotion of a compelling state interest. A showing is required that the compelling state interest cannot be promoted by [a] . . . less onerous (less segregative) alternative action . . . .

Many argue that the fourteenth amendment merely requires "color-blindness", preventing decision makers from considering race at all. On the contrary, the fourteenth amendment places states under an affirmative obligation not to disadvantage blacks as a class and requires courts [to] closely scrutinize any explanation proffered to justify results that are seriously discriminatory on their face. Given the visible distinction between many blacks and whites, the history of this century suggests that "color-blindness" is a concept that has often been used by public officials, including judges, to legitimize discrimination against minorities. In fact, the only way that courts can determine whether blacks have been disadvantaged or discriminated against by an act is not to be "color-blind", but rather honestly color conscious. Once that fact is accepted, courts will be able to review allegations of racial discrimination without regard to mere appearance . . . .

The objective [should be] a system of pupil assignment that does not discriminate against blacks as a race by imposing segregation through acts by a dominant white majority. The affirmative standard of review here proposed suggests that given the complexity and number of decisions made in assigning pupils to schools, the best way to determine whether a non-discriminatory system exists is to require the defendant school authorities to come forward with an adequate justification once plaintiffs have shown substantial racial impact.

[S]chool authorities . . . know that they do much to establish and maintain the racial composition of schools by their construction and location of schools and their assignment of students and teachers. They can be held accountable for the natural, foreseeable, and actual effects of such actions.

Some will . . . argue that housing patterns, not school boards, are responsible for school segregation. While it is only a half truth to suggest that school authorities are not responsible for housing patterns, it is wholly untrue to suggest that school authorities are not responsible for pupil and teacher assignment. Under the proposed standard, such factors as housing patterns, a neighborhood school policy, and transportation difficulties could be proffered by school authorities as explanations of existing school segregation. Such explanations must then be closely scrutinized to determine the extent, if any, they adequately justify the existing school segregation in light of the affirmative fourteenth amendment obligation . . . .

[A different theory] used to challenge . . . racial segregation . . . .looks at educational resources, inputs, and outcomes for predominantly white schools as compared with black and searches for a resulting denial of "equal educational opportunity." Insofar as [this] theory relies in part on educational outcomes, especially to prove that either inequality or harm result from disparate inputs, it is suspect. Sketchiness of data, apparently undecipherable relationship between educational inputs and outcomes, suspicions about cultural bias in many test instruments, and [the] possibility that any conclusion may be read by some as proof of the inferiority of blacks rather than the inequality of schools make use of such evidence a difficult task for the lawyer and the court.

2. JUSTICE DOUGLAS' MEMORANDUM ON *KEYES* (APRIL 19, 1971)

[I]s desegregation a permissible remedy for *de facto* segregation? On these findings it clearly is. The District Court's reliance on *Plessy v. Ferguson*, 163 U.S. 537, was not misplaced. After all, desegregation was a permissible remedy even under *Plessy* when the separate facilities were not equal . . . . Naturally *Plessy's* authorization of state-enforced segregation has been thoroughly and properly repudiated. But this does not mean that schools which are not "*de jure*" segregated are immune from all constitutional restrictions. A city may not channel all its utilities or services into the white area of town even if all blacks voluntarily choose to live in a separate area. Similarly a school board may not channel all the better resources of the system into the white schools even if the racial imbalance in the schools is constitutionally permissible. Whether the Constitution reaches certain types of school segregation is one question. It must be answered under our cases since *Brown v. Board of Education.* Whether schools are providing an equal educational opportunity for their students is another question. *Plessy* is relevant to this latter question.

Mr. Justice Black disputes both the factual findings of the District Court and the remedy selected . . . . [He] would hold [that] the only proper remedy for denial of equal educational opportunity is "an order that the teaching staffs and facilities be equalized." Clearly such an order, if it promised to be effective, would be constitutionally unassailable . . . . But the District Court here ordered desegregation as a remedy. Under *Sweatt v. Painter* this remedy is entirely proper. And nothing in the intervening years has limited the power of the District Courts to fashion appropriate equitable relief. Their duty is to select an appropriate method to remedy the constitutional wrong and they have great latitude in selecting an effective remedy . . . .

APPENDIX (From Judge Doyle's opinion, 313 F. Supp. 90, 96, 97.)

2. The evidence clearly established that the segregated setting stifles and frustrates the learning process. One of the expert witnesses made the matter clear when he said that the isolation of any group develops a homogeneous mass which brings out the worst in the individual members and establishes a low standard of achievement. When, in addition, the group is from a socioeconomic group which is deficient, the bad results are intensified. Add to this the minority factor with the attendant lack of pride and hope, and the task of raising achievement levels becomes insurmountable. The minority citizens are products, in many instances, of parents who received inferior educations and hence the home environment which is looked to for many fundamental sources of learning and knowledge yields virtually no educational value. Thus, the only hope for raising the level of these students and for providing them the equal education which the Constitution guarantees is to bring them into contact with classroom associates who can contribute to the learning process; it is now clear that the quality and effectiveness of the education process is dependent on the presence within the classroom of knowledgeable fellow students.

3. To seek to carry out a compensatory education program within minority schools without simultaneously developing a program of desegregation and integration has been unsuccessful. Experience has shown that money spent in these programs has failed to produce results and has been, therefore, wasted . . . . [Desegregation] must be carried out in an atmosphere of comprehensive education and preparation of teachers, pupils, parents and the community. It also must be coupled with an intense and massive compensatory education program for the students if it is to be successful.

3. JUSTICE BRENNAN'S MEMORANDUM TO THE CONFERENCE, APRIL 3, 1973

MEMORANDUM TO THE CONFERENCE

RE: *No. 71-507 Keyes v. School District*
    At our original conference discussion of this case, Lewis first expressed his view that the de jure/de facto distinction should be discarded. I told him then that I too

was deeply troubled by the distinction. Nevertheless, it appeared that a majority of the Court was committed to the view that the distinction should be maintained, and I therefore drafted *Keyes* within the framework established in our earlier cases. While I am still convinced that my proposed opinion for the Court is, assuming the continued vitality of the de jure/de facto distinction, a proper resolution of the case, I would be happy indeed to recast the opinion and jettison the distinction if a majority of the Court is prepared to do so.

Although Lewis and I seem to share the view that de facto segregation and de jure segregation (as we have previously used those terms) should receive like constitutional treatment, we are in substantial disagreement, I think, on what that treatment should be. Unlike Lewis, I would retain the definition of the "affirmative duty to desegregate" that we have set forth in our prior cases, in particular *Brown II*, *Green*, and *Swann*. Lewis's approach has the virtue of discarding an illogical and unworkable distinction, but only at the price of a substantial retreat form our commitment of the past twenty years to eliminate all vestiges of state-imposed segregation in the public schools. In my view, we can eliminate the distinction without cutting back on our commitment, and I would gladly do so. I welcome your comments.

—*W.J.B. Jr.*

4. JUSTICE POWELL'S OPINION IN *KEYES*

The situation in Denver is generally comparable to that in other large cities across the country in which there is a substantial minority population and where desegregation has not been ordered by the federal courts. There is segregation in the schools of many of these cities fully as pervasive as that in southern cities prior to the desegregation decrees of the past decade and a half. The focus of the school desegregation problem has now shifted from the South to the country as a whole. Unwilling and footdragging as the process was in most places, substantial progress toward achieving integration has been made in southern States. No comparable progress has been made in many nonsouthern cities with large minority populations primarily because of the de facto/de jure distinction nurtured by the courts and accepted complacently by many of the same voices which denounced the evils of segregated schools in the South. But if our national concern is for those who attend such schools, rather than for perpetuating a legalism rooted in history rather than present reality, we must recognize that the evil of operating separate schools is no less in Denver than in Atlanta.

I

In my view we should abandon a distinction which long since has outlived its time, and formulate constitutional principles of national rather than merely regional application. When Brown v Board of Education was decided, the distinction between de jure and de facto segregation was consistent with the limited constitutional rationale of that case. The situation confronting the Court, largely confined to the southern States, was officially imposed racial segregation in the schools extending back for many years and usually embodied in constitutional and statutory provisions.

The great contribution of Brown I was its holding in unmistakable terms that the Fourteenth Amendment forbids state-compelled or state-authorized segregation of public schools. Although some of the language was more expansive, the holding in Brown I was essentially negative: It was impermissible under the Constitution for the States, or their instrumentalities, to force children to attend segregated schools. The forbidden action was de jure, and the opinion in Brown I was construed—for some years and by many courts—as requiring only state neutrality . . . .

But the doctrine of Brown I, as amplified by Brown II, did not retain its original meaning. In a series of decisions extending from 1954 to 1971 the concept of state neutrality was transformed into the present constitutional doctrine requiring affirmative state action to desegregate school systems. The keystone case was Green v County School Board, where school boards were declared to have "the affirmative duty to take whatever steps might be necessary to convert to a unitary system in which racial discrimination would be eliminated root and branch." The school system before the Court in Green was operating in a rural and sparsely settled county where there were no concentrations of white and black populations, no neighborhood school system (there were only two schools in the county), and none of the problems of an urbanized school district. The Court properly identified the freedom-of-choice program there as a subterfuge, and the language in Green imposing an affirmative duty to convert to a unitary system was appropriate on the facts before the Court. There was, however, reason to question to what extent this duty would apply in the vastly different factual setting of a large city with extensive areas of residential segregation, presenting problems and calling for solutions quite different from those in the rural setting of New Kent County, Virginia.

But the doubt as to whether the affirmative-duty concept would flower into a new constitutional principle of general application was laid to rest by Swann v Charlotte Mecklenburg Board of Education, in which the duty articulated in Green was applied to the urban school system of metropolitan Charlotte, North Carolina . . . . Despite . . . recognition of a fundamentally different problem from that involved in Green, the Court nevertheless held that the affirmative-duty rule of Green was applicable, and prescribed for a metropolitan school system with 107 schools and some 84,000 pupils essentially the same remedy—elimination of segregation "root and branch"—which had been formulated for the two schools and 1,300 pupils of New Kent County.

In Swann, the Court further noted it was concerned only with States having "a long history" of officially imposed segregation . . . . In so doing, the Court refrained from even considering whether the evolution of constitutional doctrine from Brown I to Green/Swann undercut whatever logic once supported the de facto/de jure distinction. In imposing on metropolitan southern school districts an affirmative duty, entailing large-scale transportation of pupils, to eliminate segregation in the schools, the Court required these districts to alleviate conditions which in large part did *not* result from historic, state-imposed de jure segregation. Rather, the familiar root cause of segregated schools in *all* the biracial metropolitan areas of our country is essentially the same: one of segregated residential and migratory patterns the impact of which on the racial composition of the schools was often perpetuated and rarely ameliorated by action of public school authorities. This is a national, not a southern, phenomenon. And it is largely unrelated to whether a particular State had or did not have segregative school laws.

Whereas Brown I rightly decreed the elimination of state-imposed segregation in that particular section of the country where it did exist, Swann imposed obligations on southern school districts to eliminate conditions which are not regionally unique but are similar both in origin and effect to conditions in the rest of the country . . . .

II . . . .

A

The principal reason for abandonment of the de jure/de facto distinction is that, in view of the evolution of the holding in Brown I into the affirmative-duty doctrine, the distinction no longer can be justified on a principled basis. In decreeing remedial requirements for the Charlotte/Mecklenburg school district, Swann dealt with a metropolitan, urbanized area in which the basic causes of segregation were generally similar to those in all sections of the country, and also largely irrelevant to the existence of historic, state-imposed segregation at the time of the Brown decision. Further, the extension of the affirmative-duty concept to include compulsory student transportation went well beyond the mere remedying of that portion of school segregation for which former state segregation laws were ever responsible . . . .

[O]ne must try [therefore] to identify the [actual] constitutional right which is being enforced . . . . In Brown II, the Court identified the "fundamental principle" enunciated in Brown I as being the unconstitutionality of "racial discrimination in public education," and spoke of "the personal interest of the plaintiffs in admission to public schools as soon as practicable on a nondiscriminatory basis." Although this and similar language is ambiguous as to the specific constitutional right, it means—as a minimum—that one has the right not to be compelled by state action to attend a segregated school system. In the evolutionary process since 1954, decisions of this Court have added a significant gloss to this original right. Although nowhere expressly articulated in these terms, I would now define it as the right, derived from the Equal Protection Clause, to expect that once the State has assumed responsibility for education, local school boards will operate *integrated school sys-*

tems within their respective districts. This means that school authorities, consistent with the generally accepted educational goal of attaining quality education for all pupils, must make and implement their customary decisions with a view toward enhancing integrated school opportunities.

The term "integrated school system" presupposes, of course, a total absence of any laws, regulations, or policies supportive of the type of "legalized" segregation condemned in Brown. A system would be integrated in accord with constitutional standards if the responsible authorities had taken appropriate steps to (i) integrate faculties and administration; (ii) scrupulously assure equality of facilities, instruction, and curriculum opportunities throughout the district; (iii) utilize their authority to draw attendance zones to promote integration; and (iv) locate new schools, close old ones, and determine the size and grade categories with this same objective in mind . . . .

An integrated school system does not mean—and indeed could not mean in view of the residential patterns of most of our major metropolitan areas—that *every school* must in fact be an integrated unit. A school which happens to be all or predominantly white or all or predominantly black is not a "segregated" school in an unconstitutional sense if the system itself is a genuinely integrated one . . . .

III . . . .

B

Where school authorities have defaulted in their duty to operate an integrated school system, district courts must insure that affirmative desegregative steps ensue. Many of these can be taken effectively without damaging state and parental interests in having children attend schools within a reasonable vicinity of home. Where desegregative steps are possible within the framework of a system of "neighborhood education," school authorities must pursue them. For example, boundaries of neighborhood attendance zones should be drawn to integrate, to the extent practicable, the school's student body . . . .

C . . . .

A *constitutional requirement* of extensive student transportation solely to achieve integration presents a vastly more complex problem. It promises, on the one hand, a greater degree of actual desegregation, while it infringes on what may fairly be regarded as other important community aspirations and personal rights. Such a requirement is also likely to divert attention and resources from the foremost goal of any school system: the best quality education for all pupils . . . .

The neighborhood school does provide greater ease of parental and student access and convenience, as well as greater economy of public administration. These are obvious and distinct advantages, but the legitimacy of the neighborhood concept rests on more basic grounds.

Neighborhood school systems, neutrally administered, reflect the deeply felt desire of citizens for a sense of community in their public education. Public schools have been a traditional source of strength to our Nation, and that strength may derive in part from the identification of many schools with the personal features of the surrounding neighborhood. Community support, interest, and dedication to public schools may well run higher with a neighborhood attendance pattern: distance may encourage disinterest. Many citizens sense today a decline in the intimacy of our institutions—home, church, and school—which has caused a concomitant decline in the unity and communal spirit of our people. I pass no judgment on this viewpoint, but I do believe that this Court should be wary of compelling in the name of constitutional law what may seem to many a dissolution in the traditional, more personal fabric of their public schools . . . .

The argument for student transportation also overlooks the fact that the remedy exceeds that which may be necessary to redress the constitutional evil. Let us use Denver as an example. The Denver School Board, by its action and nonaction, may be legally responsible for some of the segregation that exists. But . . . the fundamental problem of residential segregation would persist. It is . . . a novel application of equitable power—not to mention a dubious extension of constitutional doctrine—to require so much greater a degree of forced school integration than would have resulted from purely natural and neutral nonstate causes.

The compulsory transportation of students carries a further infirmity as a constitutional remedy. With most constitutional violations, the major burden of remedial action falls on offending state officials . . . . But when the obligation . . . extends to the transportation of students, the full burden of the affirmative remedial action is borne by children and parents who did not participate in any constitutional violation . . . .

[T]he "busing issue" has profoundly disquieted the public wherever extensive transportation has been ordered. I make no pretense of knowing the best answers. Yet, the issue in this and like cases comes to this Court as one of constitutional law. As to this issue, I have no doubt whatever. There is nothing in the Constitution, its history, or—until recently—in the jurisprudence of this Court that mandates the employment of forced transportation of young and teenage children to achieve a single interest, as important as that interest may be. We have strayed, quite far as I view it, from the rationale of Brown I and II, as reiterated in Swann, that courts in fashioning remedies must be "guided by equitable principles" which include the "adjusting and reconciling [of] public and private needs."

I urge a return to this rationale . . . . As a minimum, this Court should not require school boards to engage in the unnecessary transportation away from their neighborhoods of elementary-age children . . . .

IV . . . .

The single most disruptive element in education today is the widespread use of [such] compulsory transportation . . . . This has risked distracting and diverting attention from basic educational ends, dividing and embittering communities, and exacerbating, rather than ameliorating, interracial friction and misunderstanding. It is time to return to a more balanced evaluation of the recognized interests of our society in achieving desegregation with other educational and societal interests a community may legitimately assert. This will help assure that integrated school systems will be established and maintained by rational action, will be better understood and supported by parents and children of both races, and will promote the enduring qualities of an integrated society so essential to its genuine success.

5. JUSTICE REHNQUIST'S DISSENT IN *KEYES*

I

The Court notes at the outset of its opinion the differences between the claims made by the plaintiffs in this case and the classical "de jure" type of claims made by plaintiffs in cases such as Brown v. Board of Education . . . . I think the similarities and differences, not only in the claims, but in the nature of the constitutional violation, deserve somewhat more attention than the Court gives them . . . .

[I]n a school district the size of Denver's, it is quite conceivable that the School Board might have engaged in the racial gerrymandering of the attendance boundary between two particular schools in order to keep one largely Negro and Hispano, and the other largely Anglo, as the District Court found to have been the fact in this case. Such action would have deprived affected minority students who were the victims of such gerrymandering of their constitutional right to equal protection of the laws. But if the school board had been evenhanded in its drawing of the attendance lines for other schools in the district, minority students required to attend other schools within the district would have suffered no such deprivation. It certainly would not reflect normal English usage to describe the entire district as "segregated" on such a state of facts, and it would be a quite unprecedented application of principles of equitable relief to determine that if the gerrymandering of one attendance zone were proved, particular racial mixtures could be required by a federal district court for every school in the district.

It is quite possible, of course, that a school district purporting to adopt racially neutral boundary zones might, with respect to every such zone, invidiously discriminate against minorities, so as to produce substantially the same result as was produced by the statutorily decreed segregation involved in Brown. If that were the case, the consequences would necessarily have to be the same as were the consequences in Brown. But, in the absence of a statute requiring segregation, there must necessarily be the sort of factual inquiry which was unnecessary in those jurisdictions where racial mixing in the schools was forbidden by law.

Underlying the Court's entire opinion is its apparent thesis that a district judge is at least permitted to find that if a single attendance zone between two individual schools in the large metropolitan district is found by him to have been "gerrymandered," the school district is guilty of operating a "dual" school system, and is apparently a candidate for what is in practice a federal receivership. Not only the language of the Court in the opinion, but its reliance on the case of Green v. County School Board, indicates that such would be the case. It would therefore presumably be open to the District Court to require . . . that pupils be transported great distances throughout the district to and from schools whose attendance zones have not been gerrymandered. Yet, unless the Equal Protection Clause of the Fourteenth Amendment now be held to embody a principle of "taint, " found in some primitive legal systems but discarded centuries ago in ours, such a result can only be described as the product of judicial fiat . . . .

The Court's own language in Green makes it unmistakably clear that this significant extension of Brown's prohibition against discrimination, and the conversion of that prohibition into an affirmative duty to integrate, was made in the context of a school system which had for a number of years rigidly excluded Negroes from attending the same schools as were attended by whites. Whatever may be the soundness of that decision in the context of a genuinely "dual" school system, where segregation of the races had once been mandated by law, I can see no constitutional justification for it in a situation such as that which the record shows to have obtained in Denver.

CHAPTER FIVE

MILLIKEN

The first northern case concerning interdistrict remedies came from New Jersey and was argued before a three judge federal panel in early 1971. In the wake of *Green*, as well as the explorations of the Mondale Committee, counsel for plaintiffs made the argument that all school segregation was unconstitutional, and that since school district lines, authorized by the state of New Jersey, isolated African-American students, the state must redraw them. The schools were racially skewed due to "'boundaries . . . rendering racial balance mathematically impossible in many districts.'"[1] This situation resulted in "'unequal educational opportunities,'" and New Jersey was obligated, therefore, "'to integrate all the schools.'"[2]

The three judge panel rejected such a broad claim, citing the holding in the Gary case "that segregation resulting from housing patterns [does] not require correction."[3] If the placing of school district lines by the state was "reasonable and not intended to foster segregation then that action satisfies the mandate of *Brown*."[4] It could not "be said" that the New Jersey district lines, based, as they were, on municipal boundaries, "are unreasonable."[5]

The Supreme Court summarily affirmed the lower court decision, though Justice Douglas indicated he would have set the case down for oral argument. The record, he noted, bringing together the rationale he had used in *Swann* and in the initial phase of *Keyes*, revealed the usual depressing pattern of "white exodus to the suburbs and the resultant surrender of the inner-city to . . . blacks."[6] Furthermore, evidence collected by the Commission on Civil Rights demonstrated that this "shift in residential patterns has been both encouraged and facilitated" by the actions of government officials at all levels. "If any form of state-imposed segregation is proved, then the racially homogeneous . . . neighborhoods and the consequent racial imbalance in schools would seem to be the result of state action."[7]

211

Even if the housing patterns and district lines in New Jersey were neutral in origin, the result, Justice Douglas argued, was still impermissible segregation in schools. "Our conclusion in *Brown* v. *Board of Education* . . . , that '[s]eparate educational facilities are inherently unequal,' has been convincingly borne out by scholarly studies."[8] Douglas' colleagues, however, wanted no part of a full-dress examination of the matter.

At the other end of the spectrum, lower courts in the South made it clear, by 1970, that school districts which had been created specifically for the purpose of conforming to segregation could be breached for remedial purposes, even if they were not of suspicious structural design. Many rural counties in the region, undergoing the process of educational consolidation in the days prior to 1954, found it logical to reorganize and combine school districts along strict geographical as well as strict racial lines. But this did not protect the sanctity of the boundaries thus drawn, held the Eighth Circuit, in an important 1969 decision which ordered the consolidation of all-white and all-black districts in Sevier County, Arkansas. "If segregation in public schools could be justified simply because of pre-*Brown* geographic structuring of school districts," wrote Judge Donald Lay, "the equal protection clause would have little meaning."[9] It was of no consequence that authorities had constructed district boundaries in a fairly rational fashion. "Simply to say there was no intentional gerrymandering of district lines for racial reasons is not enough."[10] Congruent views emerged in the Fifth and Sixth Circuits.

None of these disparate decisions, however, in either North or South, had yet addressed what was clearly the most important question raised in this area by the judicial and demographic cross-currents of the 1970's: How far could a court go in ordering adjustment of school district lines, even if not conceived on the basis of race, when it was seeking to remedy proven violations? This was a question quite relevant to the South, where all school districts were guilty of de jure segregation, but where the boundaries between most of the larger districts were neutral city-county or county lines, not designed with segregation consciously in mind. The question was also relevant in the North, where large city districts were often guilty of purposeful segregation, but their lily-white suburban neighbors were guiltless, largely because they did not need to stoop to such tactics. All of this was another way of asking whether the remedial imperatives of *Brown*, applied between school districts, could collapse the de jure-de facto distinction, as *Swann* and *Keyes* had collapsed that distinction within school districts.

If such questions had not required scrutiny in New Jersey or Arkansas, neither were they dealt with in the first interdistrict cases decided by the Supreme Court— *Wright* v. *City of Emporia* and *United States* v. *Scotland Neck City Board of Education* (1972). Both cases concerned the validity, in a desegregation context, of school boundary lines not inherently discriminatory in their design. But in each instance, authorities had drawn these lines, to the detriment of maximum compliance, *after* the issuance of a desegregation order.

Thus the city of Emporia, Virginia undertook to split itself off from the county school system, and to set up its own district, two weeks following a federal court order which established a pairing plan for the county schools under *Green*. The schools, as then constituted, were 66% black. The separate Emporia system would be 48% white, and its loss would increase the black ratio in the county to 72%.

The Court, albeit by a 5–4 margin, disallowed the city's attempt to isolate itself. Emporia's action might not constitute purposeful discrimination, noted Justice Potter Stewart, since as a city of the second class in Virginia, it possessed the right to set up its own school system, had sought to do so, indeed, since 1967. But "[u]nder the principles of Green and Monroe, such a proposal must be judged according to whether it hinders or furthers the process of school desegregation."[11] The Court must focus "upon the effect—not the purpose or motivation—of a school board's action in determining whether it is a permissible method of dismantling a dual system."[12]

Similarly, after the Justice Department negotiated a desegregation agreement with Halifax County, North Carolina in 1968, the state legislature created a separate school district for the city of Scotland Neck. Even with Scotland Neck, the county system was 77% black. Stripped of the city's students, who were 57% white, the number would go to 89%. In line with *Wright*, the five-person majority invalidated the legislature's act, since "we cannot but conclude that [its] implementation . . . would have the effect of impeding the disestablishment of the dual school system that existed in Halifax County."[13] (Justice Blackmun joined Chief Justice Burger, Justice Powell, and Justice Rehnquist in dissenting.)

While *Wright* and *Scotland Neck* applied a strict "effects" test in determining that school district lines could not stand in the way of maximum compliance, the extremely suspicious timing of the boundary adjustments involved left open the matter of whether long-existing, neutrally drawn boundaries, often coterminous with political units, could be cast aside to achieve "the greatest possible degree of actual desegregation." Yet as the Court decided the companion cases in Virginia and North Carolina, controversies were already bubbling up through the lower courts which confronted this matter head-on, in both the North and the South. The southern case came to the Supreme Court, but yielded no decisive outcome. It was the northern case which settled the issue definitively, for all regions.

II

By 1971, Richmond, Virginia was facing the situation faced by nearly all large American cities, whether under desegregation orders or not. In the 1970–71 school year, 64% of the city's students were African-American, 36% were white. A desegregation plan, put forth in April of 1971 to replace the discredited freedom of choice option, offered only miniature replicas at most schools of this majority black demographic pattern, certain to accentuate in future years. Nonetheless, District Judge Robert Mehrige approved the plan in August.

Actually, the judge harbored other ideas. A colloquy with counsel during hearings on the proposal apparently convinced city officials he would look favorably upon a broader remedial approach.[14] Consequently, in November 1970, even before the Richmond-only plan was finished, they filed a motion demanding that suburban Henrico and Chesterfield counties be joined to the suit for purposes of further relief, though both were already operating under approved desegregation plans. Judge Mehrige granted the motion, and, after the Richmond proceedings concluded, a new trial ensued in late 1971.

On January 25, 1972, the judge issued a rambling 325 page opinion ordering consolidation of the Richmond school system with those of Henrico and Chesterfield counties to produce an over-all unit which was approximately two-thirds white. Nearly all the individual schools in the consolidated area would range between 20% and 40% black.

Judge Mehrige based his actions partly on the fact that the school boundaries in question, though admittedly laid out 100 years earlier on a neutral basis, had not been neutrally maintained, and that their manipulation had distorted attendance patterns between the districts. Along with most other school lines in Virginia, the districts' boundaries were breached numerous times for the purpose of maintaining segregation, the most notable example being the state program of tuition grants for students attending racially separate public or private schools away from their home district, enacted in the late 1950's as a follow-up to Virginia's program of massive resistance. This "resulted in mass movement of pupils across political boundaries in the Richmond area and throughout the state."[15] Virginia students in fact could always transfer from one school district to another, Judge Mehrige pointed out, although the numbers he produced for metropolitan Richmond were meager, and their racial effect usually undiscoverable. (He documented, for certain, only 100 African-American students from Chesterfield County attending school elsewhere, some in Richmond, between 1949 and 1951, and 80 in 1971.)[16]

More significant, in the judge's view, were the housing violations perpetrated by local, state, and federal officials, hemming African-Americans within the ghettos of Richmond, while guaranteeing white suburbs. FHA-sponsored housing projects in the Richmond metropolitan area were completely segregated, the carry-over from an open policy of tolerating segregation which the agency practiced until 1962. The Richmond Redevelopment and Housing Authority had constructed low-income public housing projects exclusively in the black areas of the city. Though the agency possessed authority to build such projects in Chesterfield and Henrico counties, virulent opposition from county authorities rendered "it a vain act" even to seek permission.[17] There were no public housing programs in either county, and both forbade the federal rent supplement program to operate within their borders.

Realtors, licensed by the state, greatly exacerbated housing discrimination. Until passage of the Fair Housing Act of 1968, listings in the real estate section of newspapers announced baldly that residences were intended only for "colored."[18] School segregation, quite obviously, was "related to strict housing segregation patterns, maintained by public and private enforcement," which "contained blacks on one side of the city line."[19]

Judge Mehrige did not attempt to quantify the effects of these violations on inter-district segregation, however, because, for all his zeal in recording them, he did not really think such offenses were essential to imposing a metropolitan remedy. Such remedies, he felt, flowed automatically from the strictures of *Green* and *Swann*. Their logic, by definition, endowed federal courts of equity with the power to set aside individual school districts in seeking full compliance with *Brown*.

These decisions, stood, after all, for the principle that "[a]ttendance zone lines formulated by adhering to the most natural bounds of neighborhoods . . . will not pass muster if the effect is to prolong the existence . . . of racially identifiable schools."[20] *Davis* established that even barriers such as an "interstate highway"[21] must not restrict efforts to achieve maximum desegregation. Surely then, if such "physical demarcations do not limit the duty of [a] court to use 'all available techniques,' . . . so much the less should political boundaries, when they coincide with no tangible obstacles and are unrelated to any administrative or educational needs."[22] This part of Judge Mehrige's analysis came across as a bit curious, since it downplayed the necessity for those causal connections between offense and remedy which purportedly lay at the heart of *Swann* and *Davis*, and which he had labored to establish in Richmond.

As a jurisdictional matter, Judge Mehrige derived his authority to set aside district lines from the fact that the fourteenth amendment was addressed solely to the states, and that all state constitutions, including Virginia's, declared education a state responsibility. Consequently, "no amount of delegation of authority"[23] could deflect the courts from enforcing the guarantee of equal protection against state officials. The dominant thrust of Mehrige's opinion flowed, however, from the reading of *Brown* which asserts that all racial separation in schools deprives African-American children of equal educational opportunity.

> Racial identifiability of schools and school systems is both a legal concept—a conclusion of law, ultimately—and a fact of major significance to educators and lay persons. For the law's demands parallel those of educators. Although some school authorities have been slow to accept the fact, it is true that the constitutional wrong condemned in *Brown* imposed, and continues to do so, genuine damage upon children in schools that educators see as racially identifiable. The goals long considered by educators to be necessary and valid purposes of public education cannot be achieved in them.[24]

Equal opportunity was "denied when [a] pupil is exposed to the sort of segregation existing in the Richmond area, just as it was by that which drew the Supreme Court's condemnation in *Brown*."[25]

In this connection, Judge Mehrige was much influenced by the testimony at trial of Professor Thomas Pettigrew, who again asserted that genuine integration could never take root in majority black schools.[26] Under his metropolitan consolidation plan, the judge announced, 97% of African-American students would go to schools ranging from 20% to 40% black.

The Fourth Circuit, sitting *en banc*, zeroed in on the sociological interests expressed by Judge Mehrige. What the appeal essentially involved, felt the circuit judges (Judge Harrison Winter dissenting), was whether the lower court could "compel joinder" of separate school systems, themselves in compliance with *Brown*, solely in order to achieve "a greater degree of integration and racial balance"; for the 20–40 ratio in the metropolitan schools represented, in their view, "the equivalent . . . of the imposition of a fixed racial quota."[27]

Swann, they firmly noted, proscribed such demands. "[I]mposition as a matter of substantive constitutional right of any particular degree of racial balance is beyond the power of [the courts]."[28]

Interdistrict remedies could flow only from interdistrict violations, the circuit majority held. District boundaries could be set aside only if they were established or maintained "for the purpose of perpetuating racial discrimination in the public schools,"[29] and the court brushed aside Judge Mehrige's findings of interdistrict manipulation as wholly inadequate. It took more seriously the notion that violations by housing authorities might have illegally confined African-Americans to Richmond's inner city. But while accepting these findings as "not clearly erroneous,"[30] the judges subjected them to a stringent conspiratorial criterion, which rendered them insufficient as a predicate for interdistrict relief. "[N]either the record nor the opinion of the district court . . . suggests that there was ever *joint interaction between any two of the units involved* (or by higher state officers) for the purpose of keeping one unit relatively white by confining blacks to another."[31] This standard of guilt, presumably, would allow housing and school officials in any single unit, say, Chesterfield County, to combine in all the discrimination they wanted without fear of an interdistrict decree, even if the manifest effect of this discrimination was to wall African-Americans out of the county. In truth, Judge J. Braxton Craven, who wrote the majority opinion, took a dim view of efforts to link school and housing segregation. "We think," began a much-quoted passage,

> that the root causes of the concentration of blacks in the inner cities of America are simply not known and that the district court could not realistically place on the counties the responsibility for the effect that inner city decay has had on the public schools of Richmond. We are convinced that what little action, if any, the counties may seem to have taken to keep blacks out is slight indeed compared to the myriad reasons, economic, political and social, for the concentration of blacks in Richmond and does not support the conclusion that it has been invidious state action which has resulted in the racial composition of the three school districts. Indeed this record warrants no other conclusion than that the forces influencing demographic patterns in New York, Chicago,

Detroit, Los Angeles, Atlanta and other metropolitan areas have operated in the same way in the Richmond metropolitan area to produce the
same result. Typical of all of these cities is a growing black population
in the central city and a growing white population in the surrounding
suburban and rural areas. Whatever the basic causes, it has not been
school assignments, and school assignments cannot reverse the trend.[32]

The Supreme Court accepted certiorari in the Richmond case, and heard it in late
April of 1973.

The petitioners' brief followed the formal logic of Judge Mehrige's opinion
rather than probing his facade of interdistrict violations. The judge's actions, they
argued, were a simple extension of *Brown*, as amplified by *Green* and *Swann*. He
found that the schools in metropolitan Richmond "had been immemorially segregated in violation of the Constitution," and that a "remedial decree confined within
the limits of one division would be ineffective" in eliminating racially identifiable
schools. "We submit . . . that these two predicates amply sustain federal judicial
power to extend the remedial process . . . across state-created school division boundary lines."[33]

This view of the issues allowed petitioners' to distinguish legitimately between
racial balance and compliance, while still largely compounding the two on the remedial level. The court of appeals' "characterization" of Judge Mehrige's order "as
having 'the purpose of achieving racial balance'"[34] was mistaken, they argued, since
the judge did not seek such balance as an end in itself, and, in any event, had not
imposed a "fixed racial quota" on each school in metropolitan Richmond. It was
wholly "unwarranted," therefore, to charge that he used the term "racial balance" to
connote "anything other" than "that 'degree of actual desegregation' which the
Constitution as construed in *Brown* commands."[35]

The petitioners cited the housing violations documented by Judge Mehrige to
buttress their case, but, even here, they viewed these discriminatory actions more as
part of the psychological legacy of racism than as the major *cause* of metropolitan
separation. "Widespread discrimination [in housing] attests eloquently to racial attitudes in whose light the continuation of predominantly black Richmond school
facilities will be perceived as the perpetuation of a dual system of inferior Negro
and superior white schools."[36]

Virginia's brief, written in part by one of the great constitutional scholars of our
time, Professor Phillip Kurland of the University of Chicago Law School, paralleled
the court of appeals decision in its contention that the desire for racial balance per
se really inspired the Richmond litigation. "Whatever rationalization is offered . . . ,"
argued Professor Kurland, "there can be no doubt that the deficiency to be cured, as
seen by the petitioners and the trial court, is that the racial balance in Richmond
schools is different from the racial balance in the schools of the adjacent counties."[37]

It was obvious from the beginning that Justice Powell would not participate in
the Richmond case, as Justice White had not participated in *Keyes* (still being ham-

mered out at this point). Powell had served on both the Richmond and Virginia state school boards. White, in fact, played a major role in the Court's consideration of *Richmond*, showing a good deal of sympathy for Judge Mehrige's actions. At the initial conference on the case, on April 24, 1973, he suggested that the Fourth Circuit had used an improper legal standard in arriving at its decision, and proposed a remand. Blackmun, and even the chief justice, professed interest in his arguments.[38]

The more detailed exposition of these views, contained in a memorandum of April 30, aligned Justice White with those who believed that meaningful integration was the indispensable command of *Brown*. The appeals court, White agreed, was correct to condemn Judge Mehrige's plan based on any belief that it ordered racial balance for its own sake. "I could easily agree with [the court] that, as a matter of substantive constitutional right, or even as a matter of remedy for an adjudicated violation, strict racial quotas are not obligatory and very likely erroneous."[39] The circuit judges had not explored, however, what White regarded as a separate "intermediate ground."[40] This involved whether the desegregation plans of "the three counties as a unit . . . fell short" of producing a level of integration sufficient to "remedy . . . past constitutional violations," and whether these "shortcomings of the individual county plans provided a sufficient federal foundation for merging the three districts . . . so as to eliminate . . . racially identifiable schools"[41] (to be done, presumably, by a plan which would mandate, in practice, some form of racial balancing). To suggest that the goal of eliminating "racially identifiable schools" justified a merger of three districts was to dismiss as irrelevant the matter of whether past de jure offenses by state or local authorities were in any way responsible for the diverse racial configurations of Richmond and its environs.

Justice White clearly did not regard such findings as a prerequisite to further relief. Given that quotas, without more, were impermissible in metropolitan Richmond, he "nevertheless would remand for the benefit of the Court of Appeals' view of what the profile of a proper plan would be if the three districts were to be treated as a unit."[42] His analysis does not mention Judge Craven's statement that school boundary lines could be set aside only if they "have been maintained . . . for the purpose of perpetuating racial discrimination in the public schools," or if there "was . . . joint interaction between . . . two . . . units . . . (or by higher state officers) for the purpose of keeping one unit relatively white by confining blacks to another."

Like Judge Mehrige, Justice White rested his position on the fact that the state of Virginia controlled the educational process. "Historically," he noted, "Virginia has not found it impossible to merge school districts . . . . Consolidations . . . do not appear to be the impossible undertaking the Court of Appeals envisaged."[43] But under White's reasoning, the remedial duties exacted upon the state because of its responsibility went beyond those imposed in past school cases, at least those imposed openly.

Justices Brennan and Douglas immediately endorsed White's approach. (Thurgood Marshall joined later.)[44] But the effort also brought forth a reply from

Justice William Rehnquist, who articulated a criterion for determining when inter-district relief was warranted which paralleled his discussion of intradistrict remedies in *Keyes*. "I would think," he told his colleagues in a memorandum of May 3, "that [an interdistrict] remedy for a Fourteenth Amendment right would be available only where the drawing of the boundary lines or use of the boundary lines were them-selves a substantial element in the violation of the right, or where the boundary lines were observed largely in the breach."[45] Applying this standard to the record of the Richmond case led Rehnquist to conclude "that it doesn't afford a basis for any such finding."[46] The justice did not discuss the housing violations found by Judge Mehrige, apparently regarding them as immaterial under his approach.

Justice White replied to Rehnquist on May 8.[47] By this time, though, Justice Stewart had come out for affirmance of the Fourth Circuit, and, at a conference on May 11, Justice Blackmun also endorsed that approach (as, inevitably, had Burger).[48]

Neither Blackmun nor Stewart circulated memoranda expanding their views on the Richmond case, but their final votes indicate that, whatever reservations they harbored about the dejure-defacto distinction in Denver, they were not prepared to disregard this distinction when it would lead to interdistrict busing. Both men, feels Professor Jeffries, were surely cognizant of the political firestorm interdistrict bus-ing would set off.[49] A journalistic, sometimes accurate, account of the Court's activ-ities at this time reports that "Stewart told his clerks that he had ridden the bus on the Charlotte and Denver decisions, but that Richmond was different. 'It is where I get off' . . . ."[50]

On May 15, Justice Douglas circulated his own draft opinion to his colleagues, agreeing with Judge Mehrige.[51] A few days later, Justice Brennan tried to break the deadlock in the Court by invoking the old-time religion of causal presumptions. The district judge (and the plaintiffs), he noted, were trying to justify interdistrict inte-gration merely because the public schools of Virginia "had been purposefully seg-regated in violation of . . . *Brown*," and because "any form of remedial order con-fined to the limits of one district would be ineffective."[52] This rationale admittedly flew in the face of the Court's prior insistence "that some nexus must be shown between past actions of the State or the counties and the present incurably-segre-gated condition of the Richmond school system."[53]

But was it necessary, on the other hand, to accept the circuit court's "much too rigid . . . standard" for assessing interdistrict relief?[54] Justice Brennan felt that a sec-ond look at the record in *Richmond*, on remand, might reveal that a "nexus" did exist between past discrimination and the current cleavage between city and suburb. His suggestions along this line clearly paralleled *Swann* and *Keyes*. Thus, he hypothe-sized, if the inconvenient location of black schools in the white suburban districts had discouraged African-American families from relocating there, "that suburban school district has helped create and maintain the segregated schooling within the central city and therefore has as much an 'affirmative duty' to help desegregate those schools as does the city itself."[55] This was "nothing more than a concrete

application of what was said in *Swann*: 'People gravitate toward school facilities
... [and thus] the location of schools may influence the patterns of residential development of a metropolitan area . . . .'"[56]

Justice Brennan's effort did not budge his colleagues. On May 21, 1973, the
Court announced that, "the judgment [in the Richmond case] is affirmed by an
equally divided Court."[57]

III

Meanwhile, the case which would resolve the issues raised in Richmond was
wending its way through the courts of the North. The overall population of Detroit,
and the resulting population of its schools, had altered drastically in the 1950's and
1960's. In 1950, African-Americans comprised 16.2% of the city's population;
twenty years later the total was 43.9%. The black student population was approaching two-thirds, 75% of them in schools which were 90% black.

Tensions arose over the segregated nature of Detroit's schools. In 1970, seeking
to alleviate the situation, the school board adopted a limited plan of integration for
the city's high schools. An act of the Michigan legislature quickly frustrated this
plan, however, by canceling its execution, at least for the 1970–71 school year.
African-American plaintiffs filed suit in August, 1970, alleging that the law was discriminatory, and demanding a preliminary injunction against its effectuation. More
broadly, plaintiffs charged that the Detroit school system "was and is segregated
... as a result of the official policies and actions" of the board of education.[58]

District Judge Stephen Roth denied the motion for an injunction, but the Sixth
Circuit rendered this part of the controversy moot by declaring the Michigan act
unconstitutional.[59] On remand, plaintiffs moved for immediate implementation of
the high school integration scheme. Judge Roth ordered temporary adoption of an
alternate plan, and the circuit court upheld his actions, but also bid him proceed to
trial expeditiously on plaintiffs' claims of de jure segregation in Detroit.[60] The trial
consumed 41 days between April 6 and July 22, 1971.

Judge Roth found the usual brace of violations perpetrated in other cities—gerrymandered zone lines, optional attendance areas in changing neighborhoods, and
instances of busing African-American youngsters experiencing overcrowded conditions past white schools with available space to more distant black schools. He
placed his heaviest emphasis, however, on evidence of housing discrimination.

> Governmental actions and inaction at all levels, federal, state and local,
> have combined, with those of private organizations, such as loaning
> institutions and real estate associations and brokerage firms, to establish
> and to maintain the pattern of residential segregation throughout the
> Detroit metropolitan area . . . . The[se] policies . . . have a continuing
> and present effect upon the complexion of the community—as we
> know, the choice of a residence is a relatively infrequent affair. For

many years FHA and VA openly advised and advocated the maintenance of "harmonious" neighborhoods, i.e., racially and economically
harmonious. The conditions created continue. While it would be unfair
to charge the present defendants with what other governmental officers
or agencies have done, it can be said that the actions or the failure to act
by the responsible school authorities, both city and state, were linked to
that of these other governmental units. When we speak of governmental action we should not view the different agencies as a collection of
unrelated units.[61]

The State of Michigan had also committed unconstitutional acts designed to
"maintain the pattern of segregation in the Detroit schools."[62] State officials gave
final approval to the school site selections which exacerbated the dual system in the
city. Their school aid formula discriminated against Detroit, according to Judge
Roth, and in favor of suburban districts. Furthermore, there was the legislation of
1970, designed to "impede, delay and minimize racial integration" in Detroit.[63] All
this combined with the state's "general responsibility for and supervision of public
education."[64]

The judge dutifully piled up such de jure transgressions, but was not impressed
by the distinction he felt required to make. "It is, the Court believes, unfortunate that
we cannot deal with public school segregation on a no-fault basis, for if racial segregation in our public schools is an evil, then it should make no difference whether
we classify it de jure or de facto."[65] In this mood, the judge allowed himself to speculate on the fruitlessness of a Detroit-only remedy in the case. "How do you desegregate a black city, or a black school system?" he asked witnesses during the trial.[66]
At its conclusion, he directed the Detroit Board of Education to submit a desegregation plan confined to the city, but also ordered state officials to devise one encompassing the three-county metropolitan area, even though none of the 85 school districts in these counties were parties to the case.

The suburban districts then sought intervention, feeling they possessed the right
to demonstrate that they should not be included in the remedy, since none had committed any constitutional violations. But Judge Roth regarded any such demonstration as premature, and, as it turned out, ultimately irrelevant. He allowed the suburban districts to intervene only to advise him on the general "legal propriety or
impropriety of . . . a metropolitan plan,"[67] not to present evidence or witnesses bearing on their own past conduct. Two days after receiving intervenors' brief, he rejected the contention that interdistrict relief was dependent upon de jure acts by any of
the school districts surrounding Detroit. Four days later, the judge decided that
Detroit-only plans were indeed inadequate, and that he "must look beyond the limits of the Detroit school district for a solution to the problem."[68]

Emulating his colleague in Richmond, Judge Roth justified his right to order a
metropolitan remedy by citing Michigan's responsibility for education under the
state constitution, and its obligation under the fourteenth amendment to provide

equal protection of the laws. "School district lines are simply matters of political convenience," he asserted, "and may not be used to deny constitutional rights . . . . The State . . . cannot escape its constitutional duty to desegregate the public schools of the City of Detroit by pleading local authority."[69]

From March 28 to April 14, 1972, the district court held hearings on various metropolitan plans, confining counsel for the suburban districts at this point to a discussion only of the "size and expanse" of a proper plan.[70] The intervenors raged at this treatment, arguing it denied due process of law. Yet the district judge's conduct flowed logically from his theory of the case. As complainant's brief later put the matter:

> The power of . . . state officials to assist in providing relief to plaintiffs, even across the boundaries of school districts not parties [to this case], is clear as a matter of both state and federal law . . . . Manifestly, State defendants [having] had the authority to prevent the violation . . . now have the statutory authority . . . , subject to the District Court's injunction, to insure the implementation of complete relief . . . ."[71]

The judge finally approved a scheme involving 52 suburban school districts in the three counties. The plan combined 503,000 students in these districts with the 276,000 in Detroit; of the total of 780,000, 25% were black. The new metropolitan entity was divided into fifteen clusters, each linking the city with two or more suburban districts. The clusters ranged from 27,000 to 93,000 pupils, and from 20.5% to 30.8% black. Approximately 40% of the children in the combined district would be bused to school under the approved plan. This total compared favorably with the percentage of children already using buses in the tri-county area (42%–52%), but since there was little busing in Detroit itself, 350 new vehicles were required.

The remedy opinion reiterated the state's constitutional responsibility for desegregation. Resting beneath this jurisdictional concept, however, as in *Richmond*, was the wellspring of Judge Roth's actions.

> The message in *Brown* was simple: the Fourteenth Amendment was to be applied full force in public schooling. The Court held that "state-imposed" school segregation immeasurably taints the education received by all children in the public schools; perpetuates racial discrimination and a history of public action attaching a badge of inferiority to the black race in a public forum which importantly shapes the minds and hearts of succeeding generations of our young people; and amounts to an invidious racial classification.[72]

A Sixth Circuit panel affirmed Judge Roth's decision, in an unreported opinion. On rehearing *en banc*, a divided circuit agreed, though, like the earlier panel, it remanded the case to allow further refinement of the metropolitan remedy.[73] Both opinions were written by Chief Judge Harry Phillips.

The majority affirmed the lower court findings of illegal conduct by local and state education officials, adding a new, and, as it turned out, a significant charge to the mix. They pointed out that in the late 1950's, the Carver School District, a poor, black district near Detroit, lacked high school facilities and arranged with the city to have students go to school there. The nearest high school was a white one, yet the students were bused past it to an all-black school. These actions, felt the circuit court, not only reflected on Detroit authorities; they "could not have taken place without the approval, tacit or otherwise, of the State Board of Education."[74]

The Sixth Circuit also followed the reasoning used by Judge Roth to justify his remedy. "Like the District Judge, we see no validity to an argument which asserts that the constitutional right to equality before the law is hemmed in by the boundaries of a school district."[75] Under Michigan law, of course, education was "regarded . . . as the fundamental business of the State," and school district lines had never been "treated . . . as sacrosanct."[76] The court cited numerous instances where Michigan officials merged or reorganized school districts, reducing them from 1,438 in 1964 to 738 in 1968. The state not only bore the constitutional responsibility for correcting illegal segregation, but "controls the instrumentalities" for doing so.[77]

Like his lower court colleague, though, Judge Phillips' intimated that he would prefer to adopt a no-fault approach to a phenomenon he found inherently discriminatory. The record in the case, he noted at one point, revealed a pattern of black schools "separated only by school district boundaries" from white schools. "We cannot see how such segregation can be any less harmful to the minority students than if the same result were accomplished within one school district."[78] In his dissenting opinion, Judge Paul Weick produced a sentence from the slip opinion of the original panel which was left out of the *en banc* opinion. "Big city school systems for blacks surrounded by suburban school systems for whites cannot represent equal protection under the law."[79]

If the majority in *Bradley* v. *Milliken* challenged the de jure-de facto distinction from one perspective, they finessed any challenge to it from another. They acknowledged that the trial record contained "a substantial volume of testimony" about the discriminatory actions of housing authorities. Yet, "we have not relied at all upon testimony pertaining to segregated housing except as school construction programs helped cause or maintain such segregation."[80]

IV

The Supreme Court granted certiorari in what was now *Milliken* v. *Bradley* and heard oral arguments on February 27, 1974. At conference on March 1, the lineup in the Richmond case was replicated, for Justices Stewart and Blackmun remained set against extending the integrative reach of *Keyes* to the suburbs. His view "had not changed . . . since Richmond," Stewart averred, according to Justice Douglas' handwritten notes of the conference.[81] Blackmun felt the case for interdistrict relief in Detroit "is weaker than [in] Richmond," where all of the jurisdictions involved were "pro-segregationist."[82]

Given this arrangement of the eight justices who had decided *Richmond*, the outcome of the Detroit case was certain, for Justice Lewis Powell, whatever his comments in *Keyes* concerning the de jure-de facto distinction, strongly opposed the interdistrict remedy imposed by the lower courts. "[H]e fervently believed in local control of education"; and, as his opinion in *Keyes* clearly indicated, he felt that "[i]f some busing was bad, more was worse. [Powell] doubted that busing could achieve any durable solution, even if it were expanded to include the suburbs."[83]

The chief justice undertook to craft the majority opinion in *Milliken*, but his initial effort did not impress his potential allies. It consisted principally of a diatribe against the "'racial balance'"[84] he claimed the district judge had impermissibly decreed for metropolitan Detroit. The chief seemed less concerned that the lower courts had applied a *Swann*-type remedy to an improperly chosen area than that they had allegedly violated *Swann's* strictures against quotas. He quoted indignantly from Judge Roth's second opinion, with his own emphases added. "[P]upil reassignments shall be effected . . . to the end that . . . *no school, grade or classroom* [would be] substantially disproportionate *to the overall pupil racial composition*."[85] Burger also quoted, but paid no apparent attention to the phrase which opened this sentence. "Within the limitations of reasonable travel time and distance factors, pupil reassignments shall . . . ."[86] The fact was that Roth's orders, like the ones in *Swann*, were conceived as remedial in nature and imposed no exact racial formula; furthermore, *Swann* too covered grades and classrooms. In *Milliken*, quite clearly, the author of *Swann* was having second thoughts about his earlier willingness to draw a line of constitutional dimension between a "norm" and a "starting point."

Given his preoccupations, the chief dealt only perfunctorily with the central question which the case raised, when interdistrict remedies were and were not constitutionally appropriate. Moreover, the standard he articulated for dealing with this matter was a conspicuously narrow one, providing that "cross-district remedies presuppose a fair and reasoned determination that there has been a constitutional violation *by all of the districts affected by the remedy*."[87]

Justice Powell, the pivotal vote, endeavored to refocus the chief justice's sights.[88] He called Burger's attention to the amicus brief filed in *Milliken* by Solicitor General Robert Bork, which contained a finely-honed statement of a remedial standard applicable to metropolitan controversies.

[I]n our view, an interdistrict remedy, requiring the restructuring of state or local government entities, is appropriate only in the unusual circumstance where it is necessary to undo the interdistrict effect of a constitutional violation. Specifically, if it were shown that the racially discriminatory acts of the State, or of several local school districts, or of a single local district, have been a direct or substantial cause of interdistrict school segregation, then a remedy designed to eliminate the segregation so caused would be appropriate.

> In each instance of an interdistrict violation, the remedy should . . . be tailored to fit the violation, particularly in view of the deference owed to existing governmental structures . . . . Any modification of those structures should be narrowly framed . . . , so as to avoid unnecessary judicial interference with state prerogatives concerning the organization of local governments.[89]

Besides being more thorough and crisply stated than Burger's original effort, the solicitor general's standard was more capacious as well. It allowed school districts severely affected by violations in other jurisdictions to be implicated in a metropolitan remedy, even if not guilty of de jure segregation themselves.

Justices Stewart and Blackmun were also impressed by Bork's approach. "Inclined to go along with SG-reverse," say Douglas' notes on Blackmun.[90] Consequently, after further negotiation, a majority opinion emerged, following along the lines of the United States brief. It started from the premise that the educational structure of Michigan, "in common with most states, provides for a large measure of local control."[91] Under state law, the local district was "an autonomous political body . . . , operating through a Board of Education popularly elected"; its "day-to-day affairs . . . are determined at the local level."[92] Any suggestion, therefore, that school district boundaries, in Michigan, or in most other places, "may be casually ignored or treated as a mere administrative convenience is contrary to the history of public education in our country."[93]

This being the case, the law of interdistrict offenses and remedies followed the formal constitutional logic of *Swann* and *Keyes*.

> Before the boundaries of separate and autonomous school districts may be set aside by consolidating the separate units for remedial purposes or by imposing a cross-district remedy, it must first be shown that there has been a constitutional violation within one district that produces a significant segregative effect in another district. Specifically, it must be shown that racially discriminatory acts of the state or local school districts, or of a single school district have been a substantial cause of interdistrict segregation. Thus an interdistrict remedy might be in order where the racially discriminatory acts of one or more school districts caused racial segregation in an adjacent district, or where district lines have been deliberately drawn on the basis of race. In such circumstances an interdistrict remedy would be appropriate to eliminate the interdistrict segregation directly caused by the constitutional violation. Conversely, without an interdistrict violation and interdistrict effect, there is no constitutional wrong calling for an interdistrict remedy.[94]

Under such a rule, the state might be constitutionally responsible for all illegal segregation, but its responsibility was limited by the fact that a "remedy is necessarily designed, as all remedies are, to restore the victims of discriminatory conduct to the position they would have occupied in the absence of such conduct."[95] Consequently, the specific "constitutional right of the Negro respondents residing in Detroit" was "to attend a unitary school system *in that district*,"[96] absent the de jure violations which could geographically expand this right.

Still, the reasoning of *Swann* and *Keyes* would have automatically extended the violations in Detroit, and in other large cities, into their suburbs had Burger employed the full kit of analytical tools used for assessing Charlotte and Denver. He reached a contrary result in *Milliken*, above all, because he refused to supplement the liability principles declared in the earlier decisions with the presumptions which those decisions utilized. Buses stopped at the city-county line because the wide-sweeping assumptions about causation which characterized the opinions of 1971 and 1973 stopped at those lines.

In *Swann*, the Court held the Charlotte-Mecklenburg authorities responsible for all segregation in the school system due to presumptive conclusions about the effects of their past violations; the justices allowed themselves to deduce that the "location of schools may . . . have [had an] important impact on composition of inner-city neighborhoods."[97] These speculations, in fact, carried beyond the limits of a single city, since the Charlotte-Mecklenburg school system encompassed both Charlotte and its far-flung suburbs. Thus, the decision also suggested that school site selection "may . . . influence the patterns of residential development of a *metropolitan area*."[98] *Keyes*, too, while officially confining itself to Denver, spoke of segregative effects spreading throughout the "metropolitan" community.[99] It made equally as much, or as little, sense to assume that the school board's violations in Detroit meaningfully shaped residential patterns in adjoining suburban areas, some beginning only a few blocks from white enclaves in the city already held to be the result of these violations. Respondents' brief, indeed, tried to push the justices in the direction of the *Swann-Keyes* presumptions as the basis for a metropolitan remedy. While pleading for reinstatement of the independent housing violations found by Judge Roth, they reminded Chief Justice Burger and his colleagues of the "reciprocal effects" the Court had postulated previously, calling attention to the appropriate passages in *Keyes* and *Swann*.[100]

But in *Milliken*, the majority declined to take anything on faith. Predictably refusing to examine the material on housing discrimination, the chief justice also abjured any suppositions about the influence a black de jure system in Detroit might have exerted over residential patterns. He parsed the remaining record in the case only for evidence of interdistrict violations and their *specific, measurable* effects, an exercise which turned Judge Roth's whole approach to the case against him, since the judge's predicate for interdistrict relief flowed entirely from a trial devoted to establishing de jure segregation within Detroit.

There were no allegations at all, the chief noted, that authorities had drawn the school boundaries of Detroit or of the surrounding districts with segregative intent; nor were any of the suburban districts themselves guilty of de jure violations. This left the catalogue of unconstitutional actions by the state of Michigan. Two of these offenses—the legislature's enactment of the law undermining the Detroit desegregation plan and the state's supervision of school site selection—Burger easily dismissed as relating entirely to the situation in the city. The state's discrimination against Detroit with regard to school aid, while potentially more relevant, he also set aside, since the courts below had not pursued its racial implications. "[N]either the Court of Appeals nor the District Court offered any indication . . . as to how, if at all, the availability of state-financed aid for some Michigan students outside Detroit, but not for those within Detroit, might have affected the racial character of any of the State's school districts."[101]

Finally, there was the state's "tacit or express" approval of the arrangement whereby African-American students from the Carver district were bused past white schools in Detroit to an all-black high school. Burger conceded that this ploy "may have had a segregative effect on the school populations of the two districts involved." Yet an "isolated instance affecting two of the school districts would not justify the broad metropolitanwide remedy contemplated by the District Court."[102]

Eschewing a remand for further factual findings, a course urged, among others, by Solicitor General Bork,[103] the majority reversed the Sixth Circuit and sent the case back to the lower courts, with directions for the "prompt formulation of a decree . . . to eliminat[e] the segregation found to exist in [the] Detroit city schools."[104]

V

The principal dissents in *Milliken* by Justices Byron White and Thurgood Marshall both called attention to Michigan's constitutional responsibility for desegregation under the fourteenth amendment, but staunchly denied that this state liability was limited to correcting violations within Detroit. "The State's default," after all, was "'the condition that offends the Constitution,'" felt Justice White, and state authorities, therefore, could be required to eliminate from Detroit's schools "'all vestiges of state-imposed segregation.'"[105] The majority's opinion allowed Michigan to "successfully insulate itself from its duty to provide effective desegregation remedies by vesting sufficient power over its public schools in its local school districts. If this is the case in Michigan, it will be the case in most States."[106]

Similarly, Justice Marshall argued that the "essential foundation of interdistrict relief" in *Milliken* was not the desire to impose racial balance on blameless suburban districts for reasons of educational philosophy; rather, "relief was seen as a necessary part of any meaningful effort by the State of Michigan to remedy the state-caused segregation within the city of Detroit."[107] The justice admitted that such an obligation must coexist with considerations of feasibility; desegregation plans could not span an entire state. But the tri-county arrangement approved by Judge Roth fell easily within these limits, Marshall felt. It actually involved less expense for busing than a Detroit-only remedy, since the city would have needed 900 buses to implement such a plan. Moreover, the district judge had placed a forty minute ceiling on one-way bus trips; some students in the tri-county area already travelled one and a quarter hours each way.

Justice Marshall drew a parallel between the Detroit school controversy and the legislative reapportionment cases. Both, he argued, were properly governed by the principle that a state could not "hide behind its political subdivisions to avoid its obligations."[108] Justice White also called up the precedent he felt was established in *Reynolds* v. *Sims*.[109] Political units of a state, themselves guilty of no discrimination, could be restructured nonetheless "to remedy infringements of the constitutional rights of [other] members of its populace."[110]

There was certainly merit to these arguments about the implications of state responsibility for desegregation under the fourteenth amendment (though it would appear that the claims to autonomy of a congressional district are not on the same footing as those of a local school system). In truth, however, the competing contentions in *Milliken* v. *Bradley* flowed from more fundamental beliefs about the meaning of *Brown*. They depended finally on whether justices identified with the official liability formula of *Swann* and *Keyes*, or with the apparent concern of those decisions for the "segregated patterns themselves." The chief justice, who never really reconciled himself to the result in *Swann*, and disagreed with the outcome in *Keyes*, eagerly rammed home in *Milliken* the limitations which a stringent reading of those two decisions imposed on Judge Roth. The judge's action, he hastened to point out, could not "be supported on the grounds that it represents merely the devising of a suitably flexible remedy for the violation of rights *already established* by our prior decisions. It can be supported only by drastic expansion of the constitutional right itself . . . ."[111]

Justice White, on the other hand, identified with a remedy for the de jure violations of Detroit which struck at traditional distinctions in school law, though he attempted to cabin his thinking within conventional categories. A metropolitan remedy was necessary, he argued, even under the standard equity formula used in school cases. A Detroit-only scheme could *not* "'restore the victims of discriminatory conduct to the position they would have occupied in the absence of such conduct,'" because such a remedy would fail to "restore to the Negro community, *stigmatized as it was by the dual school system*, what it would have enjoyed" in the past had state-sponsored segregation not existed in Detroit.[112] The "maximum remedy available" within the city now would "leave many of the schools almost totally black," perpetuating the stigma created by past discrimination. "The Court's remedy, in the end, . . . will leave serious violations of the Constitution substantially unremedied."[113] Yet their legitimate remedy, as White conceived it, would implicate school authorities and students not involved in any "violations of the Constitution," as the Court had defined them up to 1974.

Justice Marshall's deeply-felt and eloquent dissent (which White joined) went further, articulating the integrationist ideal which lay behind so many of the abstruse maneuverings in school law during the previous decade.

> The rights at issue in the case are too fundamental to be abridged on grounds as superficial as those relied on by the majority today. We deal here with the right of all of our children, whatever their race, to an equal start in life and to an equal opportunity to reach their full potential as citizens. Those children who have been denied that right in the past deserve better than to see fences thrown up to deny them that right in the future. Our Nation, I fear, will be ill served by the Court's refusal to remedy separate and unequal education, for unless our children begin to learn together, there is little hope that our people will ever learn to live together.[114]

Only briefly in his dissent did Justice Marshall return to the game played in *Swann* and *Keyes* by seeking to use their presumptions as a basis for relief. The state's creation of all-black schools in the core city, he argued at one point, without offering any empirical evidence, "inevitably acted as a magnet to attract Negroes to the areas served by such schools and to deter them from settling either in other areas of the city or in the suburbs."[115] He dredged up the usual quotation from *Swann* to buttress this assertion ("People gravitate toward school facilities, just as schools are located in response to the needs of people."),[116] and adapted the phrase from *Keyes* about "reciprocal effects" to further expound his point. "The *rippling* effects on residential patterns caused by purposeful acts of segregation do not automatically subside at the school district border. [T]hese effects naturally spread through all the residential neighborhoods within a metropolitan area."[117] But Marshall's dissent had gone beyond placing priority on supposed causal connections.

Justice Douglas, of course, had dispensed with such concerns long before, and *Milliken* presented no problem for him. There was, he repeated, "so far as . . . school cases go no constitutional difference between de facto and de jure segregation."[118] School district lines, no less than intracity attendance zones, could be used to illegally separate the races, particularly since it was public authorities who contributed to the discriminatory housing patterns responsible for the separation. "It is state action when public funds are dispensed by housing agencies to build racial ghettos."[119] Michigan, like other northern states, "creates and nurtures a segregated school system, just as surely as those States involved in Brown v. Board of Education."[120]

Of the justices who joined Burger's opinion, only Potter Stewart wrote separately. His concurrence seemed to give a boost to those who still retained hope for metropolitan remedies in spite of *Milliken's* outcome. Justice Stewart stressed his agreement with the notion that interdistrict relief was not available unless interdistrict violations were proven. But in specifying the violations which could call forth such a remedy, Stewart followed somewhat along Douglas' line of argument and proposed a significant addition to the chief justice's list. "Were it to be shown . . . that state officials had contributed to the separation of the races by drawing or redrawing school district lines . . . ; *or by purposeful, racially discriminatory use of state housing or zoning laws*, then a decree calling for transfer of pupils across district lines or for restructuring of district lines might well be appropriate."[121] Chief Justice Burger's standard for determining interdistrict offenses appeared limited to the actions of school officials, though this was not certain, since his opinion did not deal with housing evidence. Stewart's language, however, offered hope that plaintiffs could utilize this kind of evidence in subsequent litigation. "[F]uture metropolitan cases," wrote Professor William L. Taylor in 1975, "may well depend upon the ability of plaintiffs to demonstrate policies of racial containment in housing sufficient to meet the standard set out by Mr. Justice Stewart."[122]

Indeed, Stewart's concurrence endorsed the argument with regard to housing which Judge Wright advanced a decade earlier, but no court had yet accepted—that such discrimination could form the *sole* basis for liability in a school case. The justice was speaking in a metropolitan setting. A month after *Milliken*, though, a Tenth Circuit panel cited his views in claiming that actions by housing authorities might constitute sufficient grounds to proceed against a single school district. The judges refused to dismiss a complaint against the school board of San Jose, California, despite the fact that the plaintiffs documented no acts of de jure segregation on its part. For even "assuming school authorities were not chargeable with acts of discrimination, relief might be granted if segregation in the schools resulted from the acts of other state agencies . . . . We are not prepared to hold at this stage of the proceeding that relief is necessarily precluded because the injury complained of . . . , segregated schools, is one step removed from the cause."[123]

Unlike Douglas, however, it is not clear that Stewart harbored much sympathy for the line of analysis he had opened. He actually reviewed the evidence in the Detroit case concerning housing violations and announced himself unimpressed. In a broader sense, the justice expressed the same suspicions as Judge Craven about attempts to explain demographic patterns. The "essential fact of a predominantly Negro school population in Detroit," he hypothesized, was "caused by unknown and perhaps unknowable factors such as in-migration, birth rates, economic changes, or cumulative acts of private racial fears."[124] Stewart's comments about housing violations in *Milliken* were confined possibly to discriminatory actions by state officials embodied in specific statutes ("state housing or zoning laws").

Somewhat surprising, therefore, was the justice's opinion in a major housing case, two terms later, which indirectly eased some of the rigors of *Milliken*. *Hills* v. *Gautreaux* involved racial discrimination in Chicago's public housing program, committed by the Chicago Housing Authority and HUD. While all of the violations took place within the city of Chicago, a Sixth Circuit panel ordered the defendants to prepare a comprehensive metropolitan plan of relief covering Chicago and several of its suburbs. HUD appealed the matter to the Supreme Court, claiming that under the holding in *Milliken* an interdistrict remedy for housing discrimination obtained only upon "a finding of an inter-district violation."[125]

But Justice Stewart, speaking for a unanimous Court of eight (Justice Stevens not participating), rejected HUD's claims. *Milliken*, it was true, had set "limitations on the exercise of the equity power of the federal courts," which were not restricted to school cases, but these limitations were aimed most directly at "judicial decree[s] restructuring the operation of local governmental entities that were not implicated in any constitutional violation."[126] In the Detroit case, the relevant units involved were the Detroit school system and the wholly separate suburban districts, and "prior cases had established that [school] violations are to be dealt with in terms of 'an established geographic and administrative school system.'"[127] In *Gautreaux*, however, the "relevant geographic area for purposes of the [plaintiffs'] housing options is the Chicago housing market, not the Chicago city limits."[128]

It was by no means certain in this context that an order requiring HUD to construct housing beyond the Chicago city limit "would impermissibly interfere with local governments and suburban housing authorities that have not been implicated in HUD's unconstitutional conduct."[129] HUD was "underestimat[ing] the ability of a federal court" to formulate an effective decree, "without overstepping the limits of judicial power established in the Milliken case."[130]

Stewart's logic, though rooted in a housing decision, carried some potential relevance for future school cases. It left open the possibility of remedies for inner city school districts, which exerted, and were designed to exert, an influence upon student patterns in surrounding suburban districts, so long as these remedies did not seek to restructure "governmental entities . . . not implicated in any constitutional violation."

Whatever the formal legal principles involved, Stewart's "authorship" of *Gautreaux* was "ironic," as Professor Dimond points out, in terms of its perception of urban realities.

> In the Detroit school case, there had been substantial evidence and express findings by the trial court that discrimination, public and private, including by HUD and its predecessor agencies, contributed substantially to segregation throughout the metropolitan area as well as within the Detroit city limits. The basic violation found by Judge Roth had been the containment of black families within an expanding blacks-only core of one-race schools and housing surrounded by an exclusionary whites-only ring. But, in his separate concurring opinion, Stewart had purported to review the record and said there was no such evidence. He had even suggested that the causes of the creation and expansion of the Negro ghetto in Detroit (and the protected white sanctuaries on the fringes of Detroit and in the surrounding suburbs) were "caused by unknown and perhaps unknowable factors." In the Chicago public housing case there was no proof of discrimination, public or private, outside the Chicago city limits, and there was an express trial judge finding that

the violation involved only the city of Chicago . . . .

Yet Stewart chose to perceive that the nature of the violation in the *Gautreaux* case was the confinement of black families to segregated public housing in the Negro ghetto and authorized a remedy against HUD based on the "real" housing market area, including Chicago's suburbs.

In the Detroit school case, fears of too intrusive judicial remedies and of massive white opposition to actual areawide school desegregation seemed to obscure Stewart's vision of the nature of the wrong and the state's responsibility for the system of racial ghettoization found by Judge Roth.[131]

Milliken v. *Bradley* did not make interdistrict remedies for school segregation impossible, to be sure. As Harvie Wilkinson noted bluntly, however, "*Milliken* . . . rejected what some believed to be the last hope for mass betterment of America's blacks."[132]

VI

Not unexpectedly, the *Milliken* decision brought forth the most sophisticated and most eloquent efforts yet attempted to surmount the de jure-de facto distinction and frame a nationwide principle of integration.

In response to *Milliken*, Professor Charles R. Lawrence, now of Georgetown Law School, articulated brilliantly a view of racial separation in schools which transported Professor Black's mode of analysis across the Mason-Dixon line, though Lawrence did not view the 1954 decision as favorably as did that great essay. Unlike Black, he took the Court to task for misreading the nature of segregation, even as they were properly condemning it. The justices had relied on questionable "psycho-sociological evidence," and displayed lack of discernment, he felt, in neglecting to spell out the true reason why African-American youngsters might well experience "'feelings of inferiority'—*the fact that they and everyone else knew*" that segregation characterized them "*as inferior*."[133] *Brown*, as written, failed to acknowledge that segregated schools were inherently unequal not so much because African-American youngsters were denied the right to sit next to whites, but because attendance at separate schools was part of a social labeling device. "The institution of segregation and the injury it inflicts on blacks is necessarily misunderstood until one recognizes that its chief purpose is to *define*, not to separate."[134]

This definition was conveyed by other institutions of a segregated society as surely as by its schools, Lawrence noted. The injury inflicted was "*systemic* rather than particular."[135] Some black schools in the pre-1954 South were actually superior to white schools, but they remained unconstitutional nonetheless, "because they were pieces of a larger puzzle which, when fitted together, plainly spelled out the words, 'if you're black, get back.'"[136]

These insights must be acknowledged "before a proper approach to desegregation cases can be developed."[137] And their validity most definitely was not limited by region, or by the presence in a school system of neutral geographic zoning. For the history of American society provided massive evidence "that the official actions of northern, midwestern and western states played a predominant role in the entrenchment of segregation within their borders." Because such "substantial state activity" entered into the creation of segregated social systems "throughout the nation, the fact that the northern states ceased official enforcement of a segregated school system prior to 1954 . . . does not appear to be an adequate rationale for exempting northern states from the mandate of *Brown*."[138]

The *Brown* Court's failure to confront the realities of segregation paved the way for the Burger Court's conclusions about Detroit. Proceeding on the assumption that the equal protection clause forbade only individual state separation of the races in public schools, Burger and his colleagues found, not unreasonably, no interdistrict violations in the Detroit metropolitan area. The Court failed to notice, however, that the state of Michigan "was involved in the creation of the socio-political system of segregation that labels segregated black children as inferior."[139] The reach of this injury was not confined "by school district lines."[140]

Professor Fiss basically conceded, in an essay of late 1974, that *Milliken* was in many ways a more honest decision than *Swann* or *Keyes*.[141] The next year he undertook a striking and meticulously constructed reassessment of the entire structure of equal protection jurisprudence.

Traditional equal protection principles, he noted, idealized the individual as their focus of concern, and concentrated on various forms of arbitrary discrimination against individuals as the constitutional violation to be attacked. While this ideal construct was partly illusory, since decisions such as *Brown* and *Hernandez* v. *Texas* certainly acknowledged the role of oft-persecuted "social groups,"[142] it was nonetheless true that, as part of traditional equal protection analysis, those decisions emphasized palpably discriminatory action, action clearly applicable to every member of the class involved.

But scholars, and judges, had increasingly come to see by the 1960's that this dominant "antidiscrimination principle" of fourteenth amendment law possessed "structural limitations" that prevented it "from adequately resolving or even addressing . . . central claims of equality . . . being advanced" in the society by racial and ethnic minorities, speaking *as groups*.[143] Foremost among these claims was the one condemning "facially innocent criteria"[144] for classifying and separating people, modes of government operation such as general testing for firemen and policemen, or neighborhood zoning of schools. Such classifications, it was argued, might not be invidious in nature, and did not offend, therefore, an individualistic equal protection standard, but their obvious effect was to exacerbate historical injustices perpetrated by the society against African-Americans and other minorities. "For example, when the state purports to choose . . . college students on the basis of performance on [SAT's], and it turns out that the only persons admitted . . . are white."[145]

The courts frequently sympathized with these grievances "as a matter of substantive justice," yet found it extremely difficult to condemn facially innocent criteria on the basis of "the original, modest conception of the antidiscrimination principle," which, for new claims of equality, "provides no framework of analysis or, even worse, provides the wrong one."[146]

This ambivalence explained, in Professor Fiss' view, why the Supreme Court of *Swann* and *Keyes* dwelled on the concept of past discrimination and its effects as a justification for finding equal protection violations in the present use of otherwise objective social means. A "ban on 'the perpetuation of past arbitrary discrimination'" represented a way for the justices to rationalize the rejection of facially neutral classifications without having to break new doctrinal ground, since such thinking "looks like a close cousin of the ban on 'arbitrary discrimination.'"[147] The Court had even conjured up a set of causal presumptions in this area in order to avoid inconvenient empirical inquiries "likely to strain the judicial system—consume scarce resources and yield unsatisfying results."[148]

> But these techniques have their own costs. The use of presumptions involves the court in fictionalizing and thereby impairing its credibility. And, more importantly, once the connections between victim and beneficiary and between past perpetrator and present cost-bearer are severed, we have ceased talking about the perpetuation of past discrimination in any individualized sense. The past discrimination that we are talking about is of a more global character—for example, that the group were slaves for one century and subject to Jim Crow laws for another. The ethical significance of this global past discrimination cannot be denied; it gives the group an identity and might explain why we are especially concerned with its welfare. But at the same time it should be understood that once we start talking of global past discrimination, the link between the proposed anti-past-discrimination principle and the original antidiscrimination principle becomes highly attenuated. We have embarked on another journey altogether . . . .[149]

In place of judicial deceptions, Professor Fiss proposed a new integrating principle under the fourteenth amendment to supplement the old one: a "group-disadvantaging principle,"[150] that would identify those groups in the society long held in a state of deprivation and decree that a law having even the *effect* of further disadvantaging them constituted a violation of equal protection. Clearly, this new form of equality would serve "primarily . . . as a protection for blacks,"[151] but the status of African-Americans in society could form a model for determining other groups entitled to similar solicitude. The position of black Americans as the country's "perpetual underclass," and what Professor Fiss regarded at the time as their "severely circumscribed" political power, stamped them as "the prototype of the protected group, [though] they are not the only group entitled to protection."[152]

Under a group-disadvantaging principle, state action "that seemed beyond the reach of the Equal Protection Clause under the antidiscrimination principle"—pure geographic zoning in student assignment, for example—"could be evaluated from the perspective of whether it had the effect of impairing the status of a specially disadvantaged group."[153] There would no longer exist the necessity to force such action "into the 'arbitrary discrimination' pigeonhole."[154] Nor would there be any need to fuss, among other things, with the distinction between de jure and de facto segregation of public schools.

Professor Robert Sedler of Wayne State Law School sought to derive a nationwide principle of integration by drawing on that language of *Brown* which had always seemed to make a stronger case for it than the "modern [psychological] authority" cited by the Court. All segregation in education was unconstitutional, Sedler argued, because it did to African-American youngsters what it had done to George McLaurin, stunted "his ability to study, to engage in discussions and exchange views with other students." The harm of racial isolation and the educational damage it inflicted was the reason integration was required in public schools, so that they would no longer "deprive black children of the intangible benefits connected with interracial education, . . . the opportunity to associate with white children during the educational process, to exchange ideas with them, and to learn how to live in a multiracial society."[155]

There was also a broader social dimension to this deprivation, Professor Sedler felt, which gave it its special constitutional relevance. Attendance at segregated schools rubbed in for minority youngsters the reality of the housing and employment discrimination so rampant in American society. Educational separation "strongly implicates the basic values of racial equality and black freedom embodied in the Fourteenth Amendment . . . because it perpetuates and reinforces ghettoization and residential racial segregation, one of the most pronounced consequences of the social history of racism in this nation."[156]

Thus the harm flowing from segregated public schools created by neutral zoning was identical, Sedler maintained, to the evils flowing from official segregation. In each case, "[i]t is the required attendance at racially identifiable schools" that caused "specific educational harm."[157] The actual difference between regions, then, lay not in the fact that one was engaging in an acceptable form of segregation, the other in an unacceptable form. It lay in the strength of the state justification for segregative practices. Northern authorities, at least, could defend school segregation on the basis of the legitimate interests advanced by geographic zoning—educational efficiency, involvement of parents, promotion, perhaps, of a sense of community.

But such justifications, while not inconsequential, were not sufficient to override the demands of *Brown*. The decision "must be interpreted to recognize a substantive constitutional right of children to attend a racially integrated school, and the state may not insist on geographic attendance zoning to compel children to attend racially identifiable schools."[158] Nor could the boundaries between individual school districts restrict this right of association. The interest in local autonomy stressed by district school officials and politicians was a reasonable one, but was not fundamentally compromised by desegregation plans which simply decreed student exchanges between districts, as was the case in Detroit. And insofar as local autonomy was a synonym for the preservation of socially and racially homogeneous schools—on the premise that suburbanites "'may be willing to tax themselves at a higher rate, knowing . . . the money will be spent for the education of their own children'"—this was a "constitutionally impermissible" reason for eschewing interdistrict desegregation. "Since the state cannot affirmatively act to enable whites to avoid association with blacks in public facilities, it cannot assert an interest related to enabling whites to avoid interracial association in opposition to its obligation to provide for attendance at racially integrated schools."[159]

Since a constitutional obligation to integrate derived from the harm of racial isolation, Professor Sedler found it unnecessary to "consider . . . whether required attendance at racially identifiable schools produces feelings of inferiority in black children."[160] (In fact, studies from the late 1960's on continued to raise doubts about whether "de facto" segregation actually caused such feelings in minority youngsters.)[161] Nor did Sedler rely on data concerning academic achievement, believing that while there was "substantial, although controverted evidence," that African-American students performed better in integrated than in segregated schools, "there is no evidence suggesting that the higher achievement level . . . is due to the racial mixture . . . in the school as such."[162] Professor Sedler's approach, then, like the others, rested on the historical realities best documented in footnote 11, not by Kenneth Clark, but by Gunnar Myrdal.

I. THE DECISION THAT NEVER WAS

While the Richmond interdistrict busing case ended in a 4–4 non-decision by the Supreme Court, the internal memoranda of the justices strike many of the chords which would later be sounded in *Milliken* v. *Bradley*. Justice Douglas emphasized the responsibility of the state for education, as a reason for breaching school district boundaries in order to achieve integration. Justice Rehnquist foreshadowed the far narrower standard that would prevail in *Milliken*.

Most arresting, perhaps, was Justice Brennan's attempt to utilize in the Richmond case the device which Chief Justice Burger so pointedly ignored in his Detroit opinion: the *Swann-Keyes* presumptions as a way of smoothing the path to interdistrict violations.

1. JUSTICE DOUGLAS' MEMORANDUM IN *RICHMOND*

The only question decided by the Court of Appeals was stated in its opinion as follows:

> "May a United States District Judge compel one of the States of the Union to restructure its internal government for the purpose of achieving racial balance in the assignment of pupils to the public schools? We think not, absent invidious discrimination in the establishment or maintenance of local governmental units, and accordingly reverse." 462 F. 2d 1058

On that issue the Court of Appeals was plainly wrong.

We start with the Fourteenth Amendment whose commands run to the States. Any officer of the State, any political division of the State is the State for Fourteenth Amendment purposes when it carries forward a state policy. Virginia's longstanding school policy was the maintenance of a dual school system based on racial lines. And it was that policy that the three school districts here involved carried out.

It seems clear that a federal court may disregard school district lines in designing a school desegregation plan.

Political subdivisions of a State are only convenient units for exercising special governmental responsibilities. They never have been allowed to deny federal rights. See *Reynolds v. Sims*, 377 U.S. 533, 575. The alignment or realignment of political divisions of a State to cut down or dilute federal constitutional rights is impermissible . . . .

The maintenance of existing school division lines is an instrument for segregation, for they help maintain the institution of the segregated school within strict housing segregation patterns. The maintenance of school division lines becomes an obstacle to pupil assignment under any desegregation plan. The housing pattern in Richmond produced increasingly black communities. The public schools in Richmond became identifiable as black schools, while those in the two counties were marked as white schools. When black schools are across the street, so to speak, from white schools separated only by a school district line that is an invisible barrier, no desegregation plan furthering the concept of the neighborhood school can be designed—unless the several school districts are considered as one.

The District Court was faced with the reality that if school district lines were to be maintained any desegregation plan would leave black public schools and white public schools facing each other across invisible division boundary lines surrounding Richmond. The result would be a mockery of *Brown* v. *Board of Education* . . . .

The District Court used the concept "viable racial mix," drawn from testimony that if a school's population is below 20% black, that component becomes only a token presence insufficient to allow them participation in most school activities. If it [rises] above 40% black, there tends to be an exodus of whites . . . .

This does not violate the disapproval of "racial mix" which we mentioned in *Swann* v. *Charlotte-Mecklenburg Board*. There cannot be desegregation of dual school systems without some racial mix. The District Court made a reasoned effort to break up a state segregated school system by disregarding school district lines, which stood as the guardians of separate schools for blacks and for whites.

The net result of the Court of Appeals' ruling is that out of 131 schools to be operated by the three local boards, 44 would be attended by more than 90% white students and 11 by more than 80% black students. All of the black schools would lie in the Richmond system and all of the white schools in the county systems.

I would reverse the Court of Appeals and remand the cases to it for consideration of the desegregation plan on the merits.

2. JUSTICE REHNQUIST'S MEMORANDUM IN *RICHMOND*

Insofar as Byron's memorandum rejects the notion that a district court may *never* fashion relief in school cases which would result in the crossing of school district boundaries, I agree. But I think I would say that it may *hardly ever* do this, and I guess he wouldn't. I would think that sort of remedy for a Fourteenth Amendment right would be available only where the drawing of the boundary lines or use of the boundary lines were themselves a substantial element in the violation of the right, or where the boundary lines were observed largely in the breach. Examples which occur are manipulative use of lines by school authorities to enforce or preserve segregation, repeated disregard of the lines by school authorities with the result that substantial parts of the pupil population were in fact interchanged, or some sort of joint action by the three school districts of a similar nature.

My understanding of the record in this case leads me to believe that it doesn't afford a basis for any such finding. The school district boundaries here were drawn a century ago, and the only occasion on which they had been significantly changed have been as a result of the annexation of parts of the two counties to the City of Richmond. As I understand Virginia law, the change in the school district boundary would be an expected concomitant of the annexation, and since the effect of the most recent change in 1970 was to increase the ratio of whites to Negroes in the one of the three school systems which has the highest percentage of Negro students, it certainly cannot be said to have been done with any invidious intent.

I don't see, either, how the fact that schools close to the common border of two districts are close to each other really advances the constitutional argument. It is difficult to imagine two metropolitan school districts having a common border in which this would not be the case to some degree . . . .

The only evidence that seems to me arguably substantial that school district boundaries have been disregarded in the past is the State statute enacted in 1960 . . . . The Virginia General Assembly authorized tuition grants to students for education "in nonsectarian private schools in or outside, and in public schools located outside, the locality where the children reside . . ." Va. Code Ann. § 22–115.29. This legislation was held unconstitutional . . . , and the scholarship program was terminated in June, 1970.

It seems to me that there is a significant difference between the State authorizing individual pupils to attend public schools outside of the district in which they reside if the pupil chooses to do so, and action by the State or by the districts which would assign pupils across district lines on the initiative of the governmental body. Had plaintiffs sought relief in the form of court authorization for individual pupils, on their initiative, to attend schools in one of the other two districts, it could have been fairly argued that this was only the converse of what the State had previously sanctioned in the form of tuition grants, and the State having been willing to permit pupils to cross district lines under its program could not constitutionally refuse them the right to cross district lines on their own initiative. But this is not the relief sought or granted by the District Court; that relief consisted of a consolidation of the three districts, with mandatory cross-district assignments to be made on the authority of the court quite apart from pupil choice. I do not think the earlier ten year operation of the tuition grant program can be said to have countenanced the same kind or extent of district boundary crossing which the District Court has mandated.

The District Court and the petitioners also rely on the fact that the State for a period of years after the *Brown* decision fostered and encouraged segregated school systems in the various school districts. There is no doubt that it did, but I do not see what this adds to the conceded fact that the three districts in question each maintained a dual system until recently. [And] the fact that the State encouraged this sort of segregation does not offer a basis for lumping these three particular districts together, unless the State had lumped them together in its effort to maintain segregation. Putting these difficulties to one side, the logical consequence of petitioners' argument must be that by reason of State involvement, the entire State is to be treated as one school district, a position which neither they nor the District Court are willing to adopt . . . .

Byron says at page 10 of his memorandum that he would "remand for the benefit of the Court of Appeals' view of what the profile of a proper plan would be if the three districts were to be treated as a unit and, in light of his opinion in this respect, to have its considered judgment as to whether the boundaries of each of the three districts must be adhered to in all respects." I do not see, since in this case the wrongs complained of by the plaintiffs were inflicted separately by three separate school districts, what constitutional basis there is for treating these three districts "as a unit." . . .

I think the language which the Court of Appeals quoted from *Swann*, 402 U.S. 1, 16, tends to support this view:

> "In seeking to define even in broad and general terms how far this remedial power extends it is important to remember that judicial powers may be exercised only on the basis of a constitutional violation. Remedial judicial authority does not put judges automatically in the shoes of school authorities whose powers are plenary."

The frequently quoted language from the Court's previous decisions—"desegregated school system", "unitary school systems", absence of any "black schools" or "white schools"—requires a reference to some governmentally defined system as a beginning point in the analysis. I do not see how, in the absence of the sort of exceptional circumstances which don't exist here, this starting point can be other than the school district in which the plaintiffs actually attend school.

If this limitation is to be disregarded solely because the command of the Fourteenth Amendment is addressed to the "State", there is no logical stopping place short of a State-wide remedy which wholly disregarded district lines, and was limited only in terms of administrative factors such as the availability of school facilities, length of travel, and the like . . . .

Under my line of reasoning, if I may call it that, I do not reach *Swann*-type issues as to whether the District Court was motivated by a desire to insure "racial balance" or a "viable racial mix", or whether it placed too much emphasis on bussing. These are questions which are reached only after the initial determination is made that the three districts are to be treated as a unit for school purposes. I think the basic thrust . . . of the Court of Appeals' opinion, with which I substantially agree, was that on the facts of this case the District Court had no constitutional basis for making this initial determination.

3. JUSTICE BRENNAN'S MEMORANDUM IN *RICHMOND*

Before we decide finally to dispose of this case by a 4–4 affirmance, I should like to suggest an approach not covered in the memoranda circulated by . . . Bill Douglas, Byron and Bill Rehnquist. This approach is premised on the view that neither the District Court nor the Court of Appeals applied the correct standard of law in considering whether district lines could be disregarded in fashioning a remedy to redress the existing segregation of the Richmond school system.

I read the District Court to say that judicial power to fashion a desegregation plan reaching beyond a single school district rests upon two essential predicates: (1) that the public schools in the area had been purposefully segregated in violation of the Constitution as construed by *Brown*; and (2) that any form of remedial order confined to the limits of one district would be ineffective "to eliminate from the public schools all vestiges of state-imposed segregation." *Swann*, 402 U.S., at 15. The Court of Appeals seems to say, however, that in addition to these two predicates, there must also exist "invidious discrimination in the establishment or maintenance" of the district lines—i.e., manipulation, cooperation, or collusion by or among the school districts or the State.

We could reasonably conclude, in my view, that the two-pronged test of the District Court falls short of the proper standard. For although Richmond and the counties operated statutorily-mandated dual school systems in the past, and although desegregation by individual districts "to eliminate all vestiges of state-imposed segregation" seems not to be possible, the thrust of *Scotland Neck* and *City of Emporia* is that some nexus must be shown between past actions of the State or the counties and the present incurably-segregated condition of the Richmond school system. The Court of Appeals properly concluded that some nexus must be shown, but it imposed much too rigid a standard by requiring a showing of deliberate collusion among the school districts, or action mandated by the State, to structure district lines to create or maintain the segregated Richmond situation. The Court of Appeals wholly disregarded the possibility that the nexus might exist if the locked-in Richmond situation were created or maintained at least in part because of the policies of state-imposed segregation followed in Henrico and Chesterfield. It may be true that the district lines were not drawn deliberately so as to exclude black students from the county school systems. It does not follow, however, that the existence of identifiably "black" and identifiably "white" school districts, separated only by political boundary lines, is adventitious. On the contrary, as we said in *Swann*:

> "People gravitate toward school facilities, just as schools are located in response to the needs of people. The location of schools may thus influence the patterns of residential development of a metropolitan area and have important impact on composition of inner-city neighborhoods."

If past practices and policies of Henrico and Chesterfield counties or of the State prevented or discouraged blacks from relocating in those districts, then it is surely fair to say that the high degree of segregated schooling in Richmond is attributable to action of the counties or of the State. Thus, if a "white" suburban school district had a policy of sending all black school children in the district to a separate school or schools in far-off reaches of the school district, thereby discouraging or, as a practical matter, prohibiting blacks from relocating in the suburbs, that suburban school district has helped create and maintain the segregated schooling within the central city and therefore has as much an "affirmative duty" to help desegregate those schools as does the city itself. This is nothing more than a concrete application of what was said in *Swann* . . . .

There are some clear indications in the record of this case that the policies and practices of the school authorities of Henrico and Chesterfield counties and of State authorities did help solidify segregation in Richmond schools. For example, there is evidence that Henrico and Chesterfield counties had a practice of building "white" schools in the most populous areas of the counties contiguous to Richmond and of transporting all black pupils to "black" schools located in far-off reaches of the counties . . . . These practices obviously imposed a heavy burden on blacks living in the counties, and they may well have discouraged blacks from moving there in the first place. Similarly, the State authorities helped solidify segregation in Richmond through the use of the tuition grant and pupil scholarship programs enacted after *Brown*. Under these programs, . . . the State provided reimbursement for tuition paid in order to attend a private school or a public school in another district if the pupil was assigned to an integrated school or a school which had been closed by order of the Governor because of integration . . . . In light of these programs, black families may have been reluctant to move into the counties, for fear that whites would withdraw from the schools and leave the Governor with the option of closing those schools.

By itself, this evidence, and other evidence to be found in the record, may or may not prove dispositive. The District Court did not, however, proceed along these lines, and therefore the case should not be permitted to rest upon the present record alone. Consequently, it seems to me that vacation of the Court of Appeals' judgment should be ordered and the case be remanded to the District Court for decision under the proper standard.

II. *MILLIKEN* AND ITS LEGACY

Chief Justice Burger's attempt to savage the lower court decisions in *Milliken* v. *Bradley* by use of *Swann* so preoccupied him in his first draft that it produced a rather weak statement of the standard for interdistrict remedies central to the case. Prodded by Justice Powell, the chief eventually built on the model furnished by the amicus brief of Solicitor General Robert Bork.

The final product, of course, deeply disappointed Justice Thurgood Marshall, who read an eloquent summary of his dissenting opinion from the bench on July 25, 1974. Following in this emotional and constitutional spirit was Professor Charles Lawrence's reassessment of *Brown*.

1. CHIEF JUSTICE BURGER'S FIRST DRAFT IN *MILLIKEN*

Viewing the record as a whole, it seems clear that the District Court and the Court of Appeals placed the primary focus on the desire to achieve "racial balance" in a city predominantly composed of Negro students, and this approach plainly equated desegregation with racial balance as a constitutionally mandated remedy. In *Swann*, we recognized that racially identifiable schools are often symptomatic of a segregated system and that

> "[w]here [a system] . . . contemplates the continued existence of some schools that are all or predominantly of one race, [school authorities] have the burden of showing that such school assignments are genuinely nondiscriminatory." . . .

There has never been, however, a constitutional requirement that a school system reflect "any particular degree of racial balancing or mixing." Moreover, there is no constitutional requirement that each school in the system reflect—either precisely or substantially—the racial composition of the entire school system . . . . Here, it was assumed by both courts [below], without supporting evidence, that a member of a racial or ethnic minority who attends a school in which his or her minority group is predominant is in some way injured and thereby receives a lesser quality of education. Assuming that racial balancing to avoid this presumed injury is desirable on broad social or educational grounds, school authorities can rationally make that choice but it is not a constitutional requirement. In *Wright* v. *Council of City of Emporia*, we were constrained to affirm desegregation plans that resulted in racial ratios of 66% Negro and 34% White. Similarly, in *Swann* we noted that although the District Court had employed the racial composition of the entire system (71%-29%) as a starting point in developing a remedy, the court

> "went on to acknowledge that variation 'from that norm may be unavoidable.' This contains intimations that the 'norm' is a fixed mathematical racial balance reflecting the pupil constituency of the system. If we were to read the holding of the District Court to require, as a matter of substantive constitutional right, any particular degree of racial balance or mixing, *that approach would be disapproved and we would be obliged to reverse.* The constitutional command to desegregate schools does not mean that every school in every community must always reflect the racial composition of the school system as a whole ." (emphasis added).

Here, in sharp contrast to *Swann*, the District Court expressly and frankly directed the use of a "fixed mathematical racial balance" which was to be based on the "overall pupil racial composition" of Detroit and the 53 outlying school districts to ensure that:

> "Within the limitations of reasonable travel time and distance factors, pupil reassignments shall be effected . . . so as to achieve the greatest degree of actual desegregation to the end that, upon implementation, *no school grade or classroom* [would be] substantially disproportionate *to the overall pupil racial composition.*" (emphasis added).

This is far from the use of the total racial composition as a "starting point" in the analysis of possible violations as envisioned in *Swann* and *Wright* . . . .

[W]hile the presence of clearly racially identifiable schools in close proximity to one another does not automatically dictate a constitutionally required remedy, it may, as we said in *Swann*, and restated in *Keyes* v. *School District No. 1*, serve to shift the burden of proof to the school authorities . . . .

However, the use of significant racial imbalance in schools within an autonomous school district as a signal which operates simply to shift the burden of proof, is a very different matter from equating racial imbalance with a constitutional violation calling for a remedy in the form of an order for some fixed racial balance accomplished by enlarging the relevant area until the hypothetically "desirable" racial mix is achieved . . . .

Federal authority to impose cross-district remedies presupposes a fair and reasoned determination that there has been a constitutional violation by all of the districts affected by the remedy. Thus, a cross-district remedy might be appropriate, for example, if it could be established that the segregatory practice of one or more districts created or maintained the segregated condition within the central city. Here, however, the record, as voluminous as it is, understandably contains evidence concerning only the segregated condition of the Detroit school district because that was the only theory upon which the case was brought and on which the court proceeded. The District Court altered the theory of the case and mandated a metropolitan area remedy before the intervenors were heard and without permitting any evidence on the intervenors' claim that they were guilty of no violation of the constitutional rights of others. Thus, to approve the remedy imposed by the District Court on these facts would make racial balance the constitutional objective and standard; a result not even hinted at in *Brown I* and *Brown II* which held that the operation of dual school systems, not some hypothetical level of racial imbalance, is the constitutional violation to be remedied. Unlike *Swann*, this case did not involve a "very limited use . . . of . . . mathematical ratios" as a "starting point", but, on the contrary, the finding of racial imbalance became the controlling standard for determining the existence of a violation.

2. SOLICITOR GENERAL ROBERT BORK'S BRIEF IN *MILLIKEN*

II

THE REMEDY FOR UNCONSTITUTIONAL SCHOOL SEG-REGATION MAY EXTEND BEYOND THE BOUNDARIES OF A SINGLE DISTRICT ONLY IF, AND TO THE EXTENT THAT, THE VIOLATION HAS DIRECTLY ALTERED OR SUBSTANTIALLY AFFECTED THE RACIAL COMPOSI-TION OF SCHOOLS IN MORE THAN ONE DISTRICT.

This Court held in *Swann v. Board of Education* that the task in fashioning school desegregation relief "is to correct . . . the condition that offends the Constitution." It follows that "the nature of the violation determines the scope of the remedy."

The mere co-existence, within a State, of adjacent school districts having disparate racial compositions is not itself a constitutional violation. *Spencer v. Kugler*, 404 U.S. 1027, affirming 326 F. Supp. 1235. As Solicitor General [Erwin] Griswold explained last Term in the Memorandum for the United States as Amicus Curiae in *School Board of the City of Richmond, Virginia v. State Board of Education,* at pp. 13–15.

"In determining that one school system for the entire region should be created, the district court relied upon this Court's statement in *Swann* that for remedial purposes there is "a presumption against schools that are substantially disproportionate in their racial composition." But disproportionate in relation to what? Surely not to some absolute standard, for the Constitution does not establish any fixed ratio of black students to white students that must be achieved. Instead, whether a particular school is racially imbalanced or identifiable can be determined only by comparing it with "the racial composition of the whole school system." *Swann* v. *Board of Education*, 402 U.S. at 25 . . . .

"Thus, the question whether, for example, an elementary school having a student body 70 percent black and 30 percent white is racially imbalanced or has a substantially disproportionate racial composition is in itself unanswerable. Some frame of reference is needed and, as *Swann* indicates, the proper comparison (to the extent that racial balance is relevant) is with the racial composition of the population in the school system operating the particular school since the purpose is to ensure complete elimination of the dual system by having one set of schools for both blacks and whites. And under *Swann* there would be no presumption against schools, such as the one in the example above, if these schools reflected the black-white ratio of the entire school system.

"Why then would there be a presumption against the school system itself with the same 70:30 ratio of blacks and whites, as the district court concluded here with respect to the school system of the City of Richmond? Stated differently, on what basis could the district court conclude that its remedy should reach outside the school system of the City of Richmond? Apparently, the court believed that it must look beyond the Richmond system in fashioning relief because the City school system is racially disproportionate or imbalanced in relation to the adjacent County school systems, thereby resulting in racial identifiability of the three systems. But the court had to look beyond the Richmond system and compare it with the surrounding Counties in the first place in order to determine whether the Richmond system is racially imbalanced in comparison with the adjacent systems. This is not only circular as a reason for fashioning relief beyond the Richmond system, but also heedless of the extent of the constitutional violation being remedied."

Thus, in our view, an interdistrict remedy, requiring the restructuring of state or local government entities, is appropriate only in the unusual circumstance where it is necessary to undo the interdistrict effect of a constitutional violation. Specifically, if it were shown that the racially discriminatory acts of the State, or of several local school districts, or of a single local district, have been a direct or substantial cause of interdistrict school segregation, then a remedy designed to eliminate the segregation so caused would be appropriate.

One example of circumstances warranting interdistrict relief is where one or more school systems have been created and maintained for members of one race . . . . Similarly, where the boundaries separating districts have been drawn on account of race, an interdistrict remedy is appropriate . . . . Some form of interdistrict relief may also be appropriate where pupils have been transferred across district lines on a racially discriminatory basis.

In each instance of an interdistrict violation, the remedy should, in accordance with traditional principles of equity and the law of remedies, be tailored to fit the violation, particularly in view of the deference owed to existing governmental structures .... Any modification of those structures should be narrowly framed to eliminate the interdistrict segregation that has been caused by the particular violation, so as to avoid unnecessary judicial interference with state prerogatives concerning the organization of local governments. Thus, a single instance of discriminatory cross-district transfers between only two school districts ... would not warrant the kind of metropolitan-wide interdistrict remedy involving 54 districts that the courts below contemplate here. The appropriate relief should be limited to correcting the segregative conditions caused by the transfers.

III

THE RECORD IN THIS CASE DOES NOT SUPPORT THE BROAD METROPOLITAN-WIDE REMEDY CONTEMPLATED BY THE COURT OF APPEALS ....

[N]either the district court nor the court of appeals predicated its holding on the existence of a violation affecting the racial composition of the suburban districts. The district court determined that a metropolitan-wide remedy would be appropriate to desegregate the Detroit schools, because it concluded that any effective plan limited to Detroit "would accentuate the racial identifiability of the district as a Black school system, and would not accomplish desegregation." The court of appeals reached the same conclusion: "[A]ny Detroit only desegregation plan will lead directly to a single segregated Detroit school district overwhelmingly black in all of its schools." Such a remedy "cannot correct the constitutional violations herein found."

The prediction that massive "white flight" will result from an effective intra-Detroit desegregation plan is inherently speculative, and in any event does not change the nature of the violation to be remedied. For that reason, such a prediction does not in itself warrant interdistrict relief.

3. FROM THE BENCH: JUSTICE MARSHALL'S ORAL OPINION IN *MILLIKEN*

In *Brown* v. *Board of Education* this Court held that segregation of children in public schools on the basis of race deprives Negro children of equal educational opportunities and therefore denies them the equal protection of the laws under the Fourteenth Amendment. This Court recognized then that remedying decades of segregation would not be an easy task. Subsequent events, unfortunately, have seen that prediction bear bitter fruit. But however imbedded old ways, however ingrained old prejudices, this Court has not been diverted from its appointed task of making a "living truth" of our constitutional ideal of equal justice under law.

After 20 years of small, often difficult steps toward that great end, the Court today takes a giant step backwards. I have filed a dissenting opinion joined by Justices Douglas, Brennan, and White. The record in this case shows that there has been widespread and pervasive racial segregation in the school system provided by the State of Michigan for children in Detroit . . . .

While it is true that most of the acts of segregation in this case—though by no means all—were committed by the Detroit Board of Education, it is clear that the obligation to remedy these constitutional violations rests ultimately with the state. The command of the Fourteenth Amendment is that no *state* shall deny to any person within its jurisdiction the equal protection of the laws, and the actions of state agencies—like school boards—are in law the acts of the *state*. It is thus the *state* which bears the responsibility under *Brown* for affording a non-discriminatory system of education. The state is ordinarily free to choose any decentralized framework for education it wishes. But it should not be allowed to hide behind its delegation and compartmentalization of school districts to avoid its constitutional obligations to its children . . . .

Yet the Court today holds that the District Court was powerless to require the State to remedy its constitutional violation in any meaningful fashion. Our prior cases have not minced words as to what steps responsible officials and agencies must take in order to remedy segregation in the public schools. Where, as here, state-imposed segregation has been demonstrated, it becomes the duty of the State to eliminate root and branch all vestiges of racial discrimination. As we held in *Swann* v. *Charlotte-Mecklenburg Board of Education*, where *de jure* segregation is shown school authorities must make "every effort to achieve the greatest possible degree of actual desegregation." If these words have any meaning at all, surely it is that state school authorities must take all practicable steps to ensure that Negro and white children in fact go to school together. In the final analysis, this is what desegregation of the public schools is all about.

But a Detroit-only decree, the only remedy permitted under today's decision, cannot effectively desegregate the Detroit city schools. The Detroit school system has in recent years increasingly become an all-Negro school system, with the greatest increase in the proportion of Negro students of any major northern city. Moreover, the result of a Detroit-only decree, the District Court found, would be to increase the flight of whites from the city to the outlying suburbs, compounding the effects of the present rate of increase in the proportion of Negro students in the Detroit system. Thus, even if a plan were adopted which, at its outset, provided in every school a 65% Negro–35% white racial mix in keeping with the Negro-white proportions of the total student population, such a system would, in short order, devolve into an all-Negro system.

For these reasons, a Detroit-only plan simply has no hope of achieving actual desegregation. Under such a plan white and Negro students will not go to school together. Instead, Negro children will continue to attend all-Negro schools. The very evil that *Brown* was aimed at will not be cured, but will be perpetuated for the future.

The rights at issue in this case are too fundamental to be abridged on grounds as superficial as those relied on by the majority today. We deal here with the right of all our children, whatever their race, to an equal start in life and to an equal opportunity to reach their full potential as citizens. Those children who have been denied that right in the past deserve better than to see fences thrown up to deny them that right in the future. Our Nation, I fear, will be ill-served by the Court's refusal to remedy separate and unequal education, for unless our children begin to learn together, there is little hope that our people will ever learn to live together and understand each other.

Desegregation is not and was never expected to be an easy task. Racial attitudes ingrained in our Nation's childhood and adolescence are not quickly thrown aside in its middle years. But just as the inconvenience of some cannot be allowed to stand in the way of the rights of others, so public opposition, no matter how strident, cannot be permitted to divert this Court from the enforcement of the constitutional principles at issue in this case. Today's holding, in my view, is more a reflection of a perceived public mood that we have gone far enough in enforcing the Constitution's guarantee of equal justice than it is the product of neutral principles of law. In the short run, it may seem to be the easier course to allow our great metropolitan areas to be divided up each into two cities—one white, the other black—but it is a course, I predict, our people will ultimately regret.

4. CHARLES R. LAWRENCE III, "SEGREGATION 'MISUNDERSTOOD':

THE *MILLIKEN* DECISION REVISITED"

II. UNDERSTANDING THE INSTITUTION OF SEGREGATION

In order to recognize the full scope of the constitutional injury inflicted by a segregated school system, one must understand how the institution of segregation functions. Three underlying characteristics of segregation crucial to this understanding are: it labels black children as inferior; the existence of the institution as a whole, rather than particular acts, constitutes the injury; and the institution is self-perpetuating.

A. Segregation's Only Purpose is to Label Blacks as Inferior . . . .

The holding in *Brown* v. *Board of Education* that racially segregated schools are inherently unequal makes most sense if it is understood as a recognition of the fact that racial segregation by definition is an invidious labeling device and therefore must violate the equal protection clause. In abandoning the "separate but equal" doctrine of *Plessy* v. *Ferguson*, it should have been clear to the Court that the injury to black children did not result solely from unequal resource allocation, nor from the fact that they were refused the opportunity to sit next to white children in school, but from the fact that attendance at a separate school was part of the system that labeled blacks as inferior and whites as superior.

The institution of segregation and the injury it inflicts on blacks is necessarily misunderstood until one recognizes that its chief purpose is to *define*, not to separate. This fact is best demonstrated by a brief examination of the development of segregation in the South. Southern whites had no aversion to commingling with blacks so long as the institution of slavery made their status clear. It was only with the demise of slavery that segregation became necessary . . . .

Although historians differ in their views of when segregation became firmly established as an institution, there is virtual unanimity concerning its purpose and method. Segregation was an instrument of subordination which used a strict and rigid caste system to clearly define and limit the social, political and economic mobility of blacks. The segregation statutes and "Jim Crow" laws were the "public symbols and constant reminders" of the inferior position of blacks. (Woodward, *The Strange Career of Jim Crow*, p. 7.) It is the symbolism of segregation that operates to violate the fourteenth amendment. Unless *Brown* is understood in this light, it must fail in its purpose of insuring black children equal educational opportunity.

In response to contemporaneous attacks on the soundness of the *Brown* decision, Charles Black wrote an article that is brilliant both in its simplicity and its clarity. Professor Black pointed out that while attention is usually focused on the inequalities of the separate facilities themselves, the most significant evidence of the inherent inequality of segregation can be found in looking at what it means to the people who impose it and to the people who are subjected to it . . . .

The *Brown* Court, unfortunately, was not nearly so articulate in support of its decision as was Professor Black . . . .

It is not the . . . Court's emphasis and reliance on . . . psycho-sociological evidence rather than [on] common-sense . . . that should be faulted, but the Court's failure to spell out the condition precedent for black children's "feelings of inferiority" —*the fact that they and everyone else knew that the system of segregation defined them as inferior.*

It was the *Brown* Court's failure to confront this simple reality about segregation that allowed Chief Justice Burger and the *Milliken* majority to conclude that there was no evidence of state involvement in the violation of the Detroit plaintiffs' constitutional rights requiring an inter-district remedy.

If it is the act of separating that violates the equal protection clause, then the Detroit children's only right is to be free of specific acts of separation by the state and the scope of the remedy turns on whether there is sufficient evidence of such specific acts of separation. If, however, the equal protection clause protects the right not to be labeled or classified on the basis or race, we must look not just to whether or not the state was involved in specific separating acts but also to whether the state was involved in the creation of the socio-political system of segregation that labels segregated black children as inferior. It is this principle that must be understood before a proper approach to desegregation cases can be developed.

The *Milliken* court, having defined the plaintiffs' rights under the equal protection clause as the right not to be separated, looked only for evidence of state involvement in intentional acts of *separation* of school children by race. Because this misunderstanding of the nature of segregation caused the Court to misconstrue the scope of those rights and thus to ignore pertinent evidence, the Court found no evidence of state involvement in the violation of Detroit plaintiffs' constitutional rights.

B. Black Children Are Injured by the Existence of the System of Segregation Not by Particular Segregating Acts

A second aspect of the Court's misunderstanding of segregation is related to the Court's adoption of the requirement that evidence of particular segregative acts by a school district exist before a federal judge may order relief against that district. *Milliken* adopted this requirement from *Keyes* v. *School District No.1,* wherein the Court found that there must be evidence that the racial imbalance in the schools was brought about by discriminatory actions of state authorities.

The *Keyes/Milliken* requirement of evidence of particular segregative acts by a school district before a federal court may order relief against that district demonstrates a second and related aspect of the Court's misunderstanding of segregation. Because segregation's purpose and function is to define or classify blacks as inferior, the injury which it inflicts is *systemic* rather than particular. Black school children are not injured by the fact that a school board has placed them in a school different than that in which it has placed white school children so much as by the fact that the school exists within a system that defines it as the inferior school and its pupils as inferior persons.

Many black schools that existed within the segregated school systems of the South were in fact superior to their white counterparts. It is ironic that most of these schools achieved their excellence as a direct result of the discrimination inherent in a segregated society, in that the best black professionals were forced into teaching by their virtual exclusion from other fields. The existence of such schools violated the constitutional rights of children attending them, not because a school board or state legislature had taken steps to see that white children did not attend them, and certainly not because of the relative quality of education they provided, but because they were pieces of a larger puzzle which, when fitted together, plainly spelled out the words "if you're black, get back."

Once it is understood that segregation functions as a systemic labeling device, it should be clear that *any* state action which results in the maintenance of the segregated *system* is a direct and proximate cause of the injuries suffered by black children in segregated schools and is in violation of the equal protection clause of the fourteenth amendment. Evidence of such action would, of course, not be limited to acts directly resulting in one-race schools. Segregated housing and zoning practices are equally effective means of labeling blacks as inferior. If the state discriminates by continuing to participate in labeling blacks "not fit to live with," it is surely beside the point that it is not an active participant in particular acts labeling blacks "not fit to go to school with." . . .

Because [Chief] Justice Burger limits the right of black children to freedom from acts by the state aimed at segregating the *schools*, such specific acts are the only kind of evidence he looks for in determining that there has been no violation for which inter-district relief would be appropriate.

Once the true nature of segregation is understood, it should [also] become . . . apparent that . . . the scope of [its] injury cannot be defined by school district lines. State sanction of the purposeful segregation of schools in Detroit operates to stigmatize black children throughout the state. They do not escape that stigma merely by virtue of the fact that the defamation against them occurred in another district; its publication extends throughout the state.

C. Why Draw the Line at 1954? The Fallacy of the North/South, DeJure/DeFacto Distinction . . . .

It could be argued that the northern and southern cases are distinguishable on the basis of state action; in the South, state action is present because state laws required the operation of dual school systems, while in the North, state action is absent because segregated schools occurred as the result of segregated housing patterns. *This distinction, however, neglects the entire history of segregation in America.*

Segregation is northern, not southern, in origin and reached considerable maturity in the North before moving south . . . .

Based on historical fact, it cannot be refuted that the official actions of northern, midwestern and western states played a predominant role in the entrenchment of segregation within their borders. In view of the fact that there was substantial state activity in the promulgation of segregation throughout the nation, the fact that the northern states ceased official enforcement of a segregated school system prior to 1954, while the southern states continued to do so officially, does not appear to be an adequate rationale for exempting northern states from the mandate of *Brown*, as further elucidated by *Green*. Thus, the Supreme Court's distinction between northern and southern cases of desegregation is not really a matter of state action at all, and is simply a matter of timing.

Although the Supreme Court holdings dictate a chronological distinction between pre- and post-1954 legislation, the Court's *reasoning* in *Green* would appear to counsel the contrary conclusion that the cases be treated on the basis of their facts and not be categorized by region or date. *Green* stands for the proposition that where a system of segregation remains firmly entrenched the state must do more than cease and desist from further official support of the system; it must act *affirmatively* to disestablish that system. Once it is understood that segregation achieves its purpose by labeling blacks as inferior, it becomes clear that segregation is firmly entrenched when the label of inferiority is reflected in societal attitudes; [and] it will not be removed or alleviated by a mere discontinuance of official name-calling. This understanding applies to all instances of segregation and knows no geographic distinctions . . . .

Without doubt, it will be argued that the causal link between constitutional violations existing in northern states in the distant past and presently segregated schools is too tenuous to support the application of the *Green* standard to those districts. At the root of this argument is the belief that racial segregation in the North, as we know it today, is the result of the ingrained racial prejudice of individuals in the absence of state assistance, encouragement or compulsion. This is simply not the case. Governmental participation in and support of the system of segregation in the northern and western states was not a relic of the past at the time of the *Brown* decision. Three notable examples of modern day governmental segregation contemporaneous with *Brown*, which labeled blacks as inferior in the North as well as the South, were the continued segregation of the United States Armed Forces until 1948, the Federal Housing Administration's active encouragement of segregated housing until 1950, and the statutory segregation by Congress of Washington D.C.'s school system until 1954. State and local officials have played an equally active, although not as well-documented, part in the maintenance of the system of segregation in the North. Highways and freeways were built as barriers between black and white communities, building officials did their utmost to hamper building intended for blacks in white neighborhoods, local police and fire departments excluded blacks by discriminatory hiring practices, and until 1948 local courts consistently enforced restrictive covenants.

Once the state has effectively institutionalized racial segregation as a labeling device, only minimal maintenance is required to keep it in working order. Once the system is established, any attempt to distinguish "active" governmental involvement in racial segregation from "passive" or "neutral" tolerance of private segregation is illusory. Present passivity is merely a continuation of past action. The individual facing well-entrenched segregated housing patterns does not make a wholly "private" choice when deciding to move into a neighborhood with persons of a like race. That choice is substantially influenced by societal or institutional pressures to conform to the prevailing norm. Job security and opportunity for advancement, availability of financing, and one's family's personal comfort may all depend upon such conformity. These institutionalized attitudes or norms are directly traceable to a time when the state was actively involved in their establishment. There has not been an intervening period in which these attitudes were not present so that it could truly be said they were private in origin. They remain because the state has never met the *Green* requirement of affirmative disestablishment.

CHAPTER SIX

KEYES AND *MILLIKEN:*
THE AFTERMATH

Keyes and *Milliken* set the parameters of American desegregation law. The former underwent varying interpretations by the lower courts during the 1970's. For a time, it even looked as though the post-*Milliken* Supreme Court "might . . . draw back on *Keyes*,"[1] but by the end of the decade it was clear that the arrangements established in that case would continue to govern interdistrict litigation.

Milliken, too, was subject to differing analyses by district and circuit court judges. But it remained most significant into the 1980's for what it prevented, widespread approval of interdistrict remedies.

I

Whatever observers took to be its real import, *Keyes* had stated flatly that "the differentiating factor" between de jure and de facto segregation "is *purpose* or *intent* to segregate." The first fruit of the Court's decision, therefore, was a reconsideration of opinions, such as the ones in Oxnard and San Francisco, which dispensed with the need for assessing intent. Thus a Ninth Circuit panel sent Judge Harry Pregerson's Oxnard decision back to him for another hearing. Judge Pregerson's statement that school board actions and omissions cast "'de jure overtones'" was "inconclusive and vague on the question of . . . segregative intent," the panel felt, since the indispensable prerequisite for a de jure finding, it had now been decided, was a determination that school officials "practice a deliberate policy of racial segregation."[2] By holding the Oxnard board accountable for the probable results of its actions, "regardless of any discriminatory motives behind such acts," the lower court "applied on improper legal standard."[3]

255

Another panel of Ninth Circuit judges called for a review of the San Francisco decision, since it too condemned mere knowledge of the consequences which neighborhood zoning wrought. Judge Stanley Weigel's opinion, the panel noted, was filed before *Keyes* came down, and "[q]uite understandably, therefore, . . . made no finding as to whether the School Board possessed the requisite segregatory intent."[4] Nonetheless, as *Keyes* had "now made clear," the lower court used an "erroneous" criterion.[5]

Other circuits, however, took the "knowing" or "foreseeing" of results as sufficient to make a case of segregative purpose. Parsing what they took to be the actual meaning of *Keyes*, some judges, in 1974 and 1975, bridged the gap between de jure and de facto segregation by relying on a familiar concept in tort law: people are deemed responsible for, and culpable for, the natural and foreseeable consequences of their acts. Intent or purpose, then, was deduced purely from effect. In education cases, this standard could serve to condemn the neighborhood school, no less than the gerrymandered attendance zone, as evidence of purposeful discrimination.

The transition to this concept of liability is best illustrated in the Second Circuit's consideration of *Hart* v. *Community School Board*. *Hart* concerned a single junior high school in Coney Island, the first New York City controversy to reach a federal court. Despite *Keyes*, trial Judge Jack Weinstein (one of the authentic legal giants of our time) persisted in the criterion utilized by *Soria* and *Johnson*. A condition of segregation undoubtedly existed in Mark Twain Junior High, he pointed out: the school district was 83% white, African-American and Hispanic enrollment at Mark Twain 76%. Self-evidently, this situation resulted from state action. "Just as a public school would not exist but for the state, the character of the public school is determined by the school board"; a "board which neglects to avoid racial segregation . . . is itself causing [it] . . . as an agency of the state," and was answerable for it.[6]

Judge Weinstein mixed a little of the tort standard into his opinion, taxing the board with responsibility "for the natural, foreseeable, and avoidable consequences of its . . . policies."[7] But he did not regard foreseeability as evidence of segregative intent, a concept he seemed to associate with the subjective motivations of individual school board members, and regarded, in any event, as unnecessary in establishing a constitutional violation. "Segregative design is not material . . . in proving a violation of the Constitution in a case such as this . . . ."[8] The presence of segregated schools created by state action was enough to prove liability.

In reviewing Judge Weinstein's opinion, the Second Circuit hastened to square it with *Keyes* by making the most of his references to foreseeability. In *Keyes*, the circuit panel admitted, Justice Brennan definitely spoke of the need to establish intent as part of a de jure violation. Yet because he was dealing with a case involving open and deliberate racial segregation, there was no occasion to decide "whether intentional action leading foreseeably to discrimination, but taken without racial motivation, might not also constitute *de jure* discrimination."[9] Since this question was not definitively settled, the Second Circuit held "that a finding of *de jure* segregation may be based on actions taken, coupled with omissions made, by governmental authorities which have the natural and foreseeable consequence of causing educational segregation."[10] The concept of de jure segregation must encompass an element of purposefulness, but purpose was not limited "only to acts which are provably motivated by a desire to discriminate."[11] The circuit panel upheld Judge Weinstein's decision, while admitting that, "somewhat inconsistently" in view of his findings, he had failed to charge school officials "with segregative design."[12]

District Judge John Curtin in upstate New York strongly approved the *Hart* rationale in the Buffalo school case. "In deciding the question of intent," Judge Curtin ruled, "the court is not required to find guilt or innocence, prejudice or evenhandedness, or even 'badness' or 'goodness' on the part of the defendants . . . . It is enough, as the Second Circuit explained in *Hart* v. *Community School Board* . . . to show that the probable and foreseeable result of the defendants' acts was segregation."[13]

District Judge Arthur Garrity's decision in the Boston school case also stated a rationale similar to *Hart's,* although the First Circuit, in affirming his decision, did not specifically endorse it. "The paramount issue in this case," wrote Judge Garrity, "is whether the defendants acted with a 'purpose or intent to segregate' . . . , i.e., either with a desire to bring about or continue segregation in the Boston schools *or* with knowledge that such segregation was certain, or substantially certain, to result from their actions."[14]

Other circuit courts played variations on this theme. The Sixth Circuit, affirming District Judge Noel Fox's decision in *Oliver* v. *Kalamazoo Board of Education,* developed a seemingly less stringent version of the tort standard, under which known effects greased the skids for de jure violations, but did not actually comprise them. "A presumption of segregative purpose arises," held Judge Anthony Celebrezze, "when plaintiffs establish that the natural, probable, and foreseeable result of public officials' action or inaction was an increase or perpetuation of public school segregation. The presumption becomes proof unless defendants affirmatively establish that their action or inaction was a consistent and resolute application of racially neutral policies."[15]

This standard still cast a shadow over racial imbalance. And it pretty much stood *Keyes* on its head: the burden fell on the school board in Kalamazoo to prove a neutrality which was assumed in Denver until the plaintiffs carried the burden of proving de jure violations in a meaningful portion of the school system. Still, unlike *Hart,* this approach appeared to give a school board some room for maneuver. The post-presumption debate in Kalamazoo might logically focus, as was appropriate in school cases, on whether officials maintained an honest neighborhood system, or deliberately rigged it for segregatory purposes.

In fact, the circuit court was upholding a decision largely inconsistent with the standard it set up, for the proof which Judge Fox offered to show that the Kalamazoo school board did not resolutely follow neighborhood policies, and could not rebut, therefore, any presumptions raised by segregative effect, was itself cast largely in terms of such effect. The judge actually cited a number of blatant viola-tions committed by Kalamazoo officials, but did not think it necessary to use lan-guage which distinguished between invidious departures from a neutral neighbor-hood setup, and the adverse racial impact which served, supposedly, as the mere trigger to his inquiry. The two things meant pretty much the same thing to him. Thus the Kalamazoo board's habit of adding classrooms to overcrowded white schools when space existed in contiguous minority schools was unconstitutional, since it "had the obviously foreseeable and actual effect of perpetuating the segregated con-ditions which prevailed."[16] Creating optional zones between all-white junior high schools and nearby ones rapidly becoming black "had the effect of allowing White students to opt out of" changing neighborhoods.[17]

That the terms "effect" and "intent"—presumption and violation—were synony-mous to Judge Fox is revealed in his discussion of school construction policies in the northern section of Kalamazoo. These policies, he charged, "intentionally creat-ed, maintained and perpetuated segregated schools," because the "foreseeable and actual effect of this phase of the Kalamazoo program was to contain" the black stu-dent population, when the construction projects presented "many rational alterna-tives" for attendance area changes "which would not have had the effect of perpet-uating segregation."[18]

The Eighth Circuit, overruling a district court decision in *United States* v. *School District of Omaha*,[19] laid down a more exacting version of foreseeability theory.

> We hold that a presumption of segregative intent arises once it is estab-lished that school authorities have engaged in acts or omissions, the nat-ural, probable and foreseeable consequence of which is to bring about or maintain segregation. When that presumption arises, the burden shifts to the defendants to establish that "segregative intent was not among the factors that motivated their actions." *Keyes* v. *School District No 1*.[20]

The final words echo *Keyes*, but they presented to a school board a situation even more unfavorable than the one presented in Denver or Kalamazoo, since under the Omaha standard racial imbalance kicked off presumptions which were virtually irrebuttable.

Much of the evidence against Omaha authorities was quite strong, by any mea-sure of segregative intent. They had distorted the system's transfer program, allow-ing whites to transfer to overcrowded white high schools, while the city's black high schools, from which these students transferred, possessed unused capacity. They delayed conversion of K–8 schools to K–6 schools (part of a city-wide movement toward establishment of seventh to ninth grade junior highs), when many of the affected students turned out to be white youngsters who would have been required to attend identifiably black schools; officials then created optional zones for these students, allowing them to go to more distant white junior highs.

Yet the well-known presence of several anti-integrationist members of the school board probably would have sufficed to convict Omaha, granting the presumptive burden imposed, for how could one then demonstrate that "segregative intent" was not "among the factors" infecting the board's decisions? In any event, the violations found by the circuit panel demanded "that racial discrimination in the Omaha public schools must be eliminated root and branch."[21] Under its direction, the district court imposed a systemwide remedy, aimed at racial balance, which the Eighth Circuit approved in August of 1976.[22]

Chief Judge John Reynolds of the Eastern District of Wisconsin avoided discussion of presumptions and foreseeability in the Milwaukee school case, but wound up articulating thereby the most uncluttered version of the viewpoint with which those terms were implicated. Judge Reynolds found that Milwaukee officials had "consistently and uniformly adhered to a 'neighborhood school policy,' first developed in 1919," and that it was the "gross imbalance in the city's racial residential patterns" which produced segregated attendance in the city's schools.[23] The opinion suggested that not all school board actions were absolutely pristine, documenting some suspicious busing policies and questionable school site selections. Still, the board's "fundamental purpose" was clearly "the maintenance and preservation of the neighborhood school policy"; it "believed, in good faith, that such a policy would produce the best possible educational opportunities for all students in the system, regardless of race."[24]

The whole, however, differed drastically from the sum of its parts, in Judge Reynolds' view. Standing by itself, he noted, "any one act or practice" of Milwaukee officials "may not indicate a segregative intent."[25] Yet when strung together, they "constituted a consistent and deliberate policy of racial isolation and segregation."[26] In short, Milwaukee officials were culpable because they tolerated the segregation resulting from a neighborhood school system instead of consciously pursuing integration.

The judge averred that his findings did not rest on "evidentiary presumptions and/or the much discussed test of foreseeability."[27] Indeed, he stated the underlying reason for his decision with refreshing candor. "It is hard to believe that out of all the decisions made by school authorities . . . over a twenty-year period, mere chance resulted in there being almost no decision that resulted in the furthering of integration."[28]

On review, a Seventh Circuit panel admitted to being disturbed by the possibility that Judge Reynolds was pronouncing neighborhood schools unconstitutional. The lower court decision contained "an unexplained hiatus between specific findings of fact and conclusory findings of segregative intent," noted Judge Phillip Tone.[29] It could undoubtedly be interpreted as conceding that Milwaukee officials maintained a neutral, non-discriminatory neighborhood system, and, "if so read," did not prove "segregative intent."[30] Finally, though, the circuit panel chose to read Judge Reynolds' findings and his conclusions as "presumably harmonious," and sustained him.[31]

A few of these post-*Keyes* decisions also expanded the challenge to *Deal*, encouraged, it seemed, by *Swann*, and implicated housing violations in the illegal segregation charged to northern officials. Judge Weinstein allowed the defendant school board in the *Hart* case to include city, state, and federal housing authorities as third party defendants, and ruled that their policies had "exacerbated the situation" in the Coney Island schools "by applying housing policies mechanically, discouraging integrated occupation of new housing by child-rearing families of a variety of socio-economic levels."[32] Judge Curtin in Buffalo compiled discriminatory practices by the federal government, the Buffalo Municipal Housing Authority, and the local real estate industry. To these, he added the actions of the Buffalo City Council, which, he found, had used urban renewal projects to cram African-Americans into already segregated areas of the community. "Given the purposeful residential segregation in the City of Buffalo, the School Board's 'neighborhood school policy' was not, and could not be, racially neutral."[33]

II

By 1976, the Supreme Court was casting considerable doubt on some of the lower court approaches to segregative intent in school cases. The justices' decisions in *Washington* v. *Davis* and *Arlington Heights* v. *Metropolitan Housing Corporation*, though dealing with discrimination in employment and housing, contained some pointed reminders of what *Keyes* had said. And clearly it had "not embraced the proposition," Justice White pointed out in *Davis*, "that a law . . . is unconstitutional *solely* because it has a racially disproportionate impact."[34] To be sure, plaintiffs often demonstrated equal protection violations using a wide variety of pertinent facts, "including the fact . . . that the law bears more heavily on one race than another."[35] But rarely could impact comprise "the sole touchstone of . . . invidious racial discrimination."[36] Plaintiffs must prove that deliberate bias was at work.

Justice Lewis Powell amplified these points in *Arlington Heights*. While the Court was not demanding that an official action rest *entirely* on a discriminatory purpose to be invalid, proof of such purpose "is required to show a violation of the Equal Protection Clause."[37] This need not lead to subjective inquiries into the motives of individual government officials, Justice Powell stressed. Rather, the search for intent "demands a sensitive inquiry into such circumstantial and direct evidence . . . as may be available"—including the historical background of actions attacked as discriminatory, substantive or procedural departures from normal practices in approving those actions, or relevant aspects of legislative and administrative history.[38]

Powell admitted impact or effect was relevant to inferring discriminatory purpose. But, like White, he insisted that very seldom could such a factor stand alone. "Sometimes a clear pattern, unexplainable on grounds other than race, emerges from the effect of . . . state action . . . . But such cases are rare."[39] Impact by itself almost never made a prima facie case of racial bias.

A majority of the Court feared that the *Omaha* and *Milwaukee* opinions, among others, had employed just such a test. In a pair of decisions of June, 1977, the justices remanded the cases for reconsideration in the light of *Davis* and *Arlington Heights.* Justice William Rehnquist, writing for the majority, contrasted the Eighth Circuit's approach to liability in *Omaha* with *Davis'* denial that a constitutional violation could rest "solely" on "racially disproportionate impact." He also observed that the rejected district court decision in the case applied a legal standard "which regarded the natural and foreseeable consequences of [a school board's] conduct as . . . but . . . 'one . . . factor to be weighed.'"[40] With respect to the Milwaukee case, Rehnquist noted the circuit court's reference to the "unexplained hiatus between specific findings of fact and conclusory findings of segregative intent."[41]

In a memorandum sent to his colleagues while considering the remands, Justice Rehnquist stated bluntly that the court of appeals' invocation in *Omaha* of "a presumption of law based on 'natural and foreseeable consequences' is . . . inconsistent with the spirit of *Washington* v. *Davis,* which [holds] that the burden of proving discriminatory intent rests on the plaintiffs."[42] The Omaha decision in question, it was true, had come down prior to *Davis,* but the Eighth Circuit's decision approving a systemwide remedy, issued two months after *Davis,* showed "no indication that the CA 8 gave any reconsideration . . . to the legal standard it applied previously."[43]

In *Milwaukee,* Justice Rehnquist's memorandum called attention to the paradox of the district court finding "that the school board had engaged in intentional segregative conduct, notwithstanding its own observation that the actions found to be segregative in effect were adequately explained as aspects of . . . a consistent neighborhood school policy."[44] As to the court of appeals opinion, it came down after *Davis,* yet, Rehnquist claimed, took no notice of *Davis'* conclusions. "While one cannot say that the decision of the Court of Appeals cannot be reconciled with *Washington* v. *Davis,* it is certainly arguable that it might have reached a different result had it had the 'benefit' of that decision . . . ."[45]

Justice Brennan, who dissented on the remands, pointed out to his colleague that the Milwaukee decision did in fact mention *Davis,* and had explicitly pronounced its own findings congruent with that holding. "Clearly, Judge Tone [author of the *Milwaukee* opinion] understands the significance of *Washington* v. *Davis,* and a remand for reconsideration in light of that case would be inappropriate."[46] In the meantime, Rehnquist had admitted his original memorandum was "inaccurate in one respect . . . . [T]he CA 7 did discuss *Washington* v. *Davis*"; nonetheless, he insisted, the panel "fail[ed] to correctly construe the requirement of the *Davis* case that discriminatory intent be proven."[47]

On remand of the Omaha case, before the entire membership of the Eighth Circuit, the Justice Department admitted "that statistics 'plus' supportive historical or circumstantial evidence of intent" were necessary "to establish a *prima facie* case of intentional discrimination."[48] But the original circuit court opinion actually satisfied this standard, the department argued, "even if some of the language in [the] opinion may not have anticipated every nuance of the intervening Supreme Court opinions."[49] The circuit panel had not deduced a presumption of segregative intent merely from actions having the foreseeable effect of creating or maintaining segregation. Instead, the panel "carefully analyzed all of the evidence and only applied a presumption of segregative intent requiring rebuttal by the School District to those . . . actions which deviated from the normal School District policy *and* had a foreseeable racially disproportionate impact."[50]

Thus the optional attendance zones and the delays in converting to an educationally preferred system of junior high schools were, in the circuit panel's own words, "inexplicable unless in furtherance of a single coherent policy: the unwillingness to assign white students to schools perceived as black, the 'neighborhood school' [policy] . . . notwithstanding."[51] Similarly, the transfer of white students to an overcrowded white high school from an underutilized black one represented exactly the departure from accepted administrative practice identified by *Arlington Heights* as probative of discriminatory purpose. Overall, the circuit court decision was "a precursor of *Arlington Heights*," because it stipulated that only when adverse racial impact was joined to more deliberate acts of bias did this create the prima facie case which "shift[s] the burden to the defendant to establish that its actions were not intentionally discriminatory."[52]

The Justice Department lawyers actually rearranged the panel's opinion to square with *Davis* and *Arlington Heights*. The panel had not in fact used the evidence on optional zones and the analysis of discrimination in the transfer program to *establish* a presumption of segregative intent; it used these actions to prove the Omaha school board had not *rebutted* this all but irrebuttable presumption—a presumption raised wholly by the racial imbalance flowing from the "natural and foreseeable" effects of board action.

The extremely brief Eighth Circuit decision on remand did not get into these complexities. It simply reaffirmed the original decision, concluding "that the evidence is clear that a discriminatory purpose has been a motivating factor in the School District's actions, . . . because the natural and foreseeable consequence of the acts . . . was to create and maintain segregation . . . , which evidence was not effectively rebutted."[53]

Judge Reynolds in Milwaukee, to whom the Seventh Circuit sent the Supreme Court remand,[54] offered a reading of *Davis* and *Arlington Heights* composed in equal parts, it appeared, of the Justice Department brief in *Omaha* and his own earlier opinion. A presumption of segregative purpose arose, he held, "from a showing that increased or continued racial segregation was the foreseeable result of official action or inaction that did not further avowed governmental policies *or* that ignored less segregative options which were equally consistent with governmental policies."[55] Both sides of the presumption were largely irrebuttable. Yet one side pointed toward condemnation of the classical de jure method of preserving segregation, by frank manipulations of a neighborhood school policy. The other side pointed back toward the decision Judge Reynolds was supposedly reconsidering.

The judge used both of the arrows in his quiver to find systemwide violations, in the new trial he ordered on remand. A revisiting of transportation policies in Milwaukee, for instance, revealed some shady practices with regard to what was known as the intact busing of students to alternate schools, when their home school was temporarily overcrowded or undergoing modernization. (Intact busing was the policy of keeping students together in their own separate classes at the receiving school.) Officials justified the policy because students would attend the receiving school for but a short time, and in the 1960's and early 1970's it applied to both races. However, Judge Reynolds discovered that intact busing *began* as a policy in 1958, only when African-American students first became involved in such busing, and, that for a few years thereafter, a number of white students bused to all-white receiving schools still mixed with the other students. In the case of one white school, this practice stopped as soon as African-American students were brought in.

Once intact busing became the invariable rule in the early 1960's, students at receiving schools were sometimes allowed to stay there for lunch, and sometimes were returned to their school of origin, whether they were white students bused into white schools or African-Americans brought into black schools. *"However, in no instance did students from a black school bussed into a white school remain at the white school for lunch."*[56] There were also cases in which African-American youngsters at predominantly white receiving schools were required to take recess at a different time from the white students. These blatant deviations from "avowed governmental policies" on transportation "reveal that the defendants were acting with intent to discriminate."[57]

But Judge Reynolds was ready to find violations whenever Milwaukee officials countenanced racial imbalance. Thus he condemned Milwaukee's student transfer plan, which was totally permissive in nature, and was maintained, apparently, without manipulation, because of its unfavorable outcome for integration. "[W]here the foreseeable and actual result of a transfer policy is to increase the racial identifiability of schools with large minority enrollment, continuation of the policy gives rise to a presumption of segregative intent."[58] Judge Reynolds claimed that the policy was adopted over the objections of the local NAACP, whose leaders "proposed that . . . racial integration should be added as a criterion for granting student transfers."[59] But the initial opinion on liability contained a different version of how this open transfer plan came about.

> During the early 1960's, a number of civil rights groups in the community suggested that the opportunities for students to transfer from one school might be enhanced by eliminating the requirement of having a reason therefor. In 1964, Board member Golightly (who is black) and the NAACP made such a proposal. It was argued that affording students an opportunity to choose to attend schools located outside their residential neighborhoods would lead to racial integration in the system's schools. The Board adopted the Open Transfer proposal upon the recommendation of the Committee on Equal Educational Opportunity . . . .[60]

The judge described the transfer system as "an open invitation to white students to flee from black schools," and called attention to Milwaukee officials' awareness that "their . . . policy was exacerbating racial imbalance."[61] But this really amounted to the authorities being cognizant, as was Judge Reynolds, that the "transfer procedure [was] not . . . utilized by a sufficient number of black students . . . to . . . achieve racial balance in the [Milwaukee] schools."[62] If the transfers had brought increased integration to Milwaukee, it is clear that no suggestion of illicit intent would have arisen.

Judge Curtin in Buffalo was similarly obliged to return to his earlier opinion, and he now distanced himself from the pure tort standard he had propounded. He "may have overstated the law," the judge admitted, in holding that it was "enough . . . to show that the probable and foreseeable result of the defendants' acts was segregation."[63] Upon reconstructing his liability opinion, however, Judge Curtin assured himself that he had proven "purposeful or intentional segregative acts" by Buffalo authorities.[64] These ranged from the blatantly discriminatory use of transfer policies and the setting up of optional attendance zones in changing neighborhoods to the unwillingness of the school board to affirmatively adopt an integration plan, and the failure of the state regents to force them to do so.

The mixture of full-blooded discriminatory offenses and instances of racial imbalance characterized by various courts as exhibiting "segregative intent" in the wake of *Keyes* was bewildering, perhaps, yet true to the bifurcated nature of the decision itself. *Keyes* demanded a sub-stratum of deliberate discrimination before liability was established, consistent with its caution that "the differentiating factor between de jure segregation and so-called de facto segregation . . . is *purpose* or *intent* to segregate." But under the *Keyes* presumptions, these proven violations opened the way for an assault on what many saw as the decision's real target, "the segregated patterns themselves."

III

The presumptions themselves now came directly under attack from those, like Justice Rehnquist, who believed that desegregation plans should scrupulously reflect the degree of past discrimination they were designed to correct, that de jure violators should bear the remedial costs of only the palpable results of their actions. The case which brought this dispute over remedy to a head was *Brinkman* v. *Dayton Board of Education*.

Brinkman arose in the southern district of Ohio in 1971. Judge Carl Rubin's initial decision in the case came down in February of 1973, four months before *Keyes*. The judge showed no compunction, therefore, about equating segregative effect with constitutional infringement. He found the "racially imbalanced schools" of Dayton an instance of de jure segregation, and, like Judge Doyle, held that the Dayton school board's rescission, a la Denver, of an integration plan previously approved was "an independent violation" of fourteenth amendment rights.[65] These offenses, along with some suspiciously drawn optional zones for the city's high schools, were "cumulatively in violation of the Equal Protection Clause. We hold that the totality of these findings require intervention by this Court under the mandate of *Brown* v. *Board of Education.*" (Judge Rubin ignored evidence of housing violations which the plaintiffs claimed were relevant to the case.)[66]

The judge's remedy was modest, in lieu of the "cumulative" violations. With regard to student assignment, he ordered merely the abolition of optional attendance zones and reorganization of Dayton's transfer program "for [the] purpose of improving racial balance."[67]

Meanwhile, *Keyes* was decided, but the Sixth Circuit did not seem to regard it as casting doubt on whether racial imbalance per se comprised de jure segregation, for a panel headed by Chief Judge Harry Phillips upheld the district court's finding that "racially imbalanced schools" offended the Constitution.[68] So, of course, did the optional attendance zones. Reneging on the obligation to correct this situation, especially the racial imbalance, added another "element" of illegality,[69] although, contrary to the lower courts in Dayton and Denver, Judge Phillips held that taken by itself the rescission could not comprise a constitutional violation.

Having basically affirmed the lower court's findings of illegal segregation, the circuit went on to decree, however, that, under *Keyes* and *Swann,* the limited remedy which Judge Rubin ordered would not do, and that a systemwide remedy was necessary. After two trips back to the district court, the Court of Appeals approved a plan requiring all schools in Dayton to have student populations within 15% of the 52/48 white-black ratio in the district.[70]

The Supreme Court which had recently decided *Davis* and *Arlington Heights* overturned the Sixth Circuit judgment and sent the case back to the district court for further review. The vote was 8–0; Justice Marshall did not participate.

In the light of "Washington v. Davis, 426 U.S. 229," it was clear, held Justice Rehnquist, that racial imbalance, "standing by itself, is not a violation of the Fourteenth Amendment in the absence of a showing that this condition resulted from intentionally segregative actions."[71] Furthermore, retraction of an integration plan did not represent a freestanding constitutional offense. Reproducing the words of the circuit court, Justice Rehnquist definitively settled the matter of a rescission's independent potency.

> The question of whether a rescission of previous Board action is in and of itself a violation of . . . constitutional rights is inextricably bound up with the question of whether the Board was under a constitutional duty to take the action which it initially took . . . . If the Board was not under such a duty, then the rescission of the initial action in and of itself cannot be a constitutional violation. If the Board was under such a duty, then the rescission becomes a part of the cumulative violation . . . .[72]

Creation of the optional zones was the only unarguable de jure violation, and it was confined to the high schools. "Judged most favorably to the [Dayton plaintiffs], then, the District Court's findings of constitutional violations did not, under our cases, suffice to justify the remedy imposed."[73]

None of this sparked any controversy among the justices. But in ordering the remand, Justice Rehnquist included a set of remedial instructions which carried high explosive capability. With nary a mention of the *Keyes* presumptions, Rehnquist stipulated, in language reminiscent of Chief Justice Burger's frustrated efforts in *Swann*, that

> The duty of both the District Court and the Court of Appeals in a case such as this, where mandatory segregation by law of the races in the schools has long since ceased, is to first determine whether there was any action in the conduct . . . of the school board which was intended to, and did in fact, discriminate against minority pupils, teachers, or staff . . . . If such violations are found, the District Court in the first instance, subject to review by the Court of Appeals, must determine how much incremental segregative effect these violations had on the racial distribution of the Dayton school population as presently constituted, when that distribution is compared to what it would have been in the absence of such constitutional violations. The remedy must be designed to redress that difference, and only if there has been a systemwide impact may there be a systemwide remedy.[74]

Read against the background of Rehnquist's *Keyes* dissent, this directive raised the possibility of a fundamental shift in the law of desegregation remedies. Plaintiffs would now be burdened, it appeared, with demonstrating the exact demographic consequences of each violation committed by school authorities, unaided by any momentum-building presumptions. They would revert to the position of the Denver plaintiffs seeking to convince Judge Doyle of de jure segregation in the core city, a position in which segregative intent, even if proven, could be rendered nugatory by lack of segregative impact.

Commentators speculated about the continued viability of *Keyes* in light of *Dayton*. One of them, misquoting Justice Rehnquist's words slightly, but catching their author's likely meaning, rendered the sentence on incremental segregative effect as beginning with the phrase,

> *[R]ather than presuming that all segregative effects are caused by the violation*, the district court must determine how much incremental segregative effect these violations had on the racial distribution of the Dayton school population as presently constituted, when that distribution is compared to what it would have been in the absence of such constitutional violations. The remedy must be designed to redress that difference . . . .[75]

Such an "emphasis on actual proof of the demographic effects caused . . . by a constitutional violation," felt the writer (Stephen Barrett Kanner), "clearly marks the demise of the *Keyes* presumptions."[76]

The author of *Keyes* obviously did not see Rehnquist's strictures as going that far, or he would not have agreed to the result in *Dayton*. "[C]oncurring in the judgment,"[77] Justice Brennan gave no indication he thought the *Keyes* framework jeopardized. Indeed, he seemed confident that on remand its mechanisms would set off the chain reaction producing "incremental segregative effect," and the "systemwide impact"[78] consistent with a systemwide remedy. Clearly, deliberate segregation and its results had been found in part of the Dayton school system. Upon reconsideration, therefore, "the District Court may more readily conclude that not only blatant, but also subtle actions—and in some circumstances even inaction—justify a finding of unconstitutional segregation that must be redressed by a remedial busing order."[79]

Still, Brennan was disturbed by Justice Rehnquist's tone and language. While the decision was in draft, he wrote his colleague, suggesting changes to its most important paragraph. In the reference to "conduct of . . . the school board which was intended to, and did in fact, discriminate against minority pupils, teachers, or staff," Brennan wanted to add after the words "did in fact," *"perpetuate or increase the consequences of past de jure segregation or otherwise"* ["discriminate against . . . ."].[80] Above all, he sought to delete the most important sentence in the Rehnquist draft, the one speaking of "incremental segregative effect." Brennan would have changed this critical sentence to read, "If . . . violations are found, the District Court . . . must *tailor its remedial decree to the harm resulting from those violations."*[81]

Rehnquist was unwilling to submit to either of the changes, believing he could not do so "without somewhat altering the focus of the opinion."[82] The final substitution in particular, he felt, "replaces what seems to me to be a useful reference to the relation of population distribution and 'segregation.'"[83]

Justice Brennan's apprehensions were borne out by Judge Carl Rubin's conduct on remand. Judge Rubin saw "the concept of incremental segregative effect" as "a more precise formulation" of the principle which properly governed all desegregation cases, that the scope of a remedy dare not exceed the severity of the violation it was designed to redress.[84] Applied to Dayton, he read "this language as imposing a burden upon the plaintiffs" to document the present influence of any deliberate segregation, *"not merely on a theoretical basis*, but on a *factual* basis."[85]

The judge's resultant findings showed how difficult it would be for complainants to prevail under such standards. His threshold for segregative intent was admittedly stratospheric. He saw no discriminatory design, for example, behind faculty assignment policies in Dayton, since by 1969 every school "had at least one black faculty member."[86] He neglected to mention that, in 1969, 85% of the African-American teachers in Dayton were still assigned to schools 90% black, or that the school had just ceased maintaining teacher applications on a racially separate basis, and color-coding substitute teacher files. In fact, an HEW investigation of 1968–69 found the district guilty of continuing to "pursue a policy of racially motivated assignment of teachers and other professional staff."[87]

But findings of segregative intent seldom mattered, it turned out, if their segregative effect was dissipated by what the judge regarded as impersonal demographic forces. Thus Judge Rubin conceded that an illicit purpose lay behind the establishment and administration of an all-black high school (Dunbar) between 1933 and 1962. The school was the only one in Dayton with a citywide attendance zone, and African-American students from all over town were coaxed or coerced into attending it. The few students intrepid enough to choose white high schools found themselves subjected to myriad indignities, unable to use the school swimming pool, or relegated to separate locker rooms. "Indeed, black students living in the eastern-most portion of the school district traveled across town to attend Dunbar, although they could have attended schools closer to their homes."[88]

Yet to assess the "incremental segregative effect" of all this demanded exploration of an "'alternate universe theory,' i.e., what would have happened if Dunbar had not been maintained with a district-wide enrollment."[89] And, in truth, the neighborhood around Dunbar was already approaching 70% black in 1940; by 1960, it was 100% black. "The effects of the Board of Education's segregative acts . . . were totally subsumed in the effects of five to six decades of housing segregation in which the Board played no part."[90]

Judge Rubin's approach to causation was as pinched as the *Keyes* approach was overly capacious. The shameful situation with regard to Dunbar and the other high schools might well have discouraged African-American parents from moving out of predominantly black neighborhoods, if further discouragement was needed. Expert testimony at trial documented other effects which school policy might exert over neighborhood development (much of it available since the time of *Swann*). The distinguished demographer Karl Taeuber of the University of Wisconsin, noting that parents looked carefully at schools when they chose areas to live in, demonstrated how assigning a spate of African-American teachers and administrators to a school in a changing neighborhood, let alone gerrymandering in a disproportionate number of black students, would designate the school as certain to become all-black, discourage white parents from considering the neighborhood, and accelerate the shift of the existing white population.[91] "Assignment of a black principal and the shifting of a school attendance boundary," Professor Taeuber had written a few years earlier, "are highly visible deliberate acts that may imply racial consequences to homeseekers, landlords with vacancies, and banks with funds to loan."[92]

However, this pattern, as Taeuber admitted, was endemic to transitional neighborhoods, where whites were unlikely to move anyway. And Professor Taeuber failed to deal with the embarrassing question of whether identifiably black schools in such neighborhoods were not created so that contiguous schools would be identifiably white, slowing down white flight from the area.

Unless the legacy of public (and private) housing discrimination beyond the reach of a school board figured into a demographic analysis of school segregation, something Judge Rubin refused to do, it was hard to deny that such an analysis, free from causal inferences, could reasonably lead to the judge's conclusion about Dayton, however narrow some of his thinking. The plaintiffs, he held, had "failed to meet" the "burden of proof" justifying a systemwide remedy.[93]

The Sixth Circuit overruled Judge Rubin and ordered systemwide relief,[94] sparking a successful school board attempt to get the controversy moved to the Supreme Court. The justices heard the Dayton case on April 24, 1979, along with a case from Columbus raising similar issues.

In their briefs and arguments, the Dayton plaintiffs (now the respondents) presented in greater detail a striking new approach to desegregation law which they had been urging on the justices since *Dayton I*. Despairing that the Court would order a systemwide remedy under the *Keyes* presumptions, even assuming it still considered them valid, petitioners now placed their emphasis not on current demographic or sociological trends, but on history.

At one level, this involved the boldest parallel between North and South ever drawn. In 1954, respondents now argued, the school system of Dayton, Ohio was as much of a dual system as Charlotte or Mobile, in fact, if not by formal statute, and it did not take the aid of presumptions to prove this. By means of blatant segregative devices, Dayton officials had isolated nearly three-quarters of the city's African-American students in schools virtually identical in their origins and effect to the schools in Alabama or Mississippi; 54.3% were in all-black schools, about 20% in schools heading inexorably toward that status. Repeated acts of discrimination reinforced this separation in ensuing years. The parallel with a southern system might not be exact. But a study of past events in Dayton proved that its "state-imposed system of intentional segregation was probably as perfect as it could have been without the aid of a state law mandating absolute apartheid."[95]

During a period of "forty years prior to *Brown*," therefore, "the Dayton Board . . . created and operated, pursuant to plain old-fashioned racially discriminatory purpose, a segregated school system."[96] And as a dual system, Dayton must achieve the same remedial end as Richmond or Oklahoma City, "the greatest possible degree of actual desegregation."

This parallel made some sense, but, ultimately, it was a bit of a stretch, as Dayton's attorneys pointed out. "If a dual system is one in which separate schools are maintained for black students and for white students," they asked, how could the Dayton of 1954, "in which almost half of the black students attend[ed] schools in the company of white students—regardless of the percentage mix in each school—be characterized as a dual system?"[97]

The Dayton plaintiffs possessed an ingenious fall back position, however. *They* believed the *Keyes* presumptions still valid, and used them, in cleverly altered form, to buttress their case. These presumptions, they claimed, applied not just to a *present* condition of racial segregation, but to the segregation existing in 1954, and since segregative intent operated at that time in a significant portion of the Dayton system, "these facts result in a *prima facie* case of systemic intentional discrimination . . . [u]nder the *Keyes* evidentiary principles."[98] School officials manifestly

failed the test of showing that segregative intent was "not among the factors" motivating their other decisions in 1954, and this kicked off the *Swann* presumption and
the *Swann* obligation, imposing on these officials, both in 1954 and at the present
time, the obligation to eradicate all racial separation. "At this juncture of the *Keyes*
framework, the remedial principles of *Green* and *Swann* come into play and, to the
extend that [Dayton officials] contend that less than a systemwide remedy will eliminate all vestiges of intentional discrimination . . . , they bear the burden of proving
'that a lesser degree of segregated schooling . . . would not have resulted even if the
Board had not acted as it did.'"[99]

It was this approach which Justice Byron White employed when, speaking for a
5–4 majority, he found for the respondents in a decision issued on July 2, 1979.
Obviously, White noted, deliberate segregation had flourished in a significant part
of the Dayton system at the time of *Brown*, and, under *Keyes*, this "warranted an
inference . . . that segregation in other parts of the system was also purposeful."[100]
The school board could not rebut this inference, and, given the presence of a dual
system, the board had been "under a continuing duty to eradicate the effects of that
system."[101]

Being applicable to illegal segregation in 1954, the *Keyes* presumptions certainly remained applicable to more recent de jure offenses. Consequently, Judge Rubin
had taken a misguided approach toward such offenses in Dayton (though they were
not now essential to resolution of the Dayton case). The judge had acted on the discredited notion that plaintiffs must "prove with respect to each individual act of discrimination precisely what effect it has had on current patterns of segregation."[102]

Justice White's opinion, therefore, made the 1954 baseline for northern school
systems constitutional doctrine, while reaffirming and even expanding the *Keyes*
presumptions. As one astute commentator put it,

> The *Keyes* presumption is predicated on the concept of space, not time.
> It stands for the proposition that where plaintiffs show that intentional
> or de jure segregation exists in a meaningful portion of a school system,
> the burden of proof shifts to the school authorities to show that other
> . . . actions and policies in other parts of the system having segregative
> impact are not also motivated by an intent to segregate. *Columbus* and
> *Dayton II,* on the contrary, are predicated on the concept of time. They
> stand for the proposition that where plaintiffs can prove that [a dual
> school system existed] at the time *Brown I* was decided in 1954, the
> school board was automatically charged (as of 1954) with an affirma-
> tive duty to effectuate a transition to a racially nondiscriminatory school
> system. When *Keyes* is combined with the doctrines of *Columbus* and
> *Dayton II,* the concepts of space and time are also combined.[103]

Dayton found the justices more divided in an interdistrict desegregation case
than they ever had been. Not unexpectedly, the chief justice joined Justice

Rehnquist and Justice Powell in opposing extension of a line of thinking he had apparently signed on to inadvertently in *Swann.* Justice Potter Stewart also joined the minority; only the vote of his partner in *Richmond* and *Milliken* swung the balance in favor of the Dayton respondents.

In his vigorous dissent, Justice Rehnquist had no occasion to treat the issue of whether *Dayton I* was supposed to displace *Keyes,* because he believed Justice White's new dispensation distorted even the latter. *Keyes* (and *Swann* as well) took its starting point, he noted, from *current* segregation in a significant part of a school system, and the implications of that fact. Therefore, in form at least, "Causality plays a central role in Keyes as it does in all equal protection analysis."[104] Now, however, a northern school district was condemned to a systemwide remedy because of acts committed before 1954, "despite the plaintiff's failure to demonstrate a link between those past acts and current racial imbalance." . . .

> As a matter of history, case law, or logic, there is nothing to support the novel proposition that the primary inquiry in school desegregation cases involving systems without a history of statutorily mandated racial assignment is what happened in those systems before 1954. As a matter of history, 1954 makes no more sense as a benchmark—indeed it makes *less* sense—than 1968, 1971, or 1973. Perhaps the latter year has the most to commend it, if one insists on a benchmark, because in Keyes this Court first confronted the problem of school segregation in the con text of systems without a history of statutorily mandated segregation of the races . . . .

> The analytical underpinnings of the concept of discriminatory purpose have received their still incomplete articulation [only] in the 1970's. It is sophistry to suggest that a school board in Columbus [or Dayton] in 1954 could have read [*Brown I*] and gleaned from it a constitutional duty "to diffuse black students throughout the system" or take whatever other action the Court today thinks it should have taken. And not only was the school board to anticipate the state of the law 20 years hence, but also to have a full appreciation for discrete acts or omissions of school boards 20 to 50 years earlier.[105]

Yet where did this newly conceived burden really place Dayton or Columbus if not in the same position occupied by Charlotte and Mobile in 1971, required, as Justice Powell had suggested, "to alleviate conditions which in large part did *not* result from historic, state imposed de jure segregation."? If southern communities which maintained dual school systems in 1954 were automatically assessed the responsibility for residential patterns existing twenty years later, it seemed equally as plausible, or equally as far-fetched, to hold Dayton's officials responsible for current residential patterns, because twenty five years before violations had occurred in what were then "substantial" portions of its school system.

IV

Meanwhile, inspired by Justice Stewart's concurrence, some of the Detroit plaintiffs from *Milliken* had refused to give up the battle for an interdistrict remedy. They filed motions for additional relief in 1975. Their complaint placed heavy emphasis on official housing policies which kept African-Americans penned into Detroit, though it also alleged interdistrict violations by educational authorities. The defendants fell back on *Deal's* view that "all allegations of discrimination in the public and private housing markets . . . should be stricken as immaterial to school desegregation issues."[106] But District Judge Robert DeMascio refused to go that far. He felt that "while allegations of housing discrimination standing alone are insufficient to support a finding of school segregation necessary to justify interdistrict relief, ... [such] allegations . . . are material if other separate acts of *de jure* segregation by the defendants are alleged and proved."[107] The Detroit plaintiffs did not take this case to trial, however, and the city-only remedy for school segregation went forward. In the wake of *Milliken* v. *Bradley*, as Professor Robert Sedler notes, "efforts to achieve metropolitan desegregation [were] not . . . pursued in Detroit, and generally [were] not . . . pursued elsewhere."[108] Certainly, the large-scale effort to breach the walls between city and suburb, envisioned by some before 1974, never materialized.

Still, the *Milliken* line was not totally impenetrable. While no court ever held that the conduct of housing officials alone justified metropolitan desegregation (or intradistrict desegregation for that matter), the combination of rigged or disregarded boundaries, housing violations, and other assorted transgressions did lead to interdistrict remedies in four sizable suburban areas in the decade following *Milliken*. Three were in the border South—Louisville, Wilmington, and Little Rock. One was in the "border" North, Indianapolis, Indiana. Several smaller communities, in both North and South, were also ordered to consolidate school districts or to set aside district boundaries.[109]

The most significant issue raised by these controversies was how extensive metropolitan remedies should be in light of *Milliken's* demand that relief address only the ascertainable effects of constitutional violations. The presumptions of *Swann* and *Keyes* may have pushed remedial actions well beyond the sins for which they were supposedly atoning, but those cases did provide a reasonably consistent rationale for judicial action. The presumptionless world of interdistrict remedies, on the other hand, posed enormous imponderables for lower court judges, yet also allowed freer play to their social and educational philosophies, as they went about deciding what it would take to "restore the victims of discriminatory conduct to the position they would have occupied in the absence of such conduct."

The major southern cases revealed the diversity of approach to which the search for "current interdistrict effects" could lead. *Little Rock* was an example of where both district judge and circuit court went pretty much by the book, their views on remedy reflecting a fairly literal assessment of the demographic fallout from the offenses proven in the case (violations perpetrated against the Little Rock school district by the state of Arkansas and by the surrounding systems in North Little Rock and Pulaski County.) That this was not an exact science, however, can be garnered from the fact that the Eighth Circuit, sitting *en banc*, found it necessary to overrule the district judge, finding his consolidation of the three school systems overbroad. Expanding the school system of Little Rock to the city line, which should have been its boundary originally, was, in the circuit's view, the remedy best "designed to restore the victims of segregation . . . to the position they would have occupied" if interdistrict violations had not occurred.[110]

The judges in both Louisville and Wilmington went in a very different direction, though still professing allegiance to the strictures of *Milliken*. In the first phase of the Louisville case, decided eight months before *Milliken*, a Sixth Circuit panel, consisting of Judges Harry Phillips, Wade McCree, and William Miller, assumed that they obviously possessed the power to order consolidation of the school system of Louisville and the surrounding system of Jefferson County, since neither was in compliance with *Brown*. Where there were "separate school districts," the panel held, "and the districts are not unitary systems, a federal . . . court may fashion an appropriate remedy without being constrained by school district lines created by state law . . . . There is nothing so sacrosanct about the school district lines in this case that they may be permitted to curtail the broad equity powers of [a] federal court in implementing a mandate of the . . . Constitution."[111]

The Supreme Court decision in *Milliken* manifestly brought this conclusion into question. In a brief order issued the same day as the decision, the majority remanded the Louisville case "for further consideration in light of Milliken v. Bradley."[112]

Yet, on remand, the circuit judges stuck to the view that an interdistrict remedy was justified because both Louisville and Jefferson County continued to operate dual school systems. "A vital distinction between *Milliken* and the present case," they felt, "is that in the former there was no evidence that the outlying school districts had committed acts of de jure segregation or that they were operating dual school systems. Exactly the opposite is true here since both the Louisville and Jefferson County School Districts . . . are guilty of maintaining dual . . . systems."[113] But that reasoning did not square with *Milliken*, which clearly held that even if the outlying school districts of suburban Detroit had committed acts of de jure segregation, there could still be no interdistrict remedy without interdistrict violation and effects.

The Sixth Circuit judges did go on to pinpoint such violations, noting that in pre-*Brown* days Jefferson County ran no high schools for African-Americans, and these youngsters were sent to a black high school in the inner city of Louisville. This offense itself "might be insufficient to invoke the equitable power of the court," the judges noted, mindful, no doubt, of the Carver incident in Detroit, but there were "other instances in [this] case of disregarding school district lines."[114] Before *Brown*, for example, the Louisville school board relocated a high school (called Atherton) from the central city to the confines of Jefferson County, and while the school was a segregated white institution at the time, had officials rebuilt it within its proper jurisdiction, Atherton would have been desegregated by the late 1950's instead of remaining an all-white enclave, as it was in 1973. Furthermore, the school district lines of Louisville, unlike those in Detroit, were not coterminous with the political boundaries of the city. Consequently, more than 10,000 students, overwhelmingly white, lived in areas annexed by Louisville, yet still attended schools in the Jefferson County system. This situation "materially aggravates the difficulties in disestablishing the dual city school system."[115]

Having uncovered these violations, however, the judges did not think it necessary to assess their exact effects, in order to see if the scope of the offenses justified the consolidation remedy they continued to insist upon. They did not consider, for example, whether the interdistrict segregation might be adequately redressed simply by moving the boundary lines of the Louisville school district to the city limits, as some of the plaintiffs originally proposed, and integrating Atherton High School.[116] The fact that authorities had manipulated district lines at all for segregative purposes, in districts yet to achieve unitary status, satisfied the panel of the need for metropolitan consolidation.

The situation in the Wilmington metropolitan area was more analogous, in its southern way, to the one in Detroit. By the 1970's, the suburban school districts of New Castle County had long complied with *Brown*, but, in 1974, a three judge federal panel held "that segregated schooling in Wilmington has never been eliminated and that there still exists a dual school system."[117] At the time, suburban school enrollment was 94% white; Wilmington schools were 83% black.

During this phase of the case, the Wilmington plaintiffs alleged, and the next year the panel affirmed, a number of serious interdistrict violations which had intensified segregation in Wilmington, and pointed toward some sort of metropolitan remedy. Thus the state subsidized interdistrict transportation of youngsters to private and parochial schools, helping middle class white students from Wilmington attend non-public institutions in New Castle County. The Wilmington Housing authority, though given the power to build public housing projects up to five miles beyond the city limits, had built only forty such units in the suburbs, compared to 2,000 in the inner city.

The judges also accepted the claim that state authorities were implicated in discrimination affecting private housing. The Delaware Real Estate Commission, the state licensing agency, published a primer which, until 1970, reprinted an infamous passage from the Code of Ethics of the National Association of Real Estate Boards, warning against "introducing into a neighborhood . . . any race or nationality . . . whose presence will clearly be detrimental to property values in that neighborhood."[118] Until 1968, the multi-list established by the Greater Wilmington Board of Realtors distinguished openly between those willing to sell their houses to minority purchasers and those who would not do so. Residential segregation in the

Wilmington area, felt the panel, "resulted not exclusively from individual residential choice and economics, but also from assistance, encouragement, and authorization by governmental policies."[119]

Most important was the court's finding about the issue which triggered the 1974–75 litigation in the first place, the circumstances surrounding passage of Delaware's Educational Advancement Act of 1968. The legislation was designed to facilitate reorganization of the state's school districts by temporarily suspending a state law which required that consolidation of separate districts be approved by both parties involved. Though the act aimed primarily at eradicating small, inefficient units, and while many Delaware educators believed no school district should contain over 12,000 students, Wilmington was originally included in the legislation, despite containing nearly 15,000 pupils. Before final passage, however, legislative leaders added amendments excluding the city from any consolidation plan.

This meant, argued the panel, that in its final form the Educational Advancement Act "precluded the State Board [of Education] from considering the 'integrative opportunities' of redistricting in New Castle County in any meaningful way . . . . [T]he Board could not have significantly reduced the growing racial isolation in New Castle County schools had it chosen to do so."[120] The act constituted, therefore, a "suspect racial classification," which could "withstand scrutiny under the fourteenth amendment only if . . . justified by a 'compelling' state interest."[121] And the argument from size was not sufficiently compelling, the judges concluded, because there was "substantial disagreement among professional educators as to the desirable maximum size for school districts."[122] (In these days before *Davis* and *Arlington Heights,* the panel did not think it necessary to find deliberate segregative intent, but the Supreme Court's summary affirmance of its decision in 1975 shut off later exploration of this matter.)[123]

Much less significant, apparently, was a finding by the panel that before *Brown* African-American students from the suburban districts attended high school in Wilmington because no black high schools existed in New Castle County. Some elementary and junior high school students from the county also went to "'colored'" schools in the city.[124] The total in both categories was 190 in 1954–55, a conspicuous percentage of the 845 African-American students then living in New Castle County, but the practice ceased soon after *Brown.* Meanwhile, 910 white students crossed into Wilmington in 1954–55 to attend schools thought academically superior. This practice too stopped a few years after *Brown.*

The sum of these violations pointed toward significant remedial action, even toward a consolidation of Wilmington and large parts of the county. But having developed this evidence, the three judge panel gave it short shrift in devising a remedy. Two simple facts overrode all others, according to the judges, and were sufficient to dictate their conclusion. The state had never "fulfilled its mandate" to operate a unitary school system in Wilmington; and "in the past the area comprising the suburban and city districts was treated jointly for many school purposes, including the transportation of black students to *de jure* segregated schools."[125] This was enough to require consolidation of the Wilmington school system and most of the suburban districts in New Castle County.

The court saw such a conclusion as entirely consistent with *Milliken's* command "that the remedy to be ordered must be commensurate with the scope of the violation which has been found."[126] For past practice, it held, rendered the Wilmington metropolitan area a single dual school system, and, in this situation, "Prior opinions of the Supreme Court have [ruled] unequivocally that where the violation found resulted in the operation of a dual . . . system, the Court must order the 'greatest possible actual degree of desegregation.'"[127] Although Wilmington proper was overwhelmingly white in 1954, "a desegregation decree . . . at that time . . . could properly have considered city and suburbs together for purposes of remedy."[128]

But the courts had not ordered metropolitan consolidation in 1954, and to order it now, on the basis of violations totally submerged by larger demographic developments, and, where, furthermore, the Wilmington and New Castle school districts had been functioning as separate entities for twenty years, was to signal that the judgment in this phase of *Evans* v. *Buchanan* rested on hostility to educational segregation per se, rather than on any concern with the process by which it came about.

Judge Caleb Wright wrote this remedy opinion, but observers at the time believed the panel was dominated by Chief Judge John Gibbons. A native of Newark, Judge Gibbons had seen black in-migration and white flight turn a city into a one-race ghetto. One of the lawyers for the suburban school districts felt, "'Gibbons had it in his mind all along that racial imbalance was a condition that the State had an affirmative constitutional obligation to change.'"[129]

The Indianapolis school case displays most completely the permutations, computations, and the rank confusions in school law wrought by *Milliken* v. *Bradley*— appropriate for a city which was technically "northern" at the time of *Brown*, but in fact straddled the line between northern and southern style segregation. Racial separation by statute no longer existed in Indianapolis, or in Indiana, by 1954; it had been abolished, though, only five years earlier.

The initial district court opinion in the Indianapolis controversy actually preceded Judge Roth's effort in Detroit by a month. And Judge Hugh Dillin took the same "integrationist" view his colleague would take. Having found de jure segregation in the Indianapolis school system, Judge Dillin pronounced himself dissatisfied with the prospect of a city-only remedy. The African-American student population of the city already exceeded 33%, and the judge was convinced that 40% constituted the "tipping point," at which "white exodus becomes accelerated and irreversible."[130] Therefore, while "the easy way out for this Court . . . would be to order a massive 'fruit basket' scrambling of students within the School City . . . , to achieve exact racial balancing," there was "just one thing wrong with this simplistic solution: in the long haul, it won't work."[131] For purposes of determining remedy, Judge Dillin ordered inclusion of the ten suburban school districts of Marion County; except for school administration, the county was already governed jointly with the city of Indianapolis under an arrangement known as Uni-Gov. He also brought in the school officials of systems in other surrounding counties.[132]

The judge admitted, while pondering remedy at a hearing in late 1973, that none "of the added defendant school corporations have committed acts of *de jure* segregation directed against Negro students living within their respective borders."[133] Treading, however, on what was by this time previously-plowed ground, since the process in Detroit had now moved ahead of him, Dillin noted that the illegal segregative acts in Indianapolis "can be, and are imputed, to the State of Indiana," and that the sole "feasible desegregation plan" in this situation involved "the crossing of the boundary lines between [Indianapolis] and adjacent . . . school districts." Therefore, "paraphrasing the holding of the Sixth Circuit in *Bradley* v. *Milliken,* . . . the State controls the instrumentalities whose action is necessary to remedy the harmful effects of the State acts."[134] Judge Dillin ordered interim relief for Indianapolis, and gave the Indiana legislature the option of working out a plan for interdistrict relief.

The Supreme Court's action in *Milliken* v. *Bradley* interrupted this progression. Less than a month after the decision, the Seventh Circuit reversed Judge Dillin's orders relating to a metropolitan remedy outside of Marion County, pointedly recalling *Milliken's* contention "that even if state agencies participated in the maintenance of the Detroit system, . . . it [does] not follow that an interdistrict remedy would be constitutionally justified."[135] The circuit panel remanded Dillin's order of metropolitan relief within the Uni-Gov area, however, cognizant of some observations in his earlier opinions about suspicious events preceding formation of the Uni-Gov arrangement.

Judge Dillin was in fact ready in this connection with state action of a sort consistent with Chief Justice Burger's standards. Historically, he pointed out in his opinion of August 1, 1975, it was well established under Indiana law that the school boundaries of a city or a town followed its civic boundaries; when the city expanded, so did the school system. But just before the Uni-Gov act passed the Indiana General Assembly in 1969, legislators amended it to provide that school systems would not fall under its coverage.

These amendments, argued Judge Dillin, were added to mollify "the suburban school corporations within Marion County," which "have consistently resisted the movement of black citizens or black pupils into their territory."[136] The circumstances surrounding the establishment of Uni-Gov, Judge Dillin held, warranted an "interdistrict remedy within all of Marion County."[137]

The judge also found conduct of the Housing Authority of the City of Indianapolis a cause for metropolitan relief. In a rerun of a familiar tale, he noted that HACI possessed power to construct public housing units as much as five miles from the city, yet had placed all of them within the city limits. The residents of these units were 98% black, "obviously tend[ing] to cause and to perpetuate the segregation of black pupils" within Indianapolis.[138] (Judge Dillin had to rephrase all these charges in 1978 when the Supreme Court remanded the case once more in light of *Davis* and *Arlington Heights,* but he effortlessly altered his language to read that the actions of the legislature in designing Uni-Gov "were done, at least in part, with the *racially discriminatory intent and purpose* of confining black students" to Indianapolis.[139] Similarly, the actions of HACI "were *racially motivated* with the *invidious purpose* to keep the blacks within pre-Uni-Gov Indianapolis.")[140]

When it came to segregative effect, however, and the precise remedy that dictated for metropolitan Indianapolis, Judge Dillin took a far less expansive approach than while determining violation. In first sending the controversy to the Indiana General Assembly for implementation of interdistrict relief, in 1973, he had given legislators the choice either of consolidating all of Marion County into one school system or of providing a mechanism for interdistrict transfers. The assembly naturally chose the transfers, and in his August, 1975 opinion Judge Dillin set up a distinctly conservative, not to say inequitable, version of this option. He ordered one-way transfers of African-American students (grades 1–9) from Indianapolis to Marion County school districts in numbers sufficient to bring African-American enrollment in each district to 15%—thus approximating the 17% black population in the county. The plan initially involved 6,533 youngsters.

In justifying this remedy, Judge Dillin launched into an assessment of the effect of the housing violations which was so painfully exact as to seem almost a parody of the notion of segregative impact. A detailed accounting of the students implicated by discrimination in public housing convinced the judge that the number totaled just about 7,000, which "would approximate the number of students . . . the court proposes to transfer."[141] This was because the HACI owned 2,395 public housing units exclusive of those for the elderly. "Estimating three school age children per unit"[142] brought the total to the 7,000 figure (though that number would also include, presumably, high school students not transported under the court's plan).

Indeed, after a full-dress remedy hearing in July, 1979, the judge concluded that his initial figures were "somewhat high."[143] New material allowed him to calculate much more precisely the total increase of African-American students in schools serving ten of the eleven public housing projects in Indianapolis. By the time suit was brought in 1968, the projects had contributed 2,500 additional minority pupils to the non-high school grades of nearby ghetto schools, and this figure, Judge Dillin noted, could be extrapolated to all grades in the Indianapolis school system by taking account of the fact that in 1968–69 the schools "had an enrollment of 98,363 in grades 1–12, of which 72,244 or 73.45% were [in grades 1–9]. Applying the formula 2,500/73.25 (sic) x 100 = total students, grades 1–12, we arrive at a total of 3,404 public housing students residing in the ten projects."[144] The ten projects contained, 1,644 units, so that the average number of students per unit came out to 2.07. "[A]pplied to the total of 2,395 units owned by HACI [this] yields a grand total of 4,958 black students from all eleven housing units who would have received their education in a desegregated suburban school had all public housing been located outside" Indianapolis[145] (though high school students still did not fall under the final plan which emerged from this remedy hearing).

His figures were corroborated, the judge proudly pointed out, by an actual count of the school age children, 6–18, living in the ten housing projects, made in July, 1978. The total was 2,586. And since the ten projects then showed a vacancy rate of 19.2%, "application of the formula 2,586/80.8 X 100"[146] would equal the total number of school children when the units were filled to capacity, as they were in the late 1960's. The calculation produced 3,200 children, meaning that the "correlation between this figure and the figure of 3,404 arrived at by the Court's first method speaks for itself."[147]

The 4,958 students segregated by public housing fell short, Judge Dillin admitted, of the 8,711 children he was now ordering bused to Marion County (the original 6,533, plus 2,178 over the following three years). But he also cited evidence suggesting that when black- occupied housing projects were constructed in or near formerly white neighborhoods, as was the case in Indianapolis, additional African-Americans moved into private housing in the area, thus deepening the racial concentration. "The Court's estimate is that the total number of black children affected by all [housing] violations, both directly and indirectly, . . . is from 8,000 to 8.500 children."[148]

Having strained at these demographic gnats, the judge then proceeded to shun the camels offered him by the plaintiffs. He brushed aside evidence of broader housing violations alleged to be instrumental in creating the pattern of black inner cities and white suburbs in metropolitan Indianapolis. More glaringly, he refused to countenance the argument which carried the greatest remedial clout of all, and would render his transfer schemes, one-way or otherwise, seriously inadequate: that if the Indiana General Assembly had acted in a non-discriminatory manner in creating Uni-Gov, Marion County would have operated as a single school system from 1971 on, subject to the remedial strictures of *Keyes* and *Swann*. Yet having found segregative motive in the drawing of the school district boundaries, Judge Dillin now argued that such discrimination carried no remedial significance at all, because "sans those [discriminatory] provisions, . . . Uni-Gov would not have been enacted."[149]

The Seventh Circuit refused to accept this bizarre logic. It was simply not "relevant," a circuit panel proclaimed, "that without the . . . legislation freezing [the Indianapolis school] boundaries Uni-Gov never would have been enacted. Once the state chose to act it was obligated to do so in a non-discriminatory manner."[150] The panel admitted that in this instance the remedy "most closely tailored" to the violation "would likely be one that would allow [the Indianapolis school system] to expand to [Uni-Gov's] borders," but it upheld Judge Dillin's limited remedy, nonetheless, on the ground that he had not "abused his discretion."[151]

The district judge was on firmer ground in rejecting plaintiffs' claim that a sweeping interdistrict remedy was demanded because of the ripple effects of the school violations committed by Indianapolis authorities. Their optional attendance zones, gerrymandered boundary lines, and racially-tilted use of temporary classrooms, plaintiffs argued, justified countywide integration due to the fact that "each violation" tended "to identify certain schools and neighborhoods inside [Indianapolis] as black, and that this . . . cause[d] whites to live in the suburban areas."[152] Here was a form of the *Swann-Keyes* presumptions. But in the presumptionless world of interdistrict remedies, they must carry their own empirical weight. Judge Dillin was not impressed, and offered a counterargument which, whatever its merits or demerits, had been effectively precluded by the premises of *Swann* and *Keyes*.

> The [plaintiffs], of course, must begin with the assumption that many whites do not want their children to go to school with black children, or at least not with large numbers of black children. This assumption will be taken to be true. Now, assume that city school corporation X has a student population 40% black and, in the same county, adjoining suburban school corporation Y has a student population 1% black. Assume that the schools of X are desegregated, with the racial balance being approximately equal in the various schools. Under these circumstances the white family head with school children (W), having the racial bias assumed by the [plaintiffs'] witnesses, upon moving into the county for the first time would, as a matter of logic, always elect to locate in Y, other things being equal. Assume, on the other hand, that the schools of X are segregated, with many all-white schools. In these circumstances, W could logically decide to locate inside X, near one of such white schools, if he believed that the situation would remain the same for a substantial period of time. It may therefore be seen that segregation in X would be more likely to attract W to X, or to keep a white family from leaving X, than the reverse, as testified by the experts.[153]

"The truth of the foregoing exercise in logic" was corroborated, Judge Dillin pointed out, by statistical evidence demonstrating that when the Indianapolis schools were illegally segregated, in 1968–69, white pupil enrollment was 72,025. Since desegregation, the total had fallen to 38, 693, "a catastrophic decrease of . . . 46.3%."[154]

Needless to say, this situation characterized nearly every major American metropolitan area by the 1980's, with or without desegregation plans.

I. SEGREGATIVE INTENT: THE SPORT OF THE SEVENTIES

Though explicitly reinforcing the logic of *Swann*, *Keyes'* admonition that "the differentiating factor" between types of segregation "is *purpose* or *intent* to segregate" was hard to take seriously, as we have seen. Lower court judges required to find some sort of intent in the light of *Keyes* simply invoked the tort standard which Professor Dimond had employed in the wake of *Swann*. When *Washington* v. *Davis* and *Arlington Heights* demanded more deliberate intent, plaintiffs and judges stressed the violations of this sort which had always been present in their analyses, and regarbed less blatant offenses in appropriate clothing.

This point-counterpoint is best viewed in a series of exchanges between the justices and Judge John Minor Wisdom. The occasion was a controversy which stretched through the 1970's and beyond, *The United States* v. *Texas Education Agency*. The case involved unconstitutional segregation of Mexican-American students in the Austin school system (which had never segregated these youngsters by statute). Its progress touched all aspects of the game of segregative intent.

In the first incarnation of the controversy, decided between *Swann* and *Keyes*, Judge Wisdom found no need to discover segregative intent of any sort. (His opinion paralleled the logic of an opinion in a closely-related case heard the same day, *Cisneros* v. *Corpus Christi Independent School District*, an opinion with which Judge Wisdom concurred, though it was written by Judge Henry Dyer.)

Confronted with *Keyes*, Judge Wisdom merely brought *Texas Education Agency* under the rubric of the tort principle of liability (prodded willingly, it appears, by the Hispanic plaintiff-intervenors in the case). Confronted with *Washington* v. *Davis* and *Arlington Heights*, the judge still felt he did not have to dispense completely with the tort standard, but reshaped it to encompass the long history of discrimination against Hispanics in the Austin Independent School District. His various arguments on intention were sensible, to be sure, but they seemed secondary to his real reason for demanding integration, as spelled out in *Austin I*: the existence of the "segregated patterns themselves."

1. *CISNEROS* v. *CORPUS CHRISTI INDEPENDENT SCHOOL DISTRICT*

(467 F.2d 142: 1972)

Although *Brown* arose in the context of segregation by state law, . . . we think it clear today beyond peradventure that the contour of unlawful segregation extends beyond statutorily mandated segregation to include the actions and policies of school authorities which deny to students equal protection of the laws by separating them ethnically and racially in public schools . . . . Such actions are "state action" for the purposes of the Fourteenth Amendment, and result in dual school systems that cannot be somehow less odious because they do not flow from a statutory source. The imprimatur of the state is no less visible. The continuing attempt to cast segregation that results from such action as de facto and beyond the power of the court to rectify is no longer entitled to serious consideration.

Thus, we discard the anodyne dichotomy of classical de facto and de jure segregation. We can find no support for the view that the Constitution should be applied antithetically to children in the north and south, or to mexican-americans *vis-a-vis* anglos, simply because of the adventitious circumstance of their origin or the happenstance of locality . . . .

The Board . . . nevertheless maintains that . . . de facto segregation exists here, arguing that this separation is not a result of school board actions and policies but rather of housing patterns, geographic fluctuations, and other social and economic factors prevalent in the city. Moreover, it urges, even if the imbalance could be traced to Board action, it does not fall within constitutional proscription because it has not acted with a discriminatory motive or purpose . . . .

Such [arguments] are confusing and unnecessary. The decision in *Brown* is the clear embodiment of the legal framework for the resolution of these important issues.

Brown prohibits segregation in public schools that is a result of state action. It requires simply the making of two distinct factual determinations to support a finding of unlawful segregation. First, a denial of equal educational opportunity must be found to exist, defined as racial or ethnic segregation. Secondly, this segregation must be the result of state action.

We need not define the quantity of state action or the severity of the segregation necessary to sustain a constitutional violation. These factual determinations are better dealt with on a case by case basis. We need only find a real and significant relationship, in terms of cause and effect, between state action and the denial of educational opportunity occasioned by the racial and ethnic separation of public school students.

We affirm the finding of the district court that action by the school district here has, in terms of cause and effect, resulted in a severely segregated school system in Corpus Christi. We need find nothing more. Discriminatory motive and purpose, while they may reinforce a finding of effective segregation, are not necessary ingredients of constitutional violations in the field of public education. We therefore hold that the racial and ethnic segregation that exists in the Corpus Christi school system is unconstitutional—not de facto, not de jure, but unconstitutional . . . .

Here, the Board, by a rigid superimposition of a neighborhood school plan upon the historic pattern of marked residential segregation that existed in Corpus Christi equated the residential homogeny to ethnic and racial homogeny in the public school system, producing inevitable segregation. That there was an absence of state action involved in creating the city's residential patterns is of no significance. The Board imposed a neighborhood school plan . . . upon a clear and established pattern of residential segregation in the face of an obvious and inevitable result.

2. *UNITED STATES* v. *TEXAS EDUCATION AGENCY (AUSTIN I)*

(467 F. 2d 848: 1972)

B. *Mexican-Americans in the AISD.*

(1) *The Applicable Standard* . . . . Although the inferior educational status of Mexican-American students is apparent from this record, we must determine if their segregation from whites or integration with blacks resulted from constitutionally impermissible state action. "Separate educational facilities are inherently unequal."
. . .

Here school authorities assigned students, faculty, and professional staff; employed faculty and staff; chose sites for schools; constructed new schools and renovated old ones; and drew attendance zone lines. The natural and foreseeable consequence of these actions was segregation of Mexican-Americans. Affirmative action to the contrary would have resulted in desegregation. When school authorities, by their actions, contribute to segregation in education, whether by causing additional segregation or maintaining existing segregation, they deny to the students equal protection of the laws.

We need not define the quantity of state participation which is a prerequisite to a finding of constitutional violation. Like the legal concepts of "the reasonable man", "due care", "causation", "preponderance of the evidence", and "beyond a reasonable doubt", the necessary degree of state involvement is incapable of precise definition and must be defined on a case-by-case basis. Suffice it to say that school authorities here played a significant role in causing or perpetuating unequal educational opportunities for Mexican-Americans, and did so on a system-wide basis
. . . .

The [Austin Independent School District] raises several arguments in defense
. . . .

The Board discusses the special problems of children of migrant labor families who arrive at school late in the fall semester and may be withdrawn early in the spring, the language deficiencies of Mexican-American children, and the retarded educational development of many of these children . . . . Yet, we are not convinced that, to meet the special educational needs of Mexican-American children, the AISD had to keep these children in separate schools, isolate them in Mexican-American neighborhoods, or prevent them from sharing in the educational, social, and psychological benefits of an integrated education . . . . A benign motive will not excuse the discriminatory effects of the school board's actions.

3. *UNITED STATES* v. *TEXAS EDUCATION AGENCY* (*AUSTIN II*)

(532 F. 2d 380: 1976)

II

SEGREGATION OF MEXICAN-AMERICANS

A. The *Keyes* Case . . . .

The unequal educational status of . . . minorities does not constitute a violation of the Equal Protection Clause of the Fourteenth Amendment [according to *Keyes*] unless it results from "state action". The term of art that has long described the state action requirement in the school desegregation context is "*de jure* segregation", which the Supreme Court has [now] defined as "a current condition of segregation resulting from intentional state action directed specifically to the [segregated] schools". . . .

B. The *Cisneros-Austin I* Test

We found in *Austin I* that Mexican-American students in Austin had received an education inferior to that of their Anglo counterparts and that this was the result of ethnic segregation. This would constitute an equal protection violation, we held, only if the "school authorities, by their actions, [had] contribute[d] to segregation in education, whether by causing additional segregation or maintaining existing segregation. . . ." Our ultimate decision against the AISD was based in part on our finding that "[t]he natural and foreseeable consequence of [its] actions was segregation of Mexican-Americans". We held, however, that, to establish an equal protection violation, it is not necessary to prove discriminatory intent when there is discriminatory effect.

Although, in *Cisneros*, we discarded "the anodyne dichotomy of classical de facto and de jure segregation", the rationale of that decision was very similar to that of *Austin I*. The Court held that, in order to sustain a constitutional violation,

[we] need only find a real and significant relationship, in terms of cause and effect, between state action and the denial of educational opportunity occasioned by the racial and ethnic separation of public school students.

As in *Austin I*, we held that "[d]iscriminatory motive and purpose . . . are not necessary ingredients of constitutional violations in the field of public education". And, in language reminiscent of the *Austin I* "foreseeable consequences" approach, the Court found the requisite state action in *Cisneros* in the Board's imposition of "a neighborhood school plan . . . upon a clear and established pattern of residential segregation in the face of an obvious and inevitable result".

Thus, *Austin I* and *Cisneros* both applied cause-and-effect tests for finding the state action that is a prerequisite to establishing a constitutional violation. But, in both cases, this test was applied in the context of school board actions that led to the "foreseeable" and "inevitable" result of segregated schools.

C. The Impact of *Keyes* on the *Cisneros-Austin I* Test . . . .

To the extent that *Cisneros* and *Austin I* applied cause-and-effect tests and rejected the requirement of a showing of discriminatory intent, those cases were supervened by *Keyes*.

But the intervenors . . . argue that, although this Court in *Cisneros* and *Austin I* refused to search for the defendants' express or specific intent, we did not discard intent as an element of the equal protection violation. The intervenors contend that intent could be inferred in those cases from our findings that segregation was the "inevitable result" and the "foreseeable consequence" of the school boards' actions. Whatever may have been the originally intended meaning of the tests we applied in *Cisneros* and *Austin I*, we agree with the intervenors that, after *Keyes*, our two opinions must be viewed as incorporating in school segregation law the ordinary rule of tort law that a person intends the natural and foreseeable consequences of his actions. This reading of *Cisneros* and *Austin I* is faithful to the *Keyes* requirement of proof of segregative intent . . . .

Apart from the need to conform *Cisneros* and *Austin I* to the supervening *Keyes* case, there are other reasons for attributing responsibility to a state official who should reasonably foresee the segregative effects of his actions. First, it is difficult—and often futile—to obtain direct evidence of the official's intentions. Rather than announce his intention of violating antidiscrimination laws, it is far more likely that the state official "will pursue his discriminatory practices in ways that are devious, by methods subtle and illusive—for we deal with an area in which 'subtleties of conduct . . . play no small part'." *Holland v. Edwards*, 1954, 307 N.Y. 38, 45, 119 N.E.2d 581, 584 . . . . Hence, courts usually rely on circumstantial evidence to ascertain the decisionmakers' motivations . . . .

D. The Prima Facie Case of Unlawful Segregation of Mexican-Americans in Austin

. . . .

Segregative actions taken with segregative intent. It has been the AISD's policy to assign students to the schools closest to their homes. The City of Austin, with the exception of the strip between East and West Austin, has ethnically segregated housing patterns. Hence, the natural, foreseeable, and inevitable result of the AISD's student assignment policy has been segregated schools throughout most of the city. Moreover, as we found in *Austin I*, "[a]ffirmative action to the contrary would have resulted in desegregation". The inference is inescapable: the AISD has intended, by its continued use of the neighborhood assignment policy, to maintain segregated schools in East and West Austin. The plaintiffs have therefore established a prima facie case of *de jure segregation* of Mexican-Americans in all portions of the school district except the residentially integrated central city area . . . .

As articulated in *Austin I*, the case before us presents not only the use of a neighborhood assignment policy in a residentially segregated school district, but also the taking of an extensive series of actions dating back to the early twentieth century that had the natural, foreseeable, and avoidable result of creating and maintaining an ethnically segregated school system. The AISD must convert this "still-functioning dual system to a unitary, non-[ethnic] system—lock, stock, and barrel". *United States v. Jefferson County Board of Education*, 372 F.2d at 878.

4. *UNITED STATES v. TEXAS EDUCATION AGENCY (AUSTIN III)*

(564 F. 2d 162: 1977)

Washington v. Davis and *Arlington Heights* . . . establish[ed] that the disproportionate racial impact of the neutral application of a long-standing neutral policy, by itself, will rarely constitute a constitutional violation. Those decisions thus partly answered in the affirmative, one of the questions left open in *Keyes*—"whether a neighborhood school policy of itself will justify racial or ethnic concentrations, in the absence of a finding that school authorities have committed acts constituting *de jure* segregation". We are well aware that some official actions on which a plaintiff hinges an allegation of unconstitutional discrimination have historically been motivated by racially and ethnically neutral *bona fide* concerns, such as the desire to have children attend the school closest to their home, and no showing is made that those concerns were actually subordinate to, or a subterfuge for, unconstitutional discrimination. In those circumstances, that a discriminatory result was the natural and foreseeable consequence of the actions is insufficient to infuse the challenged acts with the type of discriminatory intent required by *Washington v. Davis* and *Arlington Heights*. Nevertheless, . . . we do not read *Washington v. Davis* and *Arlington Heights* as banishing from the law of racial and ethnic discrimination the venerable common law tort principle that a person intends the natural and foreseeable consequences of his actions. When the official actions challenged as discriminatory include acts and decisions that do not have a firm basis in well accepted and historically sound non-discriminatory social policy, discriminatory intent may be inferred from the fact that those acts had foreseeable discriminatory consequences. As a practical matter, in school desegregation cases we can envision few official actions, other than the decision to use a neighborhood school policy for student assignment, that would not be subject to the "natural foreseeable consequences" rule. The presumption is especially probative in assessing the official intent behind such affirmative school board decisions as those concerning school locations, the construction and renovation of schools, the closing of schools, the drawing of student attendance zones, and the assignment of faculty and staff.

There is language in our *Austin II* opinion that an official discriminatory intent adequate to support a finding of *de jure* segregation could be inferred solely from the school board's use of a neighborhood school policy for student assignment. To the extent that *Austin II* can be so read, it is inconsistent with *Washington v. Davis* and *Arlington Heights.* The Supreme Court recognized this ambiguity in vacating our decision and remanding the case to us.

In *Austin II*, however, we analyzed the cause and effect test used in *Austin I*, which was the same test applied in our earlier decision in *Cisneros v. Corpus Christi Independent School District.* [W]e expressly rejected the argument . . . that *Keyes* did not establish that segregative intent is a necessary element of unconstitutional school segregation. We held . . . that "[W]ith respect to the . . . issue [of] segregatory intent, we are governed by *Keyes* . . . which supervenes our holding in *Cisneros* . . . to the extent that *Keyes* requires as a prerequisite to a decree to desegregate a de facto system, . . . proof of segregatory intent as a part of state action". *Austin II*, 532 F.2d 380, 387. But it was apparent to us in both *Austin I* and *Austin II* that the AISD historically had used neighborhood schools to accentuate and to perpetuate segregation of blacks and Mexican-Americans, and that it was attempting now to absolve itself of responsibility for increasing segregation by taking shelter in a supposed neutral policy of assigning students to neighborhood schools. As the United States argued, "When [a neighborhood school] policy has been used in concert with obvious tools of discrimination, it may come to partake of a discriminatory quality and to be an instrument of discrimination itself."

Our finding of discriminatory intent in *Austin II* was not predicated "solely" on the AISD's use of a neighborhood student assignment policy. We thought that we had made this clear in concluding:

> As articulated in *Austin I*, the case before us presents not only the use of a neighborhood assignment policy in a residentially segregated school district, but also the taking of an extensive series of actions dating back to the early twentieth century that had the natural, foreseeable, and avoidable result of creating and maintaining an ethnically segregated school system.

Austin is not just a case of a school board's inaction or failure to reduce segregation because of the force of residential patterns unrelated to official board action. Here the school authorities produced more racial and ethnic separation in the schools than in the residential patterns of the district as a whole. [T]he AISD intentionally discriminated against Mexican-American students, adding to racial and ethnic separation.

5. *UNITED STATES* v. *TEXAS EDUCATION AGENCY* (*AUSTIN IV*)

(579 F. 2d 910: 1978)

The major thrust of the AISD's petition for rehearing is that the holding in *Austin III* that school officials are responsible for the reasonably foreseeable consequences of their acts reinstitutes the type of effect test condemned in *Washington v. Davis* and *Arlington Heights*. [But] [n]either of those decisions abrogated the principle that an actor is held to intend the reasonably foreseeable results of his actions. Given the fundamental nature of that principle, it would be out of character for the Supreme Court to have disapproved its use in discrimination cases—without explicitly saying so . . . .

Realistically, this judicial mechanism is the most reliable one for the objective determination of intent . . . .

The AISD does not suggest what type of evidence would suffice to make out a case of intentional discrimination. On historical grounds the AISD seems to say that no discriminatory intent is made out unless segregation is ordered by a statute or ordinance. Perhaps, however, the Board thinks that there must be statements by its members that "We do not want to mix whites and Mexican-Americans". Even if individual school board members made public statements favoring segregation of Mexican-Americans, this evidence of subjective intent would not necessarily be probative of the school board's intent; any public body may contain one or two extremists who do not express the sentiment of the body . . . . The AISD seems to think that because of its stated benign motives, it could not have intentionally discriminated against Mexican-Americans. This notion shows a misunderstanding of school desegregation.

The most effective way to determine whether a body intended to discriminate is to look at what it has done. This does not mean that every time a school board decision has a discriminatory effect one should infer that the board intended the result. Rather, as in *Austin III*, the school board's actions must be evaluated in the context of the totality of the board's treatment of minorities. The Board's unreceptivity to integration is clear from the factual findings spelled out in *Austin I and II* and recapitulated in *Austin III* . . . . In the context of the AISD's performance in the area of race relations, these findings demonstrate an intent to discriminate against Mexican-

Americans.

The application of the natural and foreseeable consequences test in *Austin III* was consistent with these principles. We expressly stated that the use of the neighborhood assignment policy, though it foreseeably led to segregated schools, was insufficient, standing alone, to sustain a holding of segregative intent. Instead, we regarded this board policy as one item of evidence suggesting segregative intent. The Court evaluated the use of this policy in light of "an extensive series of actions dating back to the early 20th century" and others that had occurred in more recent years. Only then did the Court hold the segregation to be *de jure*. This is in accord with *Arlington Heights* which draws a distinction between "impact alone" and impact plus "other evidence" bearing on the decision-maker's intent . . .

The opinion in *Austin III* attempted to suggest a functional basis for determining segregative intent by circumstantial evidence. But irrespective of the methodology used in determining segregative intent, the facts clearly show that the AISD segregated Mexican-Americans, except to the extent that some were integrated in black schools.

CHAPTER SEVEN
ENDGAME

In the 1980's, court orders on desegregation were inevitably lessening, though by no means were they non-existent. Yonkers, New York was the only new city for which an extensive plan was decreed following a liability trial.[1] Additional relief was ordered, however, in Buffalo, Milwaukee, St. Louis, and Kansas City.[2] Consent decrees brought some measure of integration to cities as diverse as Chicago, Bakersfield, California, and Fort Wayne, Indiana.[3]

The Reagan administration would have been happy to see the number of desegregation orders reach zero, especially those involving mandatory busing. The Assistant Attorney General for Civil Rights, William Bradford Reynolds, bitterly opposed busing on constitutional, educational, and demographic grounds, and sought to design fresh remedial initiatives where instances of illegal racial separation persisted. "Opposition to forced busing," notes Professor Raymond Wolters, "was just the starting point" for Reynolds in developing an alternate approach for achieving what he hoped would be stable integration.[4]

> In addition, Reynolds fostered *magnet schools* that offered attractive innovations or that focused on special fields like science, foreign languages, or the performing arts. The idea was to appeal to parents who otherwise would be reluctant to send their children to integrated schools .... Reynolds hoped to achieve more racial interaction than was possible through forced busing. He regarded magnets as "a reasonable and meaningful alternative" to forced busing ("a policy which we believe has proved ill-advised and ineffective").[5]

To make this program work effectively, Reynolds was willing to take "race into account when admitting students to magnet schools."[6]

In 1983, Reynolds persuaded the district court in Chicago to adopt such an approach to compliance for that city, which at the time operated a school system 61% black, 20% Hispanic, and only 16% white. (This initiative followed in the wake of a lawsuit brought against Chicago by the Carter administration, settled before trial when the school board signed a consent decree on September 24, 1980, promising to implement a systemwide plan to remedy the effects of past segregation.) Under the plan urged by Reynolds, a school would be considered "desegregated," or "integrated," if it achieved an enrollment of 30% minority pupils *and* 30% white youngsters. The goal was to be achieved by setting up numerous magnet schools and programs. There was no required busing.

To the plaintiffs' cry that the plan would leave huge numbers of virtually all-black schools, District Judge Milton Shadur affirmed what he regarded as the "value judgment . . . [i]mplicit in all this," that it "would be contrary to the public interest to devise a plan that would have a racial balance more nearly reflecting the total school population on a school-by-school basis, only to find that through 'white flight' or otherwise the already comparatively small white enrollment would be further diminished so as to make any *real* segregation unattainable."[7]

Later that year, Reynolds was back in court, successfully battling an effort by African-American plaintiffs to strike down a "controlled enrollment program" in Chicago which prevented minority youngsters from going to high schools 65% or more white. The plaintiffs claimed this was an unconstitutional quota, but Judge Shadur, agreeing with Reynolds' views, held that since the controls were part of Chicago's valid desegregation plan, restricting "black enrollment in a given school as part of a plan to desegregate an entire system is just not the same thing as imposing a black quota independently."[8]

Reynolds instituted a similar desegregation plan for Bakersfield in 1984. But the larger issue he now became part of concerned the school districts still satisfying court orders from the post-*Swann* 1970's. In that decision, Chief Justice Burger had soothed districts soon to come under busing decrees by noting that "[a]t some point, . . . school authorities" would achieve "full compliance with this Court's decision in Brown I. The systems would then be 'unitary' in the sense required by our decisions in Green and Alexander."[9]

By the early eighties, even earlier in some instances, many school districts felt that their time had finally come, the time to get out from under court supervision and busing. William Bradford Reynolds strongly agreed. The Supreme Court of *Swann* and *Keyes* had set school boards and lower court judges to playing a game involving questionable demographic presumptions, since it was unwilling or unable to articulate a forthright rationale for integration. Now the games were coming to an end.

I

The Court chose to stay largely on the sidelines after *Dayton*, while the issue of unitary status roiled the lower courts in the 1980's. As in the first decade of desegregation, when school districts were trying to defy or to finesse *Brown*, so, two decades later, when authorities sought the declarations of unity which would end its sway, the justices did not intrude decisively into the formation of the law. They left the initial process of defining unitariness to lower court judges, prodded by individual defendant districts. The school officials frequently found an ally in Assistant Attorney General Reynolds.

Still, the Court had put down a few benchmarks in 1976 and 1977. Its first intervention of 1976 restricted the high spirits of judges like McMillan, who seemed to think they could automatically rearrange student attendance patterns each year to fit the original racial balance they had decreed. The Charlotte board, McMillan ruled, while designing his desegregation plan, must "adopt and implement a continuing program . . . during [this] school year as well as at the start of each year for the conscious purpose of maintaining each school . . . in a condition of desegregation."[10]

Judge Manuel Real in Pasadena was under a more grandiose impression. In 1974, he ruled against a request that he terminate the requirement imposed four years earlier as part of Pasadena's desegregation plan—that no school in the system have a majority of any minority group (African-American or Hispanic). School authorities maintained that the demand was no longer necessary and could no longer be met by reasonable means. But the judge not only turned them down;[11] he went so far as to declare during final arguments on the plea that to him the Pasadena plan meant "there would be no majority of any minority in any school in Pasadena . . . at least during my lifetime."[12]

Speaking for a majority of seven, Justice William Rehnquist, ruled that, even aside from his excessive rhetoric, Judge Real had erred in denying relief to the school board.[13] Having brought itself fully into compliance with the judge's orders, as the district had in 1971, Pasadena did not have to adjust its student patterns to compensate for demographic changes beyond the control of school authorities. Only if board actions themselves had been responsible in some way for a fall off from the original mandate would the board have to make adjustments.

Since shifts in student population were not in fact "caused by segregative actions chargeable to" Pasadena school officials, "the District Court was not entitled to require [Pasadena] to rearrange its attendance zones each year so as to ensure that the racial mix desired by the court was maintained in perpetuity."[14] Having successfully put into place a "racially neutral attendance pattern in order to remedy . . . perceived constitutional violations . . . , the District Court had fully performed its function of providing the appropriate remedy for previous racially discriminatory attendance patterns."[15]

The Supreme Court seemed to be saying, and later concluded it *did* say, that the student assignment aspect of desegregation in Pasadena had actually reached unitary status, meaning that such status could be realized in stages. Thus, at one point in his opinion, Justice Rehnquist noted that because of disputes over the procedure for hiring and promoting teachers, "It may well be that [school authorities] have not yet *totally achieved* the unitary system contemplated by . . . Swann."[16]

Explicitly, however, the majority did not go beyond the pronouncement that Pasadena had been in "compliance"[17] in its pupil assignments, and for the next decade lower courts interpreted unitary status as an all or nothing proposition, not realizable in increments. School districts, they held, must attain simultaneously the elements of a desegregated system specified as early as *Green*: They must end the vestiges of past discrimination not only in student assignment, but in faculty and staff appointment, facilities, transportation, and extra-curricular activities.[18] This meant that even after compliance in student assignment took place a school board not adjudged unitary in other ways still bore the burden, as in *Spangler* itself, of proving that demography was wholly responsible for adverse shifts in assignment trends, that the board's past discrimination was in no way responsible for the reseg-regation. Indeed, a Fifth Circuit panel of 1980 held, contrary to *Spangler*, that before a school district achieved unitary status it could *not* rely upon population shifts to justify attendance patterns. "Not until all vestiges of the dual system are eradicated can demographic changes constitute legal cause for racial imbalance in the schools."[19]

In any event, supervising judges, especially in the late 1970's, could often juggle desegregation plans around on the premise that school districts under their jurisdiction had yet to reach the point of compliance in assigning students. Judge McMillan for instance, had ample reason to believe that the difficulties he continued to witness in Charlotte, even after he approved a definitive desegregation plan in 1974, merited a finding of non-compliance which freed him up to entertain alterations in the plan. The situation in Charlotte, he concluded in 1979, "wholly fails to support a finding, or the promise of one, on the first essential element of a claim under the *Pasadena* decision—. . . complete implementation of a judicial remedy relating to . . . pupil assignment . . . .'Racially neutral attendance patterns' have never been achieved."[20] (Actually, Judge McMillan had ended active supervision of Charlotte in 1975. He was endorsing changes in the 1974 plan introduced by the Charlotte school board itself, and opposed by a group of parents and their children.)

The Supreme Court also expatiated somewhat on the content of the remedial burden falling on a school board. And here the justices ruled that the vestiges of segregation which must be cured to gain a declaration of unitariness could go beyond the areas delineated in *Green*. While considering a Detroit-only desegregation plan in 1977, during a later phase of *Milliken* v. *Bradley*, the Court held that remedial and compensatory education comprised a valid part of a court-ordered remedy. Chief Justice Burger brushed aside the state of Michigan's contention that such programs, for which the state in this case bore half the cost, "exceed[ed] the scope of the constitutional violation."[21] The "'condition'" violating the Constitution, Burger stressed, was "Detroit's de jure segregated school system,"[22] and the evils bred by that system were not always confined to visible manifestations such as skewed student assignment patterns or one-race faculties. "Children who have been . . . educationally and culturally set apart from the larger community will inevitably acquire habits of speech, conduct, and attitudes reflecting their cultural isolation."[23] They were "likely to acquire speech habits, for example, which vary from the environment in which they must ultimately function and compete, if they are to enter and be a part of that community."[24] The indicia of past bias "do not vanish simply by moving the child to a desegregated school," and "Federal courts need not, and cannot, close their eyes" to the underlying inequalities "which flow from a longstanding segregated system."[25]

But the *Milliken II* majority also alluded to the importance of ending judicial supervision of desegregation as expeditiously as possible. In devising and administering remedies, the chief justice noted, courts "must take into account the interests of state and local authorities in managing their own affairs."[26]

II

The Court's initial contributions to the law of unitary status seemed to point in several contrary directions. In practice, however, it was the very tangible issue of one-race schools, their elimination, and their re-emergence after compliance, which was the decisive issue faced by judges who must decide if unitary status had been achieved. The lower courts took varying views of this matter in the early and mid 1980's, as they struggled with demographic realities.

Thus, a Fifth Circuit panel declared the Houston system unitary in 1983, even though 70% of its African-American students attended schools 90% or more minority; this was a system, however, in which the African-American and Hispanic "minorities" constituted almost three-fourths of the student population.[27]

The panel dutifully placed a heavy burden upon the school board to justify this attendance pattern. Officials had "a continuing duty to eliminate the systemwide effects of earlier discrimination and to create a unitary school system untainted by the past . . . . They must demonstrate . . . that 'current segregation is in no way the result of [their] segregative actions.'"[28] The circuit then proceeded to uphold the unitary finding of the district judge, despite the fact that he completely "failed to require [Houston authorities] to show that the large number of one-race schools remaining was not due to housing patterns that were the result of [the school system's] past segregative actions."[29] The judge had even rejected plaintiffs' efforts to bear this burden themselves, by demonstrating "that earlier housing patterns resulted from official school segregation policy apart from other . . . economic and social influence."[30]

The circuit panel admitted that "[c]urrent housing patterns may still show the lingering effects of school board actions,"[31] which under the *Keyes* standard it had just endorsed would cause judgment to go against the school board. Yet the panel declined to find the district court conclusions clearly erroneous, because it purported to have discovered far the most important reason for segregated housing patterns in Houston. Such patterns were primarily a backlash against prior desegregation initiatives, "a reaction to court-ordained policies. The school attendance [situation] . . . is the result of good-faith efforts to dismantle the dual system, and not 'the result of past segregative actions.'"[32] Fear of white flight might not justify skimping on an original desegregation plan. But when the plan *produced* the demographic imbalances which undermined its effectiveness, further measures were not required according to the panel.

The judges presented no data to back up their demographic theorem, a reflection of the fact that, not unreasonably perhaps, they had thrown up their hands at the prospect of any more remedial action. "Even if some method were devised to spread white students equally among all schools in the system, 74% of the students in each school would be black and Hispanic."[33] Houston had achieved maximum feasible compliance in the panel's view, or, in any event, all the compliance it was going to achieve.

Judge Richard Matsch in Denver, backed up by the Tenth Circuit, took a different approach to unitary status, though he operated in a somewhat different demographic context.[34] Judge Matsch conceded that the Denver school board had brought itself into compliance with court orders concerning student assignment by 1976, but refused to make a unitary finding in this area because he held the board responsible for the fact that, by the time of trial in 1984, three schools had slipped out of compliance with a guideline requiring all of them to have a 34% minimum enrollment of Anglo students (in a system which was 40% Anglo and totaled fifty schools).

Population movement from Denver to its suburbs was undoubtedly one reason for the growing racial imbalance, but in treating this evidence, Judge Matsch faithfully adhered to the standards set in the Supreme Court's earlier treatment of the *Keyes* case. He refused to accept demographic trends as a sufficient explanation for the imbalance, since the proof on this matter was not absolutely airtight. In presenting their statistics to the court, he noted, the defendant's population experts failed to account for those people who had moved out of Denver, but, instead of taking up residence in the suburbs, left the Denver area altogether. This omission did not change the palpable fact that a lot of people had moved out of the city, but to Judge Matsch it rendered the data as a whole "not very helpful . . . . This court is not persuaded that demographic change is the reason for the development of racial imbalance in the schools."[35]

District Judge Frank Kaufman of Maryland, affirmed by the Fourth Circuit, took the same hawkish approach to demographic evidence, actually setting the Houston panel's approach on its head. Judge Kaufman refused to declare the Prince George's County school system unitary in 1983, mainly because he claimed that the county had never brought itself into compliance with the court's decree on student assignments, issued ten years earlier. But he suggested that in assessing future claims of unitary status he could appropriately use the very desegregation plans designed to bring this status about as evidence against its achievement. "'White flight,' resulting from a court decree issued to eliminate segregative practices," was often "related . . . to past discrimination and is a vestige of the same."[36] Consequently, the "'resegregation, resulting . . . in part, from the . . . good faith efforts of [a] School Board in implementation of [a] Court's order, amounts to . . . *de jure* segregation.'"[37]

A Fifth Circuit panel different in personnel from the one which heard the Houston case decided the same year to deny unitary status to Dallas.[38] This was due largely to the fact that a somewhat altered desegregation plan for the district, adopted after a remand from the circuit in 1978, had just come back before the panel, and there remained some dispute over its details. But the court let stand, as the basis for a later consideration of unity, the core of the plan, which left 77 schools with enrollments of 90% or more minority, out of a total of 255. (By 1981, the Dallas student population was 30% Anglo, 50% African-American, 20% Hispanic.)

This plan was a close cousin of the one which occasioned the remand to start with. Under the earlier plan, of 1976, students in grades 1–3 of the Dallas system remained in schools within their neighborhoods. High school students, as well, went to neighborhood schools, augmented by a magnet school program. Only in grades 4–8 was there a serious attempt to achieve integration.[39]

The circuit court had indicated strongly, in its 1978 remand, that it would not let anything of this sort stand, unless Dallas officials showed conclusively that they could not do any better. "We cannot properly review any student assignment plan that leaves many schools in a system one race without specific findings by the district court as to the feasibility of [the] techniques" used.[40] There were, for example, "no adequate time-and-distance studies in the record," and hence no way of knowing whether circumstances did or did not "preclude either the pairing and clustering of schools or the use of transportation to eliminate the large number of one-race schools."[41] Dallas must demonstrate, in short, maximum feasible compliance.

Five years later, however, the circuit was accepting what represented a less than strenuous implementation of its instructions by District Judge Barefoot Sanders, whose decision on remand left most of the original scheme intact by adopting a highly solicitous attitude toward the district's difficulties in achieving more meaningful desegregation. In evaluating the busing issue, for example, Judge Sanders noted that such complete time studies as existed in Dallas, for 32 elementary school routes in the city, showed that only nine of them involved total traveling time of a half hour or less. "By contrast," the judge called attention to an earlier Fifth Circuit decision in Atlanta which refused to consider busing feasible where "the distance would require total times of 40 minutes or more."[42] He also noted that in the Dayton case the Sixth Circuit held that no student be transported for a time to exceed twenty minutes. Where he neglected to look was into *Swann*, and its approval of trips for elementary school students totaling 35 minutes each way.

Both Judge Sanders and the circuit panel were obliged to deal in this area with a development becoming more pronounced in the 1980's, protests from African-American intervenors who wanted no busing at all. A group in Dallas called the Black Coalition urged that mandatory transportation be ended for African-American youngsters in grades 1–8, and that they be returned to their neighborhood schools. "The Coalition," Judge Sanders noted, "prefers remedies designed to improve educational quality . . . as alternatives to remedies that require pupil assignments to non-contiguous attendance zones and mandatory transportation."[43]

Sanders rejected this approach, and the circuit agreed, since both still purported to subscribe to the jurisprudence of *Green*, and were "[u]nable to reconcile the resegregative aspects of the [Black Coalition] plan with traditional constitutional principles favoring maximum desegregation."[44]

Despite this victory, the Dallas plaintiffs deplored (vainly) Judge Sanders' approach on remand, but Justice Lewis Powell had seen no need for remand in the first place. Dissenting from a denial of certiorari in 1980, when Dallas officials sought Supreme Court review of the Fifth Circuit's 1978 action, Justice Powell expanded on the view he had stated in *Keyes*.[45]

The circuit court remand, he felt, drew on prior Supreme Court jurisprudence, placing its emphasis, therefore, "almost entirely on the one-race schools remaining in the [Dallas] School District,"[46] and the school authorities' putative responsibility for them. Yet very obviously, in Dallas, and in "any major metropolitan school district . . . .the principal cause of segregation in the schools is residential segregation, which results . . . from demographic and economic conditions over which school authorities have no control."[47]

To hold these authorities responsible for black schools in Dallas was to violate the cardinal principle governing equitable remedies, that the "constitutional deprivation must be identified accurately, and the remedy must be related closely to that deprivation."[48] The Dallas remand, Powell argued, also flew in the face of *Davis'* notion that the "'measure of any desegregation plan is its effectiveness,'"[49] a phrase which he was not shy about relating to white fears and their effect on attempts to achieve maximum compliance. Anticipation of white flight must not drive desegregation plans, but neither should judges blink reality in designing them. "A court must act decisively to remove purposeful segregation, but it also must avoid the danger of inciting resegregation by unduly disrupting the public schools."[50]   The reality in Dallas was that Anglo student population had been cut in half between 1971 and the end of the decade. "In view of these . . . changes, the futility of administering larger doses of a remedy that has failed is self-evident."[51] The quest for racial balance "at any cost," Powell concluded, "is without constitutional or social justification."[52]

III

The *Swann-Keyes* presumptions, then, could buttress the claims of plaintiffs that unitary status had not been achieved in a school system, because one-race schools remained. But in the new environment of the 1980's, these presumptions pointed toward a more radical contention—one congruent with, indeed initially associated with, the deeper insight into educational segregation for which they were said to be a pretext—the contention that the vast majority of school districts under court order were incapable of achieving unitary status in the foreseeable future.

The final phases of the Norfolk case, commencing in 1983, exposed this pattern of views. Norfolk authorities, released since 1975 from active court supervision, proposed to sharply curtail the cross-district busing of elementary school students, and to place them in neighborhood schools. They asked the district court's permission for this arrangement, and over plaintiffs' objections, Chief Judge John MacKenzie granted it.[53] Judge MacKenzie claimed that eight years earlier, when relinquishing day to day supervision, he had declared Norfolk to be a unitary system in all respects. And once this status was obtained, he noted, the slate was obviously wiped clean. School officials could adopt any attendance plan they wished, including neighborhood zoning. Such a plan could be rejected only if it was inspired by overt discriminatory intent, which the judge did not find to be the case.

On appeal, the Norfolk plaintiffs (now the appellants) denied that Judge MacKenzie's 1975 order was a valid declaration of unitariness, partly because the order did not contain "any determinations of fact" to back up its conclusion.[54]

More fundamentally, however, appellants contended that Norfolk lay farther from unitary status, and a permissible return to neighborhood zoning, than was indicated by the technical defects in an eight year old court decree. This was mainly because segregated schools, they argued, still reproduced the evils of a racist system not sufficiently effaced by only a third of a generation of racial mixing. The proposed neighborhood plan would "impede the dismantling of Norfolk's dual school system, and its effect, by inflicting adverse psychological and educational harm upon the 40% of black elementary students assigned [under this plan] to schools where black enrollment exceeds 95%."[55] In this regard, the brief pointed to *Brown's* "explicit finding that racial segregation inflicts upon black children 'a feeling of inferiority as to their status in the community,'" and to *Milliken II's* acknowledgement of the fact that "'children who have been . . . educationally and culturally set apart from the larger community will inevitably acquire habits of speech, conduct, and attitudes reflecting their cultural isolation.'"[56]

The brief then summarized the trial testimony of psychologists and educators who affirmed that a resumption of neighborhood zoning "will cause psychological harm to black children at a time when they are most susceptible to learning, . . . will adversely affect racial attitudes, and . . . will create psychological distance between black and white schoolchildren."[57] Appellants also introduced evidence, hotly disputed as usual, which purported to show that integration was reducing the achievement gap between white and African-American pupils, and "that continued implementation of the current busing program"[58] would further narrow the disparity.

But accompanying this evocation of what the partisans of continued integration surely must have known to be overall their strongest and most profound set of claims, was the line of argument which, despite its strained, not to say fantastical quality, would play the most prominent role in future litigation on unitary status, because it most accurately reflected the misshapen nature of desegregation law.

The very structure of Norfolk and its school system, appellants contended, meant that it could not possibly be unitary under the *Swann-Keyes* presumptions. For according to these presumptions, school authorities of a formerly de jure system were deemed responsible for the basic housing patterns in that system; it was assumed that residential segregation was a vestige of past discrimination. "One basic finding in *Swann* is that school policies . . . 'may well promote segregated residential patterns.' . . . Because of [this] ripple effect of school segregation upon housing segregation, . . . neighborhood school plans . . . are deemed inadequate when they 'fail to counteract the continuing effects of past school segregation.' . . ."[59]

Thus any return to a neighborhood plan which produced segregated schools in a district once de jure represented a current manifestation of the old dual system, proving that the present system was not yet unitary. It could only become unitary when a proposed reorganization of school attendance patterns along neighborhood lines did not result in renewed racial separation, when, in effect, therefore, residential segregation itself was effaced in a community. And in Norfolk, the "undisputed evidence"[60] showed that this would be very far from the case. "These discriminatory results of the Board's action in terminating the busing desegregation program and adopting a neighborhood . . . plan" violated ipso facto "its obligation" to guarantee that pupil assignment policies "do not serve to perpetuate or re-establish the dual system."[61]

Appearing amicus curiae in behalf of Norfolk, William Bradford Reynolds called attention to the indefinite run which appellants' measure of unitariness would institute. "In effect, . . . [they] are arguing that the school system is not yet unitary because the Board has failed to correct housing patterns it did not create and can do nothing about."[62] Their argument on appeal "amounts to nothing more than a belated attempt to challenge the adequacy of the relief previously entered by this Court."[63]

The Fourth Circuit Court of Appeals upheld the lower court and freed Norfolk to resegregate its public schools.[64]

IV

The demographic claims of the Norfolk appellants were consistent with precedent, minimally related to urban realities, and doomed to failure in the environment of the 1980's. This was illustrated by the case which explored the competing arguments about residential causation most completely, and brought them finally to the bar of the Supreme Court. Appropriately enough, the case was *Dowell* v. *School Board of Oklahoma City*.

Even after Judge Luther Bohanon's pathbreaking decision in 1965, Oklahoma City school authorities still dithered over adopting an acceptable desegregation plan. In 1972, following *Swann*, the judge forced one on them, designed by the ubiquitous Dr. Finger. Under the Finger plan, all of the majority black elementary schools in the district, located almost exclusively in the center city, were converted into fifth grade centers, while the majority white schools served grades 1–4. White students attended their neighborhood schools for the first four grades, along with African-American pupils bused in from the areas where the fifth grade centers were located. The process was reversed for fifth graders. Elementary schools located in integrated neighborhoods constituted an exception to this rule. They were designated as "stand alone" schools, and encompassed grades 1–5. Middle and high schools in the city were desegregated by restructuring of attendance zones.

In 1977, Judge Bohanon relinquished jurisdiction and terminated the case. The school board continued to implement the original desegregation plan into the 1980's, though, until problems arose. By 1984, a dozen new elementary schools had qualified for "stand alone" status, which might have seemed like an encouraging sign. Since most of these "naturally integrated" schools were located in formerly white neighborhoods near the central city, however, this development increased the busing burden on African-American youngsters in the still segregated center area, who now were sent to schools farther to the north and west.

Under these circumstances, the school board decided to end busing and return to neighborhood schools for grades 1–4, establishing city-wide, at the same time, a racially balanced set of fifth grade centers. The new plan would produce eleven schools 90% or more black, and 22 which were 90% or more white (out of a total of 64). The identifiably black schools were the same ones which had been segregated by law in the pre *Brown* era.

The erstwhile plaintiffs protested this action and sought to reopen the case, but Judge Bohanon turned down their request. When he terminated the case in 1977, he now stated, he had "recognized that a 'unitary system' had been 'accomplished'" in Oklahoma City in all respects.[65] The plaintiffs were not entitled to additional relief, therefore, unless they could prove that the new student assignments had been adopted with discriminatory intent, and the burden rested on them to do so. "The existence of racially identifiable schools is not unconstitutional without a showing that such schools were created for the purpose of discriminating on the basis of race," and the "presence of [such] discriminatory intent may not be inferred solely from the disproportionate impact of a particular measure upon one race."[66] There was no reason, in Judge Bohanon's view, for reopening the litigation, and the neighborhood plan went into effect in September, 1985.

But the next year, a panel of the Tenth Circuit Court of Appeals, riding its own particular hobbyhorse in this area of the law, overruled Judge Bohanon. Speaking for the three judge panel, Judge John Moore noted that even though Bohanon terminated the Oklahoma City case in 1977, he had not, at the same time, dissolved the original 1972 desegregation order, which was in the form of a mandatory injunction forbidding future illegal conduct. The injunction was still in effect, therefore, and so the Tenth Circuit remanded the case to Judge Bohanon for hearings on whether it should be dissolved. In these hearings, the circuit ordered, he must "recast the burden of proof"[67] and place it upon the school board.

Judge Bohanon was very disappointed by the Tenth Circuit's action. "I was of the firm belief and conviction," he wrote in his as yet unpublished autobiography,

> that my order . . . terminating Federal Court supervision of the school board, which was based upon the creation of a unitary school district, freed the school board to take any action within its jurisdiction until a showing that the school board had willfully and intentionally discriminated against black students . . . .

> There can be no question that the order remanding for rehearing was in error and without merit. It was devastating to the Oklahoma City School Board and a revolting situation for the district court. In all my judicial work, I have never been so upset and saddened as I was with the circuit court's order of June 6, 1986 . . . . [It was] the most shocking order I had ever received from an appellate court.[68]

"Like a good soldier, however," Judge Bohanon "followed the order" of the appellate court.[69] He treated the court order as an invitation to conduct a new inquiry into whether Oklahoma City satisfied the *Green* factors. After an eight day trial in June of 1987, the judge ruled that the school board had met its burden of proving that the city ran a unitary school system in 1977, when jurisdiction was terminated, and continued to do so when the neighborhood plan was instituted in 1985.[70]

Responding to the *Swann-Keyes* presumptions, Bohanon asserted flatly that the racial imbalance which would come from a return to neighborhood zoning flowed entirely from forces apart from the actions of education officials, and was beyond their power to correct. Since desegregation was instituted, "the Oklahoma City Board of Education has taken absolutely no action which has caused or contributed to the patterns of . . . residential segregation which presently exist . . . . Neither this court nor the . . . Board of Education can govern and control where people choose to live."[71]

The board had also met the burden of demonstrating that its neighborhood plan was not motivated by discrimination. Judge Bohanon proceeded to dissolve the injunctive order.

Once again, a circuit panel disagreed, Judge Jack Baldock dissenting. This case, Judge Moore argued, was "not so much . . . one dealing with desegregation . . . as one dealing with the proper application of the federal law on injunctive remedies."[72] As such, it followed the principle that an injunction in a school controversy could not be dissolved, even *after* a finding of unitariness, unless the "party subject to the decree" did nothing less than demonstrate that "'the dangers the decree was meant to foreclose . . . have disappeared.' "[73] Accordingly, "compliance alone" could not be "the basis for . . . dissolving an injunction."[74]

Divorced from the mysteries of injunction law, the Tenth Circuit standard seemed to mean that a formerly de jure system was not really unitary so long as it could feasibly maintain a court-ordered desegregation plan, irrespective of the exact causal relationship which might exist between past discrimination and present demographic realities. This command, the circuit panel apparently felt, stemmed from the special symbolism conveyed by one-race schools in a community where they were once mandatory.

The record in Oklahoma City did "not support a return to . . . neighborhood schools in the elementary grades because the . . . neighborhoods remain predominantly white and predominantly black," and because retention of the Finger plan, with modifications, was "achievable without extreme disruption" of the school system[75]. Under these circumstances, it was illegal to adopt a neighborhood plan which "restores the effects of *past* discriminatory intent . . . by recreating racially identifiable elementary schools"; continuing to avoid this racial identification in Oklahoma City "does not overburden *Swann*'s remedial baggage."[76]

The circuit panel majority ordered the desegregation decree reinstated in the city and the neighborhood arrangement dismantled. Not surprisingly, in light of its logic, Judge Moore's opinion suggested, though rather ambiguously, that the finding of unitary status by Judge Bohanon was mistaken in the first place.[77] (A few days after the circuit court decision, Judge Bohanon was hospitalized with chest pains, and the 86 year old jurist successfully underwent heart bypass surgery.)

The Supreme Court accepted certiorari in *Dowell* on March 26, 1990, and heard the case on October 2. This was a decidedly different Court from the one which heard *Dayton* and *Columbus*, yet not as radically altered on school law as one might suppose. Three of the justices now gone —Potter Stewart, Lewis Powell, and Chief Justice Burger—were dissenters in *Dayton*. They would likely have been as ill-disposed by this time to continued busing as two of their successors—Antonin Scalia and Anthony Kennedy—and even more ill-disposed than one of them, Sandra Day O'Connor, turned out to be. Justice David Souter, who replaced Justice Brennan in October, 1990, did not participate in *Dowell*.

In their briefs and oral arguments the Oklahoma City plaintiffs (now the respondents) urged affirmance of the Tenth Circuit's "injunction" approach to the case. They also called attention to the undoubted role which "*all* governmental actions"[78] played in producing the segregated neighborhoods of Oklahoma City. But despairing, no doubt, of the outcome of a controversy argued on such premises, respondents articulated, in their purest form, the implications for unitary status which grew out of *Swann* and *Keyes*. "Any test for modifying a school desegregation decree," they reminded the justices, "must, at the least, be consistent with the general remedial principles announced" in the former.[79] And *Swann* had decreed that "when substantially one-race schools persist *or are reintroduced* in a school system 'with a history of segregation,' . . . 'the burden . . . [is] upon the *school authorities* to satisfy the court that their racial composition is not the result of present or past discriminatory action *on their part.*'"[80]

The Oklahoma City school board "neither did nor could meet that burden." There was "simply no evidence in this record that . . . demonstrat[es] that the natural effects of [board] policies from statehood to 1972 have been dissipated."[81] In fact, the district court itself held in 1965 and again in 1972 "that neighborhood schools could *not* be used [in the city] precisely because they exacerbated housing segregation by destroying integrated neighborhoods."[82] How could Judge Bohanon believe "that in a mere five to thirteen years, by 1977 or 1985," the past discrimination contributing to such segregation "had become attenuated to the point that the school board could revert to precisely the same school zones that . . . helped to create the segregation in the first place?"[83] Under applicable constitutional doctrine, "the existing residential segregation that produced the ten all-Afro-American schools was linked to the residential segregation found by the district court to be caused by official actions."[84]

At the conference on *Dowell*, all eight justices who heard the case agreed, as expected, that an injunction could not outlast a bona fide declaration of unitary status. But there the unanimity ended. A majority of five, led by Chief Justice William Rehnquist, voted to reverse the circuit court, though remanding the case to Judge Bohanon once again, with instructions to decide yet again whether he should terminate the injunction he had already terminated earlier. Justices Thurgood Marshall, Harry Blackmun, and John Paul Stevens favored sustaining the circuit, while recasting the controversy in Oklahoma City into one, not over the durability of injunctions, but over the standards which should determine when a genuinely unitary system existed in the district.

The chief justices's draft opinion in *Dowell*, circulated to the Court on November 3, 1990, was almost identical to what became the final product.[85] On behalf of all of his colleagues, he held that in Oklahoma City, or in any community under court order, a finding by a court that the district "was being operated in compliance with the commands of the Equal Protection Clause of the Fourteenth Amendment, and that it was unlikely that the Board would return to its former ways, would be a finding that the purposes of the desegregation litigation had been fully achieved. No additional showing . . . is required of the Board."[86]

The chief's reversal of the Tenth Circuit, and his suggestions for the remand, formed the bane of contention. Rehnquist obviously wished to terminate judicial control of school systems as quickly as possible. Desegregation devices, he was at pains to point out, "are not intended to operate in perpetuity."[87] He also took a dim view of the alleged relationships between housing and school separation, and the *Swann-Keyes* presumptions which magnified them. Thus, on remand, Rehnquist ordered, the "District Court should address itself to whether the Board . . . complied in good faith with the desegregation decree since it was entered, and whether the vestiges of past discrimination [have] been eliminated *to the extent practicable*."[88]

A footnote to this passage conveyed a sympathy for Judge Bohanon's original conclusions. The "District Court," it noted, "earlier found that present residential segregation in Oklahoma City was the result of private decisionmaking and economics, and that it was too attenuated to be a vestige of former school segregation."[89]

This footnote was the object of some debate between Rehnquist and two of his conference allies. Justice Byron White wrote to the chief on December 4, and, in apparent repudiation of his views in *Dayton* and *Columbus*, expressed a desire to see the footnote fleshed out by what amounted to an outright rejection of the *Swann-Keyes* presumptions. "I hope you will find it possible," White told his colleague, "to say expressly that on remand, residential segregation should not be treated as a vestige of the prior illegally segregated school system. Otherwise, I am with you."[90]

But Justice Sandra Day O'Connor, who originally wanted the case reargued,[91] told Rehnquist that she would be willing to go along with his draft only if he removed the footnote. "We granted cert in this case," she pointed out to the chief, in order to determine whether the Tenth Circuit's standard was "the proper test for dissolution of a school desegregation injunction."[92] The Court's attention was not adequately focused, therefore, on the "status of residential segregation as a vestige of discrimination, ...probably the single most contentious and complicated aspect of the dissolution question." Yet, "I fear that the footnote sends unwarranted signals concerning an issue the Court is not at present prepared to resolve . . . . I hope that in this case, we [w]ould avoid saying too much."[93]

Writing to Justice White on December 13, 1990, Rehnquist noted ruefully that "[o]ne does [not] have to have had a course in advanced mathematics to see that I am on the horns of a dilemma."[94] To preserve his majority, he told White, he had talked Justice O'Connor into retaining the footnote, "but not saying anything more about it." The "fairest" (and obviously the most practical) "thing to do at this point,"[95] the chief justice felt, was to decline White's suggestions and to "leave the opinion the way it is as to residential segregation."[96] The decision in *School Board of Oklahoma City* v. *Dowell* came down on January 15, 1991, the birthday of Dr. Martin Luther King, Jr.

Justice Marshall's dissent, his final opinion, as it turned out, on school desegregation, transposed Judge Moore's conclusions about Oklahoma City into the language of the law of unitary status. More important, in explicating the law, this last effort from the architect of *Brown* gave imperishable expression to the view of American history and society which lay behind the "integrationist" interpretation of that decision.

Oklahoma City had not achieved unitariness, Marshall contended, and the court of appeals was correct to continue the desegregation injunction, because "it is clear on this record that removal of the decree will result in a significant number of racially identifiable schools that could be eliminated."[97] Even the local authorities did "not argue that further desegregation of the one-race schools in its system is unworkable."[98]

These one-race schools, Marshall felt, were a demographic fallout from past actions of the school board to a greater degree than the chief justice was willing to concede. "The record in this case amply demonstrates [the] form of complicity in residential segregation on the part of the Board" sketched out in *Swann* and *Keyes*, where it was "well established that school segregation 'may have a profound reciprocal effect on the racial composition of residential neighborhoods.'"[99] But the continued existence of black schools perpetuated more subtle and hurtful forces.

> Our pointed focus in Brown I upon the stigmatic injury caused by segregated schools explains our unflagging insistence that formerly de jure segregated school districts extinguish all vestiges of school segregation. The concept of stigma also gives us guidance as to what conditions must be eliminated before a decree can be deemed to have served its purpose
> . . . .
>
> [T]he Equal Protection Clause demands elimination of every indicium of a "[r]acial[ly] identifi[able]" school system that will inflict the stigmatizing injury that Brown I sought to cure . . . .
>
> [And] [j]ust as [this] is central to the standard for evaluating the formation of a desegregation decree, so should the stigmatic injury associated with segregated schools be central to the standard for dissolving a decree.[100]

The final remand in *Dowell*, for which Judge Bohanon refused to hold a new trial, dramatized the limits of the *Swann-Keyes* presumptions, always shaky from an empirical standpoint, and now confronting a judiciary weary of the strictures they imposed. The *Dowell* plaintiffs persisted in the arguments presented to the Supreme Court. Neighborhood schools, they insisted, were still unconstitutional in Oklahoma City because the segregation they produced showed school authorities had not met their "burden," the burden of proving that racial composition in these schools was "not the result of present or past discriminatory action on their part."

This prodding caused Judge Bohanon to underline the view which he claimed to have always held with regard to urban housing separation, in common with most demographic experts. "[R]esidential segregation in Oklahoma City," he argued, "would have arisen absent the Board's past discriminatory policies, just as it has in virtually every other American city."[101] It was true that the neighborhood school policy adopted by the board in the 1950's added to residential segregation, when white families moved out of neighborhoods which were in the process of racial change, rather than have their children attend increasingly black schools. But this was only a blip on a demographic screen dominated by the acts of other public agencies, and of private institutions.

These larger segregatory patterns were gradually disappearing, Bohanon believed, under the impact of state and federal fair housing laws. The evidence revealed "high black mobility and major increases in residential integration since 1960."[102] If considerable segregation remained in Oklahoma City, it was "caused by the private choices of blacks and whites, based on such factors as economic status, . . . personal preferences, and social and neighborhood relationships."[103]

The judge conceded the possibility that the economic disparities which led to residential separation might flow from prior discrimination, but claimed that the plaintiffs had not presented enough evidence to prove this point. That the school board had played a prominent role in creating the situation he repeatedly dismissed as preposterous. "Neither the original pattern of residential segregation nor the residential segregation that remains today was . . . caused by past *de jure* school segregation in any significant way . . . . No one can explain how discriminatory Board policies prior to 1965 could possibly have caused the . . . pattern of residential segregation, and much greater integration, existing in Oklahoma City today."[104] To accept the plaintiffs' far-fetched position on demographic causation "would likely force busing to continue in Oklahoma City for decades and decades, if not in perpetuity."[105]

Judge Bohanon reaffirmed his finding of unitary status. Two years later, the Tenth Circuit finally upheld him.[106] The case did not go the Supreme Court again. In the meantime, the judge had gone on to render important decisions dealing with prison reform, Indian land rights, and the authority of the Food and Drug Administration to ban allegedly cancer-fighting drugs such as laetrile.[107] As one observer in Oklahoma noted, "Predictions were [when Luther Bohanon was appointed] that he wouldn't be much of a federal judge, perhaps even a disaster. He proved instead to be a disaster for segregationists, for Oklahoma's lock-'em-up Legislature, for those who disdain the Constitution except when it cuts their way."[108]

V

What was implicit in the *Dowell* footnote was made very explicit in the Court's next major decision on unitary school systems—*Freeman* v. *Pitts*. The majority opinion in *Freeman* is most significant for transmuting the intimations of *Spangler* into settled constitutional doctrine, holding that school officials might earn unitary status by degrees: their accomplishments in the areas of transportation and extracurricular activities might gain them freedom from judicial supervision, even as they still struggled to satisfy court orders concerning faculty desegregation. But *Freeman*'s discussion of the pivotal issue of student assignment was of even greater import, perhaps, than its affirmation of gradualism. The majority opinion clearly relaxed, indeed arguably repudiated, the presumptive rigors of the past.

Freeman v. *Pitts* involved the school system of De Kalb County, Georgia (suburban Atlanta), which had operated under a court-ordered neighborhood desegregation plan since 1969. In 1986, officials sought from the district court a declaration of unitary status and a release from further judicial scrutiny. By this time, 50% of the county's African-American students attended schools more than 90% black, in a system which was 47% black.

In determining the issue of unitariness, Judge William O'Kelley announced that he would hew to the doctrinal standards set up by past Supreme Court decisions. The defendant school board, he stressed, must meet its "burden of proof regarding whether the De Kalb County School System is now a unitary system."[109] In the student assignment area, this would mean, presumably, that the board must demonstrate that none of its past actions were a factor in causing present segregation. But in actually evaluating student assignment, Judge O'Kelley operated on the belief that the hard demographic realities in De Kalb County precluded the possibility that the school board had anything to do with the current segregated situation. A mere recitation of the population shifts in the county over the previous decade seemed to clinch the case, as far as he was concerned.

In 1970, he noted, 7,615 African-Americans lived in the northern part of De Kalb County, 11,508 in the southern part. Ten years later, the black population had increased to 15,365 in the north, but had gone to 87,583 in the south. Meanwhile, 37,000 white residents moved out of southern De Kalb County, while the white population in the north continued to grow. (Because of this population arrangement, cross-district busing was not thought feasible by either side to the controversy.)

Total elementary school enrollment in the county declined by 15% from 1976 to 1986, while black enrollment increased by 86%. High school enrollment went down by 16%, while black enrollment rose 119%. In this context, Judge O'Kelley did not seriously consider whether a school board could have played a tangible role in such a vast demographic transformation. It was obvious to him that the "rapid population shifts in De Kalb County were not caused by any action on the part of the [county school system]."[110]

The judge concluded "that the De Kalb County School System has done everything that was reasonable under the circumstances to achieve maximum practical desegregation in [student placement]."[111] He then proceeded to follow a path taken for the first time in 1987 by an appeals court panel in the Boston school case, and to adopt an incremental approach to the question of whether the county had achieved unitary status. Thus, O'Kelley declared it unitary in student assignment, as well as with regard to physical facilities, transportation, and extracurricular activities, but did find that authorities must do more to desegregate faculties. In doing so, he also accepted plaintiffs' argument that the quality of education for African-American students in De Kalb County was lower than for whites, because white schools had more experienced teachers with a greater percentage of advanced degrees, and were the beneficiaries of higher per pupil expenditures, which the judge ordered equalized. Interestingly enough, the plaintiffs' case for educational inequality consisted almost exclusively of material measures of this type, while it was the school board, in reply, which offered data showing "that black students who have been in the [De Kalb system] for two years achieve greater gains than white students on the Iowa Tests of Basic Skills."[112]

A Fifth Circuit panel rejected the notion that unitary status could come incrementally. "A school system," it proclaimed, "achieves unitary status or it does not. We will not permit resegregation in a school system that has not eliminated all vestiges of a dual system."[113] Until this was accomplished, the panel held, contradicting the Supreme Court's view in *Spangler*, De Kalb officials bore the responsibility of "eradicat[ing] segregation caused by demographic changes."[114] To achieve this goal, the school board and the district judge must embrace even those actions which "'may be administratively awkward, inconvenient, and . . . bizarre.'"[115] This included augmented busing, *"regardless of whether the plaintiffs support such a proposal."*[116]

In the Supreme Court, the De Kalb plaintiffs (now the respondents) offered a spirited factual critique of the district court's conclusions on student assignment, even as they defended the circuit's all or nothing approach to the issue of unitary status. The De Kalb school system, they argued, as they had at trial, was never a unitary system; from the beginning two elementary schools had majority black enrollments, serving a third of the African-American children (who totaled at that time only 6.2% of the elementary school population). Furthermore, the decisive resegregation of the system, it was claimed, took place between 1969 and 1975, before the really massive wave of population shifts hit the county. By the latter year, 73% of African-American youngsters attended majority black elementary schools, in a system where they still comprised less than 20% of the elementary school total. Students attending majority black high schools went from zero in 1969 to 51% in 1975, when they formed 13.9% of the high school population.

But the gravamen of respondents' case rested on Judge O'Kelley's failure to use *Swann* and *Keyes* for evaluating student assignment patterns. "Some portions of the district court's opinion" paid "lip service" to the proposition that the burden of proof in a school desegregation case lay with the original violators, but the court had not in fact "place[d] the burden" where it belonged.[117] Above all, O'Kelley failed to act on the principle that "in a formerly segregated school system, there is a presumption that current segregation was caused by prior segregation."[118] The "'systemwide nature'" of the past violations in De Kalb County "'furnished *prima facie* proof that current segregation . . . was caused at least in part by prior intentionally segregative acts.'"[119] Since the "presumption against [one-race] schools" was "applicable in this case," the De Kalb officials should have been required to rigorously "justify [such] schools."[120]

Respondents used analogous reasoning to support their claim that the elements comprising unitary status were inseparable from one another. The error of the district judge "in failing to consider the interconnectedness of the various facets of [the De Kalb] school system" was "similar to [the error] identified in *Keyes*."[121] In the Denver case, the Court had ruled that the plaintiffs need not "'bear the burden of proving . . . *de jure* segregation as to each and every school,'" because "'a finding of intentionally segregative school board actions in a meaningful portion of a school system . . . creates a presumption that other segregated schooling . . . is not adventitious.'"[122] What was true on a geographic basis, the respondents maintained, "applies even more strongly to segregation in one facet of a school system. It defies common sense to suppose that a school district . . . that for 20 years has engaged in bad faith defiance of the district court's orders in some areas has during that same time been acting in good faith to totally disestablish all vestiges of segregation in student assignment . . . ."[123]

Justice Anthony Kennedy's majority opinion in *Freeman* v. *Pitts* overruled the Fifth Circuit by making "explicit the rationale that was central in Spangler. A federal court in a school desegregation case has the discretion to order an incremental or partial withdrawal of its supervision and control."[124] It could relinquish jurisdiction over something such as student assignment, while retaining surveillance in other areas, so long as "retention of judicial control" in assignment was no longer "necessary or practicable to achieve compliance in [the] other facets of the school system."[125] De Kalb County, Kennedy held, had achieved unitary status in its student patterns, and "[t]here was no showing" that retention of the desegregation plan in this area "was an appropriate mechanism to cure other deficiencies," such as in faculty placement.[126]

In coming to these conclusions, Justice Kennedy clearly indicated his approval of the district court's analysis. It was true, he admitted, that a school system seeking a declaration of unitary status for its student assignments "bears the burden of showing that any current imbalance is not traceable, in a proximate way, to the prior violation."[127] But Judge O'Kelley's findings to this effect were sound, and "consistent with the mobility that is a distinct characteristic of our society."[128]

Fundamental demographic changes in school districts, and in the resulting student enrollment, were "inevitable"[129] in contemporary America, Justice Kennedy felt. In the year 1987–1988 alone, he pointed out, over forty million people changed their residences, over a third moving to different counties, and six million moving to a new state. Clearly, past school board actions could not account significantly for these extensive migrations, and judges were not responsible for coping with them. "It is beyond the authority and beyond the practical ability of the federal courts to try to counteract these kinds of continuous and massive demographic shifts. To attempt such results would require ongoing and never-ending supervision by the courts of school districts simply because they were once de jure segregated."[130]

Justice Kennedy's view on residential segregation accomplished in practice what his colleague, Antonin Scalia, and Solicitor General Kenneth Starr, sought to bring about in a more formal manner. Starr's amicus curiae brief in *Freeman* argued that skepticism about the demographic effects of school board actions be codified into an evidentiary rule for desegregation cases. "We suggest that by the time a school district . . . has removed all aspects of the [actual] dual school system, the persistence of . . . imbalances in other areas of society—whatever their initial cause— must be considered, *as a matter of law*, 'too attenuated to be a vestige of former school segregation.'"[131] Desegregation decrees were "not properly designed to alter features not inherent in the school system, such as uneven residential distribution or disparities in income."[132]

Justice Scalia also suggested that the Court promulgate a new legal structure for school desegregation cases, to do more easily what Justice Kennedy had already done effortlessly enough. Scalia felt the time had come to jettison the demand that school boards seeking unitary status in student assignment demonstrate "that no portion of [a] current racial imbalance is a remnant of prior de jure discrimination."[133]

The Court had started on this path in *Green*. And while even then, this "presumption was extraordinary in law," the recency of the violations being addressed, and the recalcitrance of southern school authorities, may have justified such "effectively irrebuttable" suppositions.[134]

But "it is now 25 years later," Scalia noted.[135] The Court must frankly admit "that it has become absurd to assume, without further proof, that violations of the Constitution dating from the days when Lyndon Johnson was President . . . continue to have an appreciable effect upon current operation of schools."[136] Logic and equity demanded that the jurisprudence of school cases "revert to the ordinary principles of our law . . . : that plaintiffs alleging equal protection violations must prove intent and causation and not merely the existence of racial disparity."[137]

Justice Kennedy remanded *Freeman* to the court of appeals. "It should determine what issues are open for its further consideration . . . ."[138] His opinion did not point to any reassessment of the issue of student assignment.

Like *Dowell*, however, *Freeman* v. *Pitts* was composed in equal parts of unanimity and discord. While all of the eight justices participating (Justice Thomas did not) agreed that unitary status could be achieved incrementally, only half of them endorsed Justice Kennedy's treatment of the student assignment aspect of the case (Scalia, White, and the chief). Justice David Souter concurred in Kennedy's opinion, giving it a majority of the Court, but added some cautionary words reminding his colleagues of the fact that the "dual school system itself" could be "a cause of the demographic shifts with which [a] district court is faced when considering a partial relinquishment of supervision."[139]

Justice Harry Blackmun, joined by Justices John Paul Stevens and Sandra Day O'Connor, refused to sign the majority opinion. Justice Blackmun concurred in the Court's judgement, since "I agree that in some circumstances the District Court need not interfere with a particular portion of [a] school system, even while . . . it must retain jurisdiction over the entire system until all vestiges of state-imposed segregation have been eliminated."[140]

But Blackmun strongly deplored the majority's friendliness toward the district court analysis of student assignment. Like respondents, he disputed many of Judge O'Kelley's factual findings in this area, but also held to the old-time religion as the basis for his critique. "Close examination" of the one-race schools in De Kalb County, he suggested, might reveal that "purely private preferences in housing may in fact have been created . . . by actions of the school district."[141] Then came a statement of the precedential tool for treating these suppositions.

> "People gravitate toward school facilities, just as schools are located in response to the needs of people. The location of schools may thus influence the patterns of residential development of a metropolitan area and have important impact on composition of inner-city neighborhoods." Swann, 402 US, at 20–21.[142]

Under the "foregoing principles," Justice Blackmun "would remand for the Court of Appeals to review . . . the District Court's finding that [De Kalb County] has met its burden of proving the racially identifiable schools are in no way the result of past segregative action."[143] Justice Blackmun continued to lean on a reed which had never been very strong, except as it was buttressed by more resilient social and constitutional materials.

VI

Freeman v. *Pitts* also suggested that plaintiffs in school cases no longer believed judges put much stock in the view of *Brown* urging integration on the basis of empirical evidence purporting to demonstrate that it raised the achievement levels of African-American students. Not only had the De Kalb County plaintiffs appealed to Judge O'Kelley in largely material terms when discussing educational inequality. Their Supreme Court brief in the case paid no attention to an amicus brief filed by a coalition of social interest groups, including the NAACP, the Children's Defense Fund, and the Southern Christian Leadership Conference, a document containing as its appendix a new "Social Science Statement" on school integration.

The statement drew on a number of influential studies of the 1980's, which had given renewed credibility to the view that "Desegregation is generally associated with moderate gains in the achievement of black students and the achievement of white students is typically unaffected."[144] The most far-reaching of these studies, published by Robert Crain and Rita Mahard in 1983, provided a meta-analysis of 93 monographs on the effect of integration on black academic progress; it concluded that achievement benefited, though the greatest effects were confined to the earliest grades.

As before, however, there was a plethora of data supporting different conclusions. A competing meta-study, published by the National Institute of Education in 1984, found that integration had no effects on math achievement among African-American youngsters, and only minimal effects on reading accomplishment.

> Desegregation did not cause any decrease in black achievement. On the average, desegregation did not cause an increase in achievement in mathematics. Desegregation increased mean reading levels. The gain reliably differed from zero and was estimated to be between two and six weeks [of a school year] across the studies examined . . . . The *median* gains were almost always greater than zero but were lower than the means and did not reliably differ from zero . . . .[145]

The debate between opposing statistical data and regression models, intensified by *Swann* and *Keyes*, went on.

The Norfolk case, as noted, had brought these scholarly controversies into the courtroom. In seeking to prevent the return of neighborhood schools to the city in

1982, the plaintiffs produced a study by Michigan State University sociologist Robert Green, arguing against the scuttling of an integration plan which, according to his evidence, raised black achievement. The Norfolk board responded with a study by Professor David Armor. It showed that achievement levels for both black and white students declined after cross-district busing was instituted in 1970, and did not regain pre-desegregation levels until 1978. The improvement in African-Americans' achievement which did occur by the early eighties, Armor maintained, was due, in large part, to intensive instructional programs initiated in 1979.[146]

Neither Judge MacKenzie nor the Fourth Circuit had paid any attention to these scholarly disputes. Justice Kennedy's majority opinion in *Freeman* said nothing of the NAACP brief.

Indeed, one perceptive observer had become convinced as early as 1982 that the evidence gathered by social science would never bear the burden of proving the denial of equal educational opportunity in racially isolated schools, and the realization of more equitable results through integrated ones. David Chang, law clerk to Judge Arthur Garrity, felt that such data was superfluous, however, because Professor Fiss' pioneering essay of two decades before had not gone far enough in its reading of *Brown*. For the *Brown* decision, Chang felt, derived as a constitutional imperative not only the general principle of equal educational opportunity, but the specific demand for equal educational *outcomes*. ". . . *Brown* can be interpreted as requiring the government to remedy any characteristic of the educational process that exacerbates, or fails to compensate for, those aspects of a group's disadvantage that render the group's educational performance inadequate."[147] The state, as a matter of law, "must provide minority children with the opportunity to learn as effectively as white children learn."[148]

The 1954 judgement, Chang recalled, did not flatly repudiate the doctrine of separate but equal in education; rather, it found the doctrine constitutionally infirm because the statutorily-imposed segregation at issue there damaged "the educational potential of minority children."[149] Had the Court not invoked "its factual theory," state segregation would, presumably, have remained legal.[150]

An equally obvious factual predicate extended the reach of *Brown* to all segregated schools, Chang believed. That predicate derived far less from evidence on achievement tests than from the nature and history of American society. The deeper "spirit of [the] *Brown* [decision]" compelled the integration of all aspects of this society, because it recognized that, "Race in America, like caste in India, can pose insurmountable social, economic, and political barriers."[151] Consequently, if "the Constitution does not impose an affirmative duty on the government to ensure that the educational system does not perpetuate pervasive social disadvantage, it deems caste to be acceptable in the American social structure."[152]

In this new articulation of the integrative ideal, comparative test scores were an obvious but superficial sign of inequality, defining the condition, but not the cause or the remedy. Empirical studies had never demonstrated that integration "alone could cure the performance gap between blacks and whites,"[153] because they had never isolated segregation as "the *sole* cause of unequal educational performance. In any event, "[a]lthough . . . segregation may contribute to educational harm, it clearly does not define the nature and extent of that harm."[154]

Thus, while integration of schools formed a part of any plan to produce equal educational outcomes, other tools, such as wide-ranging curriculum reform and compensatory education, must be employed, under judicial supervision if necessary, to realize the goal of true equality. "If . . . the caste-like quality of race is to be eliminated [from American society], the impetus must come from values imposed on the polity. The source must be constitutional."[155]

Chang's thesis actually got some semblance of a hearing in the most recent desegregation case decided by the Supreme Court to date, the controversy involving the schools of Kansas City.

Missouri v. *Jenkins* did not deal with claims to full unitary status on the part of school officials. Neither of the defendants in the case, the Kansas City school district and the state of Missouri, were ready to go that far in 1995, even after a decade of judicial supervision. (They were held jointly responsible in 1977 for continuing to operate an illegally segregated school system in the city; interdistrict violations were also alleged in the Kansas City metropolitan area, but were rejected.) State authorities did argue, however, that the Kansas City schools had achieved unitariness with respect to compensatory education programs, for which Missouri was assessed financial liability.

The district court judge administering the case disagreed. Judge Russell Clark rejected the state's contention without fully stating why he was doing so. But the Eighth Circuit Court of Appeals, affirming Judge Clark, put emphasis on some comments Clark made from the bench while hearing the state's argument. The panel found particularly significant the judge's finding that while "there ha[s] been a trend of improvement in academic achievement, . . . the school district [is] far from reaching its maximum potential because [it] is still *at or below national norms at many grade levels.*"[156] Here was a forthright assertion, if that is what Judge Clark actually meant, that only equal educational outcomes, or some approximation thereof, justified the termination of the integration plan.

The Supreme Court, though, casually brushed the notion aside. "[T]his clearly is not the appropriate test to be applied in deciding whether a previously segregated district has achieved partially unitary status," Chief Justice Rehnquist remarked, and ordered that on remand of the case the district court confine itself to determining "whether the reduction in achievement by minority students attributable to prior de jure segregation has been remedied *to the extent practicable.*"[157]

Indeed, the African-American respondents in the case themselves shied away from the district judge's rhetoric. As the chief justice noted just a few paragraphs after his condemnation of Clark's purported test. "[A]ll . . . parties agree that improved achievement on test scores is not necessarily required for the State to achieve partial unitary status as to the quality education programs . . . ."[158]

Justice David Souter agreed also that "it would be error to require that the students in a school district attain the national average test score as a prerequisite to a finding of partial unitary status,"[159] though Souter dissented on the test score issue, denying that either the district or the circuit court had required any definite standards in this area.

VII

Justice Souter found broader grounds for his dissenting opinion, however, a dissent which made clear that the Supreme Court of the mid-nineties was not firmly embarked on the path in desegregation law excavated by William Bradford Reynolds. By this time, President Clinton's appointees, Ruth Bader Ginsburg and Stephen Breyer, had come onto the Court. While Breyer's replacement of Harry Blackmun seemed unlikely to be crucial in desegregation decisions, Ginsburg's replacement of the later Justice White clearly did. Ginsburg and Breyer joined Justice Souter's dissent—along with Justice John Paul Stevens.

The real contention aroused by *Jenkins*, of which the test score matter was just a part, centered on the ambitious efforts made by Judge Clark to reverse the flight of white students from Kansas City to the suburbs, and the relation of these efforts to *Milliken* v. *Bradley* and *Hills* v. *Gautreaux*.

Judge Clark had followed the general approach to remedy advocated by Assistant Attorney General Reynolds, though in the opinion of Reynolds and others he had carried it to extremes. Instead of trying to further desegregate a school district already approaching two-thirds black by 1985, the judge ordered a vastly extensive and costly educational program, designed to lure suburban whites back into the city. He demanded that student-faculty ratios be lowered in all Kansas City classrooms, instituted full-day kindergartens, expanded summer school sessions, established before and after school tutoring, and early childhood development initiatives.

This re-creation of the Kansas City system was capped by a comprehensive program of magnet schools, ordered in 1986, encompassing every senior high school in the district, all of the middle schools, and half of the elementary schools. The program projected, by the early 1990's,

> high schools in which every classroom [would] have air conditioning, an alarm system, and 15 microcomputers; a 2,000-square-foot planetarium; green houses and vivariums; a 25-acre farm with an air-conditioned meeting room for 104 people; a Model United Nations wired for language translation; broadcast capable radio and television studios with an editing and animation lab; a temperature controlled art gallery; movie editing and screening rooms; a 3,500-square-foot dust-free diesel mechanics room; 1,875-square-foot elementary school animal rooms for use in a zoo project; swimming pools; and numerous other facilities.[160]

Judge Clark believed the magnet school plan "so attractive that it [will] draw non-minority students from the private schools who have abandoned or avoided [Kansas City], and draw in additional non-minority students from the suburbs."[161]

Chief Justice Rehnquist and his majority of five found this scheme in direct conflict with *Milliken*. Judge Clark's remedial scheme, they held, had turned aside from its proper objective, redistributing students within Kansas City in order "to eliminate racially identifiable schools."[162] In place of that, the judge was pursuing the purely "*inter*district goal"[163] of gaining white students from surrounding suburban counties, areas not themselves implicated in Kansas City's violations. Essentially then, "the District Court has devised a remedy to accomplish indirectly what it admittedly lacks the . . . authority to mandate directly: the interdistrict transfer of students."[164]

Milliken did not permit such easy shuffling of its principles. Nothing in that case suggested "that the District Court . . . could have circumvented the limits on its remedial authority by requiring the State of Michigan . . . to implement a magnet program designed to achieve the same interdistrict transfer of students that we held was beyond its remedial authority. Here, the District Court has done just that . . . ."[165]

Rehnquist pronounced his conclusions "fully consistent" with *Hills* v. *Gautreaux*, emphasizing Justice Stewart's assertion that the "'relevant geographic area for the purposes of the [plaintiffs'] housing options [was] the Chicago housing market, not the Chicago city limits'"; this was in sharp contrast to the situation in Detroit, where prior precedent had established that racial discrimination in schools was "to be dealt with in terms of 'an established geographic and administrative school system.'"[166]

In response, Justice Souter invoked what appears to have been the real doctrinal core of Justice Stewart's opinion in *Hills* v. *Gautreaux*. Measured against that standard, Judge Clark's orders fell "entirely within the scope of equitable authority recognized in Gautreaux," for they did not seek to "'consolidate or in any way restructure'" the suburban school districts (as Judge Roth basically had done in devising his remedy).[167] The measures implicated "only . . . the operation and quality of schools within [Kansas City], and [their] burden . . . accordingly falls only on the two proven constitutional wrongdoers in this case, the [Kansas City school district] and the State."[168]

To talk about the "'relevant geographic area for the purposes of . . . housing options'" constituted "only half the explanation" of the Court's actions in *Gautreaux*, Souter maintained.[169] It had found a metropolitan approach proper in Chicago, not simply because of the nature of the housing market, "but also because the . . . court[s] could order a remedy in that market without binding a governmental unit innocent of [any] violation."[170]

Justice Souter's position was backed up in an amicus brief submitted by the American Civil Liberties Union. Suburban school districts near Kansas City, the ACLU noted, were "not being restructured or indeed required to take any steps."

Similarly, Missouri was "not . . . being required to take . . . steps" outside of the confines of Kansas City.[171] "Only wrongdoers are . . . required to act in this case and the only actions they [must] take are within [city] boundaries."[172] Missouri's lawyers, the ACLU argued (and Chief Justice Rehnquist as well, Souter might have added), seemed to think "that any remedy that has any effect on any person beyond the school district at issue is by definition an interdistrict remedy."[173]

VIII

Missouri v. *Jenkins* was most significant, perhaps, for the concurring opinion contributed to it by Justice Clarence Thomas, his first in the area of elementary and secondary school desegregation law. Justice Thomas' effort, composed four years after Thurgood Marshall's last desegregation opinion, measured the difference, not only between the judicial philosophies of the two men, but between the cultural viewpoints within the African-American community from which each took his inspiration.

Justice Marshall articulated to the last the passion for integration, a goal still precious to him despite the disappointments of the 1980's.

> Consistent with the mandate of Brown I, our cases have imposed on school districts an unconditional duty to eliminate any condition that perpetuates the message of racial inferiority inherent in the policy of state-sponsored segregation. The racial identifiability of a district's schools is such a condition. Whether this "vestige" of state-sponsored segregation will persist cannot simply be ignored at the point where a district court is contemplating the dissolution of a desegregation decree. In a district with a history of state-sponsored school segregation, racial separation, in my view, *remains* inherently unequal.[174]

This ideal had barely been disturbed by the wave of black separatism which swept through the African-American community during the sixties. The cry of "separate and superior" might have conditioned events in the schools of the Ocean Hill-Brownsville district during that time, but it exerted scant influence on African-American constitutional scholars, judges, and litigators.[175] Indeed, the 1960's saw the great turning toward mandatory integration in desegregation law. But by the 1980's, the view of the dissident black parents in the Dallas and De Kalb County cases reflected a broader movement in American constitutional scholarship. A group of younger thinkers (both African-American and white) were questioning, even denouncing, the legacy of *Brown* v. *Board of Education.*

In part, this disillusionment flowed from the same disappointments which strained even Justice Marshall's faith. It was clear that by the late seventies, if not earlier, the progress of African-Americans toward genuine social and economic equality in a bi-racial society had hit a massive snag. The "white backlash" against civil rights produced a series of legislative and judicial retreats, from anti-busing riders to *Milliken* v. *Bradley*. Furthermore, several major studies of the late eighties and early nineties (though challenged since) painted a bleak portrait of the economic and social plight of African-Americans, noting the astronomical unemployment rates for young blacks, and the pitifully slow progress which the nation had made toward truly integrated neighborhoods.[176]

Yet the challenge to *Brown* went deeper, disputing the entire integrationist ideal the decision had inspired. In their desire to eliminate racial barriers, it was argued, integrationists were championing an assertive, "coercive assimilation[ism],"[177] a doctrine willing and even anxious to extirpate uniquely black cultural achievements and institutions, to kill off the very culture which must be preserved for genuine integration to occur in American society.

The goal of an "assimilationist color-blind society," argued Professor Neil Gotanda, was "by definition" a form of "cultural genocide," because it sought the "successful abolition of 'Black' as a meaningful concept, . . . abolishing the distinctiveness that we attribute to Black community, culture, and consciousness."[178]

Furthermore, color-blindness had been ineffective, in Gotanda's view, in promoting significant and long-lasting social change. While it could attack glaring forms of discrimination, such as Jim Crow laws, it "offers no vision for attacking less overt forms of racial subordination. The color-blind ideal of the future society has been exhausted since the implementation of *Brown* . . . and its progeny."[179]

Only a new equal protection jurisprudence which did not "devalue or ignore Black culture" could "begin to address the link between the cultural practices of Blacks and the subordination of Blacks, elements that are, in fact, inseparable in the lived experience of race."[180] This new jurisprudence, Professor Gotanda felt, must abandon the notion that all uses of race by government were subject to the virtually impassible "strict scrutiny" test under the fourteenth amendment (the test validating racial categories only if they served a compelling state interest and were narrowly tailored to serve such an interest). By discarding this "ill-advised and ultimately malicious" criterion, the constitutional jurisprudence of race would realize perhaps its deepest purpose, to "accommodate legitimate governmental efforts to address white racial privilege."[181]

"When you are on trial," noted Professor Mari Matsuda, in a seminal essay of 1987, " . . . your lawyer will want black people on your jury."

> Why? Because black jurors are more likely to understand what your lawyer will argue: that people in power sometimes abuse law to achieve their own ends, and that the prosecution's claim to neutral application of legal principles is false.[182]

Those who lived with prejudice and oppression, Professor Matsuda argued, spoke "with a special voice" to which everyone should listen. "Looking to the bottom—adopting the perspective of those who have seen and felt the falsity of the liberal promise" could greatly assist legal scholars in "defining the elements of justice."[183]

Geneva Crenshaw, the mythical civil rights lawyer and protagonist of Professor Derrick Bell's remarkable book, *And We Are Not Free*, echoed the protesters of Dallas and of suburban Atlanta in denouncing the view that integration was the royal road to educational progress, and defending the preference, in some cases, for black institutions offering high quality education combined with a nurturing cultural atmosphere.

> "[I]f the issue and the goal are as the Dallas [intervenors] suggested— 'whether or not we are going to educate the children and youth'—you simply have to agree, first, that racial balance and integration—[though] 'a noble idea in 1954'—is of very limited value today; and, second, that our priority must be to gain educationally effective schools for our children.". . .

> "What Dr. DuBois said over half a century ago is still pertinent to all the black parents in this damned country who care more about their children's schooling than about their long-lost noble dreams. Listen!

> A mixed school with poor and unsympathetic teachers, with hostile public opinion, and no teaching of truth concerning black folk, is bad. A segregated school with ignorant placeholders, inadequate equipment, poor salaries, and wretched housing, is equally bad. Other things being equal, the mixed school is the broader, more natural basis for the education of all youth. It gives wider contacts; it inspires greater self-confidence; and suppresses the inferiority complex. But other things seldom are equal, and in that case, Sympathy, Knowledge, and Truth, outweigh all that the mixed school can offer."[184]

A seminal essay of 1993, by Professor Alex Johnson of the University of Virginia Law School, summarized this contra-*Brown* vision of desegregation law with brilliance and forcefulness. *Brown* v. *Board of Education*, Johnson stated flatly, must be counted "a mistake,"[185] because it held up a false model of integrationism which had turned out to be both unrealistic and stigmatizing.

Because of the decision, and the subsequent glosses on it, integration was now monolithically required in educational institutions as the embodiment of a liberal conception of equality and neutrality; experience in such institutions would supposedly "replace the ignorance of racism with the knowledge that actual contact provides."[186] In fact, such conceptions flowed from a false and dreamy picture "of what society *should* look like," instead of "what modern American society actually looks like."[187] They totally ignored "the transitional steps that must be taken to ensure the evolution of society from . . . today to . . . tomorrow."[188] In practice, therefore, the "assimilationist vision" of *Brown* was ultimately "detrimental to the welfare of African-American students because they are forced to compete on a 'level playing field' . . . [on] which the chances of failure are significantly increased."[189]

Even worse, coercive assimilation required African-Americans to renounce their distinct culture and the organisms which sustained it, and to merge with white society on white terms. The black experience in America, therefore, had come "full circle"[190] by the 1990's, Professor Johnson felt. In the wake of slavery, the belief that racial separation constituted "a badge of inferiority" was "certainly understandable."[191] Now, the Supreme Court's "assimilationist brand of integration," which would shove African-Americans into the mainstream of contemporary society "without respecting the cultural, social, and institutional norms that developed in pre-*Brown* African-American society, creates as much a badge of inferiority as the doctrine of 'separate but equal' did."[192]

What was needed in the 1990's, Johnson maintained, was not the revival of an uncompromising black nationalism, but a genuine "cultural pluralism" which would honor the presence of a separate black community, and respect the right of African-Americans "to remain in or leave that community."[193] This new and higher form of tolerance would "not necessarily lead to the permanent maintenance of two separate societies"; rather, it would nourish "an expanded version of liberalism in which integrationism and nationalism can co-exist."[194]

The separate institutions Professor Johnson saw as most critical in promoting cultural pluralism were the black colleges and universities. They served not only as "transmitters and preservers" of black culture, but as "a cultural buffer," providing young African-Americans "the choices of whether or not to 'integrate' into mainstream society at all, and when to integrate, now or at a later point in life when they are ready to undertake the arduous transition into a mainstream culture that casts them as the 'other.'"[195]

Unfortunately, Johnson argued, the greatest threat to black colleges and universities came from a Supreme Court still devoted in this area to the pristine notion of integration, even as it gutted racial balance plans for elementary and secondary schools. Johnson took especially sharp issue with the Court's decision in the *United States* v. *Fordice*,[196] handed down after *Dowell* and *Freeman* v. *Pitts*, though before *Missouri* v. *Jenkins*.

The case involved a long-standing suit against the state of Mississippi, charging that it operated, and had failed to dismantle, a dual system of higher education. Five of the state schools were almost exclusively white; the three pre-1954 black institutions—Jackson State, Alcorn State, and Mississippi Valley University—remained almost 100% black, and grossly underfunded.

The justices agreed that the system maintained illegal segregation, and remanded the controversy to the district court for consideration of a desegregation plan. They brushed aside Mississippi's contention that racial separation was caused by a wholly non-discriminatory policy of requiring higher test scores on college entrance exams for admission to the formerly white colleges. While neutral on its face, the

Court admitted, the testing setup produced clearly segregatory effects, and, under established case law, could not be allowed to stand in the way of compliance, unless there was overriding pedagogical justification for it. Mississippi, Justice Byron White concluded, had failed to show that the test-oriented "admission standard is not susceptible to elimination without eroding sound educational policy."[197]

But Justice White also brushed aside the pleas of several African-American petitioners in the case, who urged that the remedy for past discrimination include equalized funding for Mississippi's black colleges, so as to make them a viable alternative to the white schools. "The State," White stated peremptorily, "provides these [educational] facilities for *all* its citizens and it has not met its burden under Brown . . . when it perpetuates a separate, but 'more equal' one."[198] Increased funding for the black colleges as part of the remedy was not precluded. But the district court should also consider "whether retention of all eight institutions *itself . . . perpetuates the segregated higher education system*, . . . and whether one or more of them can be practicably closed or merged with other existing institutions."[199] These directions scarcely indicated a sympathy for the black colleges, and, indeed, on remand, the district judge proposed to shut down Mississippi Valley University and to merge Alcorn State with predominantly white Mississippi State University.

Fordice, felt Professor Johnson, represented the persistence of "integrationism in its purest social form,"[200] a philosophy out of tune with the growing realism of black America. "Because it eliminates the African-American student's choice between a predominantly black or white college, forced integration has the painful and paradoxical result of failing to properly assimilate African-Americans into the larger society."[201] The Court was clinging stubbornly to an agenda for social change which was bound to fail.

Justice Clarence Thomas largely agreed. In his first opinion dealing with educational segregation on any level, Thomas concurred with the majority, but only because he managed to convince himself that Justice White's opinion did not "foreclose the possibility . . . [of] maintaining historically black colleges *as such*."[202] The standards set out in the case, Thomas optimistically asserted, might well allow a state to "operate a diverse assortment of institutions—including historically black institutions—open to all . . . , but with established traditions and programs that might disproportionately appeal to one race or another."[203]

Thomas' sympathy for such institutions clearly outran that of his senior associate. He quoted from a Carnegie Commission report on black colleges which cited their enormous accomplishments, and began his opinion with a quote from W.E.B. DuBois. "'We must rally to the defense of our schools. We must repudiate this unbearable assumption of the right to kill institutions unless they conform to one narrow standard.'"[204] How paradoxical it would be, Thomas mused, "if the institutions that sustained blacks during segregation were themselves destroyed in an effort to combat its vestiges."[205]

Justice Thomas also telegraphed his feelings in *Fordice* about the racial balance plans inaugurated by *Green* for elementary and secondary schools. Such reshuffling of students was obviously inappropriate in a college setting, he noted, "[w]hatever the merit of this approach in the grade-school context."[206] But the justice didn't appear to see much merit in these integration schemes, whatever the context. Thus under *Fordice*, he pointed out approvingly, lower courts "will spend their time determining whether [educational] policies have been adequately justified—a far narrower, more manageable task than that imposed under Green," where plaintiffs could obtain relief "merely by identifying a persistent racial imbalance."[207]

Justice Thomas' concurrence in *Missouri* v. *Jenkins* built on the hints offered in *Fordice*. "It never ceases to amaze me," he proclaimed, "that the courts are so willing to assume that anything that is predominantly black must be inferior."[208] The lower courts in *Jenkins*, unfortunately, "read our cases to support the theory that black students suffer an unspecified psychological harm from segregation that retards their mental and educational development. This approach not only relies upon questionable social science research rather than constitutional principle, but it also rests on an assumption of black inferiority."[209]

The hostility to *Green* and *Swann* also found explicit expression in *Jenkins*. "The mere fact that a school is black does not mean that it is the product of a constitutional violation."[210] A "'vestige'" of prior discrimination could not form the basis for an assumption of judicial authority unless it was "clearly traceable to the dual school system," and courts "must not confuse the consequences of de jure segregation with the results of larger social forces or private decisions . . . .When a district court holds the State liable for discrimination almost 30 years after the last official state action, it must do more than show that there are schools with high black populations . . . ."[211]

The contrast with Marshall's words in his *Dowell* dissent were marked and historic.

CODA:
"MARSHALL v. THOMAS"

1. JUSTICE MARSHALL'S DISSENT IN *DOWELL*

II

I agree with the majority that the proper standard for determining whether a school desegregation decree should be dissolved is whether the purposes of the desegregation litigation, as incorporated in the decree, have been fully achieved . . . . I strongly disagree with the majority, however, on what must be shown to demonstrate that a decree's purposes have been fully realized. In my view, a standard for dissolution of a desegregation decree must take into account the unique harm associated with a system of racially identifiable schools and must expressly demand the elimination of such schools.

A

Our pointed focus in Brown I upon the stigmatic injury caused by segregated schools explains our unflagging insistence that formerly de jure segregated school districts extinguish all vestiges of school segregation. The concept of stigma also gives us guidance as to what conditions must be eliminated before a decree can be deemed to have served its purpose.

In the decisions leading up to Brown I, the Court had attempted to curtail the ugly legacy of Plessy v. Ferguson by insisting on a searching inquiry into whether "separate" Afro–American schools were genuinely "equal" to white schools in terms of physical facilities, curricula, quality of the faculty, and certain "intangible" considerations . . . . In Brown I, the Court finally liberated the Equal Protection Clause from the doctrinal tethers of Plessy, declaring that "in the field of public education the doctrine of 'separate but equal' has no place. Separate educational facilities are inherently unequal."

The Court based this conclusion on its recognition of the particular social harm that racially segregated schools inflict on Afro–American children . . . .

Remedying and avoiding the recurrence of this stigmatizing injury have been the guiding objectives of this Court's desegregation jurisprudence ever since. These concerns inform the standard by which the Court determines the effectiveness of a proposed desegregation remedy . . . . In Green, ... [t]he Court held that [a freedom of choice] plan was inadequate because it failed to redress the effect of segregation upon "every facet of school operations—faculty, staff, transportation, extracurricular activities and facilities." By so construing the extent of a school board's obligations, the Court made clear that the Equal Protection Clause demands elimination of every indicium of a "[r]acial[ly] identifi[able]" school system that will inflict the stigmatizing injury that Brown I sought to cure . . . .

Concern with stigmatic injury also explains the Court's requirement that a formerly de jure segregated school district provide its victims with "make whole" relief . . . . In order to achieve such "make whole" relief, school systems must redress any effects traceable to former de jure segregation . . . . [Thus] [t]he remedial education upheld in Milliken II was needed to help prevent the stamp of inferiority placed upon Afro-American children from becoming a self-perpetuating phenomenon . . . .

Similarly, avoiding reemergence of the harm condemned in Brown I accounts for the Court's insistence on remedies that ensure lasting integration of formerly segregated systems. Such school districts are required to "make every effort to achieve the *greatest possible degree of actual desegregation* and [to] be concerned with the elimination of one-race schools." . . . This focus on "achieving and *preserving* an integrated school system" [*Keyes* at 251, n. 31 (emphasis added)] stems from the recognition that the reemergence of racial separation in such schools may revive the message of racial inferiority implicit in the former policy of state-enforced segregation.

Just as it is central to the standard for evaluating the formation of the desegregation decree, so should the stigmatic injury associated with segregated schools be central to the standard for dissolving a decree. The Court has indicated that "the ultimate end to be brought about" by a desegregation remedy is "a unitary, nonracial system of public education." We have suggested that this aim is realized once school officials have "eliminate[d] from the public schools all vestiges of state-imposed segregation." . . . Although the Court has never explicitly defined what constitutes a "vestige" of state-enforced segregation, the function that this concept has performed in our jurisprudence suggests that it extends to any condition that is likely to convey the message of inferiority implicit in a policy of segregation. So long as such conditions persist, the purposes of the decree cannot be deemed to have been achieved.

B

The majority suggests a more vague and, I fear, milder standard. Ignoring the harm identified in Brown I, the majority asserts that the District Court should find that the purposes of the degree have been achieved so long as "the Oklahoma City School District [is now] being operated in compliance with the commands of the Equal Protection Clause" and "it [is] unlikely that the school board would return to its former ways." . . .

By focusing heavily on present and future compliance with the Equal Protection Clause, the majority's standard ignores how the stigmatic harm identified in Brown I can persist even after the State ceases actively to enforce segregation. It was not enough in Green, for example, for the school district to withdraw its own enforcement of segregation, leaving it up to individual children and their families to "choose" which school to attend. For it was clear under the circumstances that these choices would be shaped by and perpetuate the state-created message of racial inferiority associated with the school district's historical involvement in segregation. In sum, our school-desegregation jurisprudence establishes that the *effects* of past discrimination remain chargeable to the school district regardless of its lack of continued enforcement of segregation, and the remedial decree is required until those effects have been finally eliminated.

III

Applying the standard I have outlined, I would affirm the Court of Appeals' decision ordering the District Court to restore the desegregation decree. For it is clear on this record that removal of the decree will result in a significant number of racially identifiable schools that could be eliminated . . . .

Nonetheless, the majority hints that the District Court could ignore the effect of residential segregation in perpetuating racially identifiable schools if the court finds residential segregation to be "the result of private decisionmaking and economics." [Furthermore], the majority warns against the application of a standard that would subject formerly segregated school districts to the "Draconian" fate of "judicial tutelage for the indefinite future."

This equivocation is completely unsatisfying. First, it is well established that school segregation "may have a profound reciprocal effect on the racial composition of residential neighborhoods." . . .

[Also] [t]he District Court's conclusion that the racial identity of the northeast quadrant [of Oklahoma City] now subsists because of "personal preference[s]" pays insufficient attention to the roles of the State, local officials, and the Board in creating what are now self-perpetuating patterns of residential segregation. Even more important, it fails to account for the *unique* role of the School Board in creating "all-Negro" schools clouded by the stigma of segregation—schools to which white parents would not opt to send their children. That such negative "personal preferences" exist should not absolve a school district that played a role in creating such "preferences" from its obligation to desegregate the schools to the maximum extent possible.

I also reject the majority's suggestion that the length of federal judicial supervision is a valid factor in assessing a dissolution. The majority is correct that the Court has never contemplated perpetual judicial oversight of former de jure segregated school districts. Our jurisprudence requires, however, that the job of school desegregation be fully completed and maintained so that the stigmatic harm identified in Brown I will not recur upon lifting the decree. Any doubt on the issue whether the School Board has fulfilled its remedial obligations should be resolved in favor of the Afro-American children affected by this litigation.

In its concern to spare local school boards the "Draconian" fate of "indefinite" "judicial tutelage," the majority risks subordination of the constitutional rights of Afro-American children to the interest of school board autonomy . . . .

[R]etaining the decree seems a slight burden on the school district compared with the risk of not delivering a full remedy to the Afro-American children in the school system.

IV

Consistent with the mandate of Brown I, our cases have imposed on school districts an unconditional duty to eliminate any condition that perpetuates the message of racial inferiority inherent in the policy of state-sponsored segregation. The racial identifiability of a district's schools is such a condition. Whether this "vestige" of state-sponsored segregation will persist cannot simply be ignored at the point where a district court is contemplating the dissolution of a desegregation decree. In a district with a history of state-sponsored school segregation, racial separation, in my view, remains inherently unequal.

I dissent.

2. JUSTICE THOMAS' CONCURRENCE IN *MISSOURI* v. *JENKINS*

It never ceases to amaze me that the courts are so willing to assume that anything that is predominantly black must be inferior. Instead of focusing on remedying the harm done to those black school children injured by segregation, the District Court here sought to convert the Kansas City, Missouri, School District (KCMSD) into a "magnet district" that would reverse the "white flight" caused by *de*segregation . . .

Two threads in our jurisprudence have produced this unfortunate situation, in which a District Court has taken it upon itself to experiment with the education of the KCMSD's black youth. First, the court has read our cases to support the theory that black students suffer an unspecified psychological harm from segregation that retards their mental and educational development. This approach not only relies upon questionable social science research rather than constitutional principle, but it also rests on an assumption of black inferiority. Second, we have permitted the federal courts to exercise virtually unlimited equitable powers to remedy this alleged constitutional violation. The exercise of this authority has trampled upon principles of federalism and the separation of powers and has freed courts to pursue other agendas unrelated to the narrow purpose of precisely remedying a constitutional harm.

I

A . . . .

When a district court holds the State liable for discrimination almost 30 years after the last official state action, it must do more than show that there are schools with high black populations or low test scores. Here, the district judge did not make clear how the high black enrollments in certain schools were fairly traceable to the State of Missouri's actions. I do not doubt that Missouri maintained the despicable system of segregation until 1954. But I question the District Court's conclusion that because the State had enforced segregation until 1954, its actions, or lack thereof, proximately caused the "racial isolation" of the predominantly black schools in 1984. In fact, . . . I would think it incumbent upon the District Court to explain how more recent social or demographic phenomena did not cause the "vestiges." This the District Court did not do.

B

Without a basis in any real finding of intentional government action, the District Court's imposition of liability upon the State of Missouri improperly rests upon a theory that racial imbalances are unconstitutional. That is, the court has "indulged the presumption, often irrebuttable in practice, that a presently observed [racial] imbalance has been proximately caused by intentional state action during the prior de jure era." [*United States* v. *Fordice*, at 120 L Ed 2d 575, 604.] . . . In effect, the court found that racial imbalances constituted an ongoing constitutional violation that continued to inflict harm on black students. This position appears to rest upon the idea that any school that is black is inferior, and that blacks cannot succeed without the benefit of the company of whites.

The District Court's willingness to adopt such stereotypes stemmed from a misreading of our earliest school desegregation case. In Brown v. Board of Education, the Court noted several psychological and sociological studies purporting to show that de jure segregation harmed black students by generating "a feeling of inferiority" in them. Seizing upon this passage in Brown I, the District Court asserted that "forced segregation ruins attitudes and is inherently unequal." 593 F Supp, at 1492. The District Court suggested that this inequality continues in full force even after the end of de jure segregation . . . . Thus, the District Court seemed to believe that black students in the KCMSD would continue to receive an "inferior education" despite the end of de jure segregation, as long as de facto segregation persisted . . . . Such assumptions and any social science research upon which they rely certainly cannot form the basis upon which we decide matters of constitutional principle.

It is clear that the District Court misunderstood the meaning of Brown I. Brown I did not say that "racially isolated" schools were inherently inferior; the harm that it identified was tied purely to de jure segregation, not de facto segregation. Indeed,

Brown I itself did not need to rely upon any psychological or social-science research in order to announce the simple, yet fundamental truth that the Government cannot discriminate among its citizens on the basis of race . . . . At the heart of [its] interpretation of the Equal Protection Clause lies the principle that the Government must treat citizens as individuals, and not as members of racial, ethnic or religious groups. It is for this reason that we must subject all racial classifications to the strictest of scrutiny, which (aside from two decisions rendered in the midst of wartime, see Hirabayashi v. United States, 320 US 81; Korematsu v. United States, 323 US 214) has proven automatically fatal.

Segregation was not unconstitutional because it might have caused psychological feelings of inferiority. Public school systems that separated blacks and provided them with superior educational resources—making blacks "feel" superior to whites sent to lesser schools—would violate the Fourteenth Amendment, whether or not the white students felt stigmatized, just as do school systems in which the positions of the races are reversed. Psychological injury or benefit is irrelevant to the question whether state actors have engaged in intentional discrimination—the critical inquiry for ascertaining violations of the Equal Protection Clause. The judiciary is fully competent to make independent determinations concerning the existence of state action without the unnecessary and misleading assistance of the social sciences . . . .

[N]eutral policies, such as local school assignments, do not offend the Constitution when individual private choices concerning work or residence produce schools with high black populations . . . . The Constitution does not prevent individuals from choosing to live together, to work together, or to send their children to school together, so long as the State does not interfere with their choices on the basis of race.

Given that desegregation has not produced the predicted leaps forward in black educational achievement, there is no reason to think that black students cannot learn as well when surrounded by members of their own race as when they are in an integrated environment. Indeed, it may very well be that what has been true for historically black colleges is true for black middle and high schools . . . . Because of their "distinctive histories and traditions," [*Fordice*, at 120 L Ed 2d 575, 606] black schools can function as the center and symbol of black communities, and provide examples of independent black leadership, success, and achievement.

Thus, even if the District Court had been on firmer ground in identifying a link between the KCMSD's pre-1954 de jure segregation and the present "racial isolation" of some of the district's schools, mere de facto segregation . . . does not constitute a continuing harm after the end of de jure segregation. "Racial isolation" itself is not a harm; only state-enforced segregation is. After all, if separation itself is a harm, and if integration therefore is the only way that blacks can receive a proper education, then there must be something inferior about blacks. Under this theory, segregation injures blacks because blacks, when left on their own, cannot achieve. To my way of thinking, that conclusion is the result of a jurisprudence based upon a theory of black inferiority.

This misconception has drawn the courts away from the important goal in desegregation. The point of the Equal Protection Clause is not to enforce strict race-mixing, but to ensure that blacks and whites are treated equally by the State without regard to their skin color. The lower courts should not be swayed by the easy answers of social science, nor should they accept the findings, and the assumptions, of sociology and psychology at the price of constitutional principle.

II

We have authorized the district courts to remedy past de jure segregation by reassigning students in order to eliminate or decrease observed racial imbalances, even if present methods of pupil assignment are facially neutral . . . . The District Court here merely took this approach to its logical next step. If racial proportions are the goal, then schools must improve their facilities to attract white students until the district's racial balance is restored to the "right" proportions. Thus, fault for the problem we correct today lies not only with a twisted theory of racial injuries, but also with our approach to the remedies necessary to correct racial imbalances.

The District Court's unwarranted focus on the psychological harm to blacks and on racial imbalances has been only half of the tale. Not only did the court subscribe to a theory of injury that was predicated on black inferiority, it also married this concept of liability to our expansive approach to remedial powers. We have given the federal courts the freedom to use any measure necessary to reverse problems—such as racial isolation or low educational achievement—that have proven stubbornly resistant to government policies. We have not permitted constitutional principles such as federalism or the separation of powers to stand in the way of our drive to reform the schools. Thus, the District Court here ordered massive expenditures by local and state authorities, without congressional or executive authorization and without any indication that such measures would attract whites back to KCMSD or raise KCMSD test scores. The time has come for us to put the genie back in the bottle.

A . . . .

Motivated by our worthy desire to eradicate segregation, . . . we have . . . given the courts unprecedented authority to shape a remedy in equity. Although at times we have invalidated a decree as beyond the bounds of an equitable remedy, see . . . Milliken [I], these instances have been far outnumbered by the expansions in the equity power. In United States v. Montgomery County Board of Education, for example, we allowed federal courts to desegregate faculty and staff according to specific mathematical ratios, with the ultimate goal that each school in the system would have roughly the same proportions of white and black faculty. In Swann v.

Charlotte-Mecklenburg Board of Education, we permitted federal courts to order busing, to set racial targets for school populations, and to alter attendance zones. And in . . . Milliken II, we approved the use of remedial or compensatory education programs paid for by the State.

In upholding these court-ordered measures, we indicated that trial judges had virtually boundless discretion in crafting remedies once they had identified a constitutional violation . . . .

It is perhaps understandable that we permitted the lower courts to exercise such sweeping powers. Although we had authorized the federal courts to work toward "a system of determining admission to the public schools on a nonracial basis" in . . . Brown II, resistance to Brown I produced little desegregation by the time we decided Green v. School Board of New Kent County. Our impatience with the pace of desegregation and with the lack of a good-faith effort on the part of school boards led us to approve such extraordinary remedial measures. But such powers should have been temporary and used only to overcome the widespread resistance to the dictates of the Constitution. The judicial overreaching we see before us today perhaps is the price we now pay for our approval of such extraordinary remedies in the past . . . .

III

This Court should never approve a State's efforts to deny students, because of their race, an equal opportunity for an education. But the federal courts also should avoid using racial equality as a pretext for solving social problems that do not violate the Constitution. It seems apparent to me that the District Court undertook the worthy task of providing a quality education to the children of KCMSD. As far as I can tell, however, the District Court sought to bring new funds and facilities into the KCMSD by finding a constitutional violation on the part of the State where there was none . . . .

The desire to reform a school district, or any other institution, cannot so captivate the Judiciary that it forgets its constitutionally mandated role . . . . At some point, we must recognize that the judiciary is not omniscient, and that all problems do not require a remedy of constitutional proportions.

CONCLUSION

By the early 1990's, a larger percentage of African-American youngsters were attending majority black schools than had attended them in the wake of *Swann* and *Keyes*, though the statistics also showed how widespread segregation had remained throughout the period of "forced busing." In 1969, 76.6% of African-American students went to predominantly minority institutions; the number fell to 63.6 in 1973 and to 62.9 in 1981; a decade later it was up to 66%. The number of black pupils in 90–100% minority schools fell from 64.3% in 1969, to 38.7% in 1973, to only 32.5% in 1987; by 1992 it edged up again to 33.9%.

Enrollment in Hispanic majority schools has continued to climb over the last two decades, from 54.8% in 1969 to 73.4% in 1992. In 90–100% Hispanic schools, the number has gone from 23.1 to 34%.

For African-American youngsters, at least, the South remains the most desegregated region in the country, even if that is no longer saying much. In 1992, 60.8% of southern Afro-American pupils went to majority black schools. By contrast, the total was 76.2 in the Northeast, almost 70% in the Midwest and the West. Not surprisingly, the ten most segregated states in terms of African-American students in majority black schools included only two southern states, Mississippi and Louisiana. The list was headed by New York (84.6%), Illinois (80.2%), and California (80%). Curiously, the South is the second most segregated region in the country in terms of majority Hispanic schools, following closely behind the Northeast.

Inner city schools, of course, are overwhelmingly segregated and growing moreso, but this does not mean that minority students who live in the suburbs are likely to attend mixed schools, especially in the larger metropolitan areas. In these areas, 92.4% of African-Americans attended majority black schools in the central cities by

1992, but 58% attended such schools in the suburbs. With Hispanics, the totals were 93.8 and 63.9. Smaller metropolitan areas exhibited figures which are less stark, though still indicative of considerable ethnic and racial separation: almost 63% of African-American students attended majority black schools in the cities, 43% in the suburbs; for Hispanics, the numbers were 70.4 and 51.4.

Most important, to attend a segregated school is to attend a school scarred by poverty. In those institutions with 90–100% minority enrollment, 57% were high poverty schools in 1992. A third of the schools with over 50% minority enrollment were in the high poverty category. At the other end of the spectrum, the 70% of schools in the low poverty category (10% or less poor students) carried minority enrollments averaging less than 10%.[1]

This situation produces subtle parallels with the pre-*Brown* era. Education officials of today might not set out to offer grossly inferior curricula to minorities. But things like the inability to find enough pupils to keep an advanced literature course going at an inner city school, and the need to spend more dollars in those schools on remedial education, inevitably shortchange gifted students. As Professor Gary Orfield notes, "The practical barriers to excellent precollegiate instruction in high-poverty schools are recognized to be so severe that the accomplishments of one teacher, Jaime Escalante, who taught Advanced Placement (AP) calculus in one Latino school in California, were celebrated across the United States. He became a hero, though the same course is routinely offered in a great many suburban schools."[2] Statistics suggest that teachers like Mr. Escalante are more likely to consider leaving teaching than their suburban counterparts if they cannot transfer eventually to prestigious academic schools away from the ghetto.[3]

II

Not all busing orders have been rescinded by any means. An inventory of some of the most celebrated desegregation cases of the post-*Green* period presents a mixed bag. Thus Dayton, Ohio continues to operate under a court-ordered busing plan, in a system now two-thirds minority.[4] Its neighbor in Columbus, however, was declared unitary in 1985. The city currently offers its students a wide variety of choice in selecting the schools they wish to attend, including the option of integrated schools. But Columbus operates within the context of a system which is approaching 60% minority (56% black).[5]

In 1995, Judge Richard Matsch declared the Denver school system unitary. The Supreme Court decisions in *Dowell* and *Freeman* made clear to him, Judge Matsch noted, that the "constitutional authority of the federal courts" in school desegregation cases was "limited to compelling the elimination of negative effects of *de jure* discrimination; it does not include the power to posit any particular affirmative achievements."[6] *Missouri* v. *Jenkins*, meanwhile, "defeat[ed] the [Denver] plaintiffs' call for compelling additional action to . . . redress racial disparities in student achievement," since the district court never specifically found that these differences were the result of deliberate discrimination by school authorities.[7] Minority enrollment in the Denver system hovers at 70%.

Judge Hugh Dillin in Indianapolis has refused requests that he terminate the city to suburb busing he instituted almost twenty years ago.[8] But the Wilmington-New Castle County school system has gained unitary status and the freedom to dispense with prior busing mandates. In 1981, while the busing plan was still in effect, the area was divided into four separate school districts. Each district, however, contained part of the city of Wilmington, and all students were required to spend three years in the city schools and nine in suburban settings. With the declaration of unitariness, school officials are gradually moving away from this requirement.[9]

Milliken v. *Bradley* guaranteed that Indianapolis and Wilmington would be among the few communities forced to implement interdistrict remedies under federal desegregation law. Plaintiffs in Hartford, Connecticut, therefore, recently took another tack. Rebuffed by the rigors of *Milliken* in their efforts to gain metropolitan relief under the fourteenth amendment, the Hartford complainants filed a new action under the Connecticut state constitution and were successful.[10] Another case raising similar claims is pending under the Minnesota constitution.[11]

One place never needing this sort of action has been Charlotte, North Carolina, where the school system included both city and suburb even before 1971, and where the relevant school area, therefore, has remained racially diverse. Indeed the "index of dissimilarity" in Charlotte-Mecklenburg County, a device used by demographers to measure the fraction of residents in a community who would have to be assigned to new residences to achieve perfect integration (an index of zero), declined from 0.69 before the *Swann* decision to 0.61 in 1990. Into the late eighties, long after court supervision ended, school officials retained and continued to revise Charlotte's integration plan, to cope with overcrowding and to adjust student ratios.[12]

In 1991, a new superintendent of the Charlotte-Mecklenburg schools, Dr. John A. Murphy, sought to institute a system of magnet schools which would eventually end the program of busing between inner city and suburban neighborhoods. The proposal envisioned the transformation of "a mandatory plan with little voluntarism to a voluntary plan with few mandatory facets."[13]

The Charlotte-Mecklenburg school board adopted the magnet plan in 1992. But elections for the board in 1995 produced "a clear rejection of Superintendent Murphy's decision."[14] Advocates of a renewed emphasis on desegregation won all but one of the school board seats.

Another community striving for increased integration, but still under court order to do so, is Topeka, Kansas. In 1987, school officials sought unitary status for the system, which had expanded to take in some of the Topeka suburbs, and was now known as Unified School District Number 501. The system's minority percentage in its 26 elementary schools was 27.2; five of those schools were 90% or more white; four had a majority of black and Hispanic pupils. The seven secondary schools contained total minority enrollments of 27%; three enrolled less than a 10% minority population.

District Judge Richard Dean Rogers declared the system unitary. His reasoning, though, left the plaintiffs potent ammunition on appeal, for the judge charged *them* with the "burden of proving that illegal segregation" still existed "in U.S.D.#501."[15] The "passage of time," he also noted, plus "demographic dynamics," detracted "from the justification for the *Keyes* presumption in this case. Nor does [it] fit the *Swann* presumption easily."[16]

The plaintiffs had not met their burden, Judge Rogers concluded. The "factors which bear on the [present] racial condition of school attendance [in Topeka] are the factors which affect residential choice . . . not matters directed by defendants . . . .The court is persuaded that *de jure* segregation either had no significant effect upon residential patterns in Topeka or that its impact . . . has attenuated to insignificance."[17]

A Tenth Circuit panel predictably held "that the district court erred in placing the burden on plaintiffs . . . rather than according plaintiffs the presumption that current [racial and ethnic] disparities are causally related to past intentional conduct."[18]

In evaluating whether the Topeka school board had met *its* burden, the circuit majority was moved primarily by the belief that the defendants in this original case of 1954 and 1955 had failed to go much beyond what they did immediately following the *Brown* decrees. The board implemented a basic neighborhood plan in the late fifties, and then "acted as if it had fulfilled its duty to desegregate."[19] It had not even adjusted contiguous school boundaries to encourage integration, except on two isolated occasions. Nor had it tried magnet schools, relying on a "minimally effective"[20] majority to minority transfer plan. Clearly, its actions fell far short of satisfying the commands of *Green* and *Swann*. The "lack of evidence or any attempt to argue that further desegregation is impracticable is perhaps the largest flaw in the school district's case."[21]

The circuit panel ordered Topeka to come up with new integrative initiatives, a determination not affected by a Supreme Court remand of 1992, for reconsideration in the light of *Dowell* and *Freeman*. Both of these cases, the panel argued, involved "comprehensive" approaches to compliance, plans allegedly seeking "to achieve maximum practicable desegregation."[22] In "Topeka, in contrast," the school authorities had done "very little to desegregate its student assignment practices."[23]

The Topeka board is now implementing a multi-stage integration plan which it hopes will secure unitary status. Focused primarily on the elementary schools, it involves boundary changes to promote integration, transportation for those who want majority to minority transfers, closing high majority and high minority schools, and opening magnet schools which will maintain a racial and ethnic mix close to the system average. Middle and high school students will also receive free transportation to aid majority to minority transfer.

Busing is not part of the plan. As of September 1996, the elementary schools of Topeka were 41% minority.[24]

In a brilliant essay analysing the decline of desegregation efforts in America, Professor Orfield finds disturbing parallels between recent developments and the forces which produced and justified the infamous decision in *Plessy* v. *Ferguson*. Now, as then, Professor Orfield argues, courts and political leaders are exalting local sovereignty over the constitutional rights of minorities, "assum[ing] today, as the *Plessy* Court did, that local agencies with a history of treating blacks unfairly [can] now be trusted to treat them fairly with no outside supervision."[25] Judges were also validating resegregation in schools and in society in the 1990's as the result of "'natural forces,'" though their polite references to "'incompatible residential preferences'" had replaced *Plessy's* invocation of "'racial instincts.'"[26] Some jurists were even holding up segregation as a positive "benefit"; Orfield inevitably pointed in this connection to Justice Thomas' suggestion "that segregated black schools might be better for their students."[27]

These trends, warned Professor Orfield, made it vital that there be a fresh "appraisal of the shift toward 'separate but equal' before a new status quo becomes so deeply entrenched that it will simply seem natural and questions will be ignored. We are perilously close to that point now."[28]

The sting of these comments is sharpened by the reflections of a civil rights leader in Oklahoma City, viewing the racially isolated schools left in that city by Judge Bohanon's final order. In Jim Crow days, recalled Rev. W.B. Parker,

> "Wasn't a white face in our classroom . . . . We couldn't get enough books, enough supplies. We couldn't even get our buildings heated . . . . Today I walk through some of these schools in the black neighborhoods, and ***nothing's*** changed. They're as run-down as ever, the paint's peeling, and some teachers have to buy books for the kids . . . . And you don't see a white child anywhere."[29]

But, of course, the regime of "separate but equal" *has* been swept away in America, and in more than merely a technical sense. Racial categories established by law were destroyed by *Brown*, and that is not an insignificant achievement. The Jim Crow system in all sections of the country is no more, and with it has gone some of the more poisonous attitudes toward race nourished by formal apartheid. Indeed, in many school systems, integration remains a valued goal of educators, and of some parents too.

Still, the mild integrationism of Justice Powell and of Judge Miller, generally in voluntary form, is as far as even sympathetic authorities are likely to go in a post-unitary world. The Supreme Court, to be sure, is ever unpredictable, and, stocked with some further Clinton appointees, could yet adopt a more stringent interpretation of Chief Justice Rehnquist's standard of practicality, which halts the rush to unitary status. It might even veer in a somewhat leftward doctrinal direction.

But it is also entirely possible that what will increasingly be restored as we approach 2000 is the educational and social order originally contemplated by those who argued and decided *Brown I*, an order where race could no longer be used to sort out pupils, but where, as Justice Frankfurter put it, "Non-segregation does not mean compulsory mixing," and where "it is likely that at least at the elementary school level, the typical pattern of [a] desegregated school district will show that most schools are almost wholly of one race . . . ."[30] Or in Thurgood Marshall's words of 1955: "Put the dumb colored children in with the dumb white children, and put the smart colored children with the smart white children- that is no problem."[31]

Justice Thurgood Marshall articulated a principled position on integration which went far beyond those sentiments he expressed so long ago. But the Supreme Court of the United States never did assert such a position, perhaps because the justices understood that American society was not yet ready to move farther than the literal professions of *Brown* v. *Board of Education*. Is it any wonder, then, that the schools of 2008 or so could well look, not like the schools of 1948 or of 1978, but remarkably like those of 1968?

Notes

Prologue (pages 1–34)

1. *Brown* v. *Board of Education of Topeka*, 347 US 483 (1954), at 495.
2. *Plessy* v. *Ferguson*, 163 US 537 (1896), at 551.
3. *Ibid.*, at 562.
4. Louis Pollak, *The Constitution and the Supreme Court* (Cleveland, 1966), p. 266.
5. *Brown* v. *Board of Education*, at 495.
6. *Ibid.*
7. *Ibid.*
8. *Brown* v. *Board of Education of Topeka*, 345 US 972 (1953).
9. "Conference Notes of Mr. Justice Clark on the Segregation Cases," printed as Appendix B of Dennis Hutchinson, "Unanimity and Desegregation: Decisionmaking in the Supreme Court, 1948–58," *Georgetown Law Journal* (Vol. 68, 1979), 1, 92.
10. Quoted in Richard Kluger, *Simple Justice* (New York, 1975), p. 603.
11. "Conference Notes of Mr. Justice Clark," 91.
12. Justice Felix Frankfurter, Notes on Conference of January 16, 1954, pp. 3–4. Felix Frankfurter Papers, Harvard Law School Library.
13. "Conference Notes of Mr. Justice Clark," 92.
14. Justice William O. Douglas, "Conference 12–13–52: No. 8 *Brown* v. *Board of Education of Topeka*" (p. 2). William O. Douglas Papers, Library of Congress. This quotation, and others from the Douglas Papers, are cited by permission of the estate of William O. Douglas.
15. Kluger, p. 600.
16. *Ibid.*
17. Quoted in Bernard Schwartz, *Super Chief* (New York, 1983), p. 86.
18. *Ibid.*, p. 86, pp. 86–87.
19. Frankfurter, Notes on Conference of January 16, 1954, p. 3.
20. "Appellants' Brief on Reargument," p. 195. *Records and Briefs of the Supreme Court*, 347 US 483 (1954).
21. *Ibid.*, pp. 191–92.
22. *Ibid.*, pp. 191, 190.
23. Daniel Berman, *It Is So Ordered* (New York, 1966), p. 121.
24. "Appellants' Brief on Further Reargument," p. 17. *Records and Briefs of the Supreme Court*, 349 US 294 (1955).
25. *Ibid.*, p. 29.
26. "Brief for the United States on Further Relief," p. 27. *Ibid.*
27. Leon Friedman (ed.), *Argument* (New York, 1969), p. 503.
28. *Ibid.*, p. 505.
29. Quoted in Kluger, p. 736.
30. Hutchinson, "Unanimity and Desegregation," 55. See also Schwartz, pp. 117–118.
31. Frankfurter, "Memorandum on the Segregation Decree" (April 14, 1955), p. 1. Felix Frankfurter Papers, Harvard Law School Library.
32. *Ibid.*, p. 2.
33. Kluger, p. 740.
34. Frankfurter, "Memorandum on the Segregation Decree," p. 1.

PROLOGUE NOTES CONTINUED

35. Quoted in Schwartz, p. 118.
36. *Brown* v. *Board of Education of Topeka*, 349 US 294 (1955), at 299.
37. *Ibid.*, at 300.
38. *Ibid.*
39. *Ibid.*, at 301 (Italics added).
40. Frankfurter, Memorandum of January 15, 1954, p. 2. Felix Frankfurter Papers, Harvard Law School Library. ("[T]he Court does its duty if it decrees measures that reverse the direction of the unconstitutional policy so as to uproot 'with all deliberate speed.'")
41. The case was *Virginia* v. *West Virginia*, 222 US 17 (1911), at 20.
42. Frankfurter, Memorandum of January 15, 1954, p. 1.
43. Robert Carter and Thurgood Marshall, "The Meaning and Significance of the Supreme Court Decree," *Journal of Negro Education* (Vol. 24, 1955), 397, 403.
44. *Ibid.*, 397.
45. *Ibid.*, 402.
46. *Ibid.*
47. *Ibid.*
48. *Ibid.*, 401.
49. *Ibid.*
50. Quoted in Kluger, pp. 746–47.
51. *Brown* v. *Board of Education*, 347 US 483, at 493.
52. *Ibid.* The original citation is in *Sweatt* v. *Painter*, 339 US 629 (1950), at 634.
53. *Ibid.*, at 493, 493–94. The original citation is in *McLaurin* v. *Oklahoma State Regents*, 339 US 637 (1950), at 641.
54. *Ibid.*, at 494.
55. *Ibid.*
56. *Ibid.*
57. The work cited in footnote eleven was "Effects of Prejudice and Discrimination on Personality Development," a paper given at the Midcentury White House Conference on Children and Youth. This brought together earlier research which Professor Clark and his wife had done. See "Segregation as a Factor in the Racial Identification of Negro Preschool Children," *Journal of Experimental Education* (Vol. 11, 1939), 161; "The Development of Consciousness of Self and the Emergence of Racial Identification in Negro Preschool Children," *Journal of Social Psychology* (Vol. 10, 1939), 591; "Skin Color as a Factor in Racial Identification of Negro Preschool Children," *Journal of Social Psychology* (Vol. 11, 1940), 159. See also, Horowitz, "Aspects of Self Identification in Nursery School Children," *Journal of Psychology* (Vol. 7, 1939), 91.
58. Frank Goodman, "De Facto Segregation: A Constitutional and Empirical Analysis," *California Law Review* (Vol. 60, 1972), 275, 278.
59. See *Henry* v. *Godsell*, 165 F. Supp. 87 (1958); *In the Matter of Skipwith*, 180 N.Y.S. 2d 852 (1958); and the discussion of the early phases of *Taylor* v. *Board of Education of New Rochelle*, found in John Kaplan, "Segregation Litigation and the Schools—Part I: The New Rochelle Experience," *Northwestern University Law Review* (Vol. 58, 1963), 1, 10–35.
60. "Grade School Segregation: The Latest Attack on Racial Discrimination," *Yale Law Journal* (Vol. 61, 1952), 730. Professor Clark replied to his critics in *Prejudice and Your Child* (Boston, 1963). Later studies, beginning in the 1960's, placed their emphasis less on childrens' attitude toward race, as Professor Clark had, than on their general estimate

of personal worth. Some studies, most notably one for Baltimore, showed students in identifiably black schools with a higher sense of self-esteem than those in desegregated schools. But these occurred after *Brown*, of course, and obviously may have been influenced by it. See David Armor, *Forced Justice* (New York, 1995), pp. 99–102; Morris Rosenberg and Roberta G. Simmons, *Black and White Self-Esteem: The Urban School Child* (Washington, D.C., 1971).

61. Edmond Cahn, "Jurisprudence," *New York University Law Review* (Vol. 30, 1955), 150, 157–58.

62. John Kaplan, "Segregation Litigation and the Schools—Part II: The General Northern Problem," *Northwestern University Law Review* (Vol. 58, 1963), 157, 172–73.

63. Charles L. Black, "The Lawfulness of the Segregation Decisions," *Yale Law Journal* (Vol. 69, 1960), 421, 424–25, 424.

64. *Ibid.*, 430, 422 (Footnote 8).

65. Cahn, "Jurisprudence," 150, 158.

66. J. Harvie Wilkinson, *From Brown to Bakke* (New York, 1979), p. 37. The case involved is *Hamilton* v. *Alabama*, 376 US 650 (1964).

67. *Mayor of Baltimore* v. *Dawson*, 350 US 877 (1955); *Holmes* v. *Atlanta*, 350 US 879 (1955); *Gayle* v. *Browder*, 352 US 903 (1956).

68. Paul Kauper, "Segregation in Public Education: The Decline of *Plessy* v. *Ferguson*," *Michigan Law Review* (Vol. 52, 1954), 1137, 1151, 1152.

69. Gunnar Myrdal, *An American Dilemma* (New York, 1944), Vol. II, p. 603.

70. Friedman, p. 47.

71. *Ibid.*, p. 402.

72. *Ibid.*, p. 528.

73. "Appellants' Brief on Further Reargument," p. 11.

74. Jack Greenberg, *Race Relations and American Law* (New York, 1959), p. 240.

75. *Brown* v. *Board of Education*, 349 US 294, at 301.

76. Frankfurter, "Districting," p. 3. Felix Frankfurter Papers, *Harvard Law School Library*.

77. *Brown* v. *Board of Education of Topeka*, 139 F. Supp. 468, 470 (1955).

78. *Ibid.*

79. *Briggs* v. *Elliott*, 132 F. Supp. 776, 777 (1955).

80. *Henry* v. *Godsell*, 90, 91.

Chapter One (pages 35–88)

1. United States Commission on Civil Rights, *Education* (Washington, D.C., 1961), p. 17.

2. *Liddell* v. *Board of Education of City of St. Louis*, 469 F. Supp. 1304, 1317 (1979); United States Commission on Civil Rights, *Public Schools in the North and West* (Washington, D.C., 1962), pp. 266, 267.

3. *Ibid.*, 30, 27, 19.

4. *Congressional Record*, 84th Congress, 2nd Session—Senate (March, 1956), 4460.

5. *Ibid.*

6. See *Bush* v. *Orleans Parish School Board*, 188 F. Supp. 916, 926 (Footnote 12) (1960). Arkansas adopted an interposition amendment to its constitution by popular referendum in 1956. See Tony Freyer, *The Little Rock Crisis* (Westport, Conn., 1984), Ch. 3.

7. The story is told mainly in the endless installments of the New Orleans school case, *Bush* v. *Orleans Parish School Board*. The most prominent are 242 F. 2d 156 (1957); 187 F. Supp. 42 (1960); 188 F. Supp. 916 (1960); 191 F. Supp. 871 (1961); 194 F. Supp.

CHAPTER ONE NOTES CONTINUED

182 (1961). See also *Hall* v. *St. Helena Parish School Board*, 197 F. Supp. 649 (1961).
8. *James* v. *Almond*, 170 F. Supp. 331 (1959); *Griffin* v. *School Board of Prince Edward County*, 377 US 218 (1964).
9. *Aaron* v. *McKinley*, 173 F. Supp. 944 (1959).
10. Raymond Wolters, *The Burden of Brown* (Knoxville, 1984). For earlier phases of the Virginia struggle, see Numan Bartley, *The Rise of Massive Resistance* (Baton Rouge, 1969); James Ely, *The Crisis of Conservative Virginia* (Knoxville, 1976).
11. A superb discussion of the pupil placement system is found in "The Federal Courts and Integration of Southern Schools: Troubled Status of the Pupil Placement Acts," *Columbia Law Review* (Vol. 62, 1962), 1448.
12. *Ibid.*, 1452–53.
13. Daniel Meador, "The Constitution and the Assignment of Pupils to Public Schools," *Virginia Law Review* (Vol. 45, 1959), 517, 571. See also Aubrey Williams, "What's Happening in the South Today," *Lawyers Guild Review* (Vol. 16, 1956), 21.
14. Robert Penn Warren, *Segregation* (New York, 1956), pp. 112–13, 114.
15. Benjamin Muse, *Ten Years of Prelude* (New York, 1964), pp. 68–69.
16. See Wolters, Part Two.
17. See J. Harvie Wilkinson, *From Brown To Bakke* (New York, 1979), p. 85; Reed Sarratt, *The Ordeal of Desegregation* (New York, 1966), p. 359.
18. *Carson* v. *Warlick*, 238 F. 2d 724 (1956).
19. *Shuttlesworth* v. *Birmingham Board of Education*, 162 F. Supp. 372, 381 (Footnote 11) (1958).
20. *Ibid.*, 383.
21. 358 US 101 (1958).
22. 162 F. Supp., 374.
23. Sarratt, p. 359.
24. Alexander Bickel, "The Decade of School Segregation: Progress and Prospects," *Columbia Law Review* (Vol. 64, 1964), 193, 202.
25. Robert L. Carter, "The Warren Court and Desegregation," *Michigan Law Review* (Vol. 67, 1968), 237, 243–44.
26. *Ibid.*, 244.
27. Kenneth B. Clark, "The Social Scientists, the *Brown* Decision, and Contemporary Confusion," in Leon Friedman (ed.), *Argument* (New York, 1969), p. xxxvii.
28. Charles L. Black, "Paths to Desegregation," *The New Republic* (October 21, 1957), 10, 14.
29. "Brief for Appellants," *Gibson* v. *Board of Public Instruction of Dade County*, 272 F. 2d 763 (1959), p. 16. NAACP Papers, Part V, Box 42, Library of Congress.
30. See the excellent studies by Herman Belz, *Equality Transformed* (New Brunswick, N.J., 1991); Hugh Davis Graham, *The Civil Rights Era* (New York, 1990).
31. *Holland* v. *Board of Public Instruction*, 258 F. 2d 730 (1958).
32. *Ibid.*, 732.
33. *Ibid.*, 731, 733.
34. *Gibson* v. *Board of Public Instruction of Dade County*, 272 F. 2d 763, 766 (1959).
35. *Ibid.*, 767.
36. *Ibid.*, 766.
37. *Ibid.*, 767.
38. "Brief for Appellees," *Parham* v. *Dove*, 271 F. 2d 132 (1959), p. 11. NAACP Papers,

Part V, Box 37, Library of Congress.

39. *Ibid.*, pp. 20, 19 (Italics added).
40. *Dove* v. *Parham*, 176 F. Supp. 242 (1959).
41. *Parham* v. *Dove*, 271 F. 2d 132 (1959).
42. *Dove* v. *Parham*, 181 F. Supp. 504, 517 (1960). See also 183 F. Supp. 389 (1960).
43. *Dove* v. *Parham*, 282 F. 2d 256, 260 (1960).
44. *Ibid.*, 259.
45. *Ibid.*, 258.
46. *Green* v. *School Board of Roanoke*, 304 F. 2d (1962); *Marsh* v. *County School Board*, 305 F. 2d 94 (1962); *Jeffers* v. *Whitley*, 309 F. 2d 621 (1962); *Wheeler* v. *Durham Board of Education*, 309 F. 2d 630 (1962); *Brunson* v. *Board of Trustees*, 311 F. 2d 107 (1962); *Bradley* v. *School Board of Richmond*, 317 F. 2d 429 (1963); *Jackson* v. *School Board*, 321 F. 2d 230 (1963); *Bell* v. *School Board*, 321 F. 2d 494 (1962), (all Fourth Circuit). *Augustus* v. *Board of Public Instruction*, 306 F. 2d 862 (1962); *Bush* v. *Orleans Parish School Board*, 308 F. 2d 491 (1962); *Potts* v. *Flax*, 313 F. 2d 284 (1963), (Fifth Circuit). *Northcross* v. *Board of Education of Memphis*, 302 F. 2d 818 (1962), (Sixth Circuit).
47. *Watson* v. *City of Memphis*, 373 US 526 (1963), at 530.
48. See *Calhoun* v. *Latimer*, 321 F. 2d 302 (1963); *Davis* v. *Board of School Commissioners of Mobile*, 322 F. 2d 356 (1963); *Armstrong* v. *Board of Education of Birmingham*, 323 F. 2d 333 (1963). The Supreme Court heard the *Calhoun* case on certiorari, 377 US 263 (1964), but by this time changes had been made in the Atlanta desegregation plan, which originally made initial assignments on the basis of race. Later versions of *Davis* and *Armstrong* indicated that dual attendance zones must be abolished as part of a desegregation plan. 333 F. 2d 47; 333 F. 2d 53.
49. *Northcross* v. *Board of Education of Memphis*, 302 F. 2d 818, 824 (1962) (Italics added).
50. *Buckner* v. *County School Board*, 332 F. 2d 452, 454 (1964).
51. *Bush* v. *Orleans Parish School Board*, 308 F. 2d 491, 499 (1962).
52. *Dove* v. *Parham*, 196 F. Supp. 944, 949 (1961).
53. *United States* v. *Jefferson County Board of Education*, 380 F. 2d 385, 404 (1967).
54. United States Commission on Civil Rights, *Survey of Desegregation in the Southern and Border States, 1965–66* (Washington, D.C., 1966), p. 36.
55. *Ibid.*, p. 38.
56. *Ibid.*, p. 33.
57. *Ibid.*, p. 51.
58. *Kemp* v. *Beasley*, 352 F. 2d 14, 17 (1965).
59. *Brown* v. *Board of Education*, 349 US 294 (1955), at 298 (Italics added).
60. 42 U.S.C., sect. 2000d (1974), 78 Stat. 252.
61. Gary Orfield, *The Reconstruction of Southern Education* (New York, 1969), p. 126.
62. "General Statement of Policies Under Title VI of the Civil Rights Act of 1964 Respecting Desegregation of Elementary and Secondary Schools" (March, 1963). Reprinted in *Price* v. *Denison Independent School District*, 348 F. 2d 1010, 1018 (1965).
63. George Foster, "Title VI: Southern Education Faces the Facts," *Saturday Review of Literature* (March 20, 1965), 60, 61.
64. *Ibid.*
65. Though one intrepid district judge in Kentucky, Hiram Church Ford, did in fact do so. See *Mason* v. *Jessamine County Board of Education*, 8 *Race Relations Law Reporter* 530 (1963); *Mack* v. *Frankfort Board of Education*, 8 *Race Relations Law Reporter* 945

CHAPTER ONE NOTES CONTINUED

(1963).

66. *Bradley* v. *School Board of Richmond*, 345 F. 2d 310, 316 (1965).
67. *Ibid.*
68. *Ibid.*, 322.
69. *Ibid.*, 323.
70. *Ibid.*, 322, 323 (Italics added).
71. *Kemp* v. *Beasley*, 21.
72. *Ibid.*
73. *Clark* v. *Board of Education of Little Rock*, 369 F. 2d 661, 665 (1966) (Italics added).
74. *Ibid.*, 666.
75. *Lockett* v. *Board of Education of Muscogee County*, 342 F. 2d 225 (1965).
76. *Singleton* v. *Jackson Municipal Separate School District*, 348 F. 2d 729 (1965) (*Singleton I*); 355 F. 2d 865 (1966) (*Singleton II*).
77. *Singleton I*, 729.
78. *Ibid.*, 730.
79. *Ibid.*, 730 (Footnote 5) (Italics added).
80. "The Decade of School Segregation," 232.
81. "Title VI: Southern Education Faces the Facts," 61.
82. *Goss* v. *Board of Education of Knoxville*, 186 F. Supp. 559, 563 (1960).
83. *Goss* v. *Board of Education of Knoxville*, 373 US 683 (1963).
84. *Northcross* v. *Board of Education of Memphis*, 333 F. 2d 661, 663 (1964).
85. *Ibid.*, 664.
86. An excellent discussion of these distortions is found in Robert Sedler, Review of Lino Graglia, *Disaster by Decree*, *Cornell Law Review* (Vol. 62, 1977), 645. See also Karl and Alma Taeuber, *Negroes in Cities* (Chicago, 1966).
87. "Brief of Appellees" (May 1966), *Board of Education of Oklahoma City* v. *Dowell*, 375 F. 2d 158 (1967), p. 25. NAACP Legal Defense Fund Archives, New York City.
88. Alexander Bickel, "Untangling the Busing Snarl," *The New Republic* (September 23, 1972), 21, 22.
89. "Petition for Writ of Certiorari," *Gilliam* v. *School Board of Hopewell*, 345 F. 2d 325 (1965), pp. 19, 28–29. NAACP Legal Defense Fund Archives, New York City.
90. Hearing in the United States District Court of Delaware, August 14, 1962, pp. 34–37.
91. See *Mapp* v. *Board of Chattanooga*, 319 F. 2d 571 (1963), Reversing in part, 203 F. Supp. 843 (1962); *Gilliam* v. *School Board of Hopewell*, 345 F. 2d 325 (1965);*Swann* v. *Charlotte–Mecklenburg Board of Education*, 369 F. 2d 29 (1966), Affirming 243 F. Supp. 667 (1965); *Goss* v. *Board of Education of Knoxville*, 270 F. 2d 903 (1967) (detailing earlier history of the case, unreported, in which a zoning plan was modified and accepted by parties).
92. *Gilliam* v. *School Board of Hopewell*, 345 F. 2d 325, 328 (1965).
93. *Evans* v. *Buchanan*, 172 F. Supp. 508, 516 (1959).
94. *Ibid.*
95. *Ibid.* (Italics added).
96. *Evans* v. *Buchanan*, 173 F. Supp. 891, 892 (1959).
97. *Evans* v. *Buchanan*, 207 F. Supp. 820, 823–24 (1962).
98. *Ibid.*, 824.
99. *Ibid.*, 825.
100. *Dowell* v. *School Board of Oklahoma City*, 244 F. Supp. 971 (1965).

101. For an excellent and overdue biography of Judge Luther Bohanon see Jace Weaver, *Then to the Rock Let Me Fly: Luther Bohanon and Judicial Activism* (Norman, Oklahoma, 1993).

102. *Dowell* v. *School Board of Oklahoma City*, 219 F. Supp. 427, 447 (1963).

103. Weaver, *Then to the Rock Let Me Fly*, p. 90.

104. *Dowell* v. *School Board of Oklahoma City*, 244 F. Supp., 975.

105. *Ibid.*

106. *Ibid.*, 976.

107. *Ibid.*

108. *Ibid.*, 978.

109. *Ibid.*

110. *Dowell* v. *School Board of Oklahoma City*, 219 F. Supp., 434.

111. *Ibid.* (Italics added).

112. *Ibid.*, 441.

113. *Dowell* v. *School Board of Oklahoma City*, 244 F. Supp., 981.

114. *Branche* v. *Board of Education of Hampstead*, 204 F. Supp. 150 (1962); *Blocker* v. *Board of Education of Manhasset*, 226 F. Supp. 208 (1964); *Barksdale* v. *Springfield School Committee*, 237 F. Supp. 543. *Branche* and *Blocker* were not appealed, and, during the course of the *Barksdale* appeal, the Springfield school board, on its own initiative, took action almost identical to the district court order. See *Barksdale* v. *Springfield School Committee*, 348 F. 2d 261 (1965).

115. Owen Fiss, "Racial Imbalance in the Public Schools: The Constitutional Concepts," *Harvard Law Review* (Vol. 78, 1965), 564.

116. *Ibid.*, 588.

117. *Ibid.*, 590.

118. *Ibid.*, 604.

119. *Ibid.*, 606.

120. *Ibid.*, 568 (Footnote 2).

121. James Coleman, et. al., *Equality of Educational Opportunity* (Washington, D.C., 1966).

122. See, for example, Henry S. Dyer, "School Factors and Equal Educational Opportunity," *Harvard Educational Review* (Vol. 38, 1968), 38; "What Difference Do Schools Make?" *Saturday Review of Literature* (January 20, 1968), 57.

123. *Blocker* v. *School Board of Manhasset*, 228.

124. John Kaplan, "Segregation Litigation and the Schools," *Northwestern University Law Review* (Vol. 58, 1963), 157, 175.

125. See Morris Rosenberg and Roberta G. Simmons, *Black and White Self-Esteem: The Urban School Child* (Washington, D.C., 1971), pp. 6–7.

126. J. Skelly Wright, "Public School Desegregation: Legal Remedies for De Facto Segregation," *New York University Law Review* (Vol. 40, 1965), 285. Judge Wright gave the gist of the article as the James Madison Lecture at N.Y.U. on February 17, 1965.

127. *Ibid.*, 296.

128. *Ibid.*, 295.

129. *Ibid.*, 301.

130. *Deal* v. *Cincinnati Board of Education*, 244 F. Supp. 572 (1965); Affirmed, 369 F. 2d 55 (1966).

131. *Dowell* v. *School Board of Oklahoma City*, 244 F. Supp., 975, 976.

132. *Ibid.*, 980.

133. *Ibid.*, 980 (Footnote 2).

CHAPTER ONE NOTES CONTINUED

134. "Revised Statement of Policies For School Desegregation Plans Under Title VI of the Civil Rights Act of 1964" (April, 1966). Reprinted in Hearings before the Special Subcommittee on Civil Rights of the Committee on the Judiciary, House of Representatives, 89th Congress, 2nd Session (1966), A25–A35.
135. *Ibid.*, A33.
136. Letter to members of Congress from HEW Secretary John W. Gardner, April 9, 1966. Reprinted in *Policies and Guidelines for School Desegregation*," Hearings before the Committee on Rules, House of Representatives, 89th Congress, 2nd Session (1966), p. 31.
137. Southern reaction to the revised guidelines is discussed in Wilkinson, pp. 102–08, and in Orfield, Ch. 5.
138. "Revised Statement of Policies," A 27 (Italics added).
139. See Orfield, pp. 135–47.
140. James Dunn, "Title VI, The Guidelines and School Segregation in the South," *Virginia Law Review* (Vol. 53, 1967), 42.
141. *Ibid.*, 68, 67.
142. *Ibid.*, 69.
143. *Ibid.*
144. *Ibid.*
145. Frank T. Read, "Judicial Evolution of the Law of School Integration," in Betsy Levin and Willis D. Hawley (eds.), *The Courts, Social Science, and School Desegregation* (New Brunswick, N.J., 1977), p. 20.
146. *United States* v. *Jefferson County Board of Education*, 372 F. 2d 836 (1966).

Chapter Two (pages 89–126)

1. Jack Bass, *Unlikely Heroes* (New York, 1981), p. 45.
2. *Ibid.*, p. 46.
3. *United States* v. *Louisiana*, 225 F. Supp. 353 (1963).
4. *Ibid.*, 393.
5. *Ibid.*
6. *Ibid.*, 396.
7. *United States* v. *Jefferson County Board of Education*, 372 F. 2d 836 (Dec. 29, 1966).
8. *Ibid.*, 847.
9. *Ibid.*, 869.
10. *Ibid.*, 846 (footnote 5).
11. *Ibid.*, 868.
12. *Ibid.*, 875.
13. *Ibid.*, 867.
14. *Ibid.*
15. *Ibid.*, 866.
16. *Ibid.*, 868. (Italics added).
17. *Ibid.*, 846.
18. *Ibid.*, 847 (footnote 5).
19. *Ibid.*, 876.
20. *Ibid.*, 868.
21. *Ibid.*, 868.

22. *Ibid.*, 876.
23. *Ibid.*
24. *Ibid.*
25. *Ibid.*
26. 42 U.S.C., sect. 2000c (b) (1974), 78 Stat. 246.
27. *Congressional Record*, 88th Congress, 2nd Session—House (1964), 1598, 2280.
28. *Civil Rights*, Hearings before Subcommittee No. 5 of the Committee on the Judiciary, House of Representatives, 88th Congress, 1st Session (1963), p. 1783.
29. *Ibid.*
30. *United States* v. *Jefferson County Board of Education*, 866.
31. *Ibid.*, 878.
32. 42 U.S.C., sect. 2000 c–6 (A) (1974), 78 Stat. 248.
33. *Congressional Record*, 88th Congress, 2nd Session—Senate (1964), 12715.
34. *Ibid.*, 12717.
35. *United States* v. *Jefferson County Board of Education*, 881.
36. *Ibid.*, 873.
37. *United States* v. *Jefferson County Board of Education*, 380 F. 2d 385, 389 (March 29, 1967).
38. *Ibid.*, 397–98.
39. *Ibid.*, 414.
40. *Bowman* v. *County School Board of Charles City County*, 382 F. 2d 326, 327 (1967).
41. *Monroe* v. *Board of Commissioners*, 380 F. 2d 955, 957 (1967).
42. *Kemp* v. *Beasley*, 389 F. 2d 178 (1968). The other three were in *Kelley* v. *Altheimer, Arkansas Public School District No. 22*, 378 F. 2d 483 (1967); *Yarbrough* v. *Hulbert-West Memphis School District*, 380 F. 2d (1967); *Jackson* v. *Marvell School District*, 389 F. 2d 740 (1968).
43. *Clark* v. *Board of Education of Little Rock School District*, 374 F. 2d 569 (1967); *Raney* v. *Board of Education of Gould School District*, 381 F. 2d 252 (1967).
44. The ultimate Supreme Court decisions in the cases are at 391 US 430, 443, 450 (1968).
45. Oral Argument in *Monroe* v. *Board of School Commissioners*, Kurland and Casper, *Landmark Briefs and Arguments of the Supreme Court*, Vol. 66, p. 240.
46. Oral Argument in *Green* v. *School Board of New Kent County*, Kurland and Casper, Vol. 66, p. 220.
47. "Brief for the Petitioners," *Green* v. *School Board of New Kent County*, p. 38. *Briefs and Records of the Supreme Court*, 391 US 430.
48. "Brief for Petitioners," *Monroe* v. *Board of School Commissioners*, p. 18. *Records and Briefs of the Supreme Court*, 390 US 450.
49. "Brief for the Petitioners," *Green* v. *School Board of New Kent County*, pp. 22, 25.
50. "Brief for Petitioners," *Raney* v. *Board of Education*, pp. 28–29. *Records and Briefs of the Supreme Court*, 391 US 443.
51. Oral Argument in *Raney* v. *Board of Education*, Casper and Kurland, Vol. 66, pp. 265–66.
52. Oral Argument of United States as *Amicus Curiae*, Casper and Kurland, Vol. 66, p. 283.
53. Casper and Kurland, Vol. 66, p. 238.
54. *Ibid.*
55. *Ibid.*
56. *Ibid.*, pp. 254–55.
57. *Ibid.*, p. 248.
58. See Bernard Schwartz, *Super Chief* (New York, 1983), pp. 703–06.

CHAPTER TWO NOTES CONTINUED

59. Quoted in Schwartz, p. 704.
60. "First Draft," *Green* v. *School Board of New Kent County*, p. 8. William J. Brennan Papers, Box 177, Library of Congress.
61. "First Draft," *Monroe* v. *Board of Commissioners*, p. 7. William J. Brennan Papers, Box 177, Library of Congress.
62. Quoted in Schwartz, p. 705.
63. *Ibid.*
64. Schwartz, p. 706.
65. *Green* v. *School Board of New Kent County*, 391 US 430, at 439.
66. *Ibid.*, at 442.
67. *Ibid.*, at 437–38.
68. *Ibid.*, at 441.
69. *Goss* v. *School Board of Knoxville*, 373 US 683 (1963), at 689.
70. *Monroe* v. *Board of Commissioners of Jackson, Tennessee*, 391 US 450 (1968), at 459.
71. Lino Graglia, *Disaster by Decree* (Ithaca, 1976), p. 73.
72. *Green* v. *School Board of New Kent County*, at 435, 437, 438.
73. *Ibid.*, at 442 (footnote 6).
74. *Monroe* v. *Board of School Commissioners*, at 453.
75. Alexander Bickel, *The Supreme Court and the Idea of Progress* (New York, 1970), p. 128.
76. *Alexander* v. *Holmes County Board of Education*, 396 US 19 (1969), at 20.
77. *Augustus* v. *Board of Public Instruction of Escambia County*, 185 F. Supp. 450, 451 (1960).
78. *Ibid.*
79. *Ibid.*, 453.
80. *Ibid.*
81. *Augustus* v. *Board of Education*, 306 F. 2d 862 (1962).
82. *Mapp* v. *Board of Education of City of Chattanooga*, 319 F. 2d 571, 576 (1963). See also *Northcross* v. *Board of Education of City of Memphis*, 333 F. 2d 661, 666–67 (1964).
83. *Ibid.* (Italics added).
84. *Ibid.*
85. George W. Foster, "Title VI: Southern Education Faces the Facts," *Saturday Review of Literature* (March 20, 1965), 60, 77.
86. *Kemp* v. *Beasley*, 352 F. 2d 14, 22 (1965).
87. *Ibid.*
88. *Bradley* v. *School Board of City of Richmond*, 345 F. 2d 310, 320 (1965).
89. *Ibid.*
90. *Bradley* v. *School Board of City of Richmond*, 382 US 103 (1965).
91. *Ibid.*
92. *Ibid.*, at 105.
93. *Wheeler* v. *Durham City Board of Education*, 363 F. 2d 738, 740 (1966).
94. *Dowell* v. *School Board of Oklahoma City*, 244 F. Supp. 971, 978 (1965).
95. *Kier* v. *County School Board of Augusta County*, 249 F. Supp. 239, 248 (1966).
96. *Ibid.*
97. *Bowman* v. *County School Board of Charles City County*, 328–29.
98. See Hal R. Lieberman, "Teachers and the Fourteenth Amendment—The Role of the

Faculty in the Desegregation Process," *North Carolina Law Review* (Vol. 46, 1968), 313, 352.

99. *Harris* v. *Bullock County Board of Education*, 253 F. Supp. 276, 278 (1966); *Carr* v. *Montgomery Board of Education*, 253 F. Supp. 306, 310 (1966); *Lee* v. *Macon County Board of Education*, 253 F. Supp. 727, 729 (1966).

100. Lieberman has an excellent discussion of the revised guidelines at 341–46.

101. *United States* v. *Jefferson County Board of Education*, 380 F 2d 385, 394.

102. *Ibid.*

103. *Ibid.* (Italics added).

104. *Yarbrough* v. *Hulbert-West Memphis School District*, 969.

105. *Kelley* v. *Altheimer, Arkansas Public School District No. 22*, 498 (Footnote 24).

106. *Yarbrough* v. *Hulbert-West Memphis School District*, 969.

107. *Carr* v. *Montgomery County Board of Education*, 289 F. Supp. 647, 654 (1968).

108. *Ibid.*, 658.

109. *Ibid.*, 654.

110. *Montgomery County Board of Education* v. *Carr*, 400 F. 2d 1, 5 (1968).

111. *Ibid.*, 7.

112. *Montgomery County Board of Education* v. *Carr*, 402 F. 2d 782 (1968).

113. *United States* v. *Montgomery County Board of Education*, 395 US 225 (1969).

114. *Ibid.*, at 236.

115. *Ibid.*, at 233.

116. *Ibid.*, at 235, 236.

117. *Ibid.*, at 234.

118. J. Harvie Wilkinson, *From Brown to Bakke* (New York, 1979), p. 118.

Chapter Three (pages 127–176)

1. *Henry* v. *Clarksdale Municipal Separate School District*, 409 F. 2d 682, 689 (1969).

2. See *Adams* v. *Matthews*, 403 F. 2d 181 (1968); *Hall* v. *St. Helena Parish School Board*, 417 F. 2d 801 (1969); *United States* v. *Hinds County School Board*, 417 F. 2d 1032 (1969).

3. *United States* v. *Greenwood Municipal Separate School District*, 406 F. 2d 1086, 1093 (1969).

4. *Brewer* v. *School Board of Norfolk*, 397 F. 2d 37, 41–42 (1968).

5. *Kelley* v. *Metropolitan County Board of Education*, 317 F. Supp. 980, 984 (1970).

6. *Ibid.*, 985, 990–91.

7. *Ibid.*, 990.

8. *Ibid.*

9. *Ibid.*, 985.

10. *Ellis* v. *Board of Orange County*, 423 F. 2d 203, 207 (1970).

11. *Henry* v. *Clarksdale Municipal Separate School District*, 433 F. 2d 387 (1970).

12. *Chambers* v. *Iredell County Board of Education*, 423 F. 2d 613 (1970).

13. *Northcross* v. *Board of Education of Memphis*, 312 F. Supp. 1150 (1970).

14. *Ross* v. *Eckels*, 317 F. Supp. 512 (1970).

15. *Clark* v. *Board of Education of Little Rock*, 316 F. Supp. 1209 (1970).

16. *Northcross* v. *Board of Education of Memphis*, 1157–58.

17. *Ross* v. *Eckels*, 434 F. 2d 1140 (1970).

18. *Pate* v. *Dade County School Board*, 434 F. 2d 1151 (1970).

CHAPTER THREE NOTES CONTINUED

19. *Ross* v. *Eckels*, 1148.
20. See *Beckett* v. *School Board of Norfolk*, 308 F. Supp. 1274, 1276 (1969); *Northcross* v. *Board of Education of Memphis*, 1156; *Ross* v. *Eckels*, 317 F. Supp., 515.
21. Gary Orfield, *Must We Bus?* (Washington, D.C., 1978), p. 243.
22. Hearings before the *Senate Select Committee on Equal Educational Opportunity*, 91st Congress, 2nd Session (1970), pp. 1644, 1646.
23. Governor Lester Maddox to Justice William J. Brennan, October 14, 1970. William J. Brennan Papers, Box 241, Library of Congress.
24. *Congressional Record*, 91st Congress, 2nd Session—Senate (1970), 2892.
25. *Ibid.*, 3560.
26. Orfield, *Must We Bus?* (Washington, D.C., 1978), p. 244.
27. *Congressional Record*, 91st Congress, 2nd Session—Senate (1970), 3560–61.
28. *Ibid.*, 3569.
29. *Ibid.*, 3574–75.
30. *Ibid.*, 8874.
31. *Ibid.*, 8885.
32. *Davis* v. *School District of Pontiac*, 309 F. Supp. 734, 739, 741 (1970).
33. *Ibid.*, 745.
34. *Spangler* v. *Pasadena City Board of Education*, 311 F. Supp. 501, 506 (Footnote 4), 1970.
35. *Ibid.*, 506 (Footnote 4), 504.
36. *Racial Isolation in the Schools* (Washington, D.C., 1967), pp. 100–114.
37. Senate Hearings, p. 777.
38. *Ibid.*, p. 113.
39. *Ibid.*, p. 106.
40. *Hobson* v. *Hansen*, 269 F. Supp. 401, 419–21 (1967).
41. *Keyes* v. *School District No. 1*, *Denver*, *Colorado*, 313 F. Supp. 90, 94 (1970).
42. *Beckett* v. *School Board of Norfolk*, 1284–86.
43. *Brewer* v. *School Board of Norfolk*, 434 F. 2d 408 (1970).
44. *Brunson* v. *Board of Trustees of School District No. 1 of Clarendon County*, 429 F. 2d 820, 826 (1970).
45. *Ibid.*
46. *Ibid.*
47. *Ibid.*
48. Frederick Mosteller and Daniel Moynihan (eds.), *On Equality of Educational Opportunity* (New York, 1972).
49. Senate Hearings, p. 2284.
50. *Ibid.*, p. 2307.
51. *Ibid*, p. 1613.
52. *Deal* v. *Cincinnati Board of Education*, 419 F. 2d 1387 (1969).
53. *Spangler* v. *Pasadena City Board of Education*, 512–13.
54. Senate Hearings, p. 2285.
55. *Ibid.*, p. 1634.
56. *Ibid.*, p. 2300.
57. *Ibid.*, p. 71.
58. *Ibid*, p. 78.
59. *Ibid.*, p. 72.

60. *Ibid.*, pp. 72, 76.
61. *Davis* v. *School Commissioners of Mobile County*, 364 F. 2d 896, 899 (1966).
62. *Davis* v. *School Commissioners of Mobile County*, 414 F. 2d 609, 610 (1969).
63. *Davis* v. *School Commissioners of Mobile County*, 430 F. 2d 883, 888 (1970).
64. *Swann* v. *Charlotte-Mecklenburg Board of Education*, 243 F. Supp. 667 (1965).
65. *Swann* v. *Charlotte-Mecklenburg Board of Education*, 300 F. Supp. 1358, 1372 (1969).
66. *Ibid.*
67. *Ibid.*, 1371.
68. *Ibid.*
69. *Swann* v. *Charlotte-Mecklenburg Board of Education*, 306 F. Supp. 1299, 1303 (1969).
70. *Ibid.*, 1312.
71. *Swann* v. *Charlotte-Mecklenburg Board of Education*, 311 F. Supp. 265, 266 (1970).
72. *Ibid.*, 268.
73. *Swann*, 300 F. Supp. 1358, 1371.
74. Quoted in *North Carolina Board of Education* v. *Swann*, 402 US 43 (1971), at 44 (Footnote 1).
75. *Swann* v. *North Carolina Board of Education*, 312 F. Supp. 503 (1970).
76. *Swann*, 300 F. Supp. 1358, 1372, 1366.
77. *Swann*, 306 F. Supp. 1299, 1304.
78. *Swann*, 300 F. Supp. 1358, 1369.
79. *Swann* v. *Charlotte-Mecklenburg Board of Education*, 306 F. Supp. 1291, 1297 (1969).
80. *Swann*, 306 F. Supp. 1299, 1309.
81. *Swann* v. *Charlotte-Mecklenburg Board of Education*, 397 US 978 (1970).
82. *Swann* v. *Charlotte-Mecklenburg Board of Education*, 431 F. 2d 138, 141 (1970).
83. *Ibid.*, 143.
84. *Ibid.*, 159.
85. "Memorandum of August 3, 1970," Br. A 10. *Records and Briefs of the Supreme Court*, 402 US 1 (1971).
86. *Ibid.*
87. Oral Argument of United States as Amicus Curiae, *Swann* v. *Charlotte-Mecklenburg Board of Education*, 402 US 1 (1971). Reprinted in Kurland and Casper (eds.), *Landmark Briefs and Arguments of the Supreme Court* (Arlington, Va., 1975–), Vol. 70, p. 629.
88. Brief of United Negro College Fund, et. al., *Swann* v. *Charlotte-Mecklenburg Board of Education*, pp. 13, 17–18. *Briefs and Records of the Supreme Court*, 402 US 1 (1971).
89. Bernard Schwartz, *Swann's Way* (New York, 1986). I have not tried, therefore, to give an exhaustive account of the justices' deliberations in *Swann*, but to focus on what I feel to be the key interpretive points.
90. "Memorandum and First Draft *Swann* Opinion" (December 8, 1970). John Marshall Harlan Papers, Box 433, Seeley G. Mudd Manuscript Library, Princeton University. Reprinted in Schwartz, pp. 207–221, p. 207.
91. *Ibid.*, p. 215.
92. *Ibid.*, p. 215 (Footnote 10) (Italics added).
93. *Ibid.*
94. *Ibid.*, p. 215.
95. *Ibid.*, p. 217.
96. *Ibid.*, p. 218.
97. *Ibid.*
98. *Ibid.*, p. 219.

CHAPTER THREE NOTES CONTINUED

99. *Ibid.*
100. *Ibid.*
101. *Ibid.*
102. *Ibid.*
103. *Ibid.*, p. 221.
104. *Ibid.*, p. 220.
105. *Ibid.*
106. *Ibid.* (Italics added).
107. *Ibid.*, p. 220 (Footnote 14) (Italics added).
108. *Ibid.*, p. 220.
109. *Ibid.*, p. 216, 215.
110. *Ibid.*, p. 221.
111. "Memorandum of Mr. Justice Harlan" (November 3, 1970), p. 14. John Marshall Harlan Papers, Seeley G. Mudd Manuscript Library, Box 433, Princeton University. Published with permission of Princeton University Library.
112. *Ibid.*, pp. 15, 14.
113. *Ibid.*, pp. 15–16.
114. *Ibid.*, p. 23.
115. *Ibid.*
116. Schwartz, p. 108.
117. "Memorandum of Justice William J. Brennan" (undated), pp. 1–2. William J. Brennan Papers, Box 241, Library of Congress.
118. "Memorandum from Mr. Justice Brennan," March, 1970, p. 1. William J. Brennan Papers, Box 241, Library of Congress.
119. Justice William J. Brennan to the Chief Justice, December 30, 1970, p. 1. William J. Brennan Papers, Box 241, Library of Congress.
120. *Ibid.*, p. 6 (Italics added).
121. "Memorandum to the Conference," January 12, 1971, p. 13. Thurgood Marshall Papers, Box 71, Library of Congress.
122. "Memorandum of Mr. Justice Stewart" (December 14, 1970), pp. 10, 13. William O. Douglas Papers, Box 1513, Library of Congress.
123. *Ibid.*, pp. 15–16.
124. *Ibid.*, pp. 18–19.
125. *Ibid.*, p. 19.
126. *Ibid.*, p. 28.
127. *Ibid.*, p. 26.
128. *Ibid.*, p. 34.
129. Schwartz, p. 129.
130. Memorandum and Second Draft of *Swann*, January 11, 1971, Frontispiece. Thurgood Marshall Papers, Box 71, Library of Congress.
131. *Ibid.*, pp. 29–33.
132. "Mr. Justice Douglas, dissenting in part" (January 13, 1971), p. 7. William O. Douglas Papers, Box 1514, Library of Congress.
133. "Mr. Justice Stewart, dissenting in part," February, 1971, p. 33. Thurgood Marshall Papers, Box 71, Library of Congress.
134. Memorandum and Third Draft of *Swann*, March 4, 1971, p. 25. William O. Douglas Papers, Box 1514, Library of Congress.

135. *Ibid.*, p. 23.
136. *Ibid.*, p. 28.
137. *Ibid.*, p. 27.
138. Justice William J. Brennan to the Chief Justice, March 8, 1971, p. 5. William J. Brennan Papers, Box 241, Library of Congress.
139. Justice William O. Douglas to the Chief Justice, March 6, 1971. William O. Douglas Papers, Box 1514, Library of Congress.
140. Justice John Marshall Harlan to the Chief Justice, March 11, 1971, p. 1. John Marshall Harlan Papers, Box 433, Seeley G. Mudd Manuscript Library, Princeton University. Published with permission of Princeton University Library.
141. *Ibid.*, pp. 2–3.
142. Memorandum and Fourth Draft of *Swann*, March 16, 1971, p. 28. William O. Douglas Papers, Box 1514, Library of Congress.
143. *Ibid.*, p. 26.
144. "Attachment to Letter of John Marshall Harlan to the Chief Justice," March 11, 1971, p. 2.
145. Memorandum and Fourth Draft of *Swann*, p. 23.
146. Justice William O. Douglas to the Chief Justice, March 16, 1971. William O. Douglas Papers, Box 1514, Library of Congress.
147. Mr. Justice Douglas (March 19, 1971), p. 3. William O. Douglas Papers, Box 1514, Library of Congress.
148. Memorandum and Fourth Draft of *Swann*, p. 28a.
149. *Ibid.*, pp. 29–31.
150. Justice William J. Brennan to the Chief Justice, March 23, 1971, pp. 2–3. William J. Brennan Papers, Box 241, Library of Congress.
151. *Swann* v. *Charlotte-Mecklenburg Board of Education*, 402 US 1 (1971), at 23.
152. Schwartz, p. 101.
153. *Ibid.*, p. 177.
154. *Davis* v. *School Commissioners of Mobile County*, 402 US 33 (1971), at 37.
155. *Ibid.*, at 38.
156. *North Carolina Board of Education* v. *Swann*, at 46.
157. *Kelly* v. *Metropolitan City Board of Nashville*, 463 F. 2d 732 (1972).
158. Orfield, p. 25.
159. *Northcross* v. *Board of Memphis City Schools*, 489 F. 2d 15 (1973).
160. *Goss* v. *Board of Education of Knoxville*, 340 F. Supp. 711 (1972); Affirmed and remanded, 482 F. 2d 1044 (1973).
161. *Clark* v. *Board of Education of Little Rock*, 328 F. Supp. 1205 (1971); 449 F. 2d 493 (1971); 465 F. 2d 1044 (1972).
162. Orfield, p. 25.
163. *Swann*, at 26.
164. Frank Goodman, "De Facto Segregation," *California Law Review* (Vol. 60, 1972), 275, 293.
165. Owen Fiss, "The Charlotte-Mecklenburg Case—Its Significance for Northern School Desegregation," *University of Chicago Law Review* (Vol. 38, 1971), 697, 700 (Italics added).
166. *Ibid.*, 705.
167. *Swann*, at 31.
168. *Winston-Salem/Forsyth County Board of Education* v. *Scott*, 404 US 1221 (1971), at 1224.

CHAPTER THREE NOTES CONTINUED

169. *Ibid.*, at 1225.
170. *Ibid.*, at 1226. Burger added the emphasis.
171. *Ibid.*, at 1227.
172. *Ibid.*
173. Lino Graglia, *Disaster by Decree* (Ithaca, N.Y., 1976), pp. 140–41.
174. Robert Sedler, Review of Lino Graglia, *Disaster by Decree, Cornell Law Review* (Vol. 62, 1977), 645, 651, 652.
175. *Ibid.*, 653.
176. *Ibid.*
177. *Ibid.*
178. Karl and Alma Taeuber, *Negroes in Cities* (Chicago, 1966), p. 40.
179. "The Charlotte-Mecklenburg Case," 705.
180. *Ibid.*, 704–05.

Chapter Four (pages 177–210)

1. *Johnson* v. *San Francisco Unified School District*, 339 F. Supp. 1315, 1325–26 (1971).
2. *Ibid.*, 1318.
3. *Davis* v. *School District of Pontiac*, 443 F. 2d 573, 575 (1971).
4. *Ibid.*, 577 (Footnote 1).
5. *Soria* v. *Oxnard School District*, 328 F. Supp. 155, 157 (1971).
6. Quoted in *Soria* v. *Oxnard School District*, 488 F. 2d 579, 582 (1973).
7. *Soria* v. *Oxnard School District*, 328 F. Supp., 157.
8. See Raymond Wolters, *Right Turn* (New Brunswick, N.J., 1996), pp. 321, 332; Gary Orfield, *Must We Bus?* (Washington, DC., 1978), pp. 115–118.
9. An excellent discussion of these developments is found in Orfield, pp. 247–55.
10. *Public Papers of the Presidents: Richard Nixon, 1972* (Washington, D.C., 1974), pp. 701–02.
11. See Nixon's "Special Message to the Congress on Equal Educational Opportunities and School Busing," March 17, 1972, *Ibid.*, pp. 429–43.
12. *Ibid.*, p. 703.
13. See *School Busing*, Hearings Before Subcommittee No. 5 of the Committee on the Judiciary, House of Representatives, 92nd Congress, 2nd Session (1972).
14. *Hernandez* v. *Texas*, 347 US 475 (1954).
15. *Keyes* v. *School District No. 1*, 303 F. Supp. 279, 281 (1969).
16. *Ibid.*
17. *Ibid.*, 285.
18. *Keyes* v. *School District No. 1*, 303 F. Supp. 289, 293 (1969).
19. *Ibid.*, 294.
20. *Ibid.*
21. *Keyes* v. *School District No. 1*, 313 F. Supp. 61, 67 (1970).
22. *Ibid.*
23. *Keyes* v. *School District No. 1*, 303 F. Supp. 289, 295 (Italics added). The last two statements are repeated at 313 F. Supp., 66–67.
24. *Keys* v. *School District No. 1*, 313 F. Supp., 64.
25. *Ibid.*, 73 (Italics added).
26. *Ibid.*

27. *Ibid.*
28. *Ibid.*, 75.
29. *Ibid.*
30. *Ibid.*, 76.
31. *Ibid.*, 74.
32. "Brief for Respondents," *Keyes* v. *School District No. 1*, p. 36. *Briefs and Records of the Supreme Court*, 413 US 189 (1973).
33. *Ibid.*, p. 61.
34. *Ibid.*, p. 94.
35. *Ibid.*, p. 61.
36. *Keyes* v. *School District No. 1*, 313 F. Supp., 81.
37. *Ibid.*
38. *Ibid.*
39. *Ibid.*
40. *Ibid.*, 83.
41. *Ibid.*
42. *Ibid.*, 82.
43. *Ibid.*, 77 (Footnote 20).
44. Quoted in *Keyes* v. *School District No. 1*, 402 US 82 (1971).
45. *Ibid.*
46. *Keyes* v. *School District No. 1*, 445 F. 2d 990, 1004 (1971).
47. *Ibid.*
48. *Ibid.*, 1005.
49. *Ibid.*
50. *Ibid.*, 1002.
51. *Ibid.*, (Italics added).
52. "Brief for Petitioners," *Keyes* v. *School District No. 1*, p. 103. *Records and Briefs of the Supreme Court*, 413 US 189 (1973).
53. *Ibid.*, pp. 101–02.
54. *Ibid.*, p. 86.
55. *Ibid.*
56. *Ibid.*
57. *Ibid.*, pp. 88–89.
58. *Ibid.*, p. 85.
59. "Mr. Justice Douglas, concurring" (April 6, 1971); Justice Thurgood Marshall to Justice William O. Douglas, April 6, 1971; Justice William J. Brennan to Justice William O. Douglas, April 7, 1971; Justice Potter Stewart to Justice William O. Douglas, April 7, 1971. William O. Douglas Papers, Library of Congress (Box 1499, as are the rest of the references to the Douglas Papers in this chapter).
60. "Mr. Justice Douglas, concurring" (April 7, 1971), p. 7. William O. Douglas Papers, Library of Congress.
61. *Ibid.*
62. *Ibid.*, pp. 8–9 (Italics added).
63. Justice Hugo Black to the Chief Justice, April 16, 1971. William O. Douglas Papers, Library of Congress.
64. "Mr. Justice Black, dissenting" (April 17, 1971), p. 3. William O. Douglas Papers, Library of Congress.
65. *Ibid.*
66. "Mr. Justice Douglas, concurring" (April 19, 1971), p. 8. William O. Douglas Papers,

CHAPTER FOUR NOTES CONTINUED

Library of Congress.
67. "Memorandum to the Conference from Mr. Justice Harlan" (April 15, 1971). William O. Douglas Papers, Library of Congress.
68. *Keyes* v. *School District No. 1*, 402 US 182 (1971).
69. Justice Harry Blackmun to Justice William J. Brennan, January 9, 1973. Thurgood Marshall Papers, Library of Congress (Box 100, as are the rest of the references to the Marshall Papers in this chapter).
70. "Memorandum to the Conference," April 3, 1973. William J. Brennan Papers, Box 285, Library of Congress.
71. John C. Jeffries, Jr., *Justice Lewis F. Powell, Jr.* (New York, 1994), p. 303.
72. *Ibid.*, pp. 304, 303.
73. Justice Harry Blackmun to Justice William J. Brennan, May 30, 1973. Thurgood Marshall Papers, Library of Congress.
74. The Chief Justice to Justice William J. Brennan, December 18, 1972. Thurgood Marshall Papers, Library of Congress.
75. The Chief Justice to Justice William J. Brennan, May 30, 1973. Thurgood Marshall Papers, Library of Congress.
76. Justice William J. Brennan to the Chief Justice, May 30, 1973. Thurgood Marshall Papers, Library of Congress.
77. The Chief Justice to Justice William J. Brennan, May 30, 1973. Thurgood Marshall Papers, Library of Congress.
78. *Ibid.*
79. Jeffries, p. 305.
80. Justice Harry Blackmun to Justice William J. Brennan, May 30, 1973. Thurgood Marshall Papers, Library of Congress.
81. The Chief Justice to Justice William J. Brennan, June 19, 1973. Thurgood Marshall Papers, Library of Congress.
82. *Keyes* v. *School District No. 1*, 413 US 189 (1973), at 208, 205.
83. *Ibid.*, at 212.
84. *Ibid.*, at 193.
85. *Ibid.*, at 199.
86. *Ibid.*, at 201.
87. *Ibid.*, at 202.
88. *Ibid.*
89. [John W. Hanley, Jr.], "*Keyes* v. *School District No. 1*: Unlocking the Northern Schoolhouse Door," *Harvard Civil Rights-Civil Liberties Law Review* (Vol. 9, 1974), 124, 132–33.
90. Owen Fiss, "School Desegregation: The Uncertain Path of the Law," in Marshall Cohen, Thomas Nagel, and Thomas Scanlon (eds.), *Equality and Preferential Treatment* (Princeton, 1977), p. 175.
91. *Keyes* v. *School District No. 1*, at 203.
92. *Ibid.*
93. *Ibid.*, at 208.
94. *Ibid.*, at 210.
95. [Hanley], 141.
96. *Keyes* v. *School District No. 1*, at 211 (Footnote 17).
97. *Ibid.*, at 197, 197–98.

98. "Brief for Petitioners," *Keyes* v. *School District No. 1*, p. 73.

99. *Keyes* v. *School District No. 1*, at 214.

100. *Ibid.*, at 216.

101. *Ibid.*

102. *Ibid.*, at 256.

103. *Ibid.*, at 256, 257.

104. *Ibid.*, at 217.

105. *Ibid.*, at 222.

106. *Ibid.*, at 225–26.

107. *Ibid.*, at 236.

108. *Ibid.*, at 226.

109. *Ibid.*, at 238.

110. *Ibid.*, at 253.

111. *Ibid.*, at 230 (Footnote 14).

112. David Armor, *Forced Justice* (New York, 1995), p. 68.

113. *Ibid.*, p. 59.

114. David Armor, "The Evidence on Busing," *The Public Interest* (No. 28, 1972), 90.

115. Nancy St. John, *School Desegregation* (New York, 1975), p. 36.

116. *Ibid.*

117. See Thomas Pettigrew, et. al., "Busing: A Review of the 'Evidence,'" *The Public Interest* (No. 30, 1973), 88. And see Professor Armor's reply, "The Double Double Standard: A Reply," *Ibid.*, 119.

118. Meyer Weinberg, *Minority Standards: A Research Appraisal* (Washington, D.C., 1977).

119. *Congressional Record*, 93rd Congress, 1st Session—House (1973), 41268.

120. *Congressional Record*, 93rd Congress, 2nd Session—Senate (1974), 14850.

121. *Ibid.*, 14909.

122. *Ibid.*, 15078.

123. *Ibid.*

124. *Ibid.*, 24919.

125. For a full account of the mushrooming pattern of racial and ethnic separation, see Gary Orfield, *The Growth of Segregation in American Schools: Changing Patterns of Separation and Poverty Since 1968* (Alexandria, VA., 1993).

126. James Coleman, Sara Kelley, and John Moore, *Trends in School Integration* (Washington, D.C., 1975).

127. See Thomas Pettigrew and Robert Green, "School Desegregation in Large Cities: A Critique of the Coleman 'White Flight' Thesis," *Harvard Educational Review* (Vol. 46, 1976), 1; Orfield, *Must We Bus?*, Ch. 3; Christine Rossell, "Desegregation and 'White Flight,'" *Political Science Quarterly* (Vol. 90, 1975), 675. Professor Rossell later modified her views. See "Applied Social Research: What Does It Say About the Effectiveness of School Desegregation Plans," *Journal of Legal Studies* (Vol. 12, 1983), 69.

128. The preceding material is found in United States Commission on Civil Rights, *Desegregation of the Nation's Public Schools: A Status Report* (1979), pp. 56–57, 35–36, 59–61, 37–38, 30–31.

129. *San Antonio School District* v. *Rodriquez*, 411 US 1 (1973).

Chapter Five (pages 211–254)

1. *Spencer* v. *Kugler*, 326 F. Supp. 1235, 1237 (1971).
2. *Ibid.*
3. *Ibid.*, 1241.
4. *Ibid.*
5. *Ibid.*
6. *Spencer* v. *Kugler*, 404 US 1027 (1972).
7. *Ibid.*
8. *Ibid.*
9. *Haney* v. *County Board of Education*, 410 F. 2d 920, 924 (1969).
10. *Ibid.*
11. *Wright* v. *Council of City of Emporia*, 407 US 451 (1972), at 460.
12. *Ibid.*, at 462.
13. *United States* v. *Scotland Neck City Board of Education*, 407 US 484 (1972), at 490.
14. See *Bradley* v. *School Board of Richmond*, 462 F. 2d 1058, 1061–62 (1972).
15. *Bradley* v. *School Board of Richmond*, 338 F. Supp. 67, 84 (1972).
16. *Ibid.*, 163.
17. *Ibid.*, 220.
18. *Ibid.*, 228.
19. *Ibid.*, 84, 99–100.
20. *Ibid.*, 82.
21. *Ibid.*, 83.
22. *Ibid.*, 84.
23. *Ibid.*, 92.
24. *Ibid.*, 80.
25. *Ibid.*, 194.
26. *Ibid.*, 193–196.
27. *Bradley* v. *School Board of Richmond*, 462 F. 2d, 1061, 1064.
28. *Ibid.*
29. *Ibid.*
30. *Ibid.*, 1065.
31. *Ibid.* (Italics added).
32. *Ibid.*, 1066.
33. "Brief for Petitioners," *Bradley* v. *State Board of Education*, p. 63. *Records and Briefs of the Supreme Court*, 412 US 92 (1973).
34. *Ibid.*, p. 58.
35. *Ibid.*, pp. 58–59.
36. *Ibid.*, p. 96.
37. "Brief for Respondents," *Bradley* v. *State Board of Education*, p. 57. *Records and Briefs of the Supreme Court*, 412 US 92 (1973).
38. Justice Harry Blackmun to the Chief Justice, April 25, 1973; "Memorandum To The Conference," April 26, 1973. William O. Douglas Papers, Box 1613, Library of Congress. (All other references to the Douglas Papers concerning the Richmond case are in Box 1613.)
39. "From: White, J." (April 30, 1973), pp. 4–5. William O. Douglas Papers, Library of Congress.
40. *Ibid.*, p. 6.
41. *Ibid.*, p. 7.

42. *Ibid.*, p. 10.
43. *Ibid.*, pp. 7–8.
44. Justice William J. Brennan to Justice Byron White, May 1, 1973; Justice William O. Douglas to Justice Byron White, May 3, 1973; Justice Thurgood Marshall to Justice Byron White, May 10, 1973. William O. Douglas Papers, Library of Congress.
45. "From: Rehnquist, J.," May 3, 1973, p. 2. William O. Douglas Papers, Library of Congress.
46. *Ibid.*, p. 3.
47. Justice Bryon White, "Memorandum For The Conference," May 8, 1973. William O. Douglas Papers, Library of Congress.
48. Justice Potter Stewart to Justice William Rehnquist, May 3, 1973; Justice Harry Blackmun to Justice William Rehnquist, May 11, 1973; "Memorandum To The Conference," May 10, 1973. William O. Douglas Papers, Library of Congress.
49. John J. Jeffries, Jr., *Justice Lewis F. Powell, Jr.* (New York, 1994) p. 316.
50. Bob Woodward and Scott Armstrong, *The Brethren* (New York, 1979), p. 267.
51. "Memorandum from Mr. Justice Douglas" (May 15, 1973). William O. Douglas Papers, Library of Congress.
52. William J. Brennan, "Memorandum To The Conference" (Undated, but undoubtedly between May 16 and May 20, 1973), p. 1. William O. Douglas Papers, Library of Congress.
53. *Ibid*, p. 2.
54. *Ibid.*
55. *Ibid*, p. 3.
56. *Ibid.*
57. 412 US 92 (1973).
58. *Bradley* v. *Milliken*, 338 F. Supp. 582, 584 (1971).
59. *Bradley* v. *Milliken*, 433 F. 2d 897 (1970).
60. *Bradley* v. *Milliken*, 438 F. 2d 945 (1971).
61. *Bradley* v. *Milliken*, 338 F. Supp., 587.
62. *Ibid.*, 589.
63. *Ibid.*
64. *Ibid.*
65. *Ibid.*, 592.
66. Quoted in *Milliken* v. *Bradley*, 418 US 717 (1974), at 728 (Footnote 8).
67. Quoted in *Ibid.*, at 731.
68. "Findings of Fact and Conclusions of Law on Detroit-Only Plans of Desegregation." Reprinted in *Bradley* v. *Milliken*, 484 F. 2d 215 (1973), at 242–45, 244.
69. *Ibid.*
70. Quoted in *Milliken* v. *Bradley*, at 733.
71. "Brief for Respondents," *Milliken* v. *Bradley*, pp. 64–65. *Records and Briefs of the Supreme Court*, 418 US 717 (1973).
72. *Bradley* v. *Milliken*, 345 F. Supp. 914, 921 (1972).
73. *Bradley* v. *Milliken*, 484 F. 2d 215 (1973).
74. *Ibid.*, 238.
75. *Ibid.*, 245.
76. *Ibid.*, 247.
77. *Ibid.*, 249.
78. *Ibid.*, 245.
79. *Ibid.*, 261.

CHAPTER FIVE NOTES CONTINUED

80. *Ibid.*, 242.
81. "Conference, March 1, 1974" (p. 2). William O. Douglas Papers, Box 1655, Library of Congress.
82. *Ibid.*
83. Jeffries, p. 312.
84. First Draft of *Milliken* v. *Bradley*, p. 20. Thurgood Marshall Papers, Box 131, Library of Congress.
85. *Ibid.*, p. 22.
86. *Ibid.* The passage appears in *Bradley* v. *Milliken*, 345 F. Supp., 918. Burger included this passage in his final draft, but its context had by that time been significantly altered.
87. *Ibid.*, p. 24 (Italics added).
88. Jeffries, p. 313.
89. "Brief for the United States," *Milliken* v. *Bradley*, pp. 13, 14–15. *Records and Briefs of the Supreme Court*, 418 US 717 (1974).
90. "Conference, March 1, 1974" (p. 2).
91. *Milliken* v. *Bradley*, 418 US 717 (1974), at 742.
92. *Ibid.*, at 742 (Footnote 20).
93. *Ibid.*, at 741.
94. *Ibid.*, at 744–45.
95. *Ibid.*, at 746.
96. *Ibid.* (Italics added).
97. *Swann* v. *Charlotte-Mecklenburg Board of Education*, 402 US 1 (1971), at 21.
98. *Ibid.*, at 20–21 (Italics added).
99. *Keyes* v. *School District No. 1*, 413 US 189 (1973), at 202.
100. "Brief for Respondents," *Milliken* v. *Bradley*, pp. 47–48. *Records and Briefs of the Supreme Court*, 418 US 717 (1974).
101. *Milliken* v. *Bradley*, at 751.
102. *Ibid.*, at 750.
103. "Brief for the United States," p. 27.
104. *Milliken* v. *Bradley*, at 753.
105. *Ibid.*, at 772.
106. *Ibid.*, at 763.
107. *Ibid.*, at 789.
108. *Ibid.*, at 808.
109. 377 US 533 (1964).
110. *Milliken* v. *Bradley*, at 777.
111. *Ibid.*, at 747 (Italics added).
112. *Ibid.*, at 779 (Italics added).
113. *Ibid.*, at 779, 780.
114. *Ibid.*, at 783.
115. *Ibid.*, at 805.
116. *Ibid.* The quotation is in *Swann*, at 20.
117. *Ibid.*, at 806 (Italics added).
118. *Ibid.*, at 761.
119. *Ibid.*
120. *Ibid.*
121. *Ibid.*, at 755 (Italics added).

122. William L. Taylor, "The Supreme Court and Urban Reality," *Wayne Law Review* (Vol. 21, 1975), 751, 760.

123. *Ybarra* v. *City of San Jose*, 503 F. 2d 1041, 1043 (1974).

124. *Milliken* v. *Bradley*, at 756 (Footnote 2).

125. *Hills* v. *Gautreaux*, 425 US 284 (1976), at 292.

126. *Ibid.*, at 294, 295.

127. *Ibid.*, at 298 (Footnote 13), quoting *Milliken* v. *Bradley*, at 746.

128. *Ibid.*, at 299.

129. *Ibid.*, at 300.

130. *Ibid.*, at 301.

131. Paul R. Dimond, *Beyond Busing* (Ann Arbor, 1985), p. 219.

132. J. Harvie Wilkinson, *From Brown to Bakke* (New York, 1979), p. 242.

133. Charles R. Lawrence III, "Segregation 'Misunderstood': The *Milliken* Decision Revisited," *University of San Francisco Law Review* (Vol. 12, 1977), 15, 28, 29.

134. *Ibid.*, 25.

135. *Ibid.*, 30.

136. *Ibid.*, 31.

137. *Ibid.*, 29.

138. *Ibid.*, 37.

139. *Ibid.*, 29.

140. *Ibid.*, 32.

141. Owen Fiss, "School Desegregation: The Uncertain Path of the Law," in Marshall Cohen, Thomas Nagel, and Thomas Scanlon (eds.), *Equality* and *Preferential Treatment* (Princeton, 1977), pp. 155–91.

142. Owen Fiss, "Groups and the Equal Protection Clause," in Cohen, et. al., p. 101.

143. *Ibid.*, p. 106.

144. *Ibid.*, p. 118.

145. *Ibid.*

146. *Ibid.*, pp. 119–120, 106.

147. *Ibid.*, p. 121.

148. *Ibid.*, p. 122.

149. *Ibid.*

150. *Ibid.*, p. 124.

151. *Ibid.*

152. *Ibid.*, pp. 127, 132.

153. *Ibid.*, p. 135.

154. *Ibid.*

155. Robert Sedler, "The Constitution and School Desegregation: An Inquiry Into the Nature of the Substantive Right," *Kentucky Law Journal* (Vol. 68, 1979), 925, 931.

156. *Ibid.*, 950–51.

157. *Ibid.*, 952.

158. *Ibid.*, 956.

159. *Ibid.*, 963–64.

160. *Ibid.*, 949.

161. See Morris Rosenberg and Roberta G. Simmons, *Black and White Self-Esteem: The Urban School Child* (Washington, D.C., 1971), esp. pp. 5–8; David Armor, *Forced Justice* (New York, 1995), pp. 99–102.

162. "The Constitution and School Segregation," 949–50.

Chapter Six (pages 255–290)

1. Owen Fiss, "School Desegregation: The Uncertain Path of Law," in Marshall Cohen, Thomas Nagel, and Thomas Scanlon (eds.), *Equality and Preferential Treatment* (Princeton, 1977), p. 183.
2. *Soria* v. *Oxnard School District*, 488 F. 2d 579, 586, 585 (1973).
3. *Ibid.*, 585.
4. *Johnson* v. *San Francisco Unified School District*, 500 F. 2d 349, 351 (1974).
5. *Ibid.*, 352.
6. *Hart* v. *Community School Board*, 383 F. Supp. 699, 733, 734, (1974).
7. *Ibid.*
8. *Ibid.*, 737.
9. *Hart* v. *Community School Board*, 512 F. 2d 37, 49 (1975).
10. *Ibid.*, 50.
11. *Ibid.*
12. *Ibid.*, 48.
13. *Arthur* v. *Nyquist*, 415 F. Supp. 904, 912–13 (1976).
14. *Morgan* v. *Kerrigan*, 379 F. Supp. 410, 478 (1974) (Italics added); Affirmed, 509 F. 2d 580 (1974).
15. *Oliver* v. *Michigan State Board of Education*, 508 F. 2d 178, 182 (1974).
16. *Oliver* v. *Kalamazoo Board of Education*, 368 F. Supp. 143, 173 (1973).
17. *Ibid.*, 167.
18. *Ibid.*, 170.
19. *United States* v. *School District of Omaha*, 389 F. Supp. 293 (1974).
20. *United States* v. *School District of Omaha*, 521 F. 2d 530, 535–36 (1975).
21. *Ibid.*, 546.
22. 418 F. Supp. 22 (1976); Affirmed and remanded, 541 F. 2d 708 (1976).
23. *Amos* v. *City of Milwaukee*, 408 F. Supp. 765, 780, 812 (1976).
24. *Ibid.*, 808.
25. *Ibid.*, 819.
26. *Ibid.*
27. *Ibid.*
28. *Ibid.*
29. *Armstrong* v. *Brennan*, 539 F. 2d 625, 636 (1976).
30. *Ibid.*
31. *Ibid.*
32. *Hart* v. *Community School Board*, 383 F. Supp., 706.
33. *Arthur* v. *Nyquist*, 415 F. Supp., 968.
34. *Washington* v. *Davis*, 426 US 229 (1976), at 239.
35. *Ibid.*, at 242.
36. *Ibid.*
37. *Arlington Heights* v. *Metropolitan Housing Corporation*, 429 US 252 (1977), at 265.
38. *Ibid.*, at 266, 266–68.
39. *Ibid.*, at 266.
40. *School District of Omaha* v. *United States*, 433 US 667 (1977).
41. *Brennan* v. *Armstrong*, 433 US 672 (1977).
42. Justice William Rehnquist, "Memorandum To The Conference," June 20, 1977, p. 2. William J. Brennan Papers, Box 452, Library of Congress.
43. *Ibid.*

44. *Ibid.*, pp. 2–3.
45. *Ibid.*, p. 3.
46. Justice William J. Brennan, "Memorandum To The Conference," June 21, 1977, p. 2. William J. Brennan Papers, Box 452, Library of Congress.
47. Rehnquist, "Memorandum To The Conference," June 21, 1977. William J. Brennan Papers, Box 452, Library of Congress.
48. "Brief for the United States," *United States* v. *School District of Omaha*, 565 F. 2d 127 (1977), p. 15. (Copy obtained from United States Department of Justice).
49. *Ibid.*, p. 12.
50. *Ibid.*, p. 20 (Italics added).
51. *Ibid.*, p. 35. The original quotation is at 521 F. 2d, 543 (Footnote 25).
52. *Ibid.*, pp. 24, 20.
53. *United States* v. *School District of Omaha*, 565 F. 2d 127, 128 (1977).
54. *Armstrong* v. *Brennan*, 566 F. 2d 1175 (1977).
55. *Armstrong* v. *O'Connell*, 451 F. Supp. 817, 824 (1978) (Italics added).
56. *Ibid.*, 843.
57. *Ibid.*, 852.
58. *Ibid.*, 857. Judge Reynolds was quoting, with evident approval, from *N.A.A.C.P* v. *Lansing Board of Education*, 559 F. 2d 1042, 1051 (1977).
59. *Ibid.*, 856.
60. *Amos* v. *City of Milwaukee*, 792.
61. *Armstrong* v. *O'Connell*, 856.
62. *Ibid.*, 855.
63. *Arthur* v. *Nyquist*, 429 F. Supp. 206, 211 (Footnote 4) (1977).
64. *Ibid.*, 211. Judge Curtin here is quoting approvingly from himself in *Arthur* v. *Nyquist*, 415 F. Supp., 912.
65. *Brinkman* v. *Gilligan*, "Findings of Fact and Memorandum Opinion of Law" (1973). Printed as Appendix A of *Brinkman* v. *Gilligan*, 446 F. Supp. 1232 (1977), at 1254–61, 1259, 1258.
66. *Ibid.*, 1259. For a fascinating account of the Dayton trials, see Paul Dimond, *Beyond Busing* (Ann Arbor, 1985), Chs. 6, 7, 12.
67. *Ibid.*, 1260.
68. *Brinkman* v. *Gilligan*, 503 F. 2d 684, 693 (1974).
69. *Ibid.*, 697.
70. See *Brinkman* v. *Gilligan*, 518 F. 2d 853 (1975); 539 F. 2d 1084 (1976).
71. *Dayton Board of Education* v. *Brinkman* (*Dayton I*), 433 US 406 (1977), at 413.
72. *Ibid.*, at 414. Quoting from *Brinkman* v. *Gilligan*, 503 F. 2d, 697.
73. *Ibid.*
74. *Ibid.*, at 420.
75. Stephen Barrett Kanner, "From Denver to Dayton," *Northwestern University Law Review* (Vol. 72, 1977), 382, 404 (Italics added).
76. *Ibid.*
77. *Dayton I*, at 421.
78. *Ibid.*, at 423.
79. *Ibid.*
80. Justice William J. Brennan to Justice William Rehnquist, June 3, 1977. Thurgood Marshall Papers, Box 193, Library of Congress.
81. *Ibid.*
82. Justice William Rehnquist, "Memorandum To The Conference," June 6, 1977.

CHAPTER SIX NOTES CONTINUED

Thurgood Marshall Papers, Box 193, Library of Congress.
83. *Ibid.*
84. *Brinkman* v. *Gilligan*, 446 F. Supp. 1232, 1236 (1977).
85. *Ibid.*, (Italics added).
86. *Ibid.*, 1238.
87. "Brief for Respondents," *Dayton Board of Education* v. *Brinkman* (*Dayton II*), p. 35. *Records and Briefs of the Supreme Court*, 443 US 526 (1979).
88. *Brinkman* v. *Gilligan*, 446 F. Supp., 1245.
89. *Ibid.*, 1246.
90. *Ibid.*
91. "Testimony of Karl Taeuber," *Dayton II*, A 176–79. *Records and Briefs of the Supreme Court*, 443 US 526 (1979). See also Professor Taeuber's testimony in *Columbus Board of Education* v. *Penick*, A 280–311. *Records and Briefs of the Supreme Court*, 443 US 449 (1979).
92. Karl Taeuber, "Demographic Perspectives on Housing and School Segregation," *Wayne Law Review* (Vol. 21, 1975) 833, 843.
93. *Brinkman* v. *Gilligan*, 446 F. Supp., 1253.
94. *Brinkman* v. *Gilligan*, 583 F. 2d 243 (1978).
95. "Brief for Respondents," *Dayton I*, p. 61. *Records and Briefs of the Supreme Court*, 433 US 406 (1977).
96. "Brief for Respondents," *Dayton II*, p. 99.
97. "Brief for Petitioners," *Dayton II*, p. 16. *Records and Briefs of the Supreme Court*, 443 US 526 (1977).
98. "Brief for Respondents," *Dayton II*, p. 137.
99. *Ibid*, p. 139.
100. *Dayton II*, 443 US 526 (1979), at 535.
101. *Ibid.*, at 537.
102. *Ibid.*, at 540.
103. Note, "Proving Segregative Intent in School Desegregation Cases," *North Carolina Central Law Journal* (Vol. 12, 1980), 219, 227–28.
104. *Columbus Board of Education* v. *Penick*, 443 US 449 (1979), at 501. Rehnquist's dissent in *Columbus* was clearly meant to be his principal attack on the Court's disposition of both cases. At the beginning of his *Dayton II* dissent, he notes: "For the reasons set out in my dissent in *Columbus Board of Education* v. *Penick* . . . , I cannot join the Court's opinion in this case." *Dayton II*, at 542.
105. *Ibid.*, at 502, 500–01.
106. *Bradley* v. *Milliken*, 411 F. Supp. 937, 940 (1975).
107. *Ibid.*, 940–41.
108. Robert Sedler, "The Profound Impact of *Milliken* v. *Bradley*," *Wayne Law Review* (Vol. 33, 1987), 1693, 1697.
109. See *United States* v. *State of Missouri*, 515 F. 2d 1365 (1975); *Morrilton School District* v. *United States*, 606 F. 2d 222 (1979); *Hoots* v. *Commonwealth of Pennsylvania*, 510 F. Supp. 615 (1981), Affirmed, 672 F. 2d 1107 (1982); *Berry* v. *School District of Benton Harbor*, 515 F. Supp. 344 (1981), Affirmed, 698 F. 2d 813 (1963).
110. *Little Rock School District* v. *Pulaski County Special District*, 778 F. 2d 404, 434 (1985). The district court remedy decision is 597 F. Supp. 1220 (1984).
111. *Newburg Area Council* v. *Board of Education of Jefferson City*, 489 F. 2d 925, 932

(1973).

112. 418 US 918.

113. *Newburg Area Council* v. *Board of Education, Kentucky*, 510 F. 2d 1358, 1359 (1974).

114. *Ibid.*, 1361.

115. *Ibid.*, 1360.

116. An excellent discussion of the Louisville matter is found in Robert Sedler, "Metropolitan Desegregation in the Wake of *Milliken*," *Washington University Law Quarterly* (1975 Volume), 535. Professor Sedler was counsel to the plaintiffs in the Louisville case.

117. *Evans* v. *Buchanan*, 379 F. Supp. 1218, 1223 (1974).

118. *Evans* v. *Buchanan*, 393 F. Supp. 428, 434 (1975).

119. *Ibid.*

120. *Ibid.*, 442.

121. *Ibid.*, 440.

122. *Ibid.*, 445.

123. *Buchanan* v. *Evans*, 423 US 963 (1975).

124. *Evans* v. *Buchanan*, 393 F. Supp., 433.

125. *Evans* v. *Buchanan*, 416 F. Supp. 328, 343 (1976).

126. *Ibid.*, 339.

127. *Ibid.*, 341.

128. *Ibid.*, 341 (Footnote 42).

129. Raymond Wolters, *The Burden of Brown* (Knoxville, 1984), p. 215.

130. *United States* v. *Board of School Commissioners of Indianapolis*, 332 F. Supp. 655, 676 (1971).

131. *Ibid.*, 678.

132. Meanwhile, The Seventh Circuit Court of Appeals affirmed Judge Dillin's findings of illegal segregation in Indianapolis. 474 F. 2d 81 (1973).

133. *United States* v. *Board of School Commissioners of Indianapolis*, 368 F. Supp. 1191, 1203 (1973).

134. *Ibid.*, 1205.

135. *United States* v. *Board of School Commissioners of Indianapolis*, 503 F. 2d 68, 79–80 (1974).

136. *United States* v. *Board of School Commissioners of Indianapolis*, 419 F. Supp. 180, 183, 182 (1975).

137. *Ibid.*, 183.

138. *Ibid.*, 182.

139. *United States* v. *Board of School Commissioners of Indianapolis*, 456 F. Supp. 183, 188 (1978) (Italics added).

140. *Ibid.*, 189 (Italics added).

141. *Ibid.*, 190.

142. *Ibid.*

143. *United States* v. *Board of School Commissioners of Indianapolis*, 506 F. Supp. 657, 664 (1979).

144. *Ibid.*

145. *Ibid.*

146. *Ibid.*

147. *Ibid.*

148. *Ibid.*, 670.

149. *Ibid.*, 666.

CHAPTER SIX NOTES CONTINUED

150. *United States* v. *Board of School Commissioners of Indianapolis*, 637 F. 2d 1101, 1113 (1980).
151. *Ibid.*, 1114.
152. *United States* v. *Board of School Commissioners of Indianapolis*, 506 F. Supp., 666.
153. *Ibid.*, 666–67.
154. *Ibid.*, 667.

Chapter Seven Notes (pages 291–330)

1. *United States* v. *Yonkers Board of Education*, 624 F. Supp. 1276 (1985); Affirmed, 537 F. 2d 1181 (1987).
2. See James S. Liebman, "Desegregation Politics: 'All-Out' School Desegregation Explained," *Columbia Law Review* (Vol. 90, 1990), 1463, 1468–69.
3. Raymond Wolters, *Right Turn* (New Brunswick, N.J., 1996), pp. 369–78, 388–94; *Parents For Equality Education With Integration, Inc.* v. *Fort Wayne Community Schools Corp.*, 728 F. Supp. 1373 (1990).
4. Wolters, *Right Turn*, p. 363.
5. *Ibid.*
6. *Ibid.*
7. *United States* v. *Board of Education of Chicago*, 554 F. Supp. 912, 920 (1983).
8. *United States* v. *Board of Education of Chicago*, 567 F. Supp. 290, 296 (1983).
9. *Swann* v. *Charlotte-Mecklenburg Board of Education*, 402 US 1 (1971), at 31.
10. *Swann* v. *Charlotte-Mecklenburg Board of Education*, 311 F. Supp. 265, 269 (1970).
11. *Spangler* v. *Pasadena Board of Education*, 375 F. Supp. 1304 (1974).
12. *Spangler* v. *Pasadena Board of Education*, 519 F. 2d 430, 438 (1975). Despite these comments, the Ninth Circuit upheld Judge Real's decision.
13. *Pasadena Board of Education* v. *Spangler*, 427 US 424 (1976). Justices Marshall and Brennan dissented.
14. *Ibid.*, at 435, 436.
15. *Ibid.*, at 437.
16. *Ibid.*, at 436 (Italics added).
17. *Ibid.*, at 431.
18. *Green* v. *New Kent County*, 391 US 430 (1968), at 435.
19. *Lee* v. *Macon City Board of Education*, 616 F. 2d 805, 810 (1980). See *Vaughns* v. *Board of Education of Prince Georges' County*, 758 F. 2d 983, 988 (1985).
20. *Martin* v. *Charlotte-Mecklenburg Board of Education*, 475 F. Supp. 1318, 1340 (1979). See also *Haycraft* v. *Board of Education of Jefferson County*, 560 F. 2d 755 (1977).
21. *Milliken* v. *Bradley*, 433 US 267 (1977), at 281.
22. *Ibid.*, at 282.
23. *Ibid.*, at 287.
24. *Ibid.*
25. *Ibid.*, at 288, 283.
26. *Ibid.*, at 280–81.
27. *Ross* v. *Houston Independent School District*, 699 F. 2d 218 (1983).
28. *Ibid.*, 225.
29. *Ibid.*, 226.
30. *Ibid.*, 227.

31. *Ibid.*, 226.
32. *Ibid.*
33. *Ibid.*
34. *Keyes* v. *School District No. 1, Denver, Colorado*, 609 F. Supp. 1491 (1985).
35. *Ibid.*, 1508.
36. *Vaughns* v. *Board of Education of Prince Georges' County*, 574 F. Supp. 1280, 1349 (1983); Affirmed, 758 F. 2d 983 (1985).
37. *Ibid.*, 1349–50. Judge Kaufman was quoting from *Kelly* v. *Metropolitan County Board of Education*, 479 F. Supp. 120, 122–23 (1979).
38. *Tasby* v. *Wright*, 713 F. 2d 90 (1983).
39. *Tasby* v. *Estes*, 412 F. Supp. 1192 (1976).
40. *Tasby* v. *Estes*, 572 F. 2d 1010, 1014 (1978).
41. *Ibid.*
42. *Tasby* v. *Wright*, 520 F. Supp. 683, 725 (1981).
43. *Ibid.*, 690.
44. *Tasby* v. *Wright*, 713 F. 2d, 97.
45. *Estes* v. *Metropolitan Branch, Dallas NAACP*, 444 US 437 (1980).
46. *Ibid.*, at 445.
47. *Ibid.*
48. *Ibid.*, at 444.
49. *Ibid.*
50. *Ibid.*
51. *Ibid.*, at 452.
52. *Ibid.*, at 450.
53. *Riddick by Riddick* v. *School Board of Norfolk*, 627 F. Supp. 814 (1984).
54. Brief of Appellants, *Riddick by Riddick* v. *School Board of Norfolk*, 784 F. 2d 521 (1986), p. 40. Federal Archives, Philadelphia, PA.
55. *Ibid.*, p. 30.
56. *Ibid.*, pp. 25–26.
57. *Ibid.*, p. 30.
58. *Ibid.*, p. 33.
59. *Ibid.*, p. 28.
60. *Ibid.*, p. 29.
61. *Ibid.*, p. 30.
62. Brief of United States, *Amicus Curiae, Riddick by Riddick* v. *School Board of Norfolk*, 784 F. 2d 521 (1986), p. 34. Federal Archives, Philadelphia, PA.
63. *Ibid.*, p. 33.
64. *Riddick by Riddick* v. *School Board of Norfolk*, 784 F. 2d 521 (1986).
65. *Dowell* v. *Board of Education of Oklahoma City*, 606 F. Supp. 1548, 1554 (1985).
66. *Ibid.*, 1556.
67. *Dowell by Dowell* v. *Board of Education of Oklahoma*, 795 F. 2d 1516, 1523 (1986).
68. Jace Weaver, *Then to the Rock Let Me Fly* (Norman, Oklahoma, 1993), pp. 103, 106.
69. *Ibid.*, p. 107.
70. *Dowell* v. *Oklahoma City Public Schools*, 677 F. Supp. 1503 (1987).
71. *Ibid.*,
72. *Dowell* v. *Board of Education of Oklahoma City Public Schools*, 890 F. 2d 1483, 1486 (1989).
73. *Ibid.*, 1491, 1493. The quotation is from *Humble Oil and Refinery Co.* v. *American Oil Company*, 405 F. 2d 803, 813 (1969).

CHAPTER SEVEN NOTES CONTINUED

74. *Ibid.*, 1491.
75. *Ibid.*, 1504, 1505.
76. *Ibid.*, 1504.
77. *Ibid.*, 1503. Judge Moore used language referring to "clear error" only in discussing Judge Bohanon's heavy use of testimony from school administrators to demonstrate that Oklahoma City's neighborhood plan was not motivated by discriminatory intent. The Supreme Court was not certain whether the "clear error" reference was confined to this matter, or applied to Bohanon's total findings.
78. Brief for Respondents, *Board of Education of Oklahoma City* v. *Dowell*, p. 43. *Records and Briefs of the Supreme Court*, 498 US 237 (1991).
79. *Ibid.*, p. 42.
80. *Ibid.* (Italics added).
81. *Ibid.*, pp. 42, 46.
82. *Ibid.*, p. 43.
83. *Ibid.*
84. *Ibid.*, p. 42.
85. First Draft of *Board of Education of Oklahoma City* v. *Dowell*, November 16, 1991. Thurgood Marshall Papers, Box 529, Library of Congress. Since the content of the published opinion parallels almost exactly this first draft, I have used references to the published opinion.
86. *Board of Education of Oklahoma City* v. *Dowell*, 498 US 237 (1991), at 247.
87. *Ibid.*, at 248.
88. *Ibid.*, at 249–50 (Italics added).
89. *Ibid.*, at 250 (Footnote 2).
90. Justice Byron White to the Chief Justice, December 4, 1991. Thurgood Marshall Papers, Box 529, Library of Congress.
91. See Chief Justice Rehnquist, "Memorandum to the Conference," November 16, 1991. Thurgood Marshall Papers, Box 529, Library of Congress.
92. Justice Sandra Day O'Connor to the Chief Justice, December 4, 1991 (p. 1). Thurgood Marshall Papers, Box 529, Library of Congress.
93. *Ibid.* (p. 2).
94. Chief Justice Rehnquist to Justice Byron White, December 13, 1996. Thurgood Marshall Papers, Box 529, Library of Congress.
95. *Ibid.*
96. *Ibid.*
97. *Board of Education of Oklahoma City* v. *Dowell*, at 262.
98. *Ibid.*, at 268.
99. *Ibid.*, at 264.
100. *Ibid.*, at 257, 258, 260.
101. *Dowell* v. *Board of Education of Oklahoma City Public Schools*, 778 F. Supp. 1144, 1170 (1991).
102. *Ibid.*, 1166.
103. *Ibid.*, at 1167.
104. *Ibid.*, 1168, 1169.
105. *Ibid.*, 1160.
106. *Dowell* v. *Board of Education of Oklahoma City*, 8 F. 3d 1501 (1993).
107. See *Battle* v. *Anderson*, 376 F. Supp. 402 (1974); 447 F. Supp. 516 (1977); 457 F. Supp.

719 (1978); 541 F. Supp. 1061 (1982). *Choctaw Nation* v. *Cherokee Nation*, 393 F. Supp. 224 (1975). *Rutherford* v. *United States*, 399 F. Supp. 1208 (1975); 424 F. Supp. 105 (1977); 429 F. Supp. 506 (1977); 438 F. Supp. 1287 (1977). Those cases are discussed in Weaver, *Then to the Rock Let Me Fly*, Chs. 5,6,7.

108. Weaver, *Then to the Rock Let Me Fly*, p. 65.

109. *Freeman* v. *Pitts* (In United States District Court, Northern District of Georgia), A 202, 206. *Records and Briefs of the Supreme Court*, 503 US 467 (1992).

110. *Ibid.*, A 221.

111. *Ibid.*, A 220, 221.

112. *Ibid.*, A 240. The Boston case was *Morgan* v. *Nucci*, 831 F.2d 313 (1987).

113. *Pitts by Pitts* v. *Freeman*, 887 F. 2d 1438, 1446–47 (1989).

114. *Ibid.*, 1449.

115. *Ibid.*, 1450.

116. *Ibid.* (Italics added).

117. Brief for Respondents, *Freeman* v. *Pitts*, p. 35. *Records and Briefs of the Supreme Court*, 503 US 467 (1992).

118. *Ibid.*, p. 36.

119. *Ibid.*

120. *Ibid.*

121. *Ibid.*, p. 31.

122. *Ibid.*, p. 29.

123. *Ibid.*, pp. 29–30.

124. *Freeman* v. *Pitts*, 503 US 467 (1992), at 489.

125. *Ibid.*, at 497.

126. *Ibid.*, at 498.

127. *Ibid.*, at 494.

128. *Ibid.*

129. *Ibid.*, at 495.

130. *Ibid.*

131. Brief for the United States, *Amicus Curiae*, *Freeman* v. *Pitts*, pp. 14–15 (Footnote 7). *Briefs and Records of the Supreme Court*, 503 US 467 (1992) (Italics added).

132. *Ibid.*, p. 14.

133. *Freeman* v. *Pitts*, at 500.

134. *Ibid.*, at 505.

135. *Ibid.*

136. *Ibid.*, at 506.

137. *Ibid.*

138. *Ibid.*, at 499.

139. *Ibid.*, at 507.

140. *Ibid.*, at 509.

141. *Ibid.*, at 513.

142. *Ibid.*

143. *Ibid.*, at 518.

144. Brief of the NAACP, et. al., *Amicus Curiae*, *Freeman* v. *Pitts*, p. 7a. *Briefs and Records of the Supreme Court*, 503 US 467 (1992).

145. Quoted in David Armor, *Forced Justice* (New York, 1995), p. 91.

146. *Ibid.*, pp. 79–81.

147. David Chang, "The Bus Stops Here," *Boston University Law Review* (Vol. 63, 1983) 1.

148. *Ibid.*, 8–9.

CHAPTER SEVEN NOTES CONTINUED

149. *Ibid.*, 9.
150. *Ibid.*
151. *Ibid.*, 33.
152. *Ibid.*, 34.
153. *Ibid.*, 39.
154. *Ibid.*
155. *Ibid.*, 58.
156. *Missouri* v. *Jenkins*, 11 F. 3d 755, 761–62 (1993) (Italics added).
157. *Missouri* v. *Jenkins*, 132 L Ed 2d 63, 88 (1995) (Italics added).
158. *Ibid.*, 88–89.
159. *Ibid.*, 121.
160. *Missouri* v. *Jenkins*, 495 US 33 (1990), at 77.
161. Quoted in *Missouri* v. *Jenkins*, 132 L Ed 2d, 73.
162. *Ibid.*, 83.
163. *Ibid.*
164. *Ibid.*
165. *Ibid.*, 84.
166. *Ibid.*, 86.
167. *Ibid.*, 132.
168. *Ibid.*
169. *Ibid.*, 131.
170. *Ibid.*
171. Brief of American Civil Liberties Union, *Amicus Curiae, Missouri* v. *Jenkins*, p. 20. *Briefs and Records of the Supreme Court*, 132 L Ed 2d 63 (1995).
172. *Ibid.*
173. *Ibid.*, p. 19.
174. *Board of Education of Oklahoma City* v. *Dowell*, at 268.
175. An excellent account of the Ocean Hill-Brownsville controversy is found in Diane Ravitch, *The Great School Wars* (New York, 1974), Chs. 28–35.
176. Two searing analyses are Gerald D. Jaynes and Robin M. Williams, Jr. (eds.), *A Common Destiny: Blacks and American Society* (New York, 1989); Douglas S. Massey and Nancy Denton, *American Apartheid: Segregation and the Making of the Underclass* (New York, 1993).
177. Alex M. Johnson, "Bid Whist, Tonk, and *United States* v. *Fordice*: Why Integrationism Fails African-Americans Again," *California Law Review* (Vol. 81, 1993), 1401, 1404.
178. Neil Gotanda, "A Critique of 'Our Constitution is Color-Blind,'" *Stanford Law Review* (Vol. 44, 1991), 1, 56, 60, 59.
179. *Ibid.*, 54.
180. *Ibid,*, 56.
181. *Ibid.*, 64, 63.
182. Mari J. Matsuda, "Looking To The Bottom," *Harvard Civil Rights-Civil Liberties Law Review* (Vol. 22, 1987), 323.
183. *Ibid.*, 324.
184. Derrick Bell, *And We Are Not Free* (New York, 1987), pp. 118, 120–21.
185. Johnson, "Bid Whist, Tonk, and *United States* v. *Fordice*," 1409.
186. *Ibid.*, 1423. Johnson is quoting here from Gary Peller, "Race Consciousness," *Duke Law Journal* (1990 Volume), 758, 770.

NOTES   369

187. *Ibid.* (Italics added).
188. *Ibid.*
189. *Ibid.*
190. *Ibid.*, 1427.
191. *Ibid.*
192. *Ibid.*, 1427, 1431.
193. *Ibid.*, 1432.
194. *Ibid.*
195. *Ibid.*
196. *United States* v. *Fordice*, 120 L Ed 2d 575 (1992).
197. *Ibid.*, 599.
198. *Ibid.*, 602.
199. *Ibid.* (Italics added).
200. Johnson, "Bid Whist, Tonk, and *United States* v. *Fordice*," 1424.
201. *Ibid.*, 1418.
202. *United States* v. *Fordice*, 605.
203. *Ibid.*, 606.
204. *Ibid.*, 603.
205. *Ibid.*, 606.
206. *Ibid.*, 604.
207. *Ibid.*
208. *Missouri* v. *Jenkins*, 132 L Ed 2d, 96.
209. *Ibid.*, 97.
210. *Ibid.*
211. *Ibid.*, 98–99.

Conclusion (pages 331–336)

1. This statistical material is found in Gary Orfield, *The Growth of Segregation in American Schools: Changing Patterns of Separation and Poverty Since 1968* (Alexandria, Va., 1993), see especially, tables 1,3,6,13,15.
2. Gary Orfield, "The Growth of Segregation," in Gary Orfield and Susan Eaton (eds.), *Dismantling Desegregation* (New York, 1996), pp. 67–68.
3. *Ibid.*, p. 69.
4. Conservation with Jill Moberley, Dayton Public Schools, April 14, 1997.
5. Conversation with Judith Rogers, Columbus Public Schools, April 14, 1997.
6. *Keyes* v. *Congress of Hispanic Educators*, 902 F. Supp. 1274, 1281 (1995).
7. *Ibid.*, 1282.
8. Conversation with Duncan Pritchett, Indianapolis Public Schools, April 16, 1997.
9. Conversation with Dr. Jack Nichols, Delaware State Board of Education, April 22, 1997.
10. *Sheff* v. *O'Neill*, 678 A. 2d 1267 (1996).
11. Conversation with Christopher A. Hansen, American Civil Liberties Union Foundation, April 30, 1997.
12. See Alison Morantz, "Desegregation at Risk," in *Dismantling Desegregation*, pp. 179–206.
13. *Ibid.*, p. 189.
14. *Ibid.*, p. 206.

CONCLUSION NOTES CONTINUED

15. *Brown* v. *Topeka Board of Education*, 671 F. Supp. 1290, 1295 (1987).
16. *Ibid.*
17. *Ibid.*, 1310.
18. *Brown* v. *Board of Education of Topeka*, 892 F. 2d 851, 854 (1989).
19. *Ibid.*, 874.
20. *Ibid.*, 885.
21. *Ibid.*, 886.
22. *Brown* v. *Board of Education of Topeka*, 978 F. 2d 585, 589 (1992).
23. *Ibid.*
24. Conversation with Scott McCulley, Unified School District No. 501, April 17, 1997.
25. Gary Orfield, *"Plessy* Parallels," in *Dismantling Desegregation*, p. 36.
26. *Ibid.*, pp. 40, 41. The reference from *Plessy* is to 63 US 537 (1896), at 551.
27. *Ibid.*, pp. 37–38.
28. *Ibid.*, p. 49.
29. Jace Weaver, *Then to the Rock Let Me Fly* (Norman, Oklahoma, 1993), p. 112.
30. Documents for Prologue, II, 3.
31. Leon Friedman (ed.), *Argument* (New York, 1969), p. 402.

List of Detailed Sources

Prologue

Chapter One

Chapter Two

I. *Jefferson County*
   1. The Fifth Circuit's Affirmance, 380 F. 2d 385, 389–90 (1967).
   2. Judge Gewin's Dissent, 380 F. 2d 385, 397, 399–400, 399, 397–98, 404–06, 409.
   3. Judge Bell's Dissent, 380 F. 2d 385, 410–14, 417.

II. The *Green* Trilogy
   1. Appellees' Brief: *Monroe*, pp. 14–16, 18, 22–25, 28, 41–44, 48–50. *Records and Briefs of the Supreme Court*, 391 US 450 (1968).
   2. Appellants' Brief: *Monroe*, pp. 21–22, 24–25, 27–28. *Ibid.*
   3. Oral Argument of Frederick Gray. Reprinted in Phillip B. Kurland and Gerhard Casper (eds.), *Landmark Briefs and Arguments of the Supreme Court* (Arlington, VA, 1975–), Vol. 66, pp. 221–24, 229–31.
   4. Oral Arguments of James Nabrit and Jack Greenberg. *Ibid.*, pp. 238, 237, 262–64.
   5. *Green* v. *New Kent County*, 391 US 430, 437–42. (Justice Brennan's deleted language is on pages 7 and 8 of his first draft. William J. Brennan Papers, Box 177, Library of Congress.)
   6. *Monroe* v. *Board of Commissioners*, 391 US 450, 456–59. (Justice Brennan's deleted language is on page 7 of his first draft. William J. Brennan Papers, Box 177, Library of Congress.)

Chapter Three

I. The Briefs
   1. Brief for Petitioners, pp. 41, 46–49; Supplemental Brief, pp. 9–14; Brief for Petitioners, pp. 51–53. *Records and Briefs of the Supreme Court*, 402 US 1 (1971).
   2. Edelman-Rauh Brief, pp. 12–22. *Ibid.*
   3. Brief of Senator Ervin, pp. 17, 24–26. *Ibid.*

II. The Justices
   1. Justice Stewart's Opinion, pp. 8, 10–11, 13–15, 22, 26–28, 30. Thurgood Marshall Papers, Box 71, Library of Congress.
   2. Memorandum of Justice Harlan, pp. 8–11, 14–18, 21–23, 28. John Marshall Harlan Papers, Box 433, Seeley G. Mudd Manuscript Library, Princeton University. Published with permission of Princeton University Library.
   3. Justice Douglas' Opinion, pp. 3–5, 11–12. William O. Douglas Papers, Box 1514, Library of Congress.
   4. Justice Brennan's Memorandum, pp. 1–4. William J. Brennan Papers, Box 241, Library of Congress.

Chapter Four

I. *Swann* and the Fallout From *Keyes*
   1. Dimond Essay, *Harvard Civil Rights-Civil Liberties Law Review* (Vol. 7, 1972), 1, 4–6, 8–11, 13–14.
   2. Justice Douglas' Memorandum, pp. 6–8, 10–11. William O. Douglas Papers, Box 1499, Library of Congress.

3. Justice Brennan's Memorandum, William J. Brennan Papers, Box 285, Library of Congress.
4. Justice Powell's Opinion, *Keyes* v. *School District No. 1, Denver, Colorado*, 413 US 189 (1973), at 218–227, 236, 240–42, 246, 249–53.
5. Justice Rehnquist's Dissent, *Ibid.*, at 254, 256–58.

Chapter Five

I. The Decision That Never Was
1. Justice Douglas' Memorandum, pp. 1–3, 5. William O. Douglas Papers, Box 1613, Library of Congress.
2. Justice Rehnquist's Memorandum, pp. 2–3, 5–10. *Ibid.*
3. Justice Brennan's Memorandum, pp. 1–5. *Ibid.*

II. *Milliken* and its Legacy
1. Chief Justice Burger's First Draft, pp. 20–24. Thurgood Marshall, Box 131, Library of Congress.
2. Solicitor General Bork's Brief in *Milliken*, pp. 11–15, 20–21. *Records and Briefs of the Supreme Court*, 418 US 717 (1974).
3. Justice Marshall's Oral Opinion, pp 1–6. Thurgood Marshall Papers, Box 131, Library of Congress.
4. Lawrence Essay, *University of San Francisco Law Review* (Vol. 12, 1977), 15, 23–33, 35–40. Reprinted by permission of the *University of San Francisco Law Review*.

Chapter Six

I. The Sport of the Seventies
1. *Cisneros* v. *Corpus Christi Independent School District*, 467 F. 2d 142, 147–49 (1972).
2. *Austin I*, 467 F. 2d 848, 862–64, 868–69 (1972).
3. *Austin II*, 532 F. 2d 380, 386–89, 390, 392 (1976).
4. *Austin III*, 564 F. 2d 162, 168–70 (1977).
5. *Austin IV*, 579 F. 2d 910, 913–14 (1978).

Chapter Seven

Coda
1. Justice Marshall's Dissent in *Dowell*, 498 US 237 (1991), at 256–262, 264–68.
2. Justice Thomas' Concurrence in *Missouri* v. *Jenkins*, 132 L Ed 2d 63, 96–7, 99–103, 111 (1995).

Selected Bibliography and Suggestions for Further Reading

Armor, David.   "The Evidence on Busing," *The Public Interest* (No. 28, 1972), 90.

Bartley, Numan.   *The Rise of Massive Resistance* (Baton Rouge, 1969).

Bass, Jack.   *Taming the Storm: The Life and Times of Judge Frank M. Johnson, Jr.* (New York, 1993).

Unlikely Heroes (New York, 1981).

Bell, Derrick.   *And We Are Not Free* (New York, 1987).

Shades of Brown (ed.) (New York, 1980).

Belz, Herman.   *Equality Transformed* (New Brunswick, N.J., 1991).

Berman, Daniel.   *It Is So Ordered* (New York, 1966).

Bickel, Alexander.   "The Decade of School Segregation," *Columbia Law Review* (Vol. 64, 1964), 193.

The Least Dangerous Branch, Second Edition (New Haven, 1986).

The Supreme Court and the Idea of Progress (New York, 1970).

"Untangling the Busing Snarl," *The New Republic* (September 23, 1972), 21.

Black, Charles.   "The Lawfulness of the Segregation Decisions," *Yale Law Journal* (Vol. 69, 1960), 421.

"Paths to Desegregation," *The New Republic* (October 21, 1957), 10.

Brown, Kevin.   "Has the Supreme Court Allowed the Cure for De Jure Segregation to Replicate the Disease?" *Cornell Law Review* (Vol. 78, 1992), 1.

"Termination of Public School Desegregation," *The George Washington Law Review* (Vol. 58, 1990), 1105.

Cahn, Edmond.   "Jurisprudence," *New York University Law Review* (Vol. 30, 1955), 150.

Carter, Robert.   "De Facto School Segregation," *Western Reserve Law Review* (Vol. 16, 1965), 502.

"The Warren Court and Desegregation," *Michigan Law Review* (Vol. 67, 1968), 237.

Chang, David.   "The Bus Stops Here," *Boston University Law Review* (Vol. 63, 1983), 1.

Clark, Kenneth.   *Dark Ghetto* (New York, 1965).

	Prejudice and Your Child (Boston, 1963).
Cohen, Marshall (ed.).	*Equality and Preferential Treatment* (Princeton, 1977).
Coleman, James.	*Equality and Achievement in Education* (Boulder, Colorado, 1990).
	Equality of Educational Opportunity (Washington, D.C., 1966).
Days, Drew, III.	"*Brown* Blues: Rethinking the Integrative Ideal," *William and Mary Law Review* (Vol. 34, 1992), 53.
	"School Desegregation Law in the 1980's: Why Isn't Anybody Laughing?" *Yale Law Journal* (Vol. 95, 1986), 1737.
Delgado, Richard.	"The Imperial Scholar," *University of Pennsylvania Law Review* (Vol. 132, 1984), 561.
Dimond, Paul.	*Beyond Busing* (Ann Arbor, 1985).
	"School Segregation in the North: There Is But One Constitution," *Harvard Civil Rights-Civil Liberties Law Review* (Vol. 7, 1972), 1.
Douglas, Davison M.	*Reading, Writing, and Race* (Chapel Hill, N.C., 1995).
Dunn, James.	"Title VI, The Guidelines and School Segregation in the South," *Virginia Law Review* (Vol. 53, 1967), 42.
Dyer, Henry S.	"School Factors and Equal Educational Opportunity," *Harvard Educational Review* (Vol. 38, 1968), 38.
Ely, James.	*The Crisis of Conservative Virginia* (Knoxville, 1976).
Fiss, Owen.	"The Charlotte-Mecklenburg Case—Its Significance for Northern School Desegregation," *University of Chicago Law Review* (Vol. 38, 1971), 697.
	"Racial Imbalance in the Public Schools: The Constitutional Concepts," *Harvard Law Review* (Vol. 78, 1965), 564.
Freyer, Tony.	*The Little Rock Crisis* (Westport, Conn., 1984).
Friedman, Leon (ed.).	*Argument* (New York, 1969).
Gewirtz, Paul.	"Choice in the Transition," *Columbia Law Review* (Vol. 86, 1986), 736.
Goodman, Frank.	"De Facto Segregation," *California Law Review* (Vol. 60, 1972), 275.
Gotunda, Neil.	"A Critique of 'Our Constitution is Color-Blind,'" *Stanford Law Review* (Vol. 44, 1991), 1.
Graglia, Lino.	*Disaster by Decree* (Ithaca, 1976).
Graham, Hugh Davis.	*The Civil Rights Era* (New York, 1990).
Greenberg, Jack.	*Race Relations and American Law* (New York, 1959).
Heyman, Ira.	"The Chief Justice, Racial Segregation, and the Friendly Critics," *California Law Review* (Vol. 49, 1961), 104.
Hirsch, H.N.	*The Enigma of Felix Frankfurter* (New York, 1981).
Hochschild, Jennifer.	*The New American Dilemma: Liberal Democracy and School*

	Desegregation (New Haven, 1984).
Hutchinson, Dennis.	"Unanimity and Desegregation," *Georgetown Law Journal* (Vol. 58, 1979), 1.
Jaynes, Gerald D. & Williams, Robin M. (eds.).	*A Common Destiny: Blacks and American Society* (New York, 1989).
Jeffries, John C., Jr.	*Justice Lewis F. Powell, Jr.* (New York, 1994).
Johnson, Alex M., Jr.	"Bid Whist, Tonk, and *United States* v. *Fordice*," *California Law Review* (Vol. 81, 1993), 1401.
	"The New Voice of Color," *Yale Law Journal* (Vol. 100, 1991), 2007.
Kanner, Stephen.	"From Denver to Dayton," *Northwestern University Law Review* (Vol. 72, 1977), 382.
Kaplan, John.	"Segregation Litigation and the Schools—Part II: The General Northern Problem," *Northwestern University Law Review* (Vol. 58, 1963), 157.
Kauper, Paul.	"Segregation in Public Education: The Decline of *Plessy* v. *Ferguson*," *Michigan Law Review* (Vol. 52, 1954), 1137.
Kennedy, Randall.	"Racial Critiques of Legal Academia," *Harvard Law Review* (Vol. 102, 1989), 1745.
Kluger, Richard.	*Simple Justice* (New York, 1975).
Kull, Andrew.	*The Color-Blind Constitution* (Cambridge, Mass., 1992).
Kurland, Phillip.	"Equal Educational Opportunity: The Limits of Constitutional Jurisprudence Undefined," *University of Chicago Law Review* (Vol. 35, 1968), 583.
Kushner, James A.	*Apartheid in America* (Frederick, MD., 1980).
Lawrence, Charles R., III.	"Segregation 'Misunderstood': The *Milliken* Decision Revisited," *University of San Francisco Law Review* (Vol. 12, 1977), 15.
Levin, Betsy & Hawley, Willis (eds.).	*The Courts, Social Science, and School Desegregation* (New Brunswick, N.J., 1977).
Liebman, James.	"Desegregating Politics," *Columbia Law Review* (Vol. 90, 1990), 1463.
	"Implementing *Brown* in the Nineties," *Virginia Law Review* (Vol. 76, 1990), 349.
Lukas, J. Anthony.	*Common Ground* (New York, 1985).
Massey, Douglas & Denton, Nancy.	*American Apartheid: Segregation and the Making of the Underclass* (New York, 1993).
Matsuda, Mari.	"Looking To The Bottom," *Harvard Civil Rights-Civil Liberties Law Review* (Vol. 22, 1987), 323.
Meador, Daniel.	"The Constitution and the Assignment of Pupils to Public Schools," *Virginia Law Review* (Vol. 45, 1959), 517.
Mehrige, Robert R., Jr.	"A Judge Remembers Richmond in the Post-*Brown* Years," *Washington and Lee Law Review* (Vol. 49, 1992), 23.

Mosteller, Frederick & Moynihan, Daniel (eds.).	*On Equality of Educational Opportunity* (New York, 1972).
Muse, Benjamin.	*Ten Years of Prelude* (New York, 1964).
Myrdal, Gunnar.	*An American Dilemma*, Two Volumes (New York, 1944).
Newman, Roger.	*Hugo Black* (New York, 1994).
Orfield, Gary.	*Must We Bus?* (Washington, D.C., 1978).
	The Reconstruction of Southern Education (New York, 1969).
Peller, Gary.	"Race Consciousness," *Duke Law Journal* (1990 Volume), 758.
Peltason, Jack.	*Fifty-eight Lonely Men* (New York, 1961).
Pettigrew, Thomas.	"Busing: A Review of the 'Evidence,'" *The Public Interest* (No. 30, 1973), 88.
Pollak, Louis.	*The Constitution and the Supreme Court* (Cleveland, 1966).
Ravitch, Diane.	*The Great School Wars* (New York, 1974).
	The Troubled Crusade: American Education, 1945–1980 (New York, 1983).
Rosenberg, Morris & Simmons, Roberta G.	*Black and White Self-Esteem: The Urban School Child* (Washington, D.C., 1971).
Sarratt, Reed.	*The Ordeal of Desegregation* (New York, 1966).
Schwartz, Bernard.	*Super Chief* (New York, 1983).
	Swann's Way (New York, 1986).
Sedler, Robert.	"Beyond *Bakke*," *Harvard Civil Rights-Civil Liberties Law Review* (Vol. 14, 1979), 133.
	"The Constitution and School Segregation," *Kentucky Law Journal* (Vol. 68, 1979), 925.
	"Metropolitan Desegregation in the Wake of *Milliken*," *Washington University Law Review* (1975 Volume), 535.
	"The Profound Impact of *Milliken* v. *Bradley*," *Wayne Law Review* (Vol. 33, 1987), 1693.
	Review of Lino Graglia, *Disaster by Decree*, *Cornell Law Review* (Vol. 62, 1977), 645.
Shane, Peter M.	"School Segregation Remedies and the Fair Governance of Schools," *University of Pennsylvania Law Review* (Vol. 132, 1984), 1041.
Simon, James.	*Independent Journey: The Life of William O. Douglas* (New York, 1980).
St. John, Nancy.	*School Desegregation* (New York, 1975).
Taeuber, Karl.	"Demographic Perspectives on Housing and School Segregation," *Wayne Law Review* (Vol. 21, 1975), 833.
Taeuber, Karl & Taeuber, Alma.	*Negroes in Cities* (Chicago, 1965).
Taylor, William L.	"The Supreme Court and Urban Reality," *Wayne Law Review*

	(Vol. 21, 1975), 751.
Tushnet, Mark.	*Making Civil Rights Law* (New York, 1994).
	The NAACP's Legal Strategy Against Segregated Education, 1925–1950 (Chapel Hill, N.C., 1987).
Warren, Robert Penn.	*Segregation* (New York, 1956).
Weaver, Jace.	*Then to the Rock Let Me Fly: Luther Bohanon and Judicial Activism* (Norman, Oklahoma, 1993).
Weinberg, Meyer.	*Minority Standards: A Research Appraisal* (Washington, D.C., 1977).
	Race and Place: A Legal History of the Neighborhood School (Washington, D.C., 1967).
White, G. Edward.	*The American Judicial Tradition* (New York, 1976).
	Earl Warren: A Public Life (New York, 1982).
Wilkinson, J. Harvie.	*From Brown to Bakke* (New York, 1979).
Williams, Patricia.	*The Alchemy of Race and Rights* (Cambridge, Mass., 1993).
Woodward, Bob & Armstrong, Scott.	*The Brethren* (New York, 1979).
Wolf, Eleanor.	*Trial and Error* (Detroit, 1981).
Wolters, Raymond.	*The Burden of Brown* (Knoxville, 1984).
	Right Turn (New Brunswick, N.J., 1996).
Wright, J. Skelly.	"Public School Desegregation: Legal Remedies for De Facto Segregation," *New York University Law Review* (Vol. 40, 1965), 285.
Yarmolinsky, Adam (ed.).	*Race and Schooling in the City* (Cambridge, Mass., 1981).

Acknowledgments

It is a distinct pleasure to thank those public figures and the people and institutions associated with them who allowed me to use and to quote from documents, for they comprise a cross-section of the great men of the law of our time: the late Justice William J. Brennan, Chief Justice William Rehnquist, Judge Robert Carter, Ms. Cathleen Douglas Stone for permission to use documents from the William O. Douglas Papers, the Princeton University Library for permission to use the John Marshall Harlan Papers. In that last connection, I want to thank my old friend Ben Primer, archivist at the Seeley G. Mudd Manuscript Library.

For permission to use some brilliant scholarly material, I am indebted to Professor Charles Lawrence, Professor Paul Dimond, the editors of the *Harvard Civil Rights-Civil Liberties Law Review* and of the *University of San Francisco Law Review*.

The librarians at the Library of Congress Manuscript Reading Room and at the University of Baltimore Law Library were, as always, marvelously courteous and knowledgeable, as were those at the Albert S. Cook Library at Towson University. In that regard, it has been an inspiration and a pleasure to have as a colleague these many years Ms. Eleanore O. Hofstetter.

I also want to thank those who were kind enough to talk to me about the most recent developments in desegregation law: Christopher A. Hansen of the American Civil Liberties Union Foundation, Scott McCully of Unified School District No. 501 (Topeka, Kansas), Ms. Jill Moberley of the Dayton Public School System, Dr. Jack Nichols of the Delaware State Board of Education, Mr. Duncan Pritchett of the Indianapolis Public School System, and Ms. Judith Rogers of the Columbus Public School System.

I have been fortunate to spend my entire academic career in the History Department of Towson University. It is that rarest and most treasured species of academia, a place where good humor, mutual support, and personal friendship have flourished. This atmosphere was created by our long-time chairperson, Mary Catherine Kahl and has been lovingly maintained by our present chair, Garry Van Osdell, my officemate and close friend since I came to Towson.

I should mention all my colleagues, no doubt. I will be forgiven, I hope, if I single out my corridor mates in Linthicum Hall, Karl and Marilynn Larew, Ronn Pineo, and Lynn Johnson, as well as Laura Eldridge, Cindy Gissendanner, and Fred and Nancy Rivers.

None of my scholarly efforts would ever have born fruit but for the encouragement of my colleague Patricia Romero. Her zest for life, her tangible aid, and her own remarkable scholarly achievements have virtually shamed me into attempting work of my own.

And then there is Professor Myron Scholnick, quite simply the best colleague and the best friend any person in academic life could ever have.

I do not believe this effort would have seen the light of day, however, but for the remarkable efforts of the most remarkable, and most competent, person I know. Emily Daugherty, our department secretary, found time to process this entire manuscript, put up patiently with my endless mistakes and "rethinkings," and do her other work magnificently as well. All this in times of great personal sorrow for her, but also, fortunately, great happiness as well. This is in great part her book, and Charlie's too.

A family forced to put up with a tiresome old bachelor these many years is entitled to reams of sympathy. They have never asked for any. No person could be more fortunate than to have in his life the family that I have: My sister Sandy Winters, my nephews Gary, Andy, and his wife Laura, my uncle, Dr. Marvin Davis, and my cousins Penny and Sol Love, and Rita and Irv Sherman.

My late parents are ever foremost in my thoughts and ever will be.